Melrose Leadership Academy
4730 Fleming Avenue
Oakland, CA 94619

ASSASSINATION CLASSROOM

TIME FOR ROBBERY

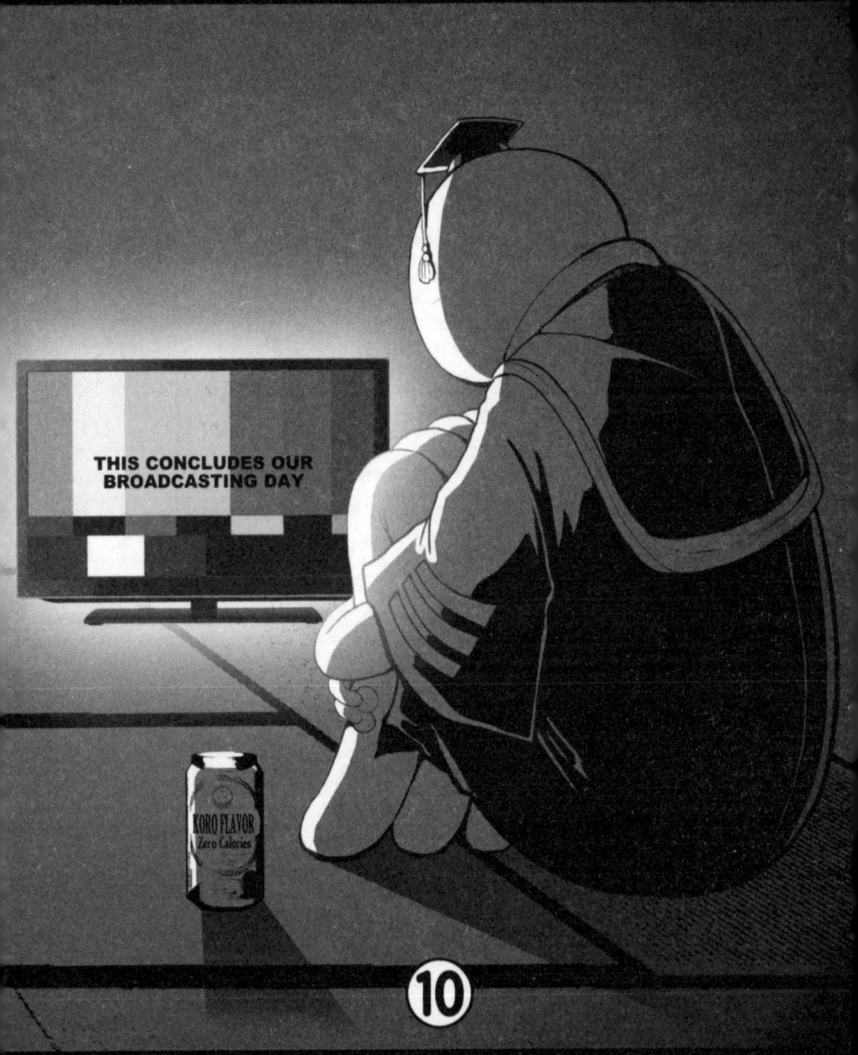
THIS CONCLUDES OUR BROADCASTING DAY
KORO FLAVOR
Zero Calories

10

YUSEI MATSUI

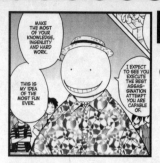

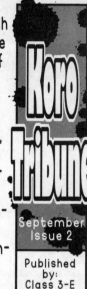

Koro Tribune

September Issue 2

Published by: Class 3-E Newspaper Staff

Although we have a lot of data on his weaknesses, we are still far from successfully assassinating Koro Sensei...

Story Thus Far

I EXPECT TO SEE YOU EXECUTE THE BEST ASSAS-SINATION ATTEMPT YOU ARE CAPABLE OF.
MAKE THE MOST OF YOUR KNOWLEDGE, INGENUITY AND HARD WORK.
THIS IS MY IDEA OF THE MOST FUN EVER.

Kunugigaoka Junior High, Class 3-E is led by a monster who has disintegrated the moon and is planning to do the same to the Earth next March.

Even the armies of the world, with the latest technology, can't kill the super-creature Koro Sensei and collect the bounty of up to 30 billion yen (300 million dollars) for a group assassination! So it comes down to his students in the so-called "End Class." Thanks to Koro Sensei's dedication, they are becoming fine students who can academically outshine the top-ranking students at their school. Likewise, their assassination skills are rapidly improving under the tutelage of Mr. Karasuma of the Ministry of Defense, who is molding them into a professional team of assassins. The first semester is over and the clock is ticking. Will the students of 3-E successfully assassinate Koro Sensei?!

Koro Sensei

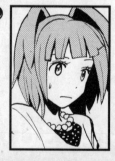

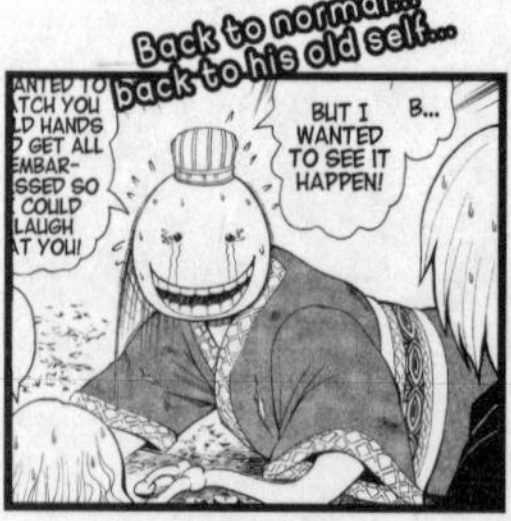

Back to normal... back to his old self...
B...
BUT I WANTED TO SEE IT HAPPEN!

A mysterious, man-made, octopus-like creature whose name is a play on the words "koro senai," which means "can't kill." He is capable of flying at Mach 20 and his versatile tentacles protect him from attacks and aid him in everyday activities. Nobody knows who created him or why he wants to teach Class 3-E, but he has proven to be an extremely capable teacher.

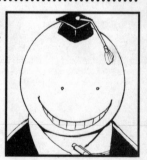

Kaede Kayano

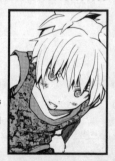

Class E student. She's the one who named Koro Sensei. She sits at the desk next to Nagisa, and they seem to get along well.

Nagisa Shiota

Class E student. Skilled at information gathering, he has been taking notes on Koro Sensei's weaknesses. He has a hidden talent for assassinations and even the Assassin Broker Lovro sees his potential.

Rinka Hayami

Smart, skilled and cute but a bit of a wallflower. There's always a person like that in a class, isn't there?

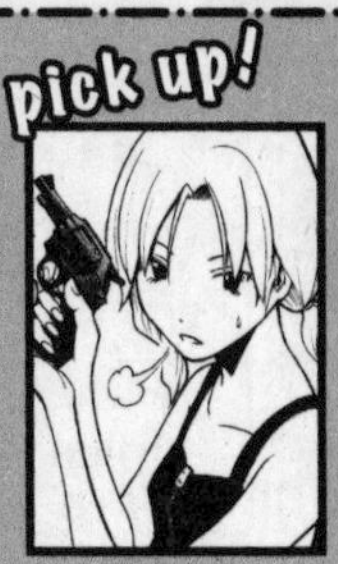
pick up!

Karma Akabane

Class E student. A natural genius who earns top grades. His failure in the final exam of the first semester has forced him to grow up and take things a bit more seriously.

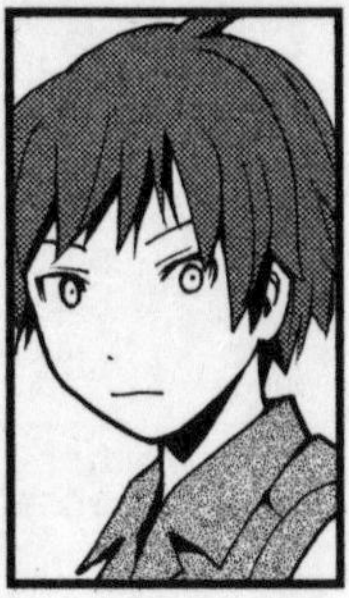

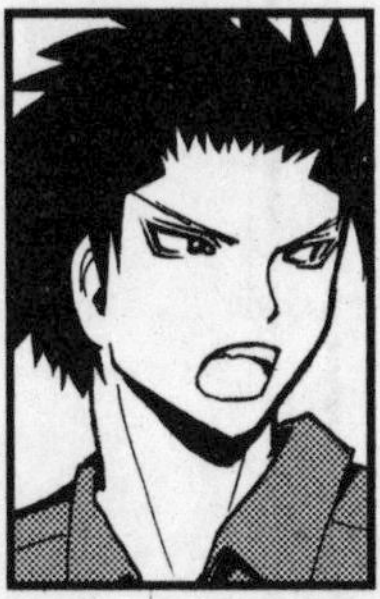

Tadaomi Karasuma

Member of the Ministry of Defense and the Class E students' P.E. teacher. Though serious about his duties, he is successfully building good relationships with his students.

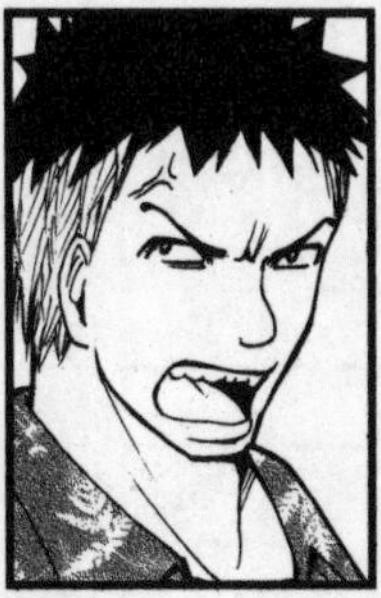

Ryoma Terasaka

Class E student. Once a rebel and an outcast, he has gradually begun to fit in and is now a dependable assassin due to his great physical strength.

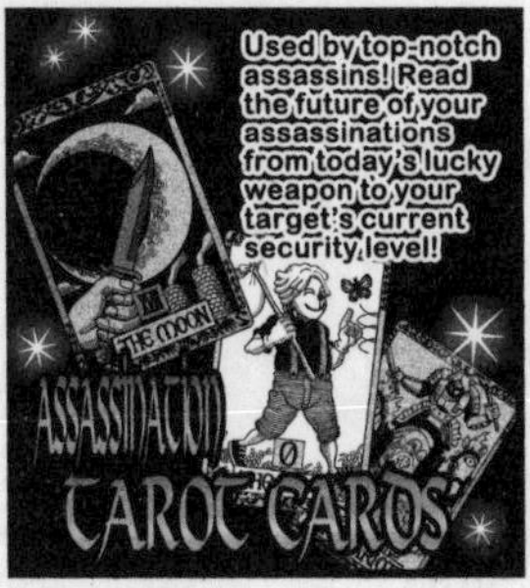
Used by top-notch assassins! Read the future of your assassinations from today's lucky weapon to your target's current security level!
THE MOON
ASSASSINATION TAROT CARDS

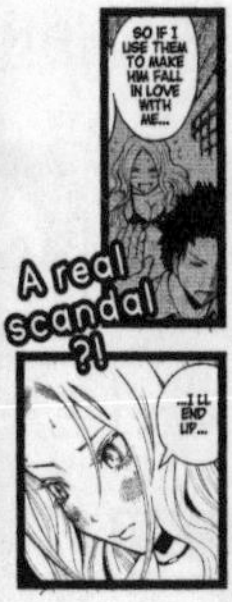
SO IF I USE THEM TO MAKE HIM FALL IN LOVE WITH ME...
A real scandal ?!
...I'LL END UP...

Irina Jelavich

A sexy assassin hired as an English teacher. She's known for using her "womanly charms" to get close to a target. She often flirts with Karasuma, but hasn't had any success so far.

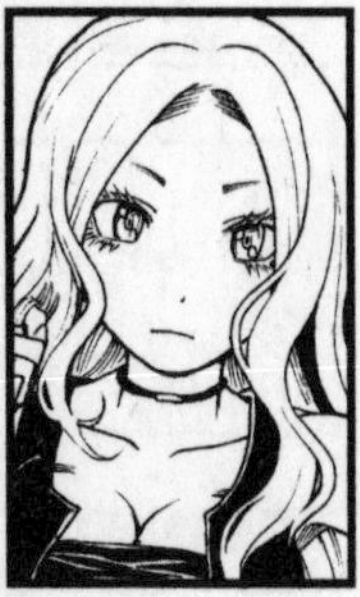

KIMURA AND MIMURA HAVE JOINED FORCES TO CREATE THE "WALLFLOWER-MURA COALITION"!

When you talk about wallflowers, you probably think of these two. They have secretly joined forces to make a big splash, but it looks like their coalition is on the verge of a breakup by vol. 11...

WALL-FLOWERS

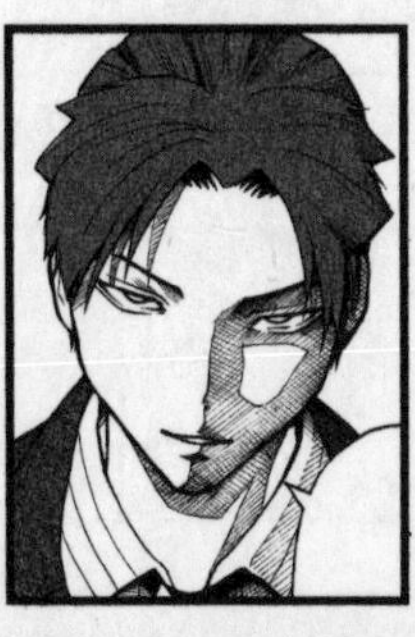

Gakuho Asano

The principal of Kunugigaoka Academy, who built this academically competitive school based on his faith in rationality and hierarchy.

Assassination Class Roster

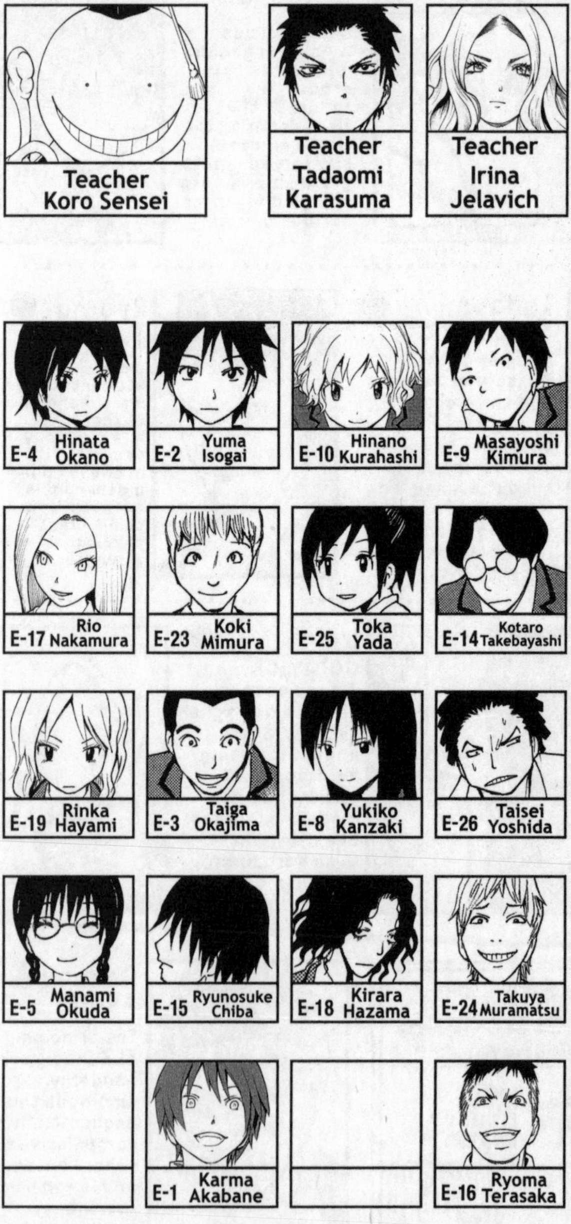
Teacher Koro Sensei
Teacher Tadaomi Karasuma
Teacher Irina Jelavich
E-4 Hinata Okano
E-2 Yuma Isogai
E-10 Hinano Kurahashi
E-9 Masayoshi Kimura
E-17 Rio Nakamura
E-23 Koki Mimura
E-25 Toka Yada
E-14 Kotaro Takebayashi
E-19 Rinka Hayami
E-3 Taiga Okajima
E-8 Yukiko Kanzaki
E-26 Taisei Yoshida
E-5 Manami Okuda
E-15 Ryunosuke Chiba
E-18 Kirara Hazama
E-24 Takuya Muramatsu
E-1 Karma Akabane
E-16 Ryoma Terasaka

Always assassinate your target using a method that brings a smile to your face.

I'm open for assassinations any time. But don't let them get in the way of your studies.

I won't harm students who try to assassinate me. But if your skills are rusty, expect a good scrubbing!

Individual Statistics

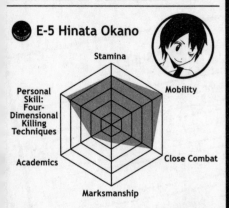

E-5 Hinata Okano

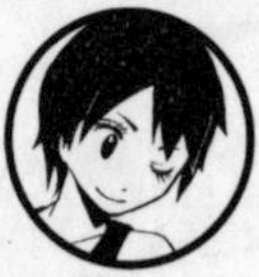

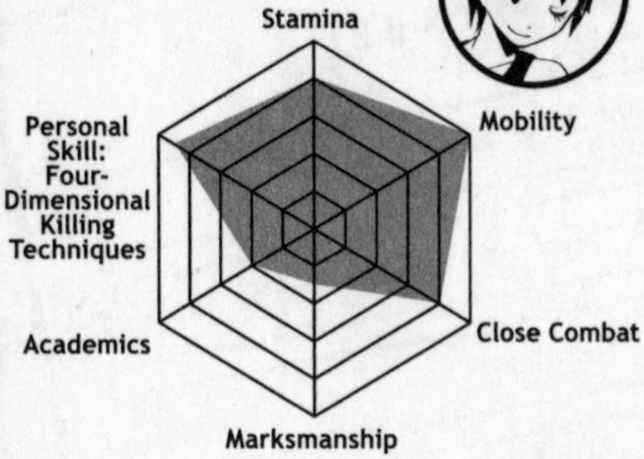

Stamina
Mobility
Close Combat
Marksmanship
Academics
Personal Skill: Four-Dimensional Killing Techniques

E-5 Manami Okuda

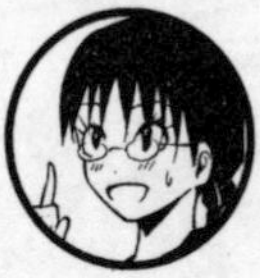

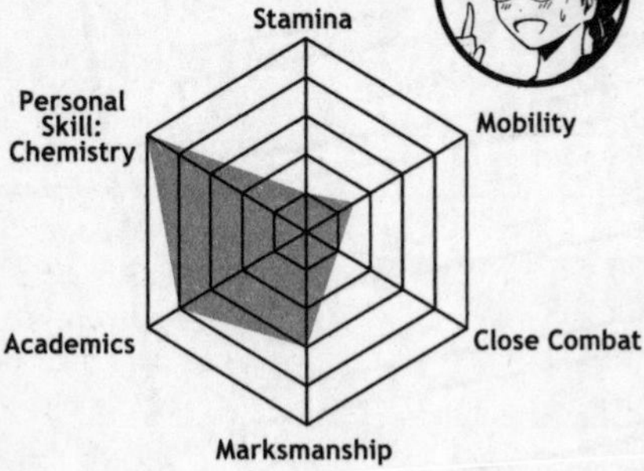

Stamina
Mobility
Close Combat
Marksmanship
Academics
Personal Skill: Chemistry

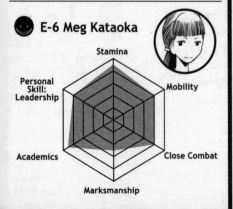

E-6 Meg Kataoka

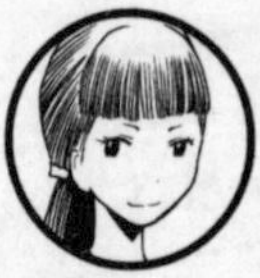

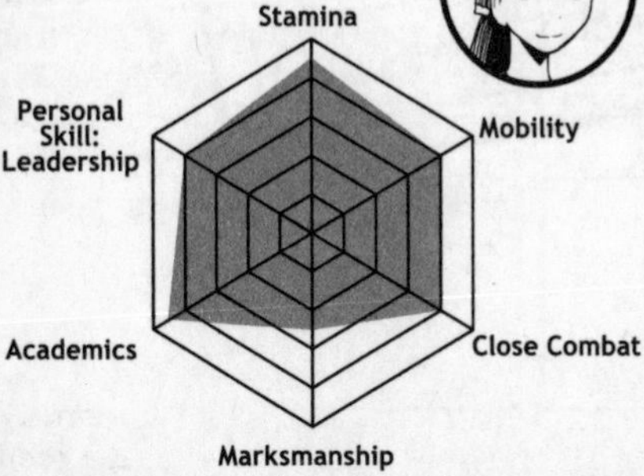

Stamina
Mobility
Close Combat
Marksmanship
Academics
Personal Skill: Leadership

Kunugigaoka Junior High
3-E
Koro Sensei Class
Seating Arrangement

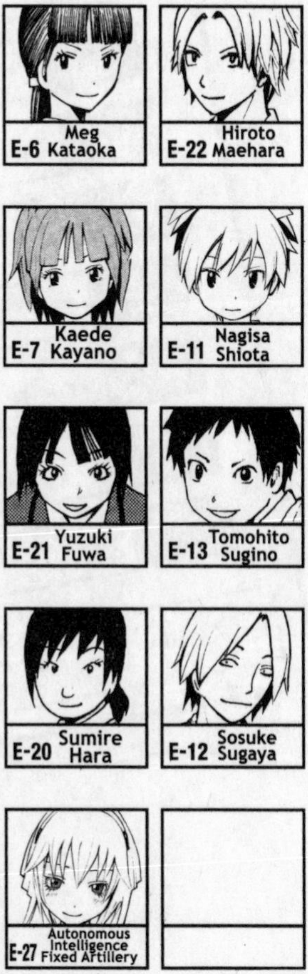

E-6 Meg Kataoka
E-22 Hiroto Maehara
E-7 Kaede Kayano
E-11 Nagisa Shiota
E-21 Yuzuki Fuwa
E-13 Tomohito Sugino
E-20 Sumire Hara
E-12 Sosuke Sugaya
E-27 Autonomous Intelligence Fixed Artillery

ASSASSINATION CLASSROOM 10 CONTENTS

(ANSWER SHEET)

Grade	3	Class	E	Name	CONTENTS	Score	

Geogra

ion. 1): Which
ations on the ri
seen from the o

B

(Que

(1)

Japan

D: Of tourism and assas
What is the nationality of the
citizens who visit Japan the most ?

(2): The citizens of which of the following forei
countries reside in Japan in greater numbers than the

Choose one.

A: Korea/North Korea B: China C: United States D: Iran E: Philippines

(3): Which of the following sentences are incorrect statements about
companies that expand their business overseas?

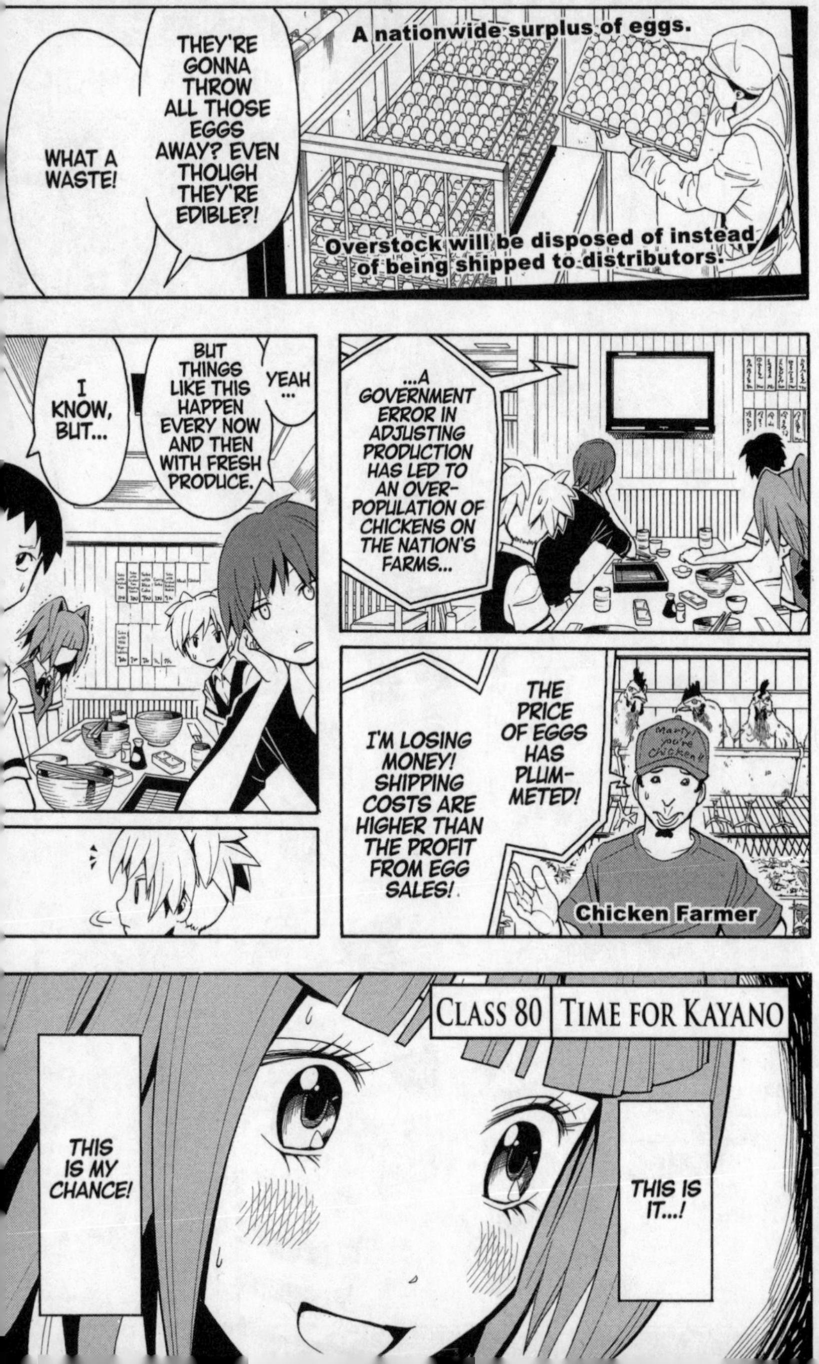
A nationwide surplus of eggs.
Overstock will be disposed of instead of being shipped to distributors.
THEY'RE GONNA THROW ALL THOSE EGGS AWAY? EVEN THOUGH THEY'RE EDIBLE?!
WHAT A WASTE!
...A GOVERNMENT ERROR IN ADJUSTING PRODUCTION HAS LED TO AN OVERPOPULATION OF CHICKENS ON THE NATION'S FARMS...
THE PRICE OF EGGS HAS PLUMMETED!
I'M LOSING MONEY! SHIPPING COSTS ARE HIGHER THAN THE PROFIT FROM EGG SALES!
Chicken Farmer
YEAH...
BUT THINGS LIKE THIS HAPPEN EVERY NOW AND THEN WITH FRESH PRODUCE.
I KNOW, BUT...
CLASS 80 TIME FOR KAYANO
THIS IS IT...!
THIS IS MY CHANCE!

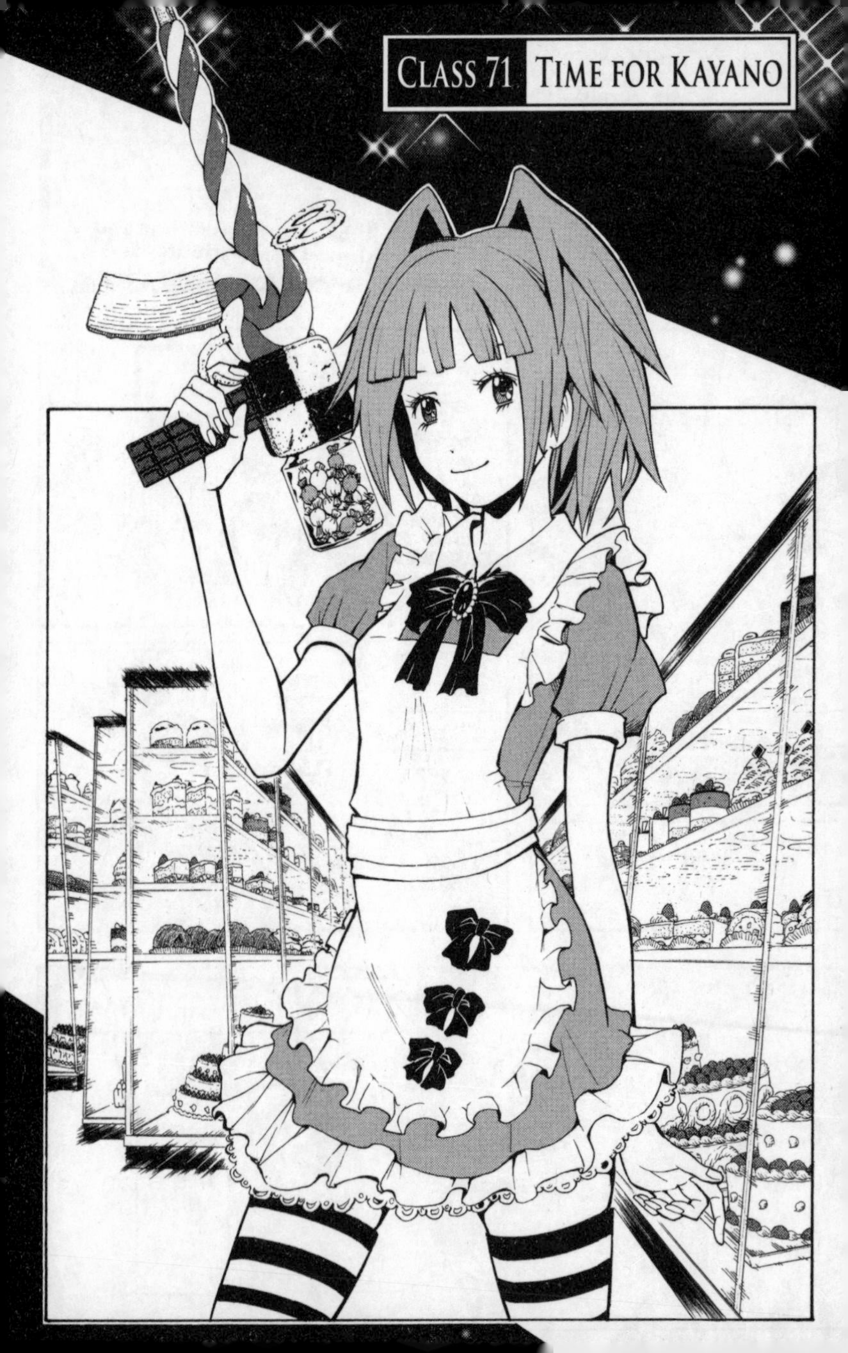
CLASS 71
TIME FOR KAYANO

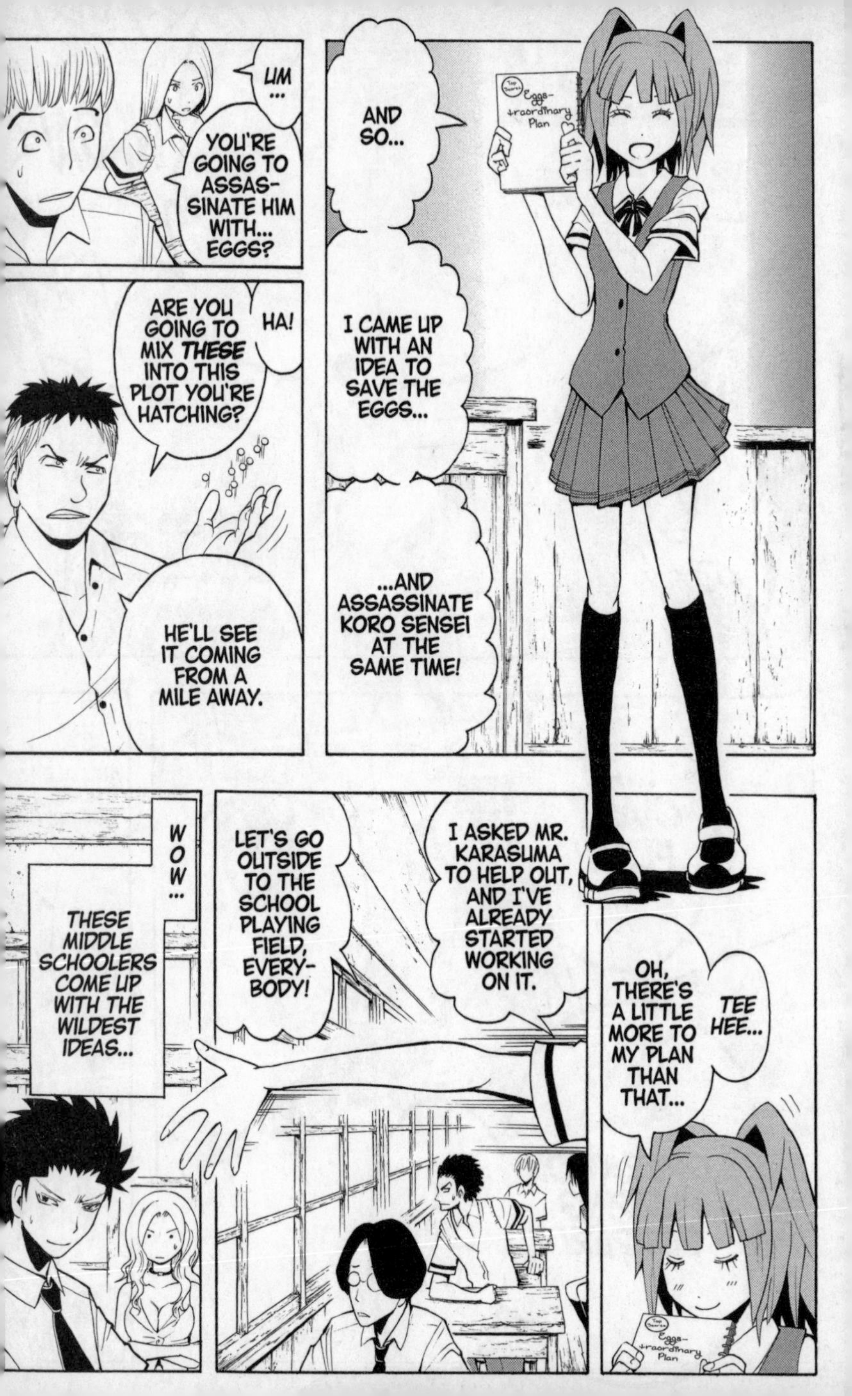
Eggs-traordinary Plan
AND SO...
I CAME UP WITH AN IDEA TO SAVE THE EGGS...
...AND ASSASSINATE KORO SENSEI AT THE SAME TIME!
UM...
YOU'RE GOING TO ASSAS-SINATE HIM WITH... EGGS?
HA!
ARE YOU GOING TO MIX *THESE* INTO THIS PLOT YOU'RE HATCHING?
HE'LL SEE IT COMING FROM A MILE AWAY.
OH, THERE'S A LITTLE MORE TO MY PLAN THAN THAT...
TEE HEE...
Eggs-traordinary Plan
I ASKED MR. KARASUMA TO HELP OUT, AND I'VE ALREADY STARTED WORKING ON IT.
LET'S GO OUTSIDE TO THE SCHOOL PLAYING FIELD, EVERY-BODY!
WOW...
THESE MIDDLE SCHOOLERS COME UP WITH THE WILDEST IDEAS...

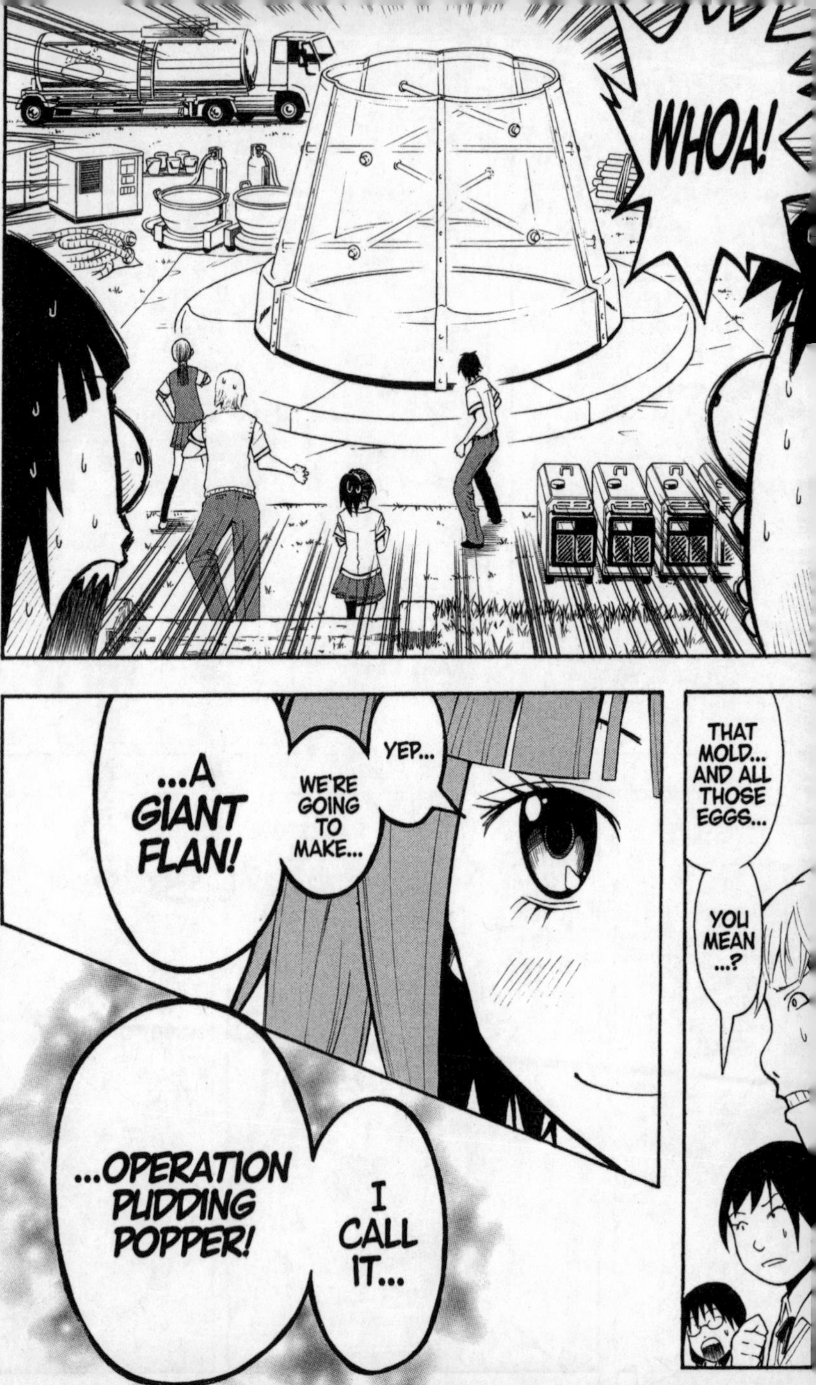
WHOA!
THAT MOLD... AND ALL THOSE EGGS...
YOU MEAN ...?
YEP...
WE'RE GOING TO MAKE...
...A GIANT FLAN!
I CALL IT...
...OPERATION PUDDING POPPER!

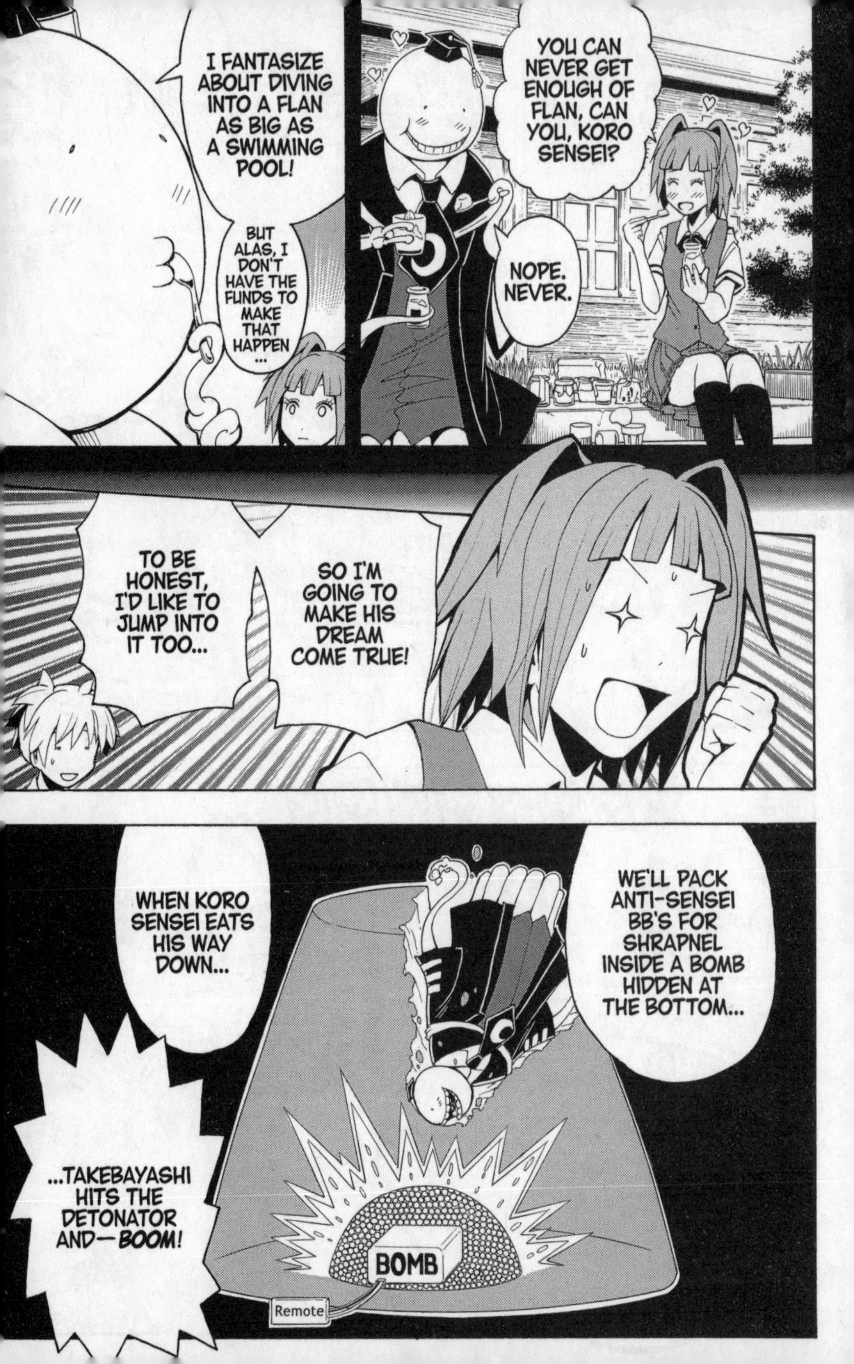
YOU CAN NEVER GET ENOUGH OF FLAN, CAN YOU, KORO SENSEI?
NOPE. NEVER.
I FANTASIZE ABOUT DIVING INTO A FLAN AS BIG AS A SWIMMING POOL!
BUT ALAS, I DON'T HAVE THE FUNDS TO MAKE THAT HAPPEN ...
SO I'M GOING TO MAKE HIS DREAM COME TRUE!
TO BE HONEST, I'D LIKE TO JUMP INTO IT TOO...
WE'LL PACK ANTI-SENSEI BB'S FOR SHRAPNEL INSIDE A BOMB HIDDEN AT THE BOTTOM...
WHEN KORO SENSEI EATS HIS WAY DOWN...
...TAKEBAYASHI HITS THE DETONATOR AND—BOOM!
BOMB
Remote

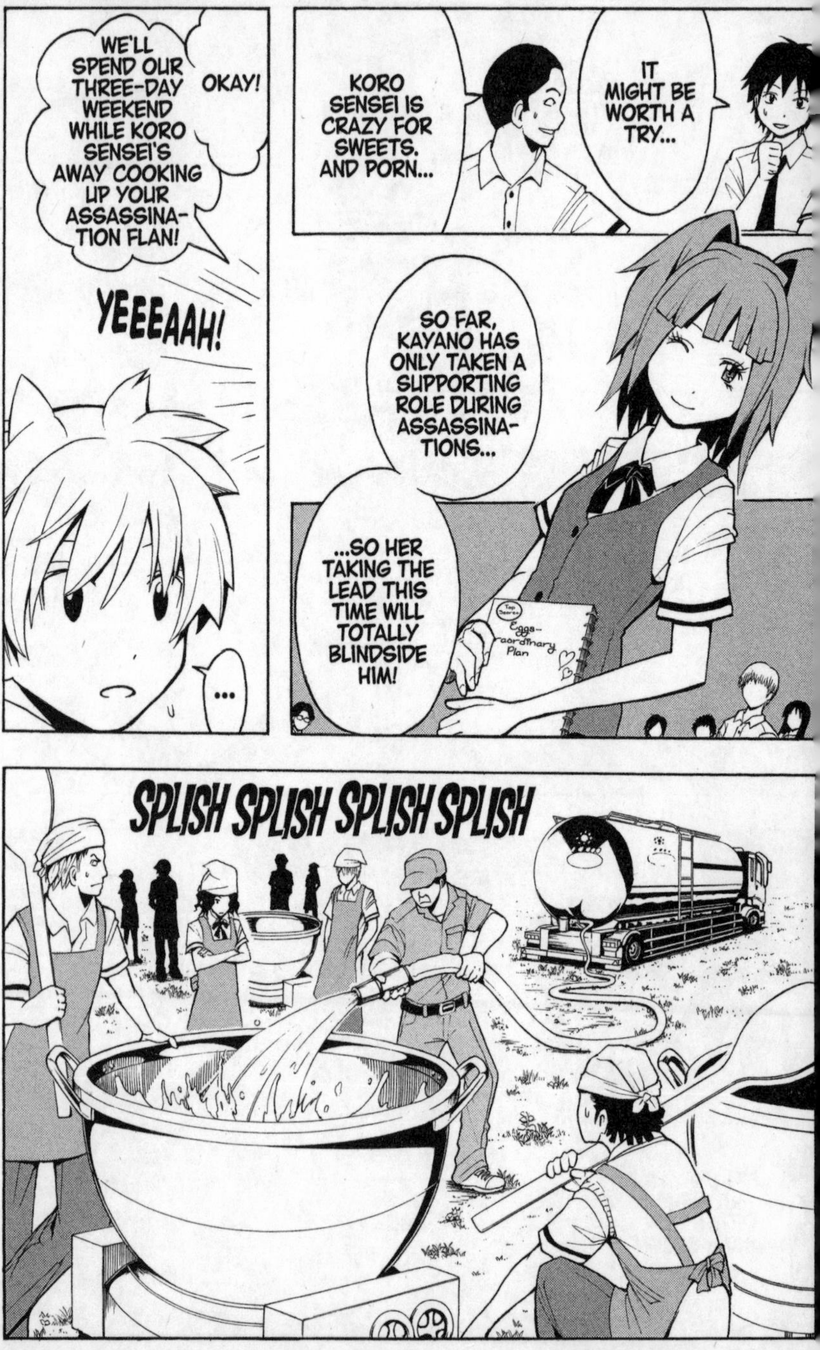
IT MIGHT BE WORTH A TRY...
KORO SENSEI IS CRAZY FOR SWEETS. AND PORN...
SO FAR, KAYANO HAS ONLY TAKEN A SUPPORTING ROLE DURING ASSASSINATIONS...
...SO HER TAKING THE LEAD THIS TIME WILL TOTALLY BLINDSIDE HIM!
Top Secret
Eggs-raordinary Plan
WE'LL SPEND OUR THREE-DAY WEEKEND WHILE KORO SENSEI'S AWAY COOKING UP YOUR ASSASSINATION FLAN!
OKAY!
YEEEAAH!
...
SPLISH SPLISH SPLISH SPLISH

WE'LL ADD SUGAR, MILK AND VANILLA EXTRACT TO THAT MIXTURE...

SPLOOSH

SPLISH

I ASKED...

...A MAYONNAISE FACTORY WHOSE PRODUCTION LINE WAS SUSPENDED TO MIX UP THE EGGS FOR ME.

THE AGAR WILL MAKE THE PUDDING HARDER.

TO COUNTER THAT PROBLEM... WE'LL MIX IN GELATIN AND AGAR AS A THICKENER.

Agar Powder

POWER FUL

IT COULDN'T SUPPORT ITS OWN WEIGHT!

I WATCHED THEM MAKE A GIANT PUDDING ON A TV SHOW ONCE. THEY FAILED.

BUT, KAEDE...

SPLORTCH

THAT'S RIGHT.

Hmm...

IT SHOULD STAND UP TO THE AMBIENT WARMTH...

...OF THIS MILD SEPTEMBER WEATHER.

Agar		Gelatin
	90°C	
	50°C	
	25°C	
	20°C	

PLUS, AGAR HAS A HIGHER MELTING POINT THAN GELATIN.

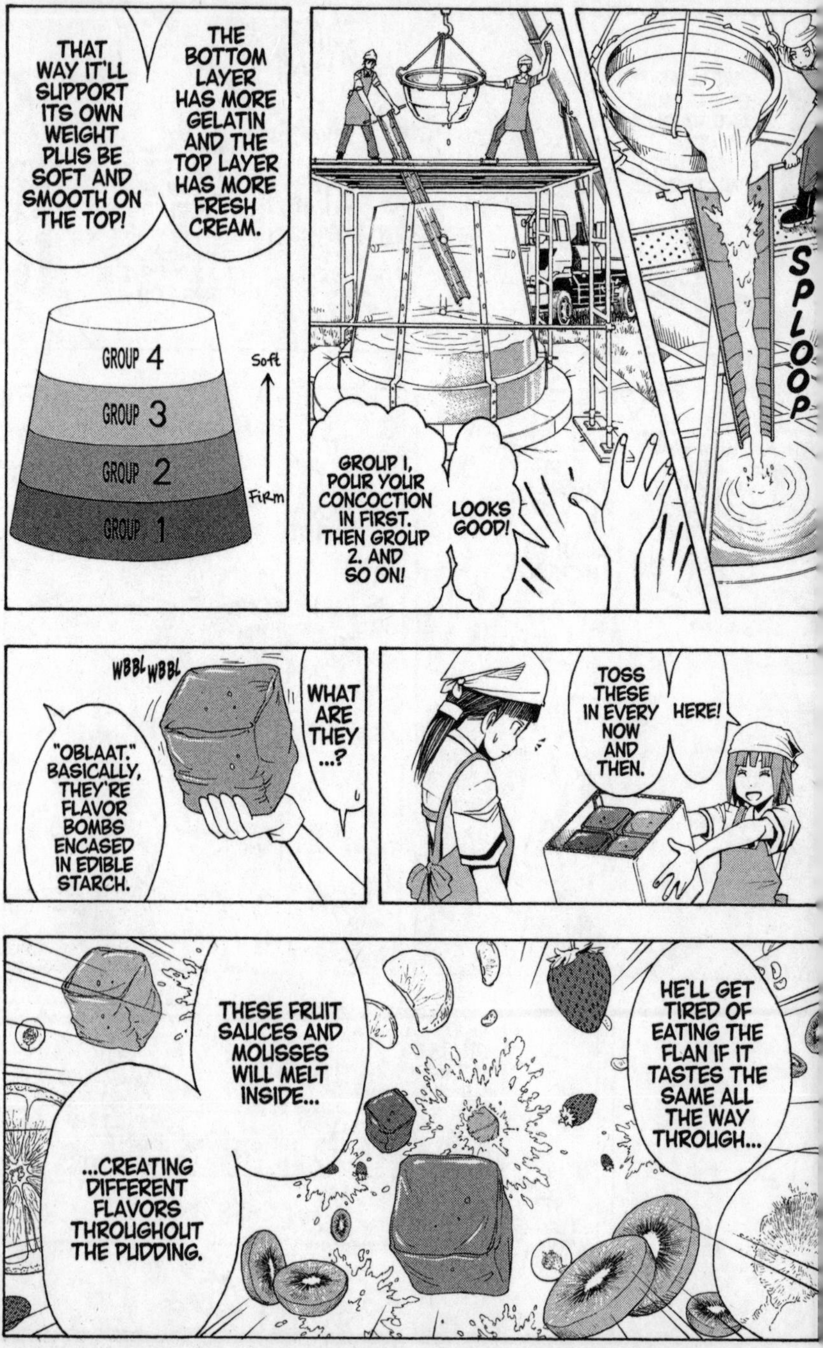
SPLOOP
LOOKS GOOD!
GROUP 1, POUR YOUR CONCOCTION IN FIRST. THEN GROUP 2. AND SO ON!
THE BOTTOM LAYER HAS MORE GELATIN AND THE TOP LAYER HAS MORE FRESH CREAM.
THAT WAY IT'LL SUPPORT ITS OWN WEIGHT PLUS BE SOFT AND SMOOTH ON THE TOP!
GROUP 4
GROUP 3
GROUP 2
GROUP 1
Soft
Firm
HERE!
TOSS THESE IN EVERY NOW AND THEN.
WHAT ARE THEY ...?
WBBL WBBL
"OBLAAT." BASICALLY, THEY'RE FLAVOR BOMBS ENCASED IN EDIBLE STARCH.
HE'LL GET TIRED OF EATING THE FLAN IF IT TASTES THE SAME ALL THE WAY THROUGH...
THESE FRUIT SAUCES AND MOUSSES WILL MELT INSIDE...
...CREATING DIFFERENT FLAVORS THROUGHOUT THE PUDDING.

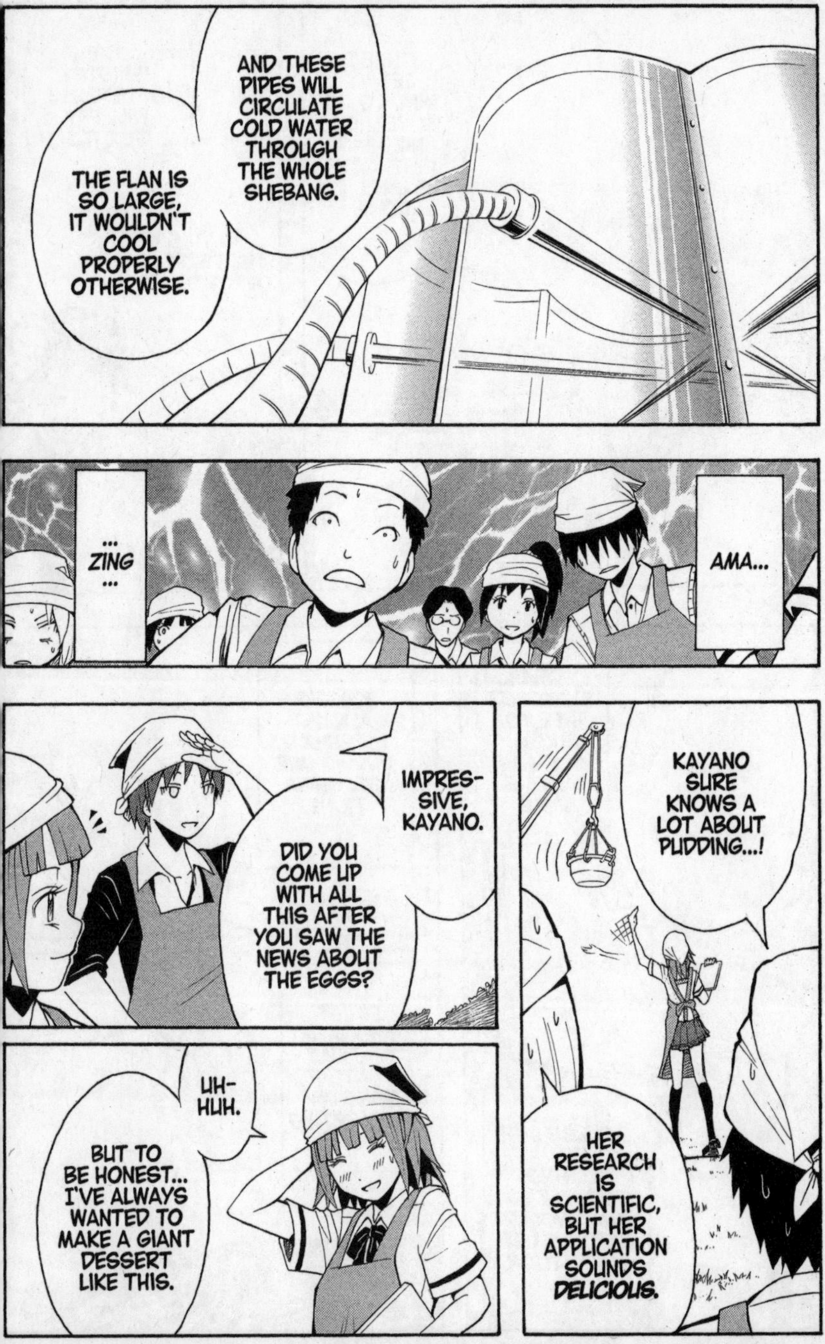
AND THESE PIPES WILL CIRCULATE COLD WATER THROUGH THE WHOLE SHEBANG.
THE FLAN IS SO LARGE, IT WOULDN'T COOL PROPERLY OTHERWISE.
AMA...
...ZING...
KAYANO SURE KNOWS A LOT ABOUT PUDDING...!
HER RESEARCH IS SCIENTIFIC, BUT HER APPLICATION SOUNDS **DELICIOUS.**
IMPRESSIVE, KAYANO.
DID YOU COME UP WITH ALL THIS AFTER YOU SAW THE NEWS ABOUT THE EGGS?
UH-HUH.
BUT TO BE HONEST... I'VE ALWAYS WANTED TO MAKE A GIANT DESSERT LIKE THIS.

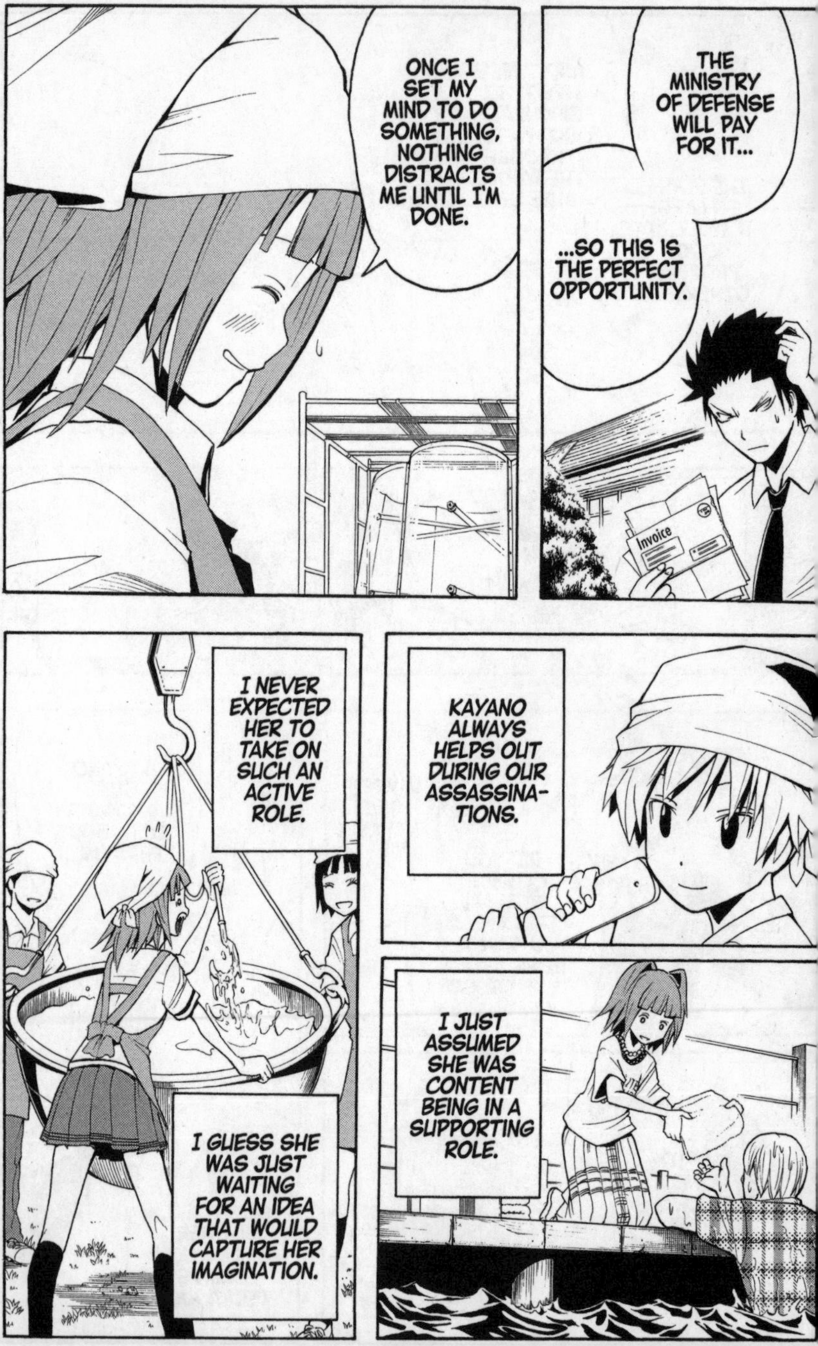
THE MINISTRY OF DEFENSE WILL PAY FOR IT...
...SO THIS IS THE PERFECT OPPORTUNITY.
Invoice
ONCE I SET MY MIND TO DO SOMETHING, NOTHING DISTRACTS ME UNTIL I'M DONE.
KAYANO ALWAYS HELPS OUT DURING OUR ASSASSINATIONS.
I JUST ASSUMED SHE WAS CONTENT BEING IN A SUPPORTING ROLE.
I NEVER EXPECTED HER TO TAKE ON SUCH AN ACTIVE ROLE.
I GUESS SHE WAS JUST WAITING FOR AN IDEA THAT WOULD CAPTURE HER IMAGINATION.

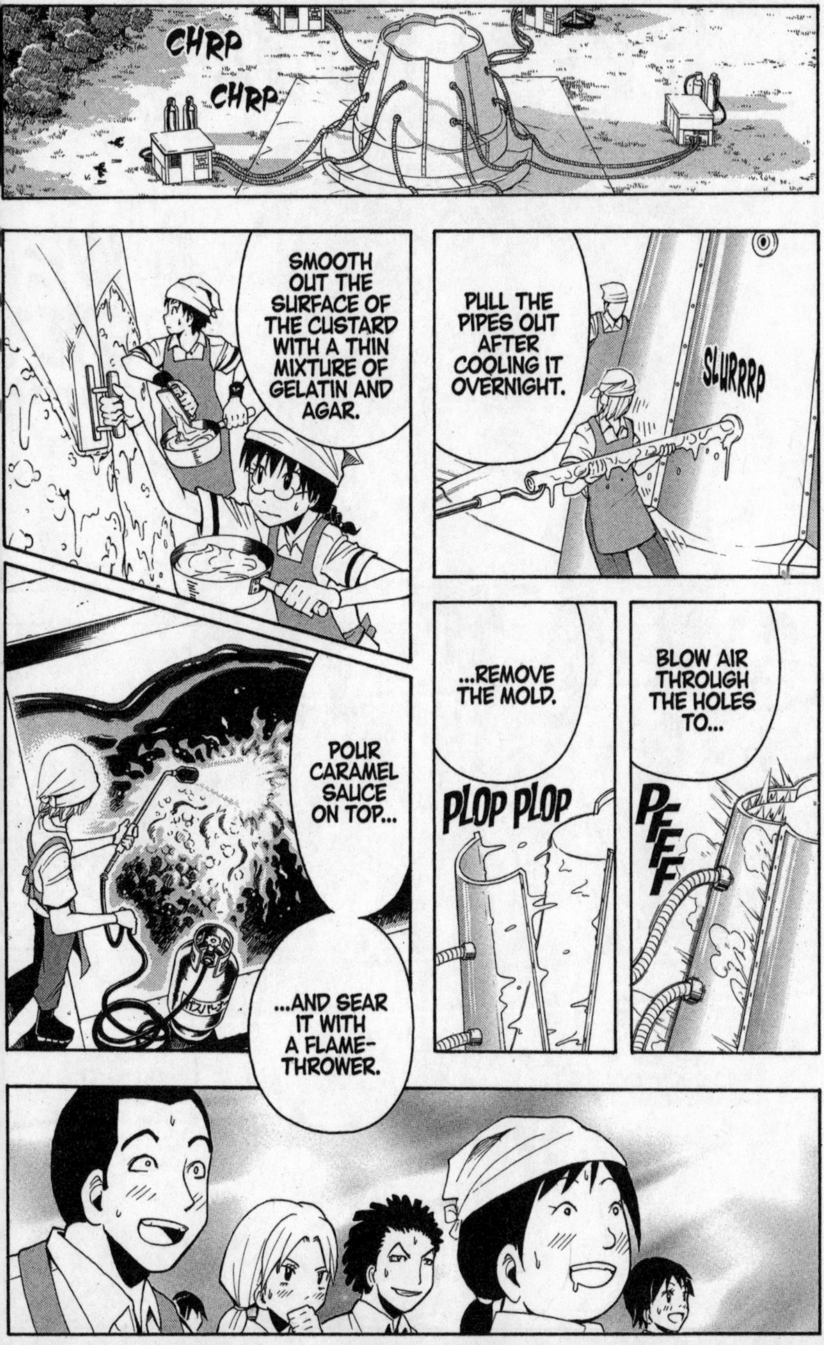
CHRP
CHRP
PULL THE PIPES OUT AFTER COOLING IT OVERNIGHT.
SLURRRP
BLOW AIR THROUGH THE HOLES TO...
PFFF
...REMOVE THE MOLD.
PLOP PLOP
SMOOTH OUT THE SURFACE OF THE CUSTARD WITH A THIN MIXTURE OF GELATIN AND AGAR.
POUR CARAMEL SAUCE ON TOP...
...AND SEAR IT WITH A FLAME-THROWER.

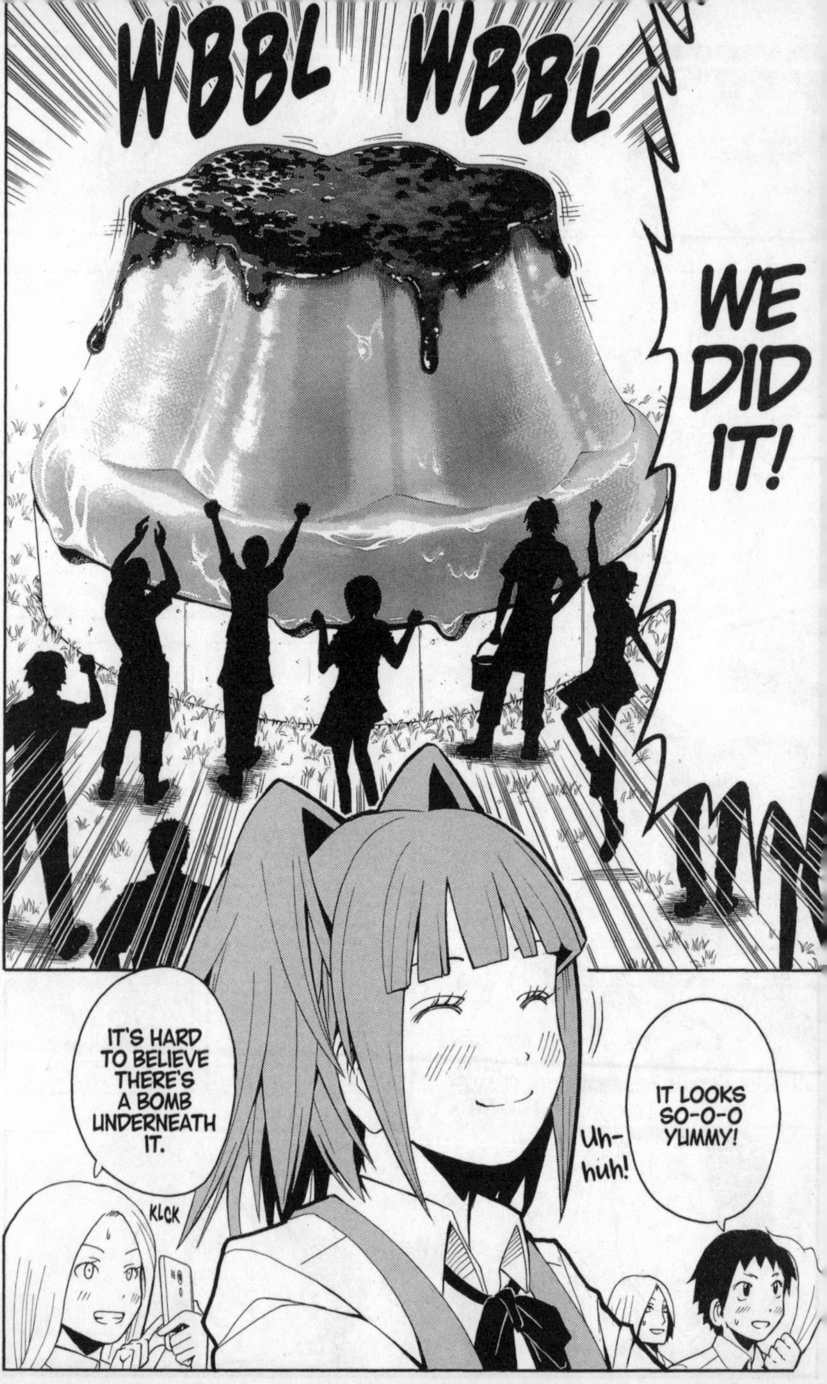
WBBL WBBL
WE DID IT!
IT LOOKS SO-O-O YUMMY!
Uh-huh!
IT'S HARD TO BELIEVE THERE'S A BOMB UNDERNEATH IT.
KLCK

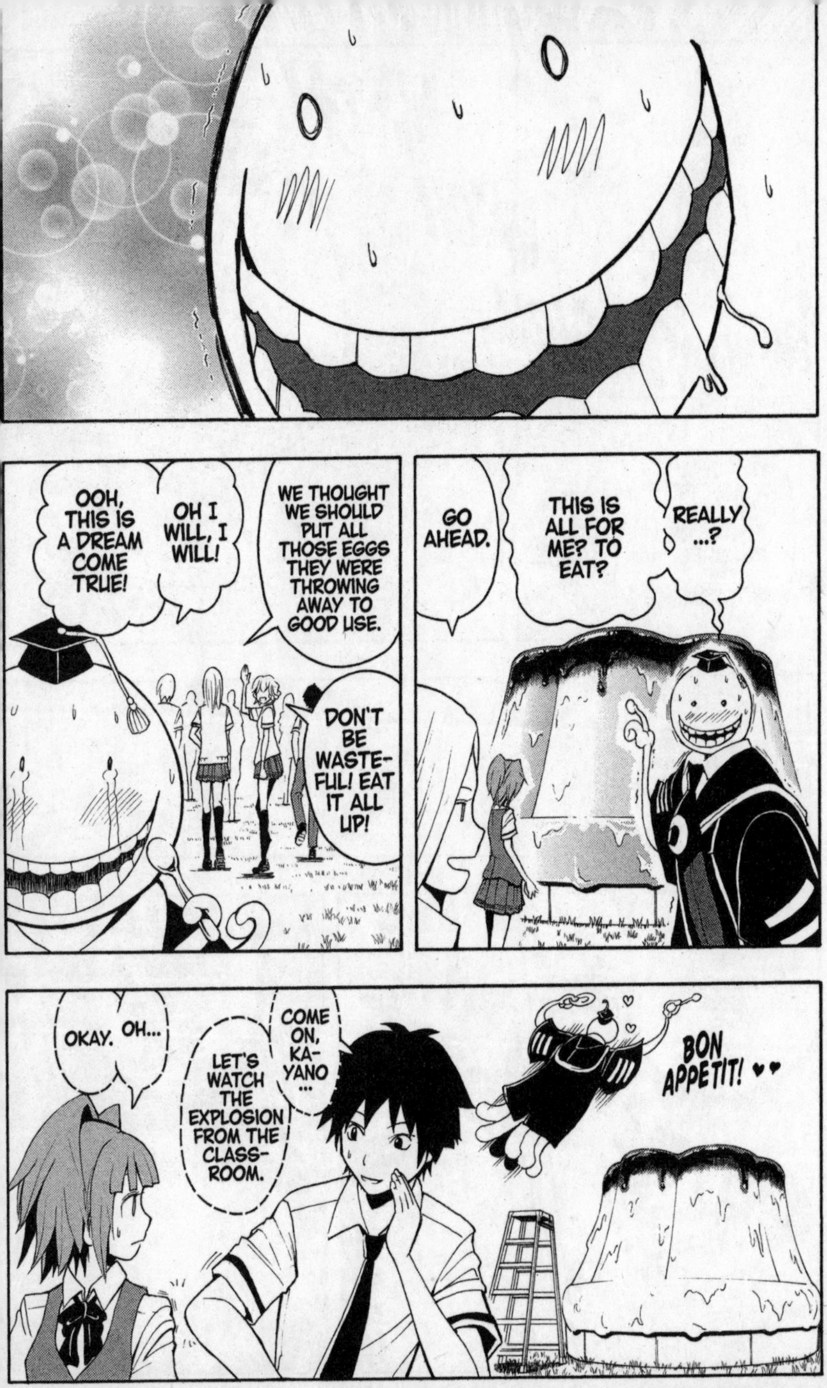
REALLY ...?
THIS IS ALL FOR ME? TO EAT?
GO AHEAD.
WE THOUGHT WE SHOULD PUT ALL THOSE EGGS THEY WERE THROWING AWAY TO GOOD USE.
DON'T BE WASTE-FUL! EAT IT ALL UP!
OH I WILL, I WILL!
OOH, THIS IS A DREAM COME TRUE!
BON APPETIT! ♥♥
COME ON, KA-YANO ...
LET'S WATCH THE EXPLOSION FROM THE CLASS-ROOM.
OH...
OKAY.

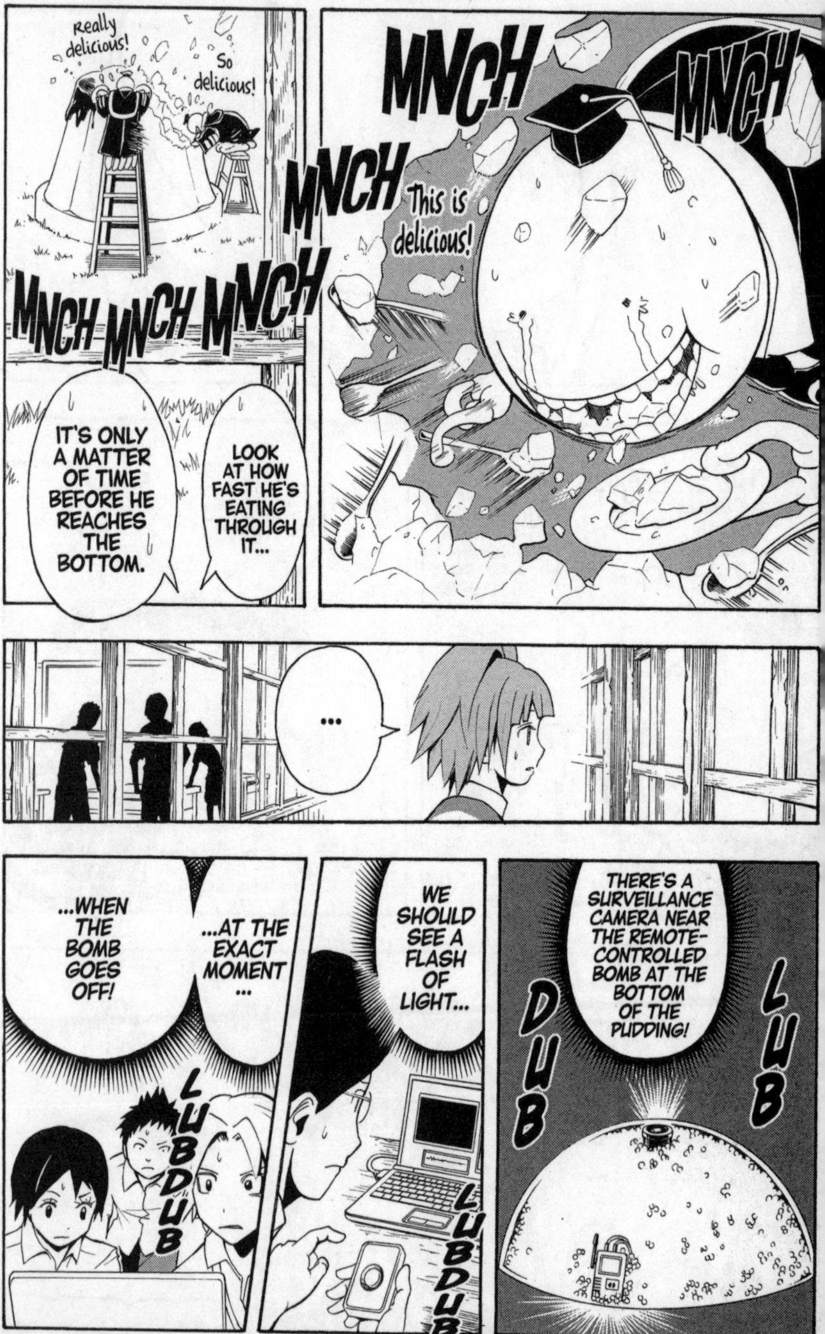
MNCH
MNCH
This is delicious!
MNCH
Really delicious!
So delicious!
MNCH MNCH MNCH
LOOK AT HOW FAST HE'S EATING THROUGH IT...
IT'S ONLY A MATTER OF TIME BEFORE HE REACHES THE BOTTOM.
...
THERE'S A SURVEILLANCE CAMERA NEAR THE REMOTE-CONTROLLED BOMB AT THE BOTTOM OF THE PUDDING!
LUB
DUB
WE SHOULD SEE A FLASH OF LIGHT...
LUBDUB
...AT THE EXACT MOMENT...
...WHEN THE BOMB GOES OFF!
LUBDUB

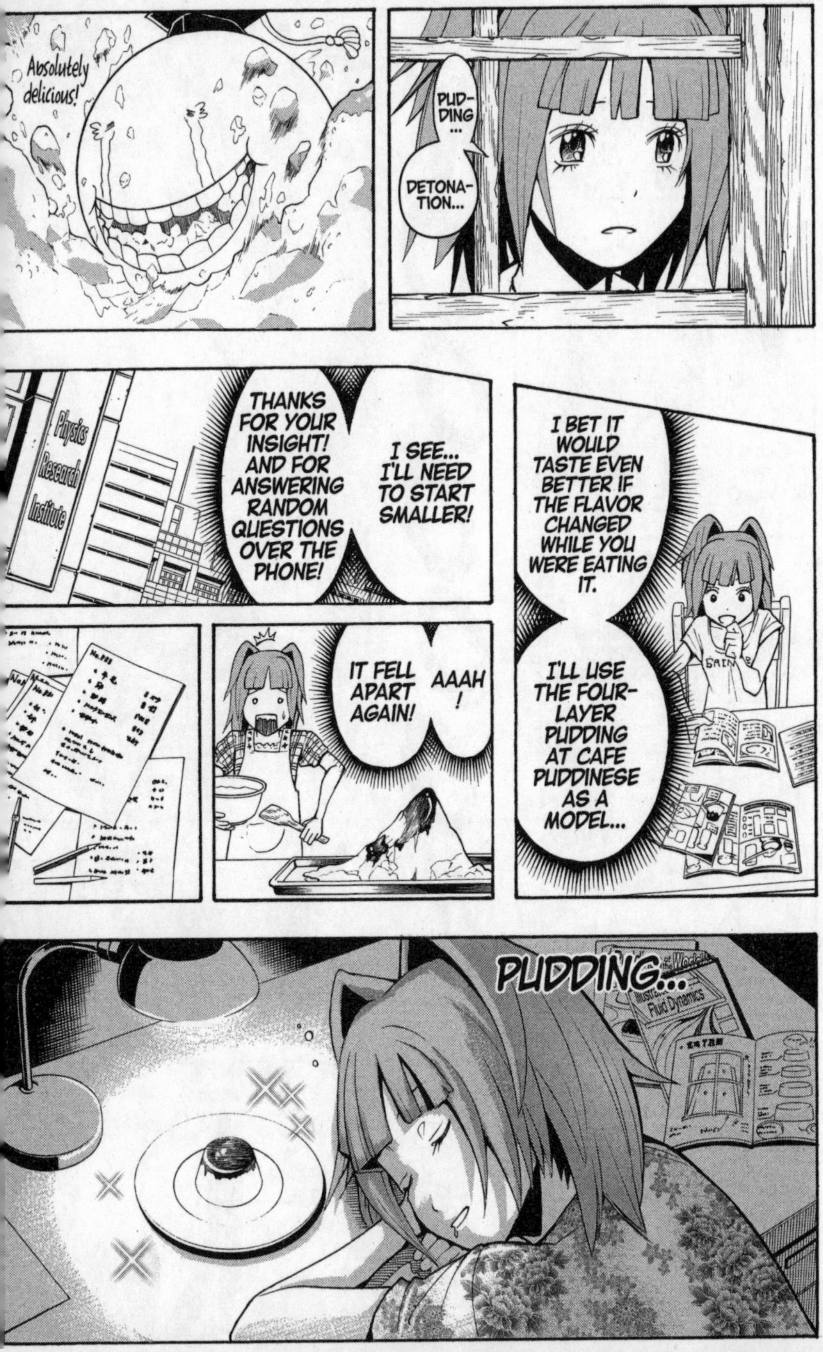
PUD-DING...
DETONA-TION...
Absolutely delicious!
I BET IT WOULD TASTE EVEN BETTER IF THE FLAVOR CHANGED WHILE YOU WERE EATING IT.
I'LL USE THE FOUR-LAYER PUDDING AT CAFE PUDDINESE AS A MODEL...
I SEE... I'LL NEED TO START SMALLER!
THANKS FOR YOUR INSIGHT! AND FOR ANSWERING RANDOM QUESTIONS OVER THE PHONE!
Physics Research Institute
AAAH!
IT FELL APART AGAIN!
PUDDING...
Fluid Dynamics

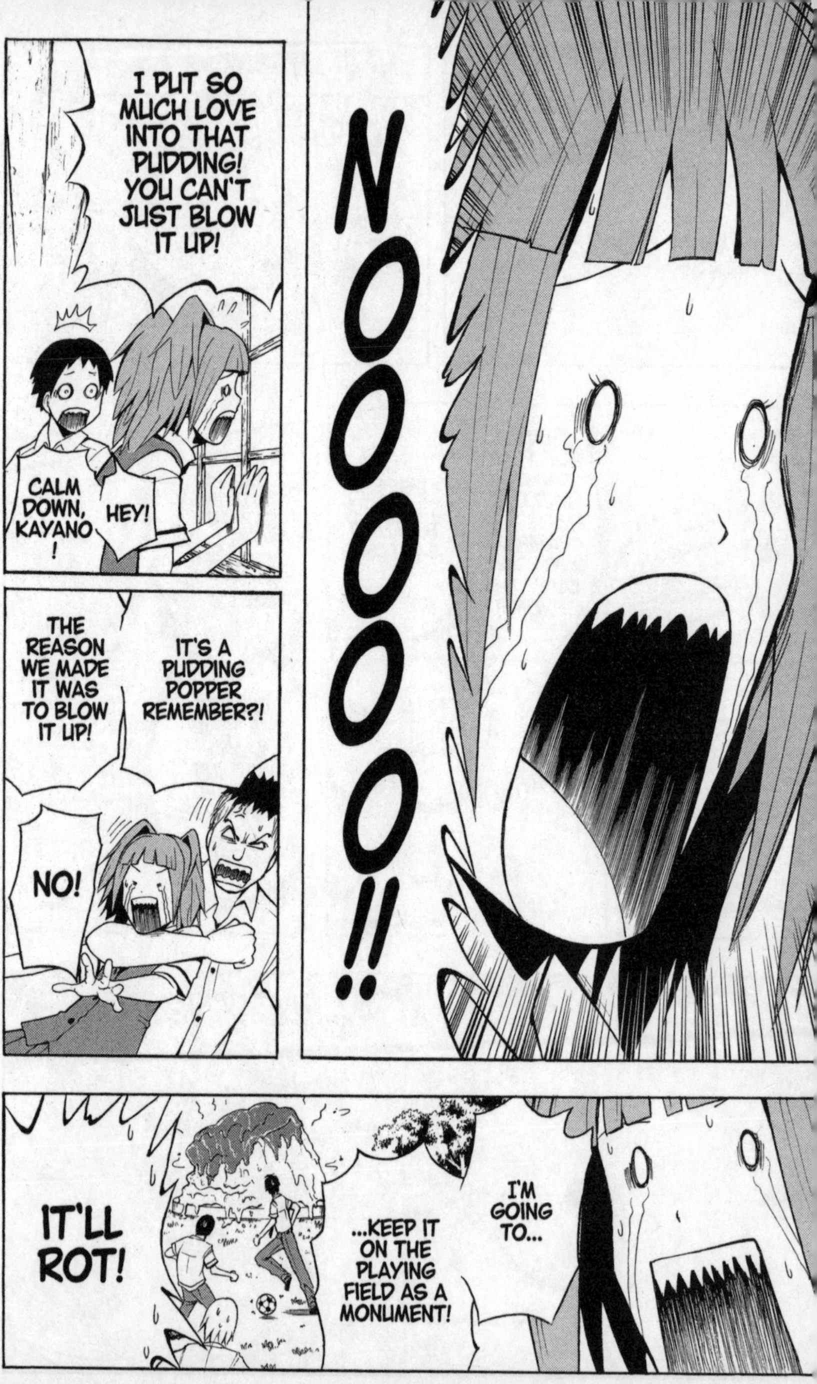

NOOOOO!!
I PUT SO MUCH LOVE INTO THAT PUDDING! YOU CAN'T JUST BLOW IT UP!
HEY!
CALM DOWN, KAYANO!
IT'S A PUDDING POPPER REMEMBER?!
THE REASON WE MADE IT WAS TO BLOW IT UP!
NO!
I'M GOING TO...
...KEEP IT ON THE PLAYING FIELD AS A MONUMENT!
IT'LL ROT!

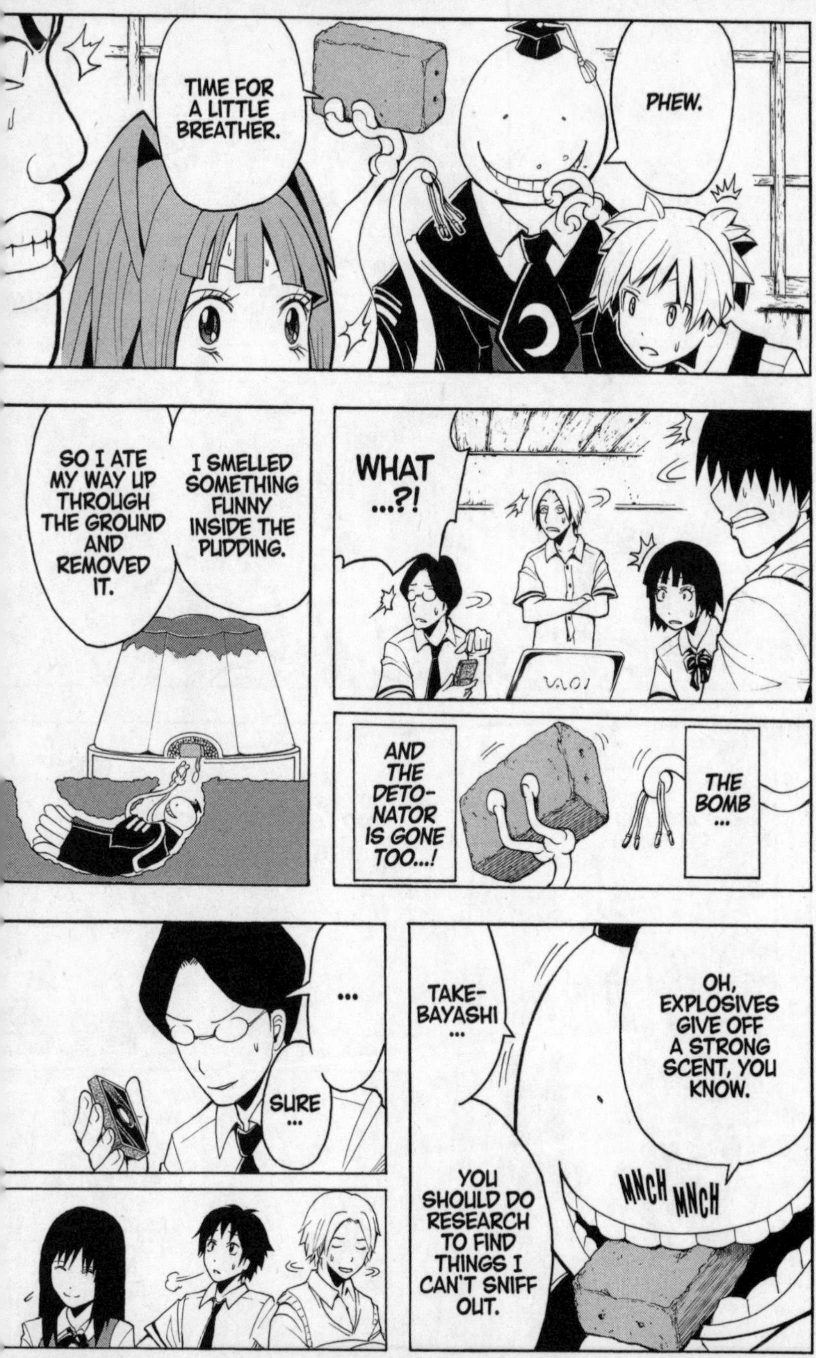
PHEW.
TIME FOR A LITTLE BREATHER.
WHAT ...?!
THE BOMB ...
AND THE DETONATOR IS GONE TOO...!
I SMELLED SOMETHING FUNNY INSIDE THE PUDDING.
SO I ATE MY WAY UP THROUGH THE GROUND AND REMOVED IT.
OH, EXPLOSIVES GIVE OFF A STRONG SCENT, YOU KNOW.
TAKE-BAYASHI ...
MNCH MNCH
YOU SHOULD DO RESEARCH TO FIND THINGS I CAN'T SNIFF OUT.
...
SURE ...

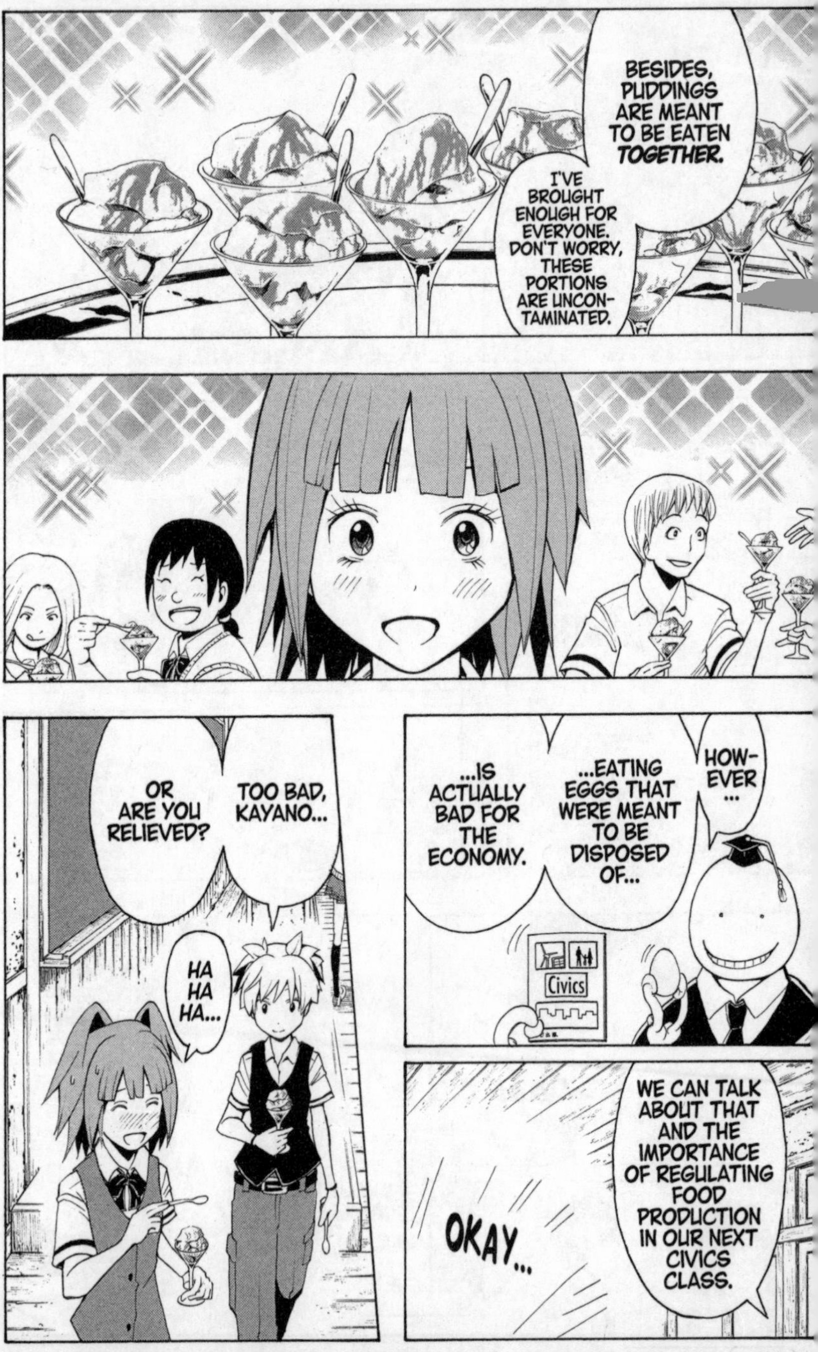
BESIDES, PUDDINGS ARE MEANT TO BE EATEN *TOGETHER.*
I'VE BROUGHT ENOUGH FOR EVERYONE. DON'T WORRY, THESE PORTIONS ARE UNCON-TAMINATED.
HOW-EVER...
...EATING EGGS THAT WERE MEANT TO BE DISPOSED OF...
...IS ACTUALLY BAD FOR THE ECONOMY.
Civics
WE CAN TALK ABOUT THAT AND THE IMPORTANCE OF REGULATING FOOD PRODUCTION IN OUR NEXT CIVICS CLASS.
OKAY...
TOO BAD, KAYANO...
OR ARE YOU RELIEVED?
HA HA HA...

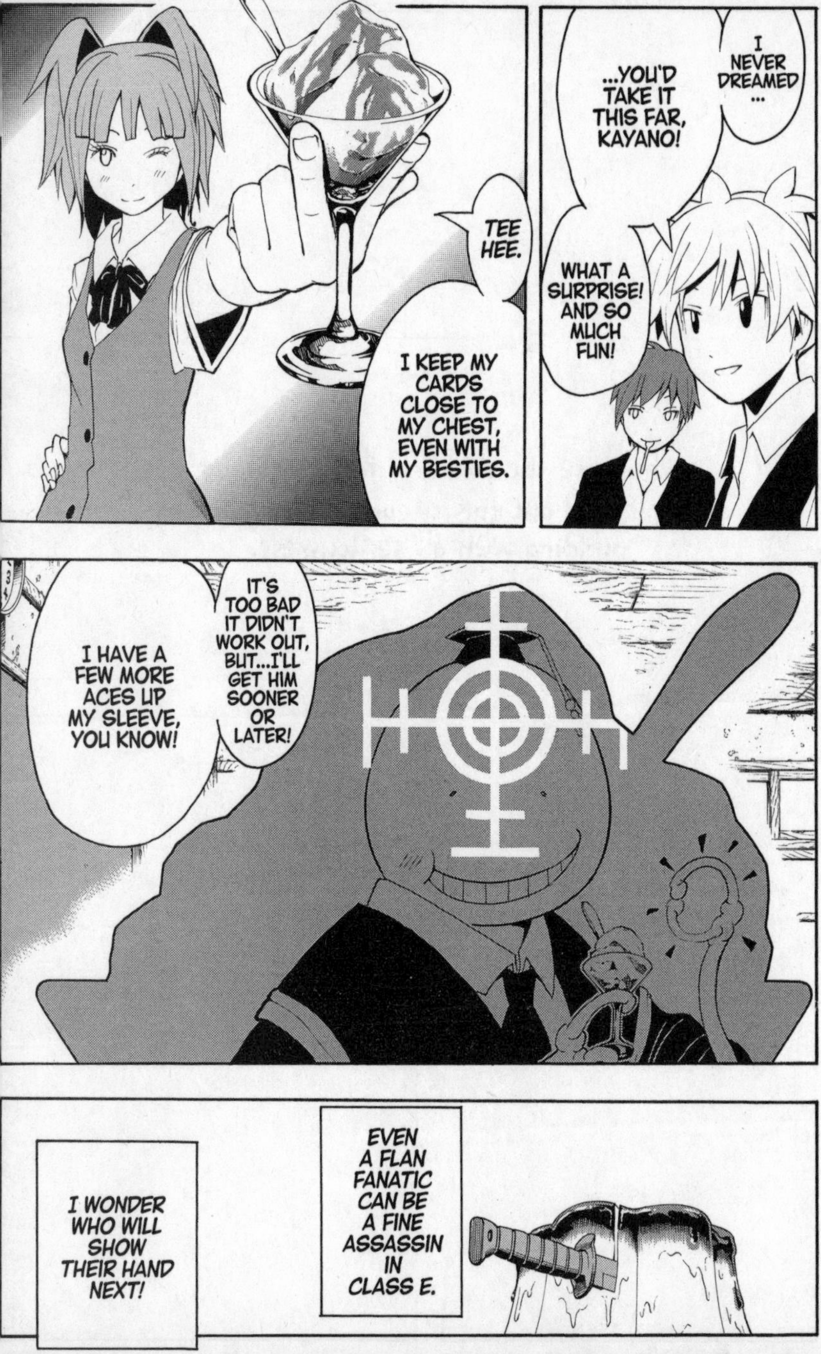
I NEVER DREAMED...
...YOU'D TAKE IT THIS FAR, KAYANO!
WHAT A SURPRISE! AND SO MUCH FUN!
TEE HEE.
I KEEP MY CARDS CLOSE TO MY CHEST, EVEN WITH MY BESTIES.
IT'S TOO BAD IT DIDN'T WORK OUT, BUT...I'LL GET HIM SOONER OR LATER!
I HAVE A FEW MORE ACES UP MY SLEEVE, YOU KNOW!
EVEN A FLAN FANATIC CAN BE A FINE ASSASSIN IN CLASS E.
I WONDER WHO WILL SHOW THEIR HAND NEXT!

I'm quite the pudding fan myself, so I planned out this creation of a giant pudding with all seriousness.

Could someone—anyone?—please test out my recipe to prove that it can be done?

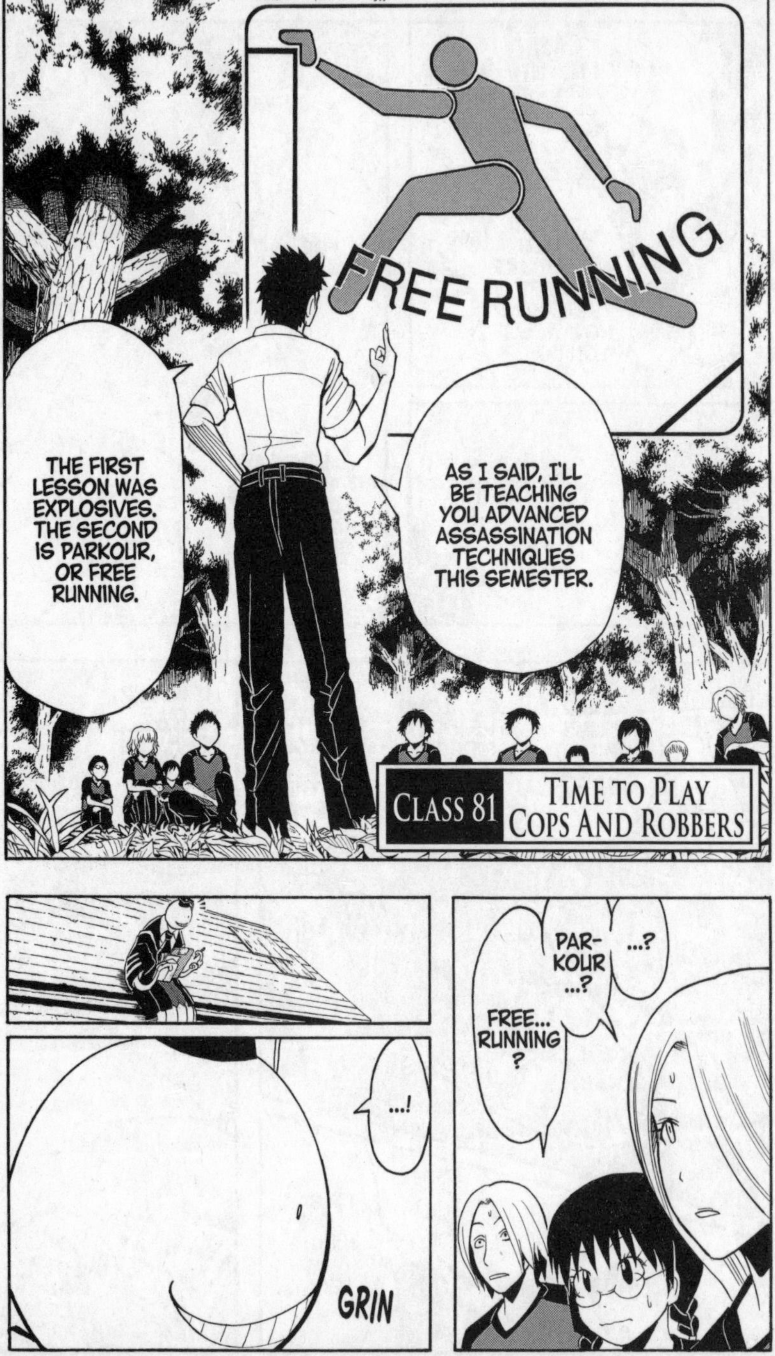
FREE RUNNING
AS I SAID, I'LL BE TEACHING YOU ADVANCED ASSASSINATION TECHNIQUES THIS SEMESTER.
THE FIRST LESSON WAS EXPLOSIVES. THE SECOND IS PARKOUR, OR FREE RUNNING.
CLASS 81
TIME TO PLAY COPS AND ROBBERS
...?
PAR-KOUR ...?
FREE... RUNNING ?
...!
GRIN

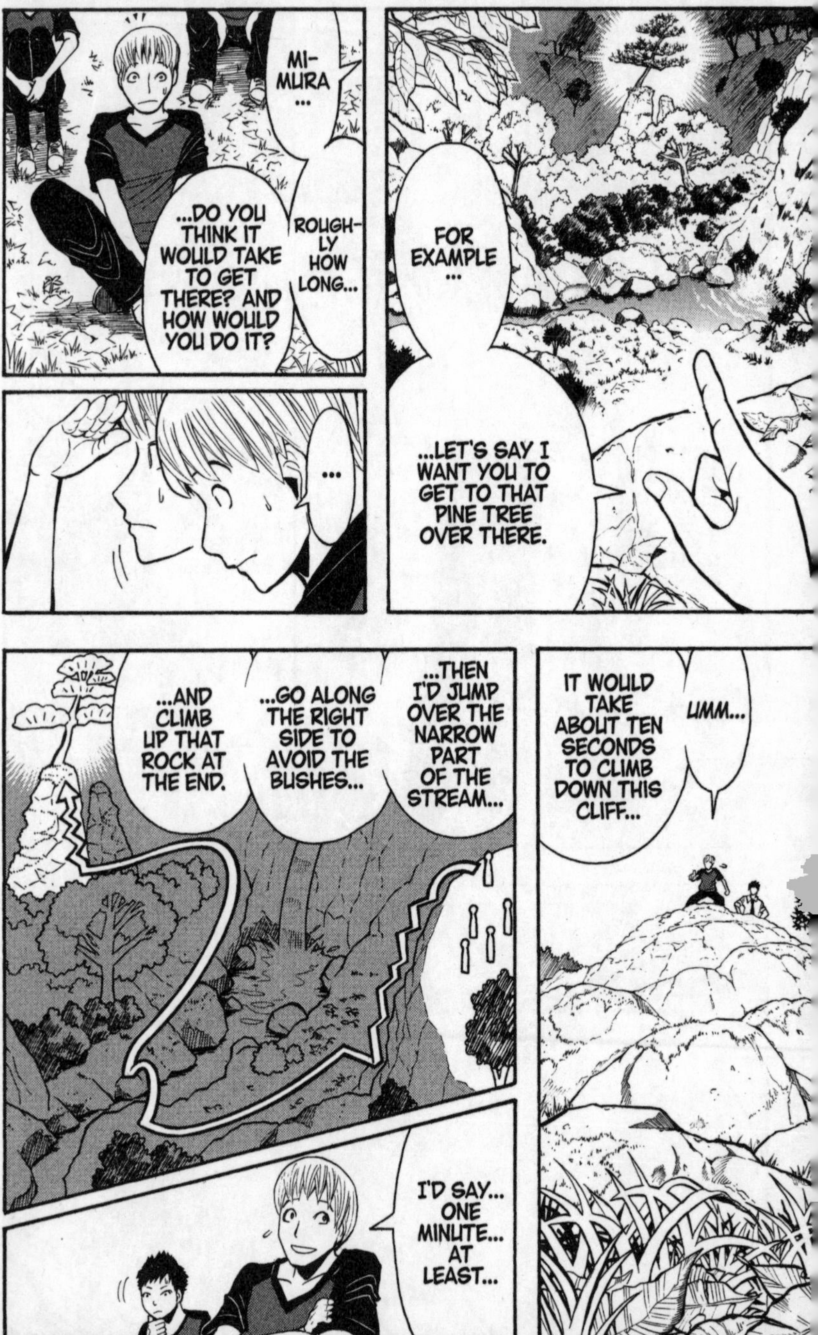
FOR EXAMPLE...
...LET'S SAY I WANT YOU TO GET TO THAT PINE TREE OVER THERE.
MI-MURA...
ROUGHLY HOW LONG...
...DO YOU THINK IT WOULD TAKE TO GET THERE? AND HOW WOULD YOU DO IT?
...
UMM...
IT WOULD TAKE ABOUT TEN SECONDS TO CLIMB DOWN THIS CLIFF...
...THEN I'D JUMP OVER THE NARROW PART OF THE STREAM...
...GO ALONG THE RIGHT SIDE TO AVOID THE BUSHES...
...AND CLIMB UP THAT ROCK AT THE END.
I'D SAY... ONE MINUTE... AT LEAST...

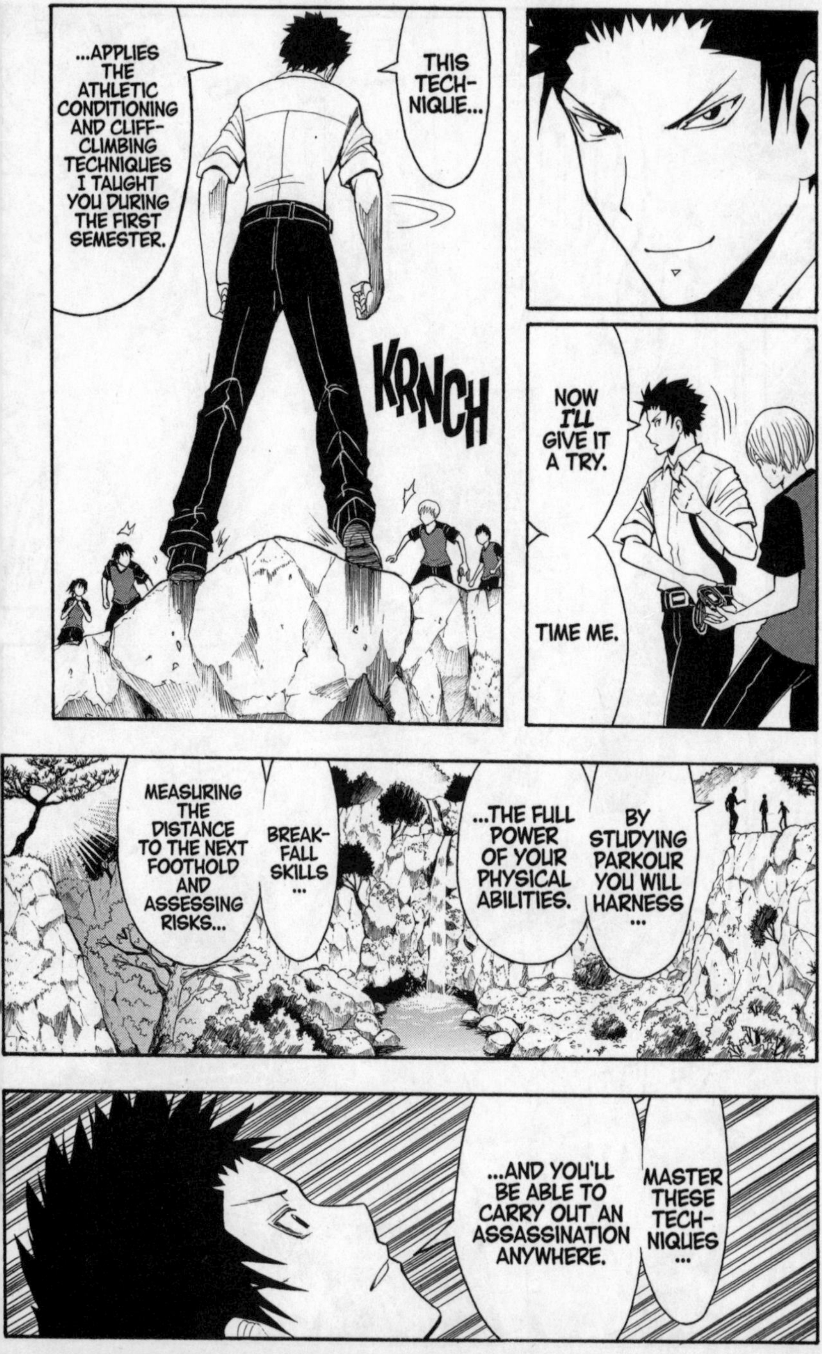
NOW I'LL GIVE IT A TRY.
TIME ME.
THIS TECH-NIQUE...
...APPLIES THE ATHLETIC CONDITIONING AND CLIFF-CLIMBING TECHNIQUES I TAUGHT YOU DURING THE FIRST SEMESTER.
KRNCH
BY STUDYING PARKOUR YOU WILL HARNESS...
...THE FULL POWER OF YOUR PHYSICAL ABILITIES.
BREAK-FALL SKILLS...
MEASURING THE DISTANCE TO THE NEXT FOOTHOLD AND ASSESSING RISKS...
MASTER THESE TECH-NIQUES...
...AND YOU'LL BE ABLE TO CARRY OUT AN ASSASSINATION ANYWHERE.

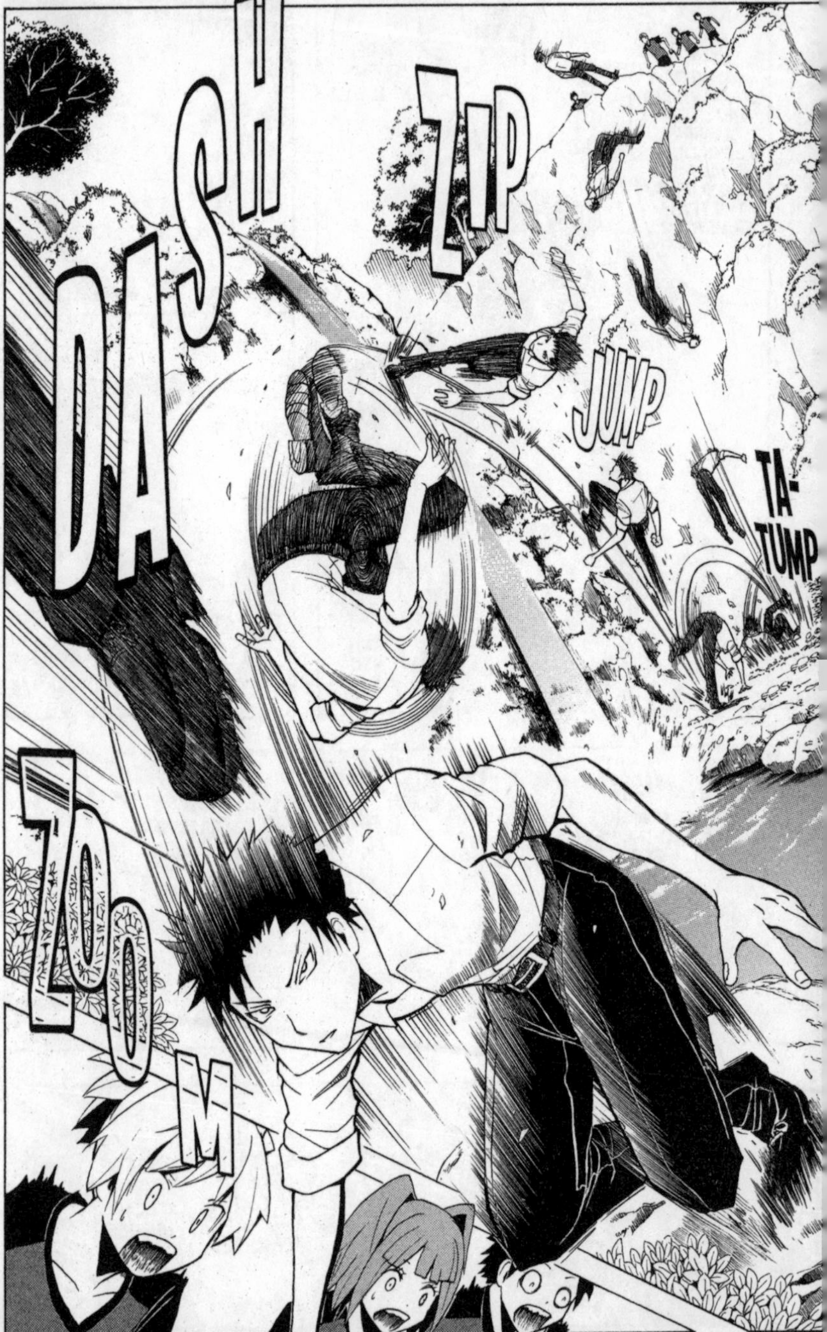
TA-
TUMP
JUMP
ZIP
DASH
ZOOM

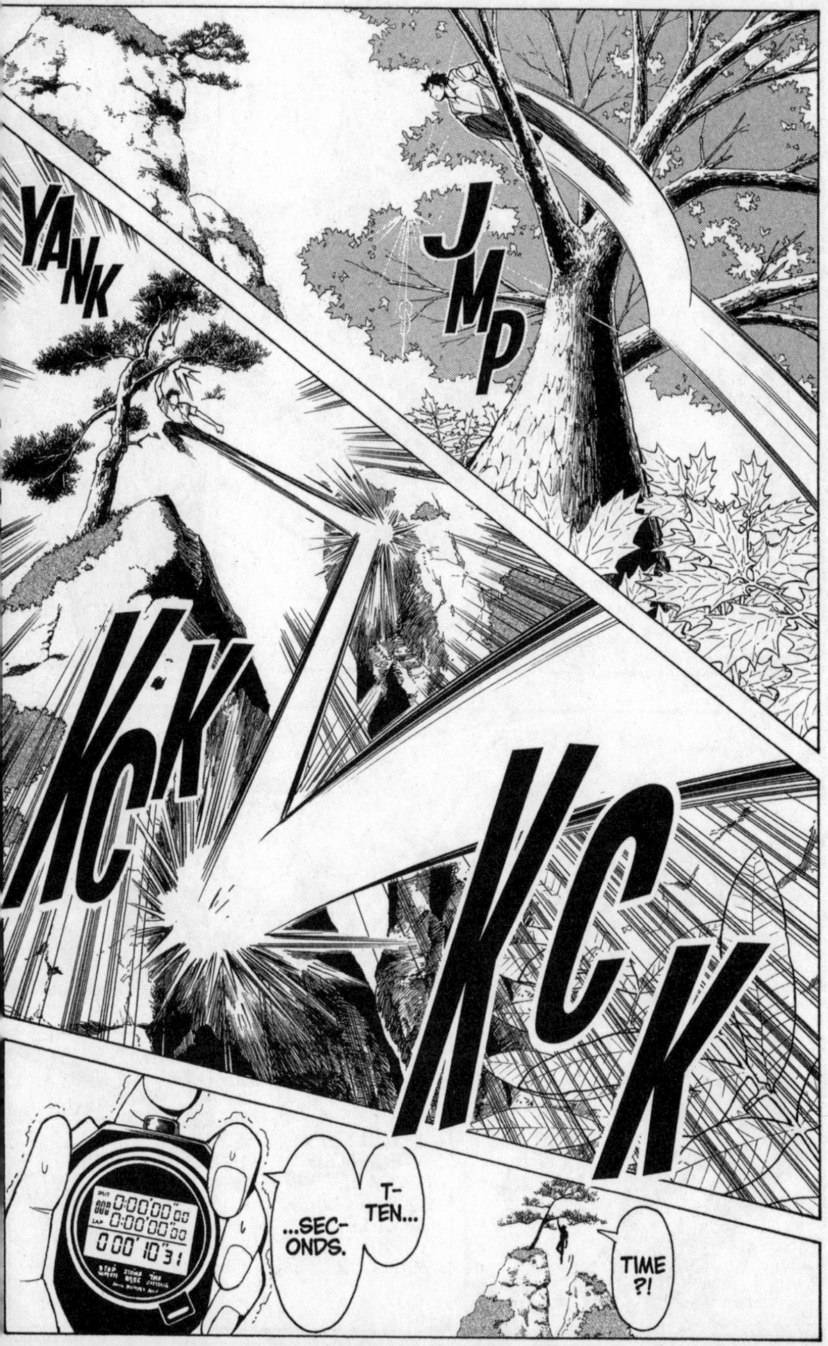
JMP
YANK
KCK
KCK
TIME ?!
T- TEN...
...SEC- ONDS.

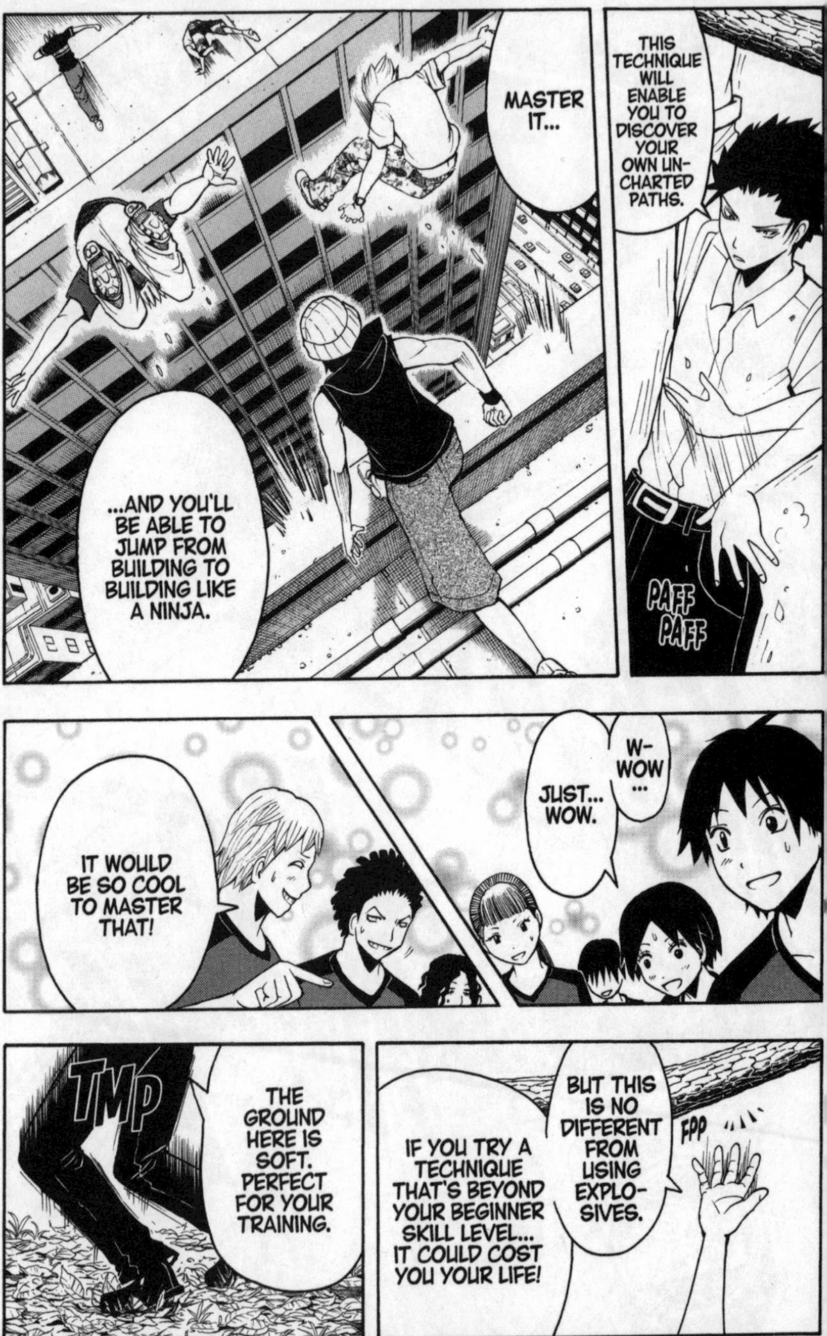
THIS TECHNIQUE WILL ENABLE YOU TO DISCOVER YOUR OWN UN-CHARTED PATHS.
PAFF PAFF
MASTER IT...
...AND YOU'LL BE ABLE TO JUMP FROM BUILDING TO BUILDING LIKE A NINJA.
W-WOW...
JUST... WOW.
IT WOULD BE SO COOL TO MASTER THAT!
BUT THIS IS NO DIFFERENT FROM USING EXPLO-SIVES.
FPP
IF YOU TRY A TECHNIQUE THAT'S BEYOND YOUR BEGINNER SKILL LEVEL... IT COULD COST YOU YOUR LIFE!
THE GROUND HERE IS SOFT. PERFECT FOR YOUR TRAINING.
TMP

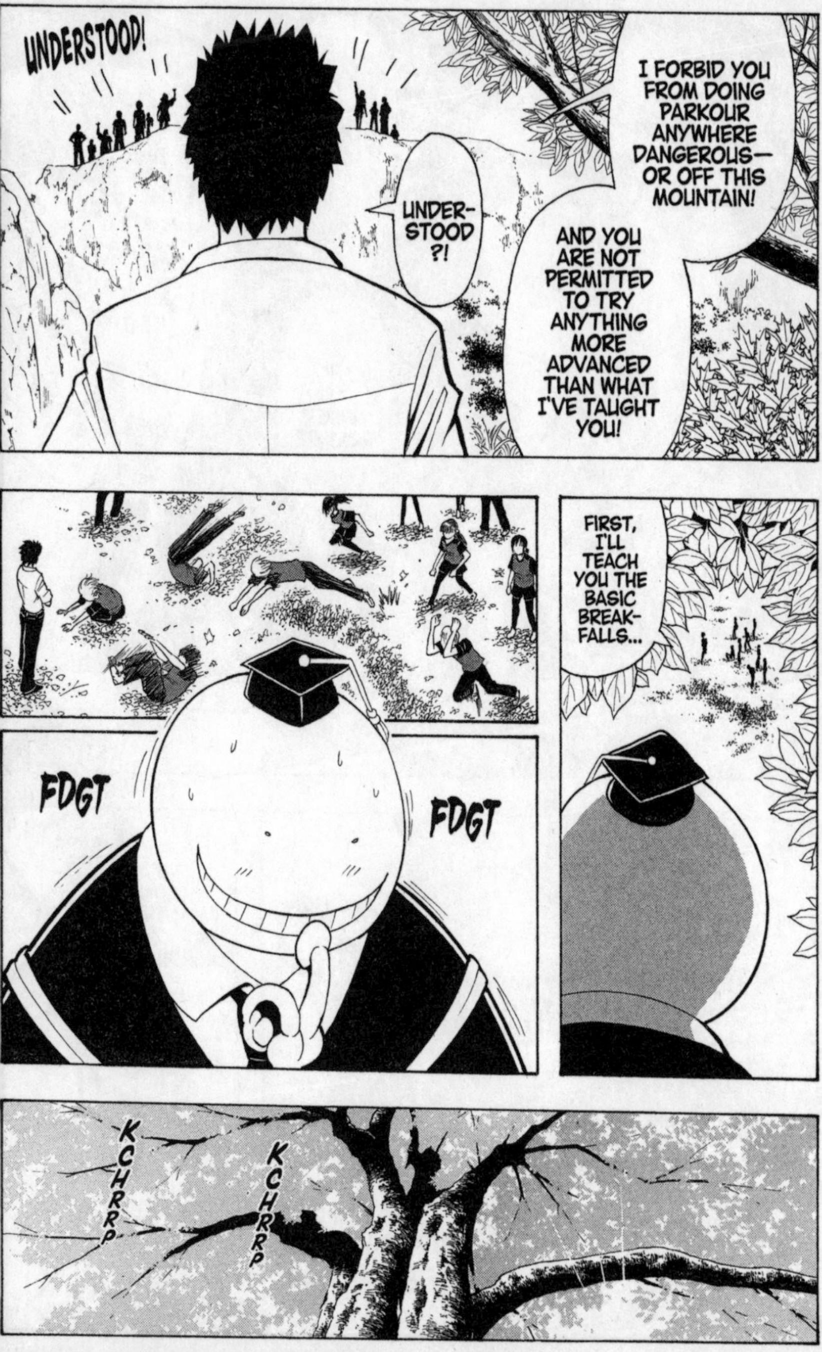
I FORBID YOU FROM DOING PARKOUR ANYWHERE DANGEROUS—OR OFF THIS MOUNTAIN!
AND YOU ARE NOT PERMITTED TO TRY ANYTHING MORE ADVANCED THAN WHAT I'VE TAUGHT YOU!
UNDER-STOOD?!
UNDERSTOOD!
FIRST, I'LL TEACH YOU THE BASIC BREAK-FALLS...
FDGT
FDGT
KCHRRP
KCHRRP

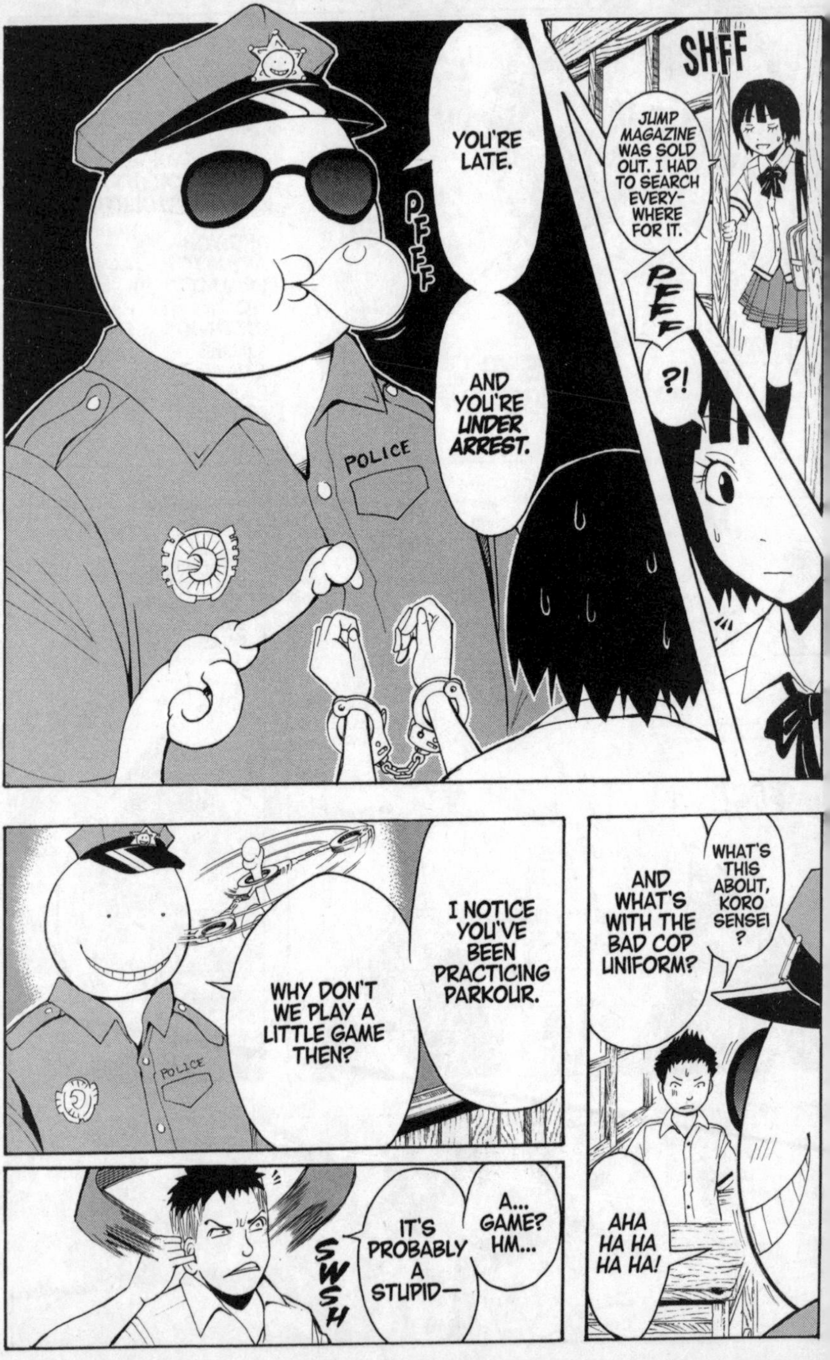
SHFF
JUMP MAGAZINE WAS SOLD OUT. I HAD TO SEARCH EVERY-WHERE FOR IT.
PFFF
?!
YOU'RE LATE.
PFFF
AND YOU'RE UNDER ARREST.
WHAT'S THIS ABOUT, KORO SENSEI?
AND WHAT'S WITH THE BAD COP UNIFORM?
AHA HA HA HA HA!
I NOTICE YOU'VE BEEN PRACTICING PARKOUR.
WHY DON'T WE PLAY A LITTLE GAME THEN?
A... GAME? HM...
IT'S PROBABLY A STUPID—
SWSH

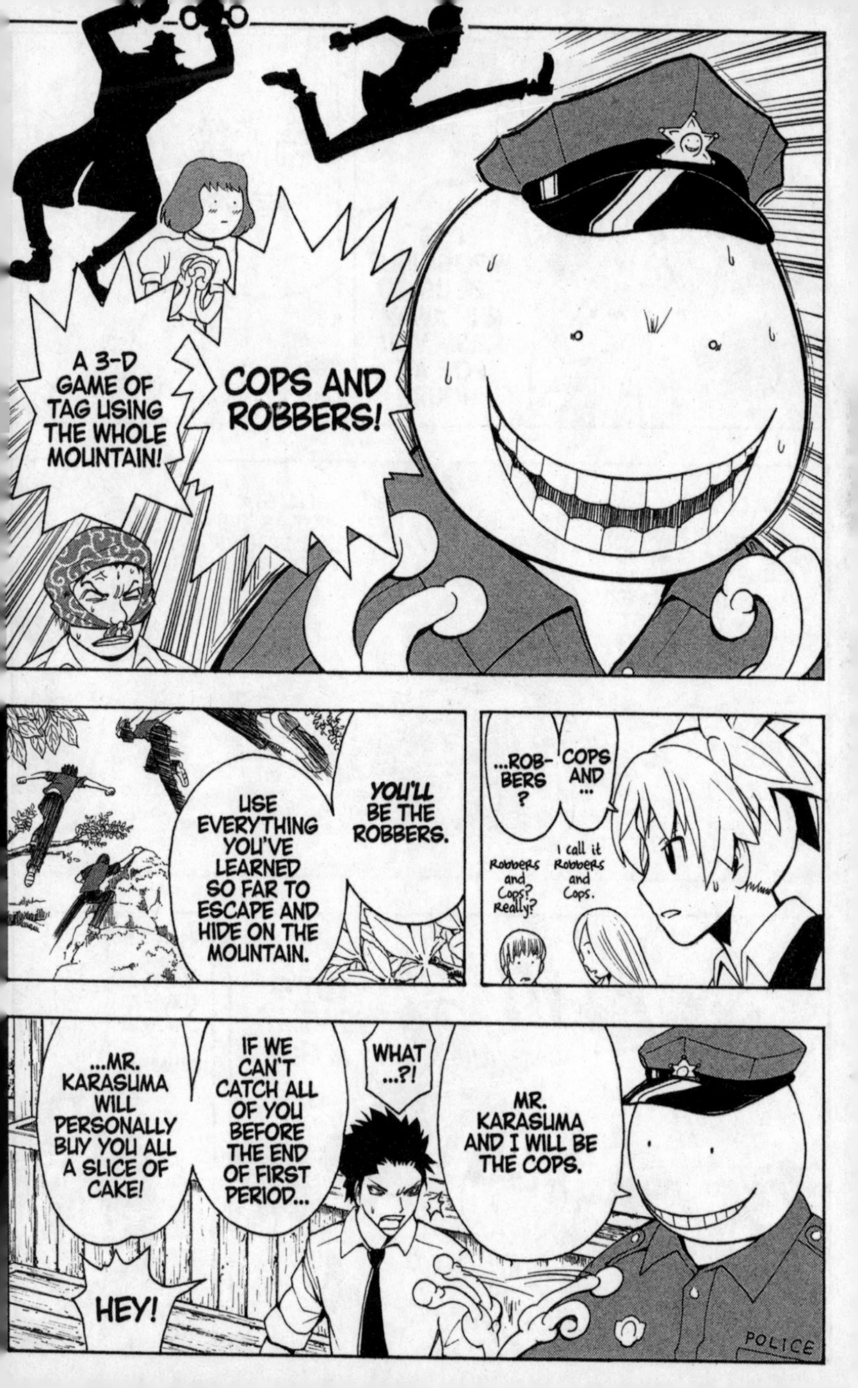
COPS AND ROBBERS!
A 3-D GAME OF TAG USING THE WHOLE MOUNTAIN!
COPS AND ...
...ROB-BERS?
I call it Robbers and Cops.
Robbers and Cops? Really!?
YOU'LL BE THE ROBBERS.
USE EVERYTHING YOU'VE LEARNED SO FAR TO ESCAPE AND HIDE ON THE MOUNTAIN.
MR. KARASUMA AND I WILL BE THE COPS.
WHAT ...?!
IF WE CAN'T CATCH ALL OF YOU BEFORE THE END OF FIRST PERIOD...
...MR. KARASUMA WILL PERSONALLY BUY YOU ALL A SLICE OF CAKE!
HEY!
POLICE

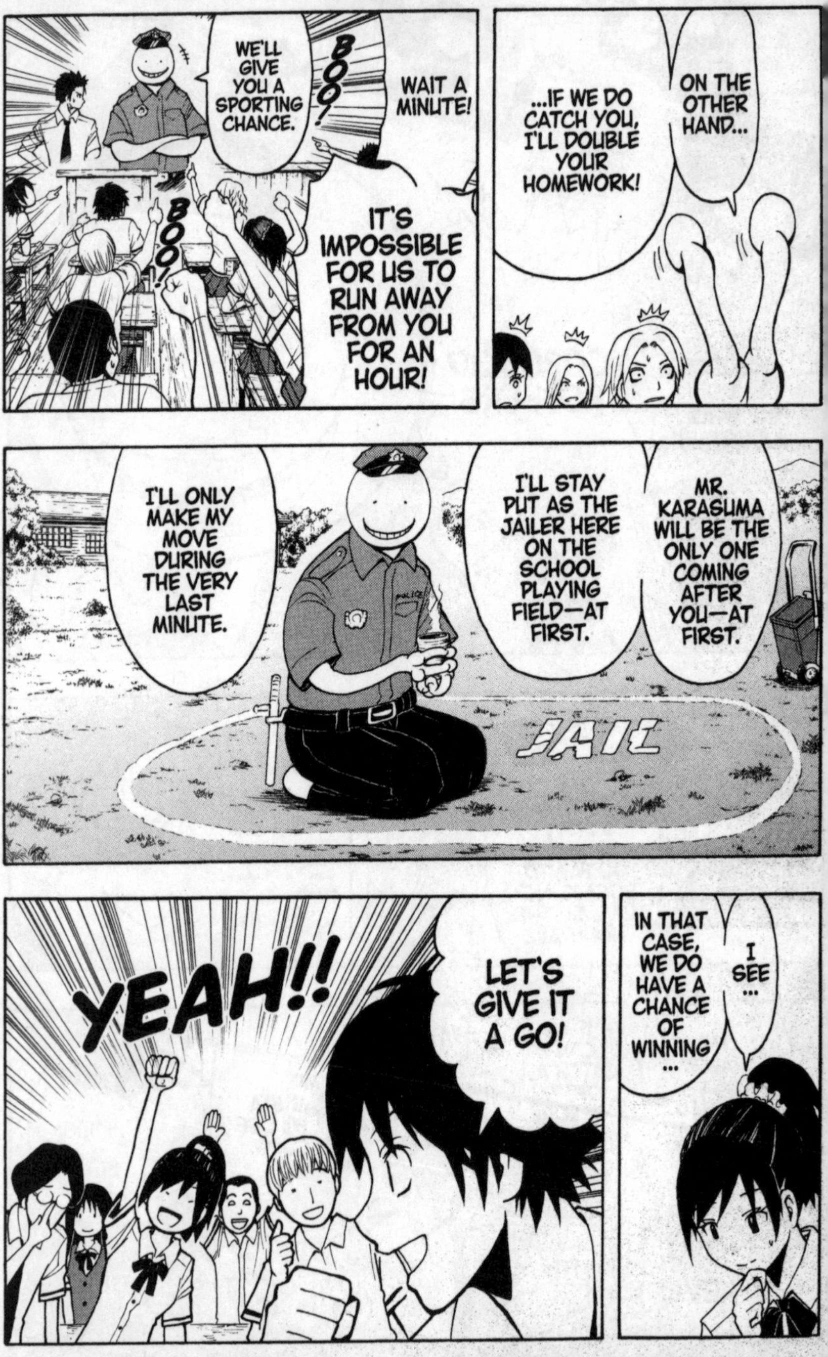
ON THE OTHER HAND...
...IF WE DO CATCH YOU, I'LL DOUBLE YOUR HOMEWORK!
WAIT A MINUTE!
BOO!
WE'LL GIVE YOU A SPORTING CHANCE.
IT'S IMPOSSIBLE FOR US TO RUN AWAY FROM YOU FOR AN HOUR!
BOO!
MR. KARASUMA WILL BE THE ONLY ONE COMING AFTER YOU—AT FIRST.
I'LL STAY PUT AS THE JAILER HERE ON THE SCHOOL PLAYING FIELD—AT FIRST.
I'LL ONLY MAKE MY MOVE DURING THE VERY LAST MINUTE.
JAIL
I SEE...
IN THAT CASE, WE DO HAVE A CHANCE OF WINNING...
LET'S GIVE IT A GO!
YEAH!!

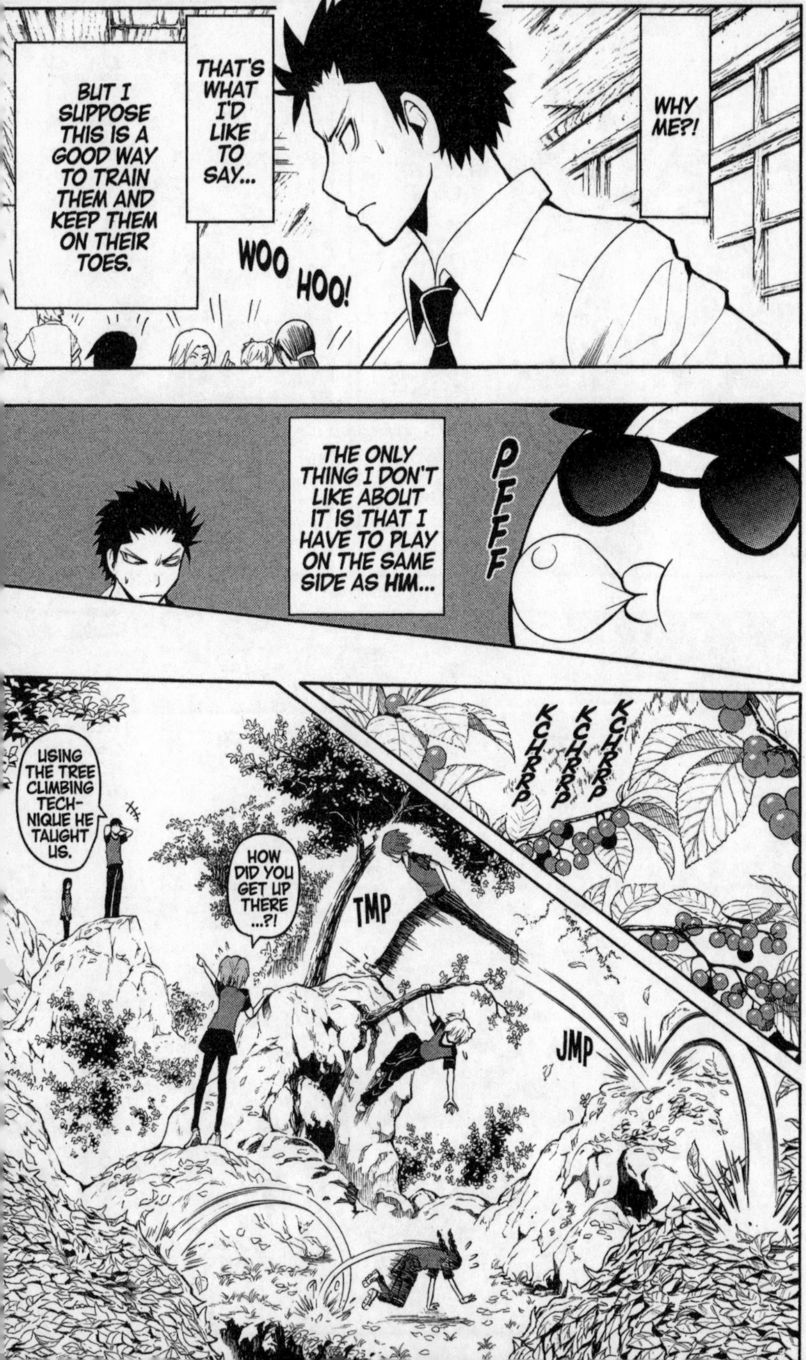
WHY ME?!
THAT'S WHAT I'D LIKE TO SAY...
BUT I SUPPOSE THIS IS A GOOD WAY TO TRAIN THEM AND KEEP THEM ON THEIR TOES.
WOO HOO!
PFFF
THE ONLY THING I DON'T LIKE ABOUT IT IS THAT I HAVE TO PLAY ON THE SAME SIDE AS HIM...
KCHRRRP
KCHRRRP
KCHRRRP
JMP
TMP
HOW DID YOU GET UP THERE ...?!
USING THE TREE CLIMBING TECH-NIQUE HE TAUGHT US.

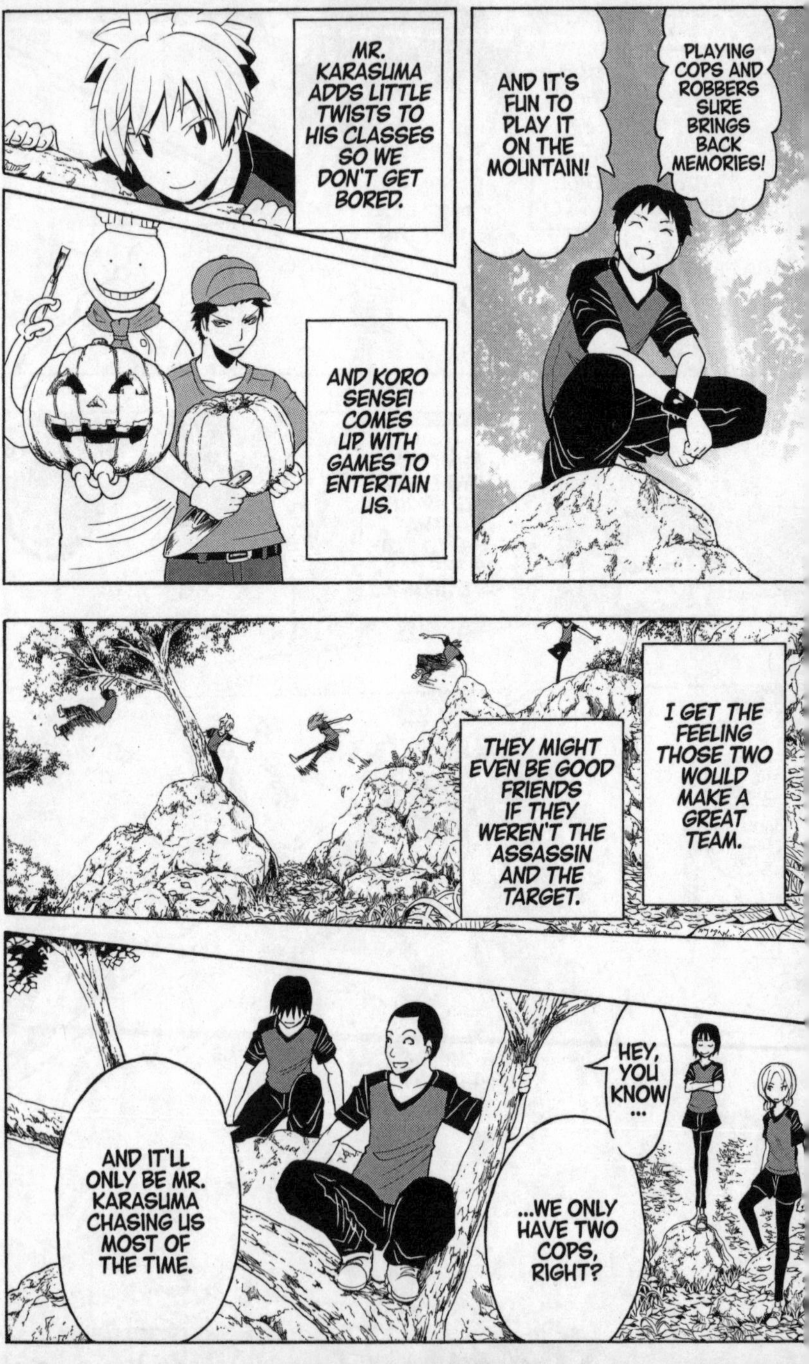
PLAYING COPS AND ROBBERS SURE BRINGS BACK MEMORIES!
AND IT'S FUN TO PLAY IT ON THE MOUNTAIN!
MR. KARASUMA ADDS LITTLE TWISTS TO HIS CLASSES SO WE DON'T GET BORED.
AND KORO SENSEI COMES UP WITH GAMES TO ENTERTAIN US.
I GET THE FEELING THOSE TWO WOULD MAKE A GREAT TEAM.
THEY MIGHT EVEN BE GOOD FRIENDS IF THEY WEREN'T THE ASSASSIN AND THE TARGET.
HEY, YOU KNOW...
...WE ONLY HAVE TWO COPS, RIGHT?
AND IT'LL ONLY BE MR. KARASUMA CHASING US MOST OF THE TIME.

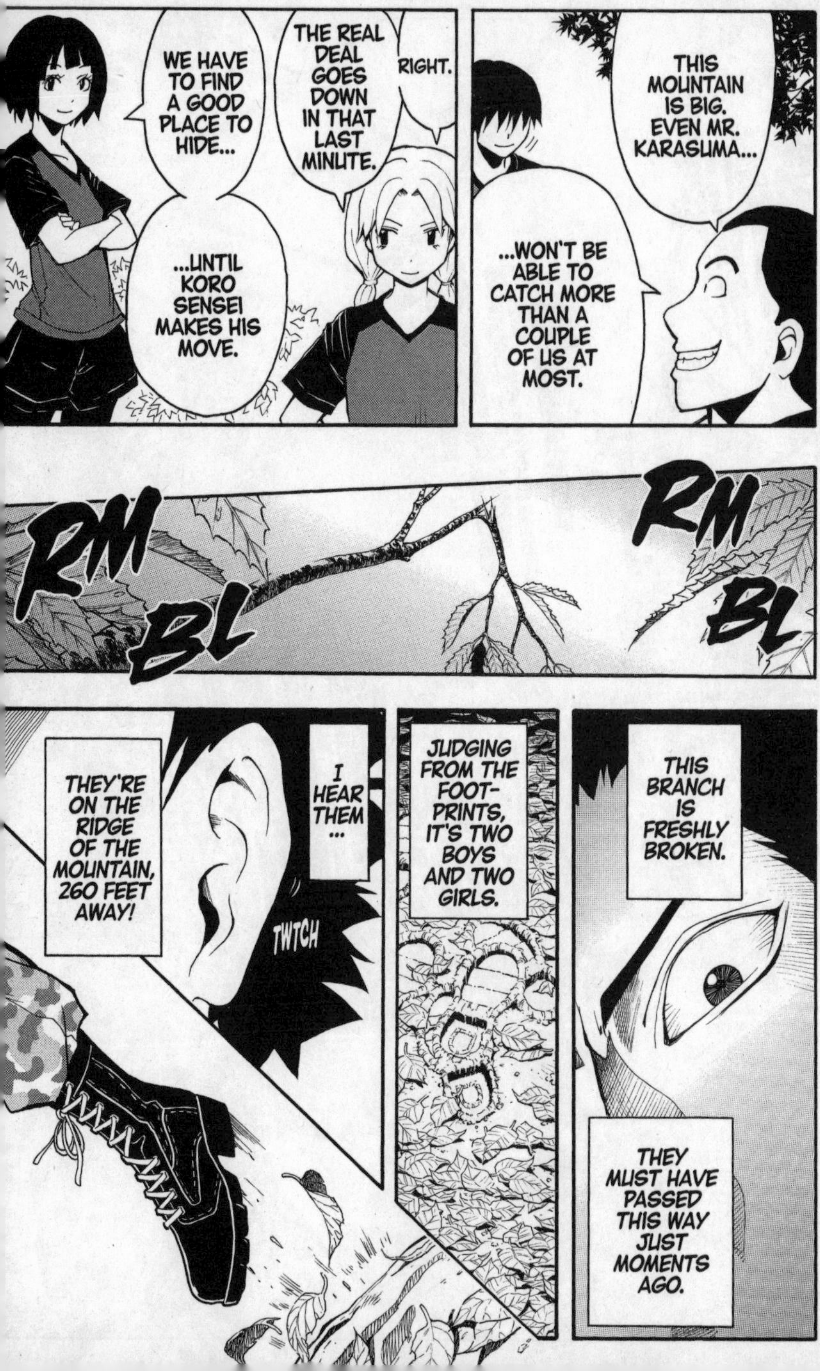
THIS MOUNTAIN IS BIG. EVEN MR. KARASUMA...
...WON'T BE ABLE TO CATCH MORE THAN A COUPLE OF US AT MOST.
RIGHT.
THE REAL DEAL GOES DOWN IN THAT LAST MINUTE.
WE HAVE TO FIND A GOOD PLACE TO HIDE...
...UNTIL KORO SENSEI MAKES HIS MOVE.
RMBL
RMBL
THIS BRANCH IS FRESHLY BROKEN.
THEY MUST HAVE PASSED THIS WAY JUST MOMENTS AGO.
JUDGING FROM THE FOOT-PRINTS, IT'S TWO BOYS AND TWO GIRLS.
I HEAR THEM...
TWTCH
THEY'RE ON THE RIDGE OF THE MOUNTAIN, 260 FEET AWAY!

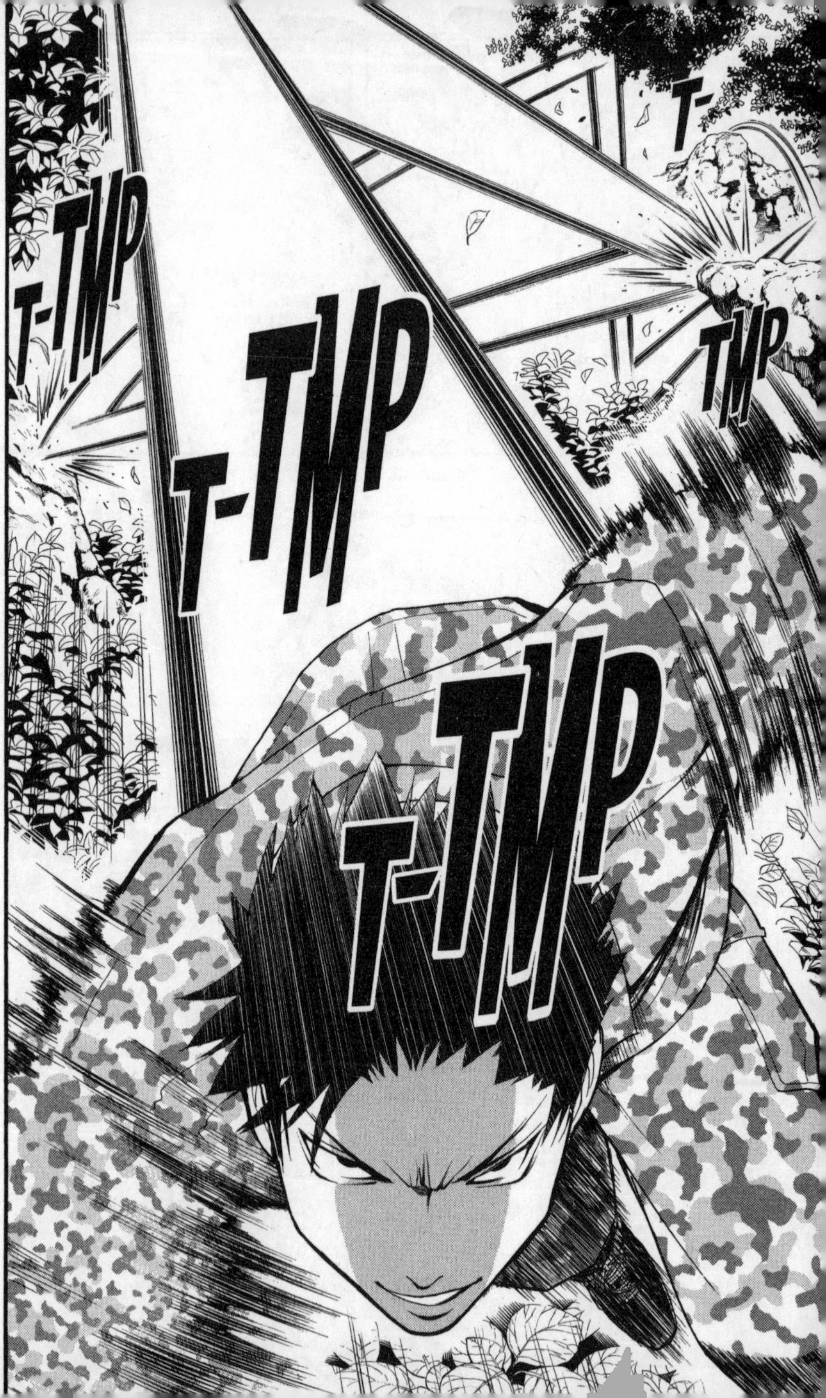
T-
TMP
T-TMP
T-TMP
T-TMP

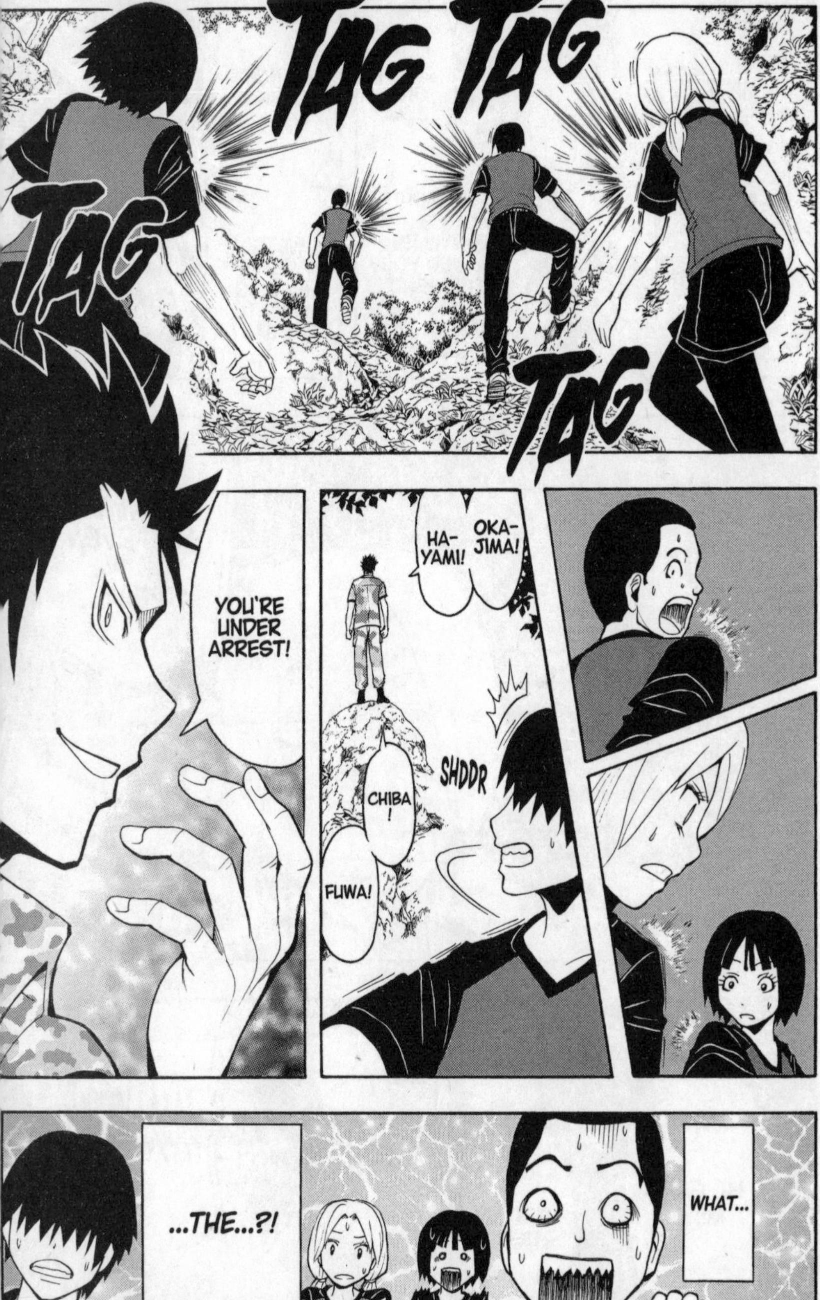
TAG TAG
TAG
TAG
OKA-JIMA!
HA-YAMI!
SHDDR
CHIBA!
FUWA!
YOU'RE UNDER ARREST!
WHAT...
...THE...?!

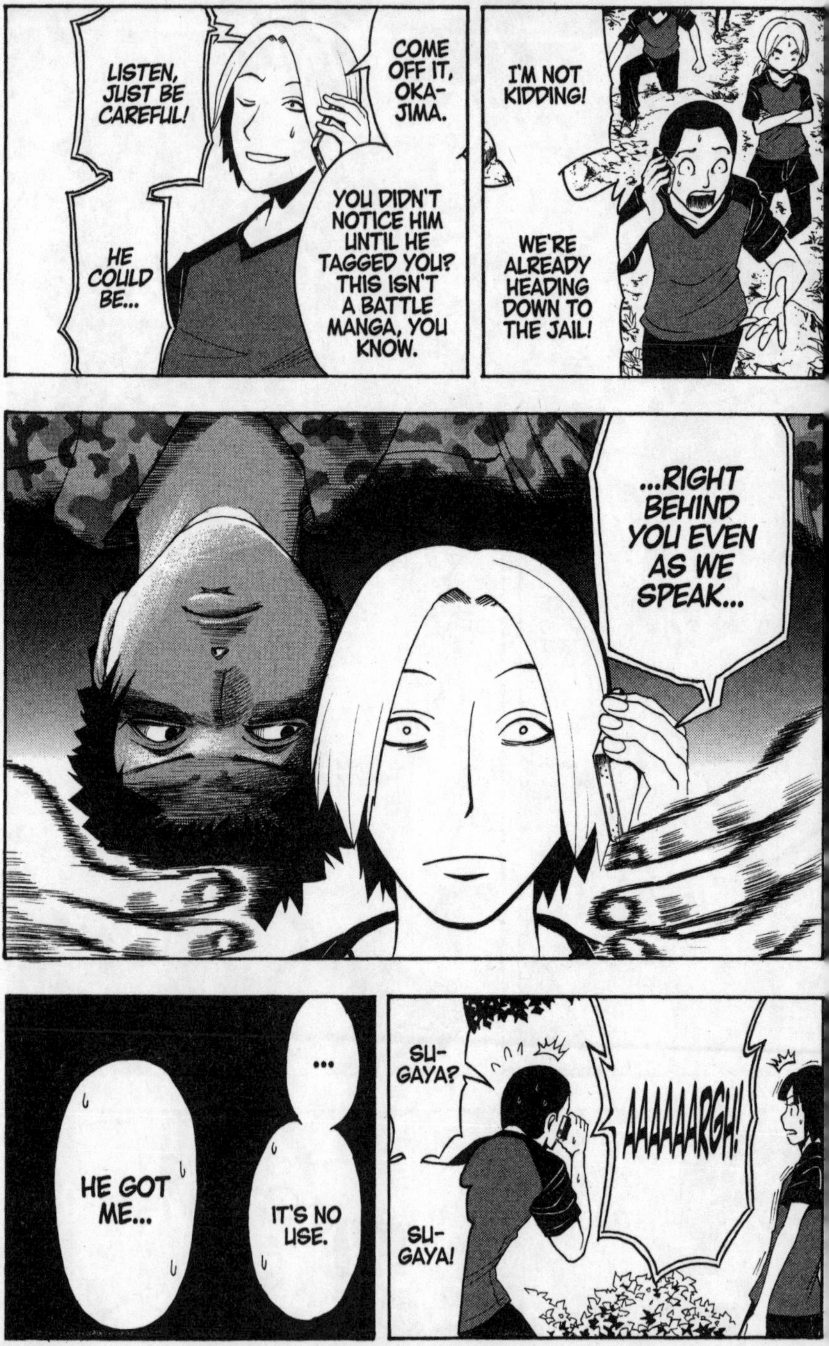
I'M NOT KIDDING!
WE'RE ALREADY HEADING DOWN TO THE JAIL!
COME OFF IT, OKA-JIMA.
YOU DIDN'T NOTICE HIM UNTIL HE TAGGED YOU? THIS ISN'T A BATTLE MANGA, YOU KNOW.
LISTEN, JUST BE CAREFUL!
HE COULD BE...
...RIGHT BEHIND YOU EVEN AS WE SPEAK...
AAAAAARGH!
SU-GAYA?
SU-GAYA!
...
IT'S NO USE.
HE GOT ME...

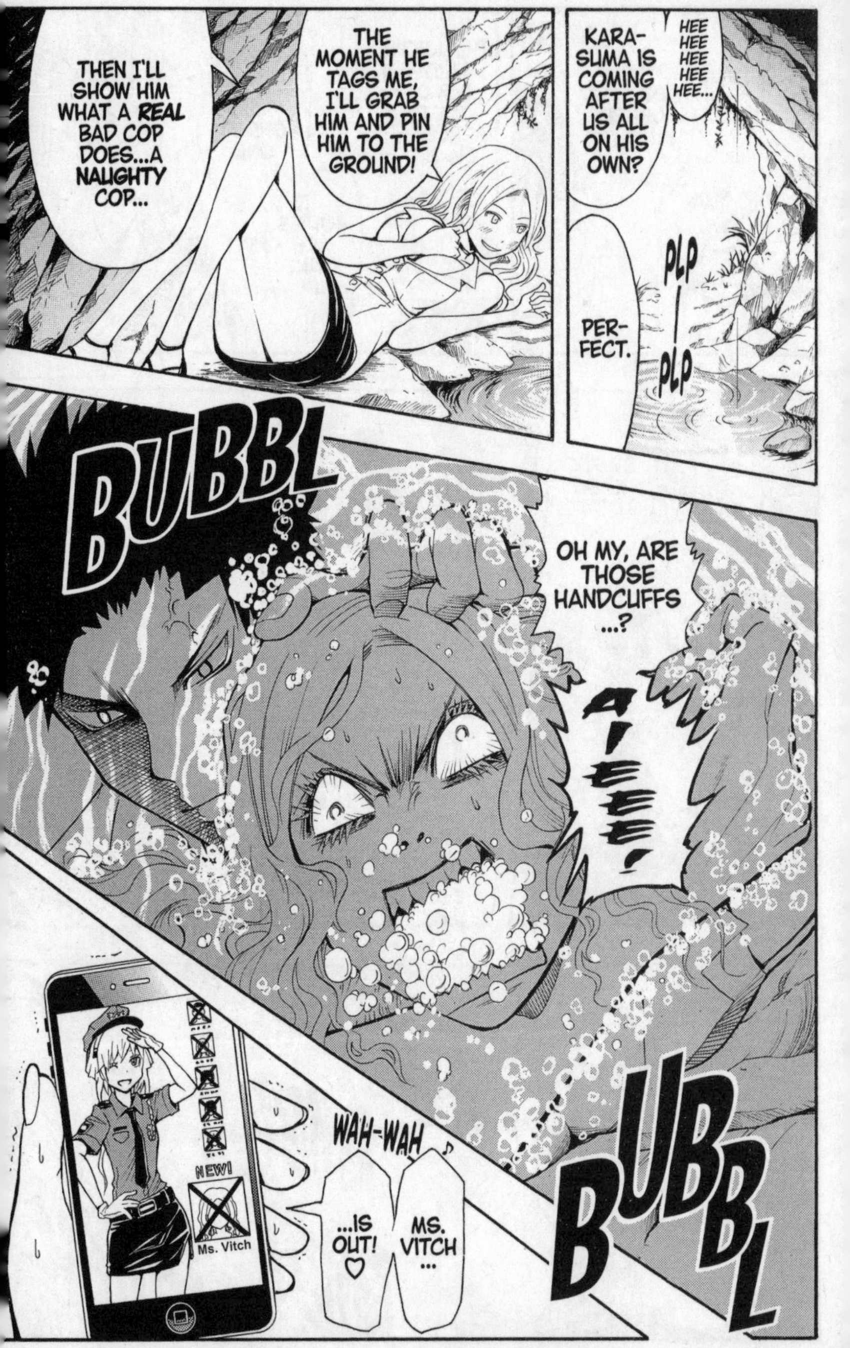
HEE HEE HEE HEE HEE...
KARA-SUMA IS COMING AFTER US ALL ON HIS OWN?
PER-FECT.
PLP PLP
THE MOMENT HE TAGS ME, I'LL GRAB HIM AND PIN HIM TO THE GROUND!
THEN I'LL SHOW HIM WHAT A REAL BAD COP DOES...A NAUGHTY COP...
BUBBL
OH MY, ARE THOSE HANDCUFFS ...?
AIEEEE!
BUBBBL
WAH-WAH ♪
MS. VITCH ...
...IS OUT! ♡
NEW!
Ms. Vitch

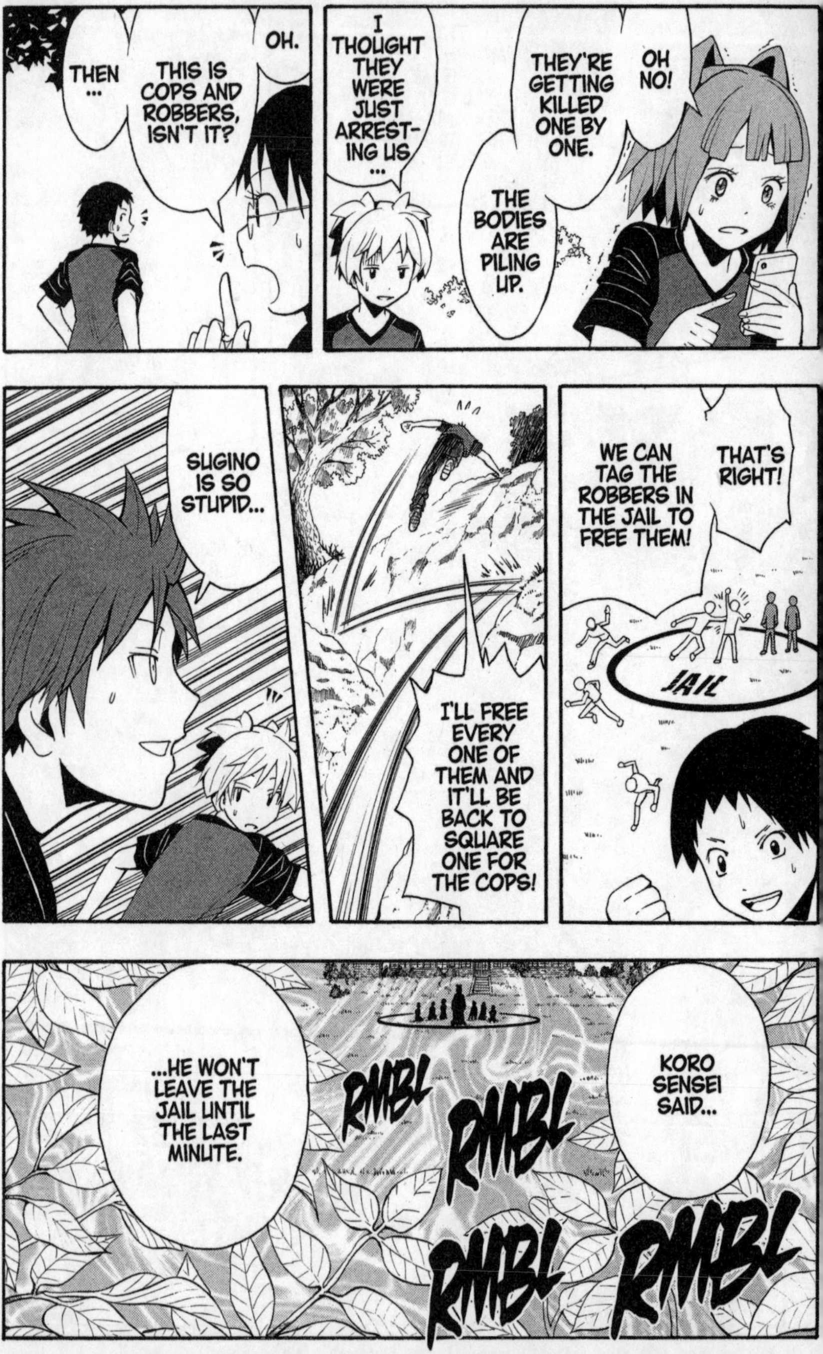
OH NO!
THEY'RE GETTING KILLED ONE BY ONE.
THE BODIES ARE PILING UP.
I THOUGHT THEY WERE JUST ARREST-ING US...
OH.
THIS IS COPS AND ROBBERS, ISN'T IT?
THEN...
THAT'S RIGHT!
WE CAN TAG THE ROBBERS IN THE JAIL TO FREE THEM!
JAIL
I'LL FREE EVERY ONE OF THEM AND IT'LL BE BACK TO SQUARE ONE FOR THE COPS!
SUGINO IS SO STUPID...
KORO SENSEI SAID...
RMBL
RMBL
RMBL
RMBL
...HE WON'T LEAVE THE JAIL UNTIL THE LAST MINUTE.

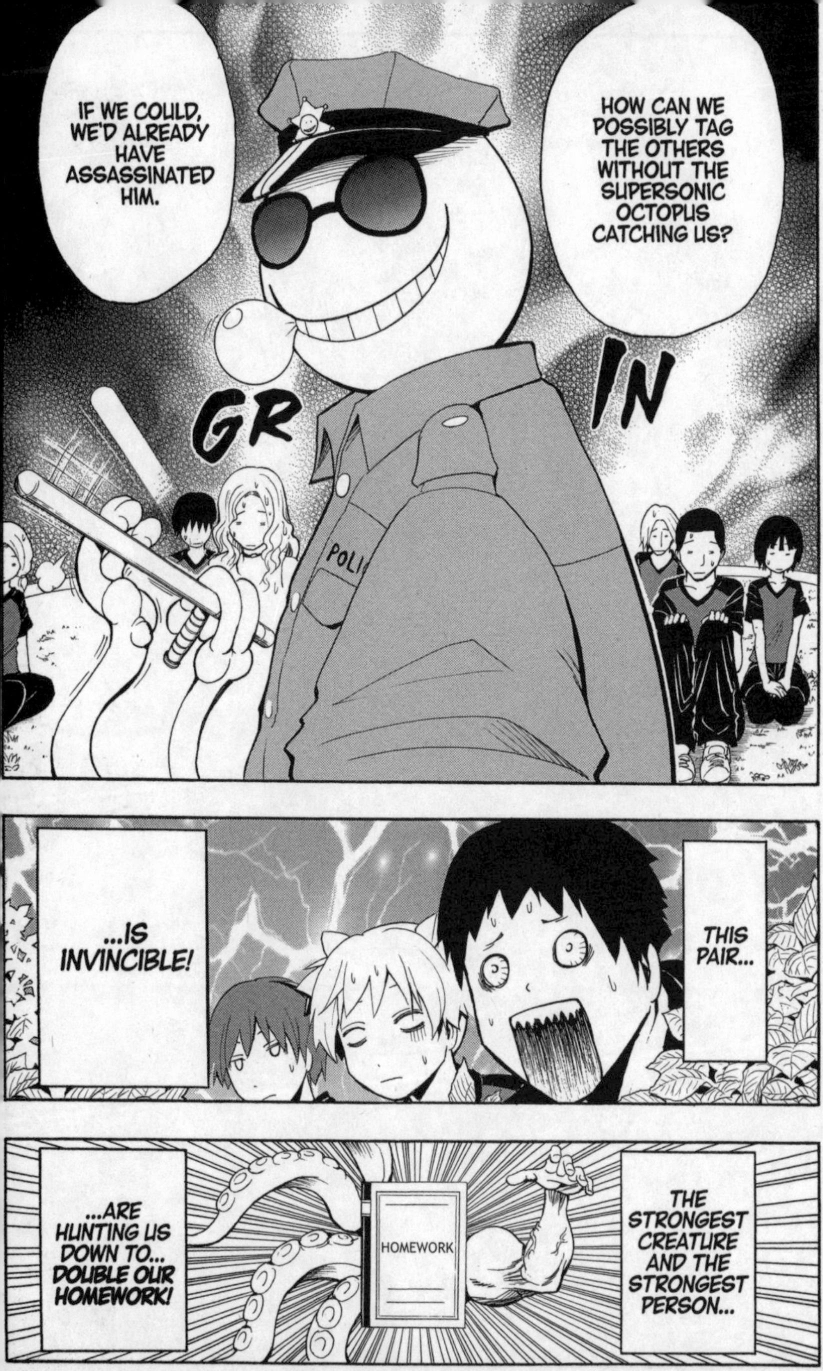
HOW CAN WE POSSIBLY TAG THE OTHERS WITHOUT THE SUPERSONIC OCTOPUS CATCHING US?
IF WE COULD, WE'D ALREADY HAVE ASSASSINATED HIM.
GR
IN
POLI
THIS PAIR...
...IS INVINCIBLE!
THE STRONGEST CREATURE AND THE STRONGEST PERSON...
HOMEWORK
...ARE HUNTING US DOWN TO... DOUBLE OUR HOMEWORK!

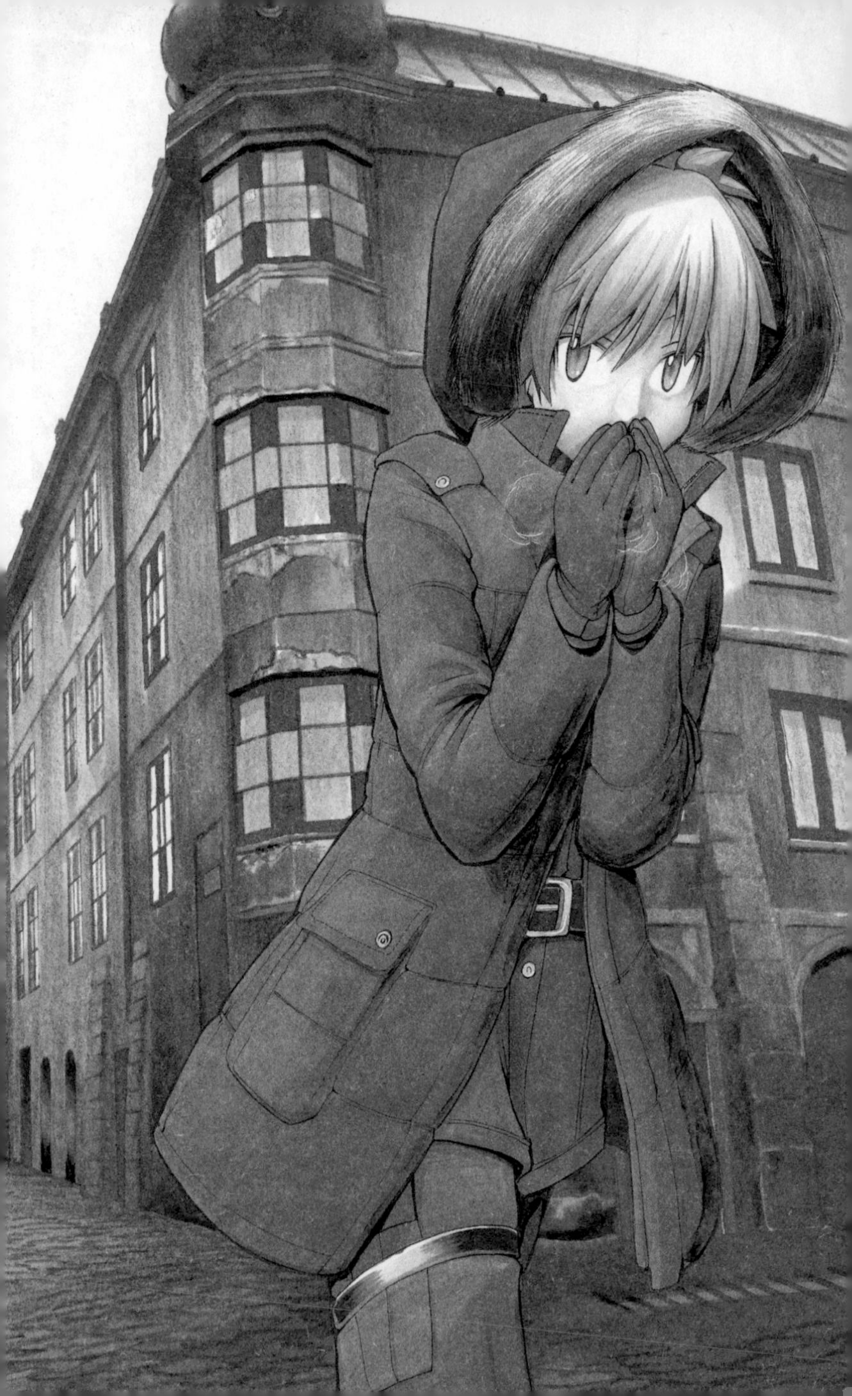

Class 82 Time for Robbery

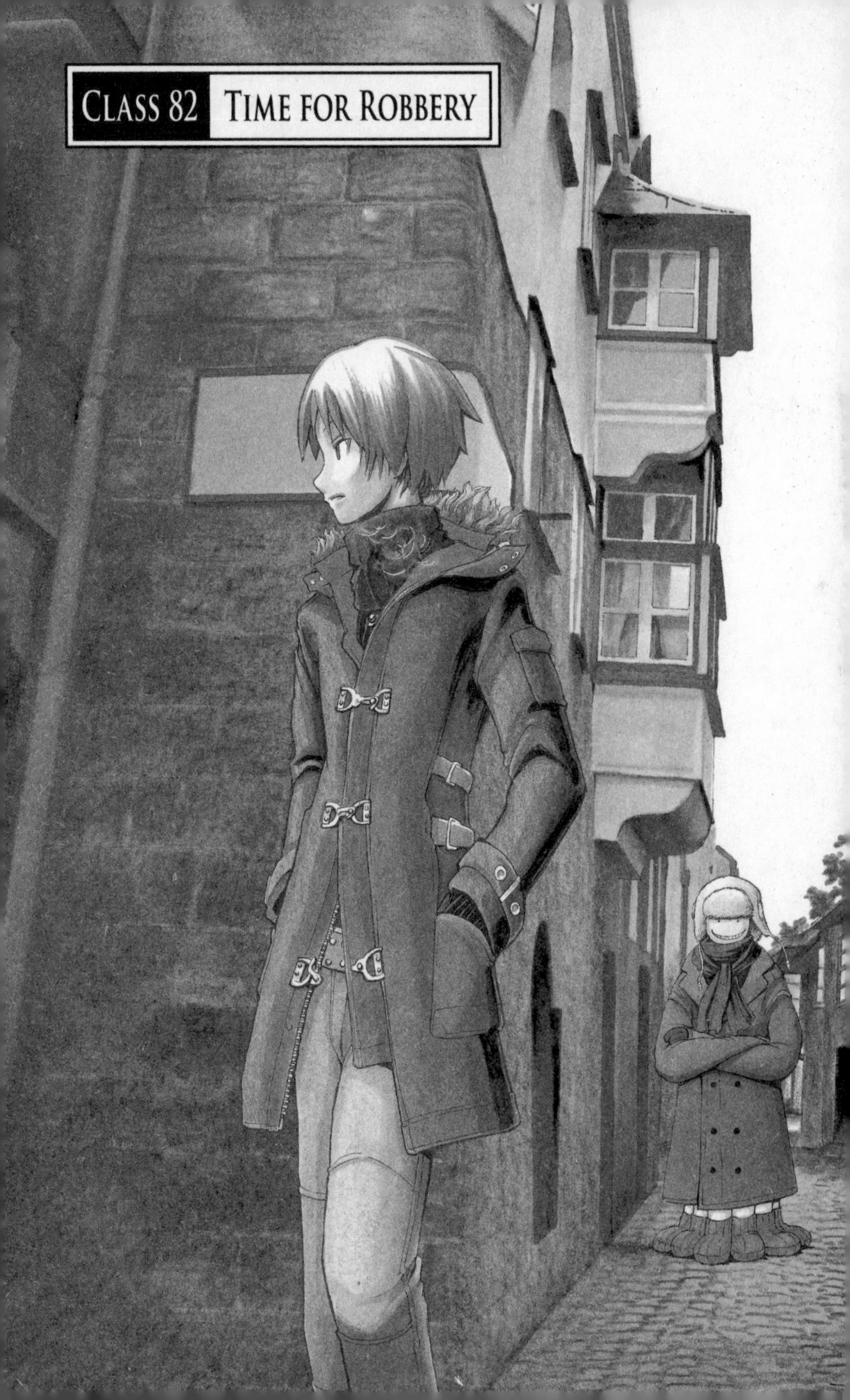

TO SMILE
WAS
ORIGINALLY
AN ACT OF
VIOLENCE.

LIKE
ANIMALS
BARING
THEIR
FANGS.

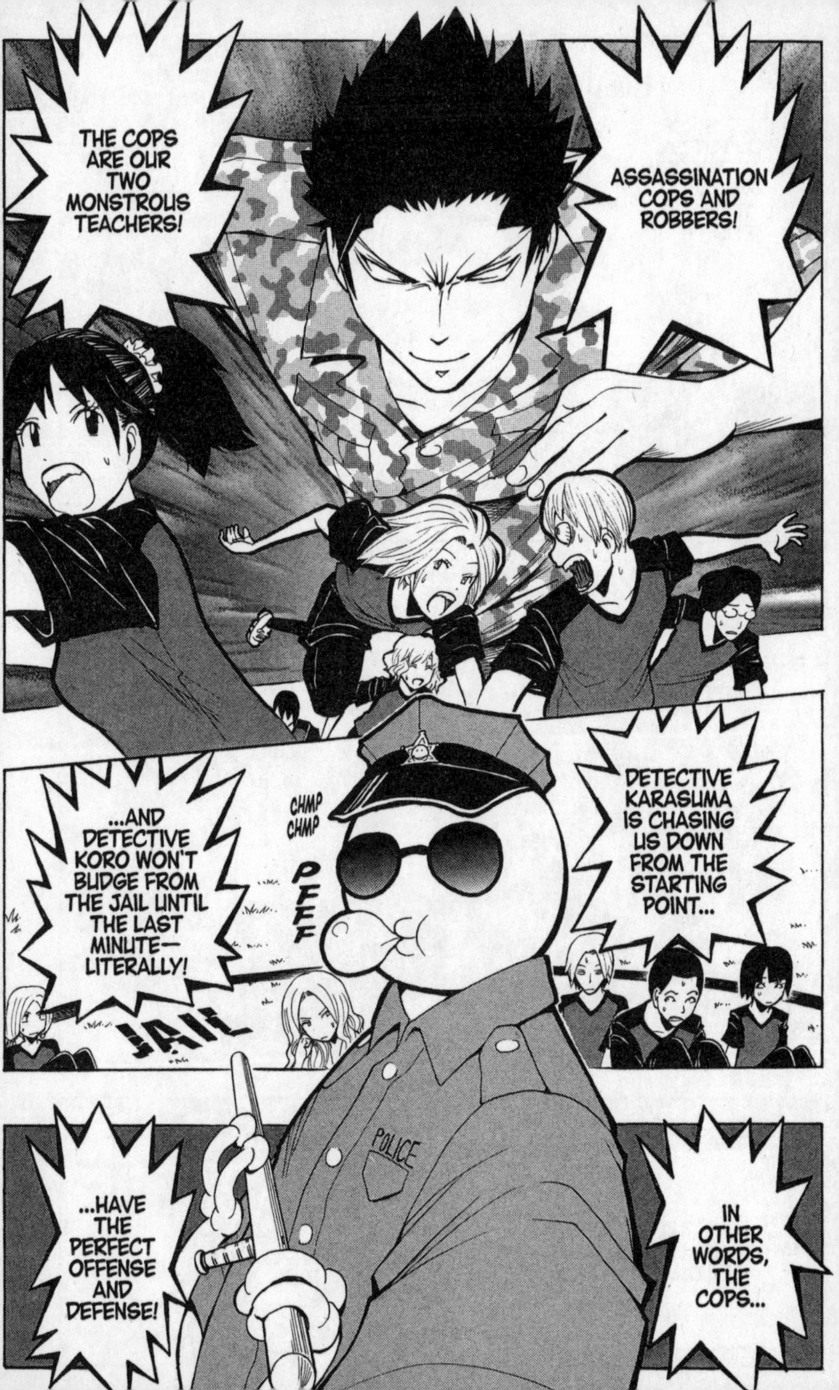
ASSASSINATION COPS AND ROBBERS!
THE COPS ARE OUR TWO MONSTROUS TEACHERS!
DETECTIVE KARASUMA IS CHASING US DOWN FROM THE STARTING POINT...
CHMP CHMP
PFFF
...AND DETECTIVE KORO WON'T BUDGE FROM THE JAIL UNTIL THE LAST MINUTE—LITERALLY!
JAIL
IN OTHER WORDS, THE COPS...
...HAVE THE PERFECT OFFENSE AND DEFENSE!
POLICE

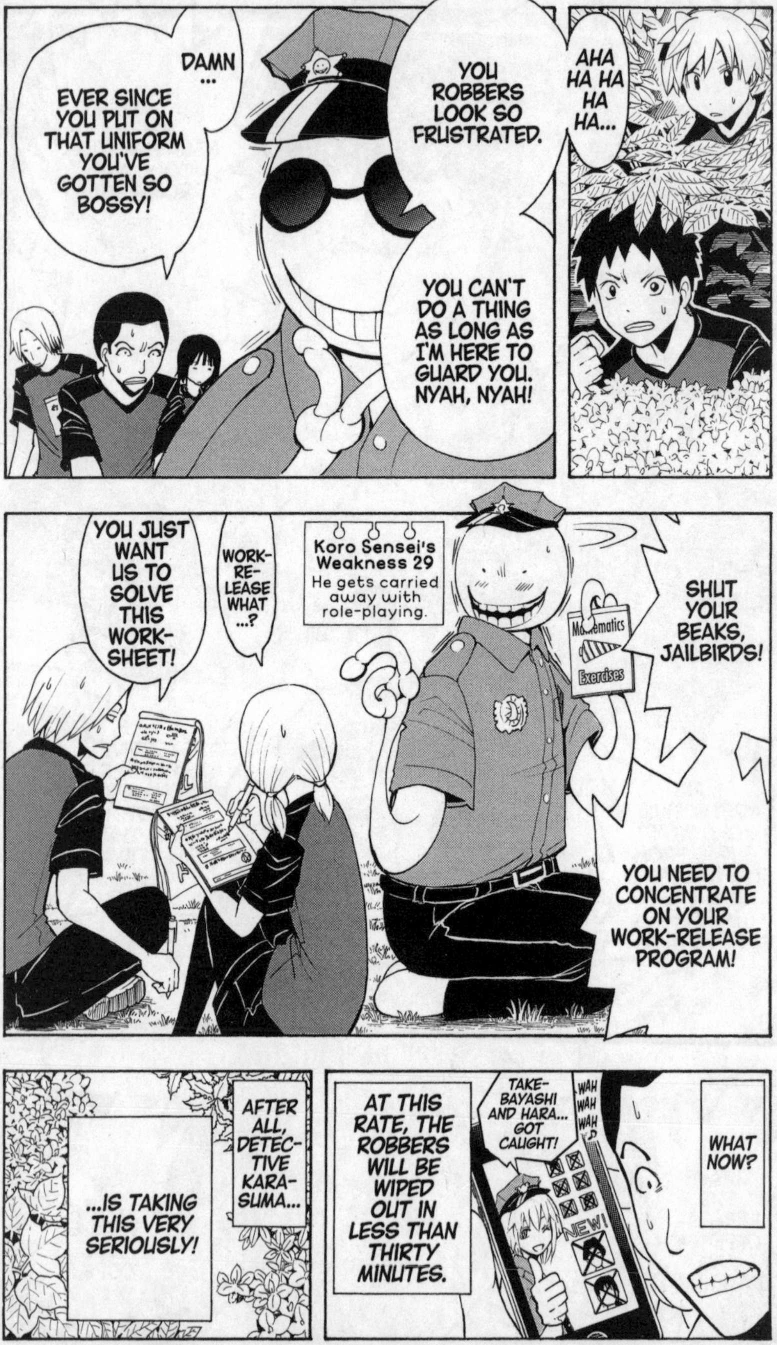
AHA HA HA HA HA...
YOU ROBBERS LOOK SO FRUSTRATED.
YOU CAN'T DO A THING AS LONG AS I'M HERE TO GUARD YOU. NYAH, NYAH!
DAMN...
EVER SINCE YOU PUT ON THAT UNIFORM YOU'VE GOTTEN SO BOSSY!
SHUT YOUR BEAKS, JAILBIRDS!
YOU NEED TO CONCENTRATE ON YOUR WORK-RELEASE PROGRAM!
Mathematics Exercises
Koro Sensei's Weakness 29
He gets carried away with role-playing.
WORK-RELEASE WHAT...?
YOU JUST WANT US TO SOLVE THIS WORKSHEET!
WHAT NOW?
WAH WAH WAH
TAKEBAYASHI AND HARA... GOT CAUGHT!
NEW!
AT THIS RATE, THE ROBBERS WILL BE WIPED OUT IN LESS THAN THIRTY MINUTES.
AFTER ALL, DETECTIVE KARASUMA...
...IS TAKING THIS VERY SERIOUSLY!

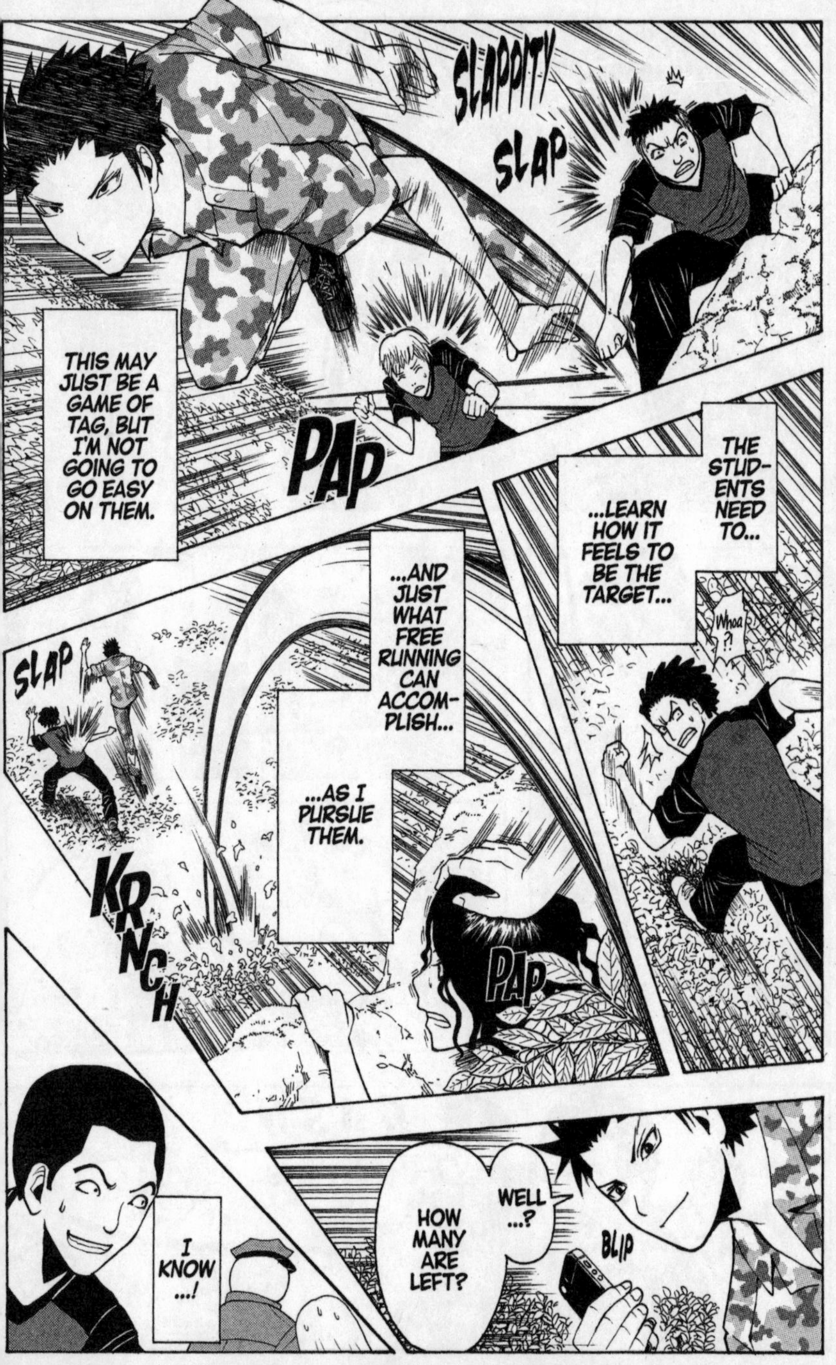
SLAPPITY
SLAP
THIS MAY JUST BE A GAME OF TAG, BUT I'M NOT GOING TO GO EASY ON THEM.
PAP
THE STUDENTS NEED TO...
...LEARN HOW IT FEELS TO BE THE TARGET...
Whoa?!
PAP
...AND JUST WHAT FREE RUNNING CAN ACCOMPLISH...
...AS I PURSUE THEM.
KRNCH
SLAP
BLIP
WELL...?
HOW MANY ARE LEFT?
I KNOW...!

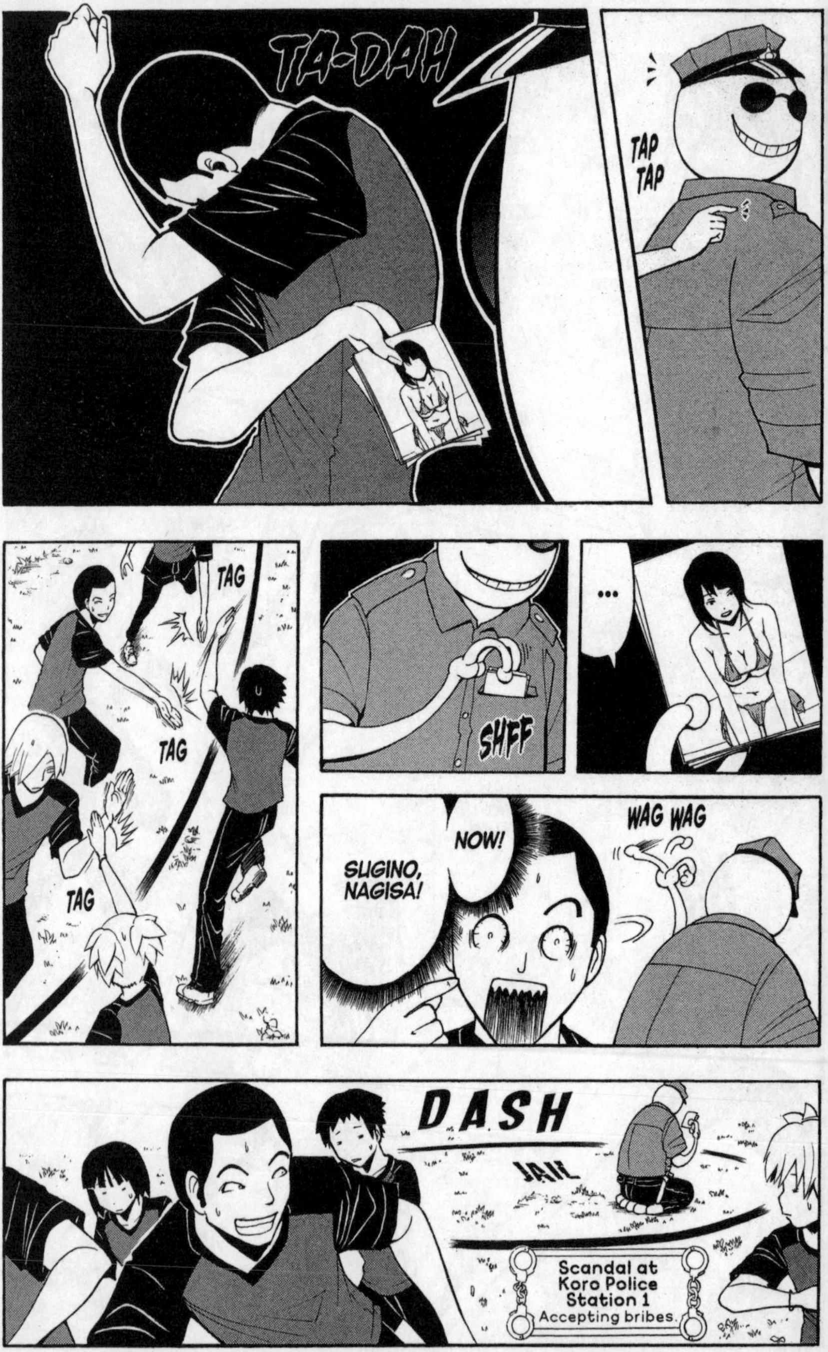
TAP TAP
TA-DAH
...
SHFF
WAG WAG
NOW!
SUGINO, NAGISA!
TAG
TAG
TAG
D.A.S.H
JAIL
Scandal at Koro Police Station 1
Accepting bribes.

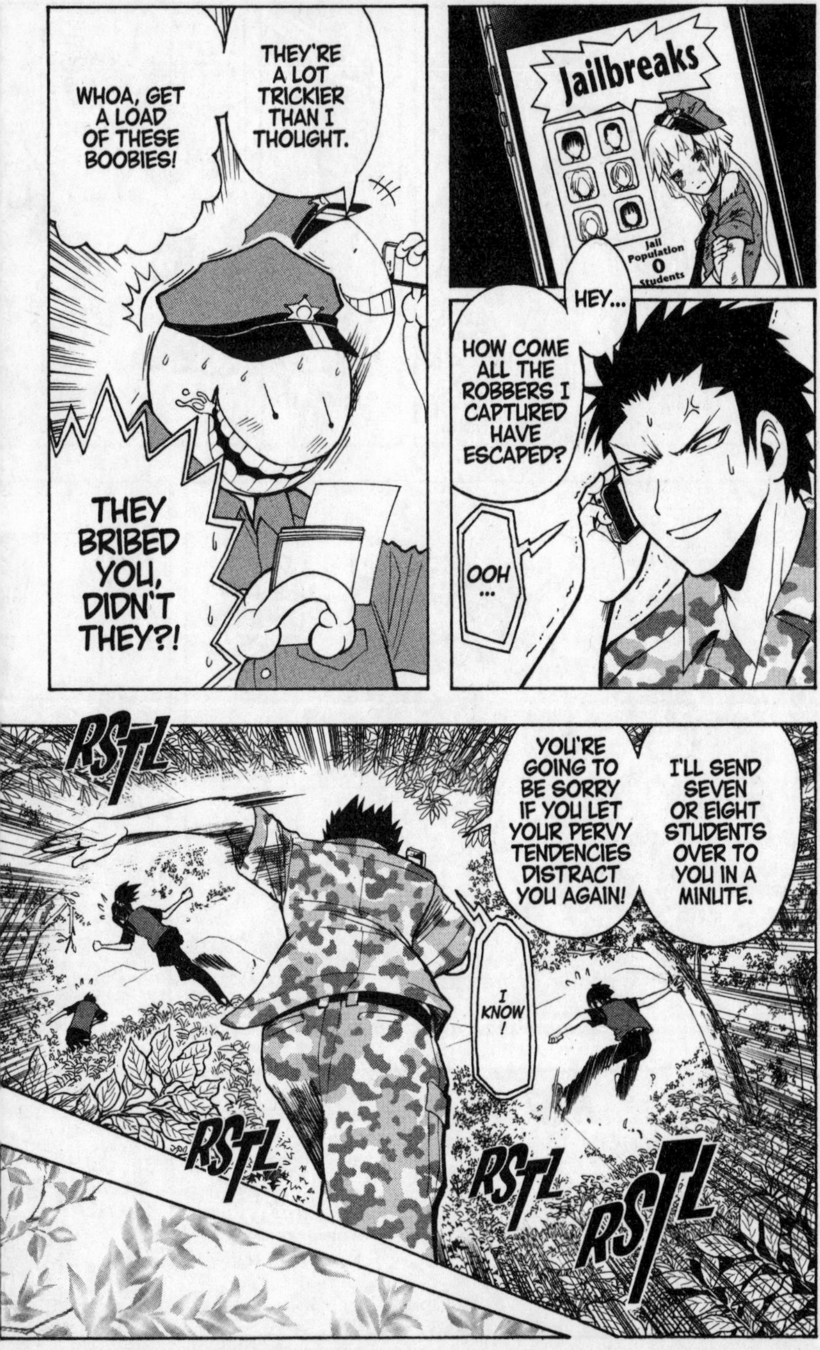
Jailbreaks
Jail Population 0 Students
HEY...
HOW COME ALL THE ROBBERS I CAPTURED HAVE ESCAPED?
OOH ...
THEY'RE A LOT TRICKIER THAN I THOUGHT.
WHOA, GET A LOAD OF THESE BOOBIES!
THEY BRIBED YOU, DIDN'T THEY?!
I'LL SEND SEVEN OR EIGHT STUDENTS OVER TO YOU IN A MINUTE.
YOU'RE GOING TO BE SORRY IF YOU LET YOUR PERVY TENDENCIES DISTRACT YOU AGAIN!
RSTL
I KNOW!
RSTL
RSTL
RSTL

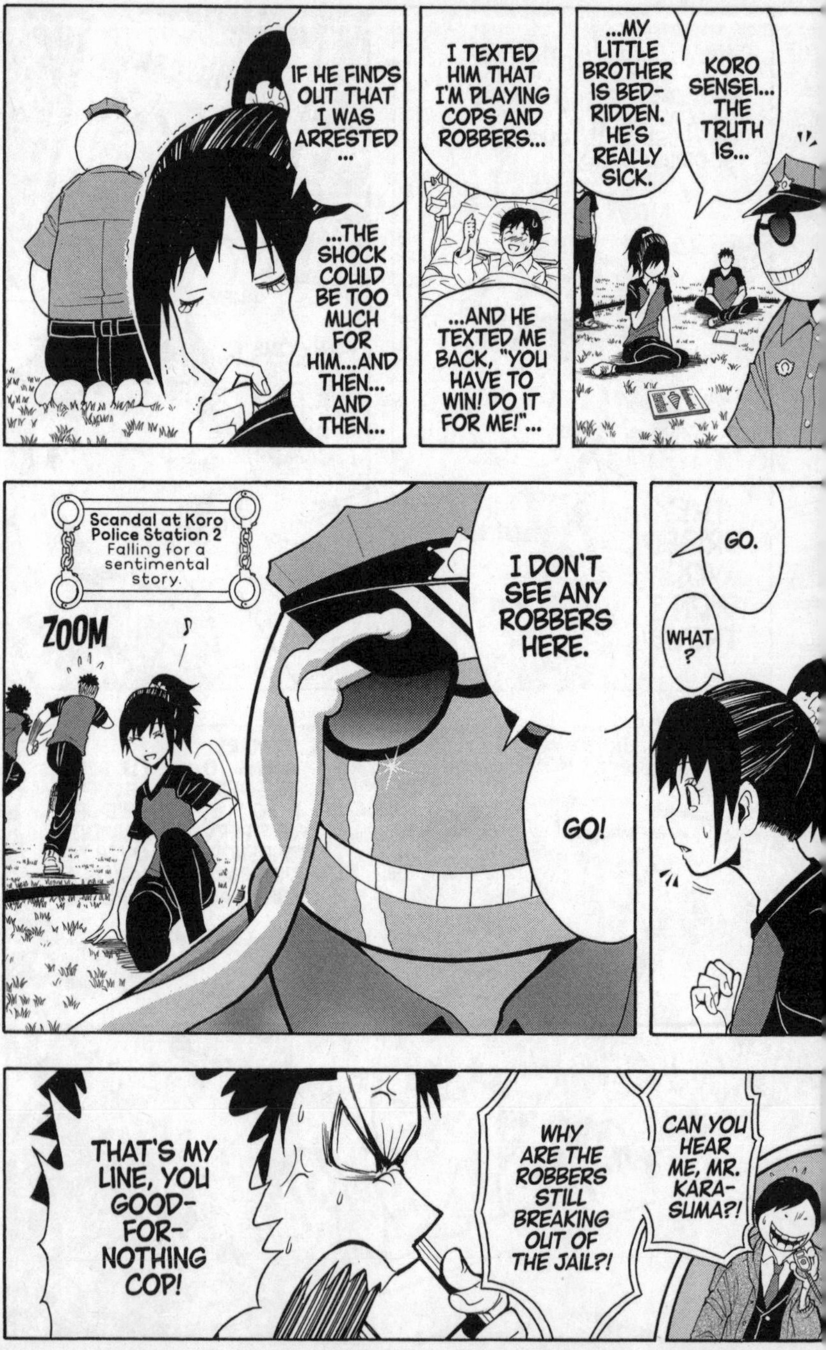
KORO SENSEI... THE TRUTH IS...
...MY LITTLE BROTHER IS BED-RIDDEN. HE'S REALLY SICK.
I TEXTED HIM THAT I'M PLAYING COPS AND ROBBERS...
...AND HE TEXTED ME BACK, "YOU HAVE TO WIN! DO IT FOR ME!"...
IF HE FINDS OUT THAT I WAS ARRESTED...
...THE SHOCK COULD BE TOO MUCH FOR HIM...AND THEN... AND THEN...
GO.
WHAT?
I DON'T SEE ANY ROBBERS HERE.
GO!
Scandal at Koro Police Station 2 Falling for a sentimental story.
ZOOM
CAN YOU HEAR ME, MR. KARA-SUMA?!
WHY ARE THE ROBBERS STILL BREAKING OUT OF THE JAIL?!
THAT'S MY LINE, YOU GOOD-FOR-NOTHING COP!

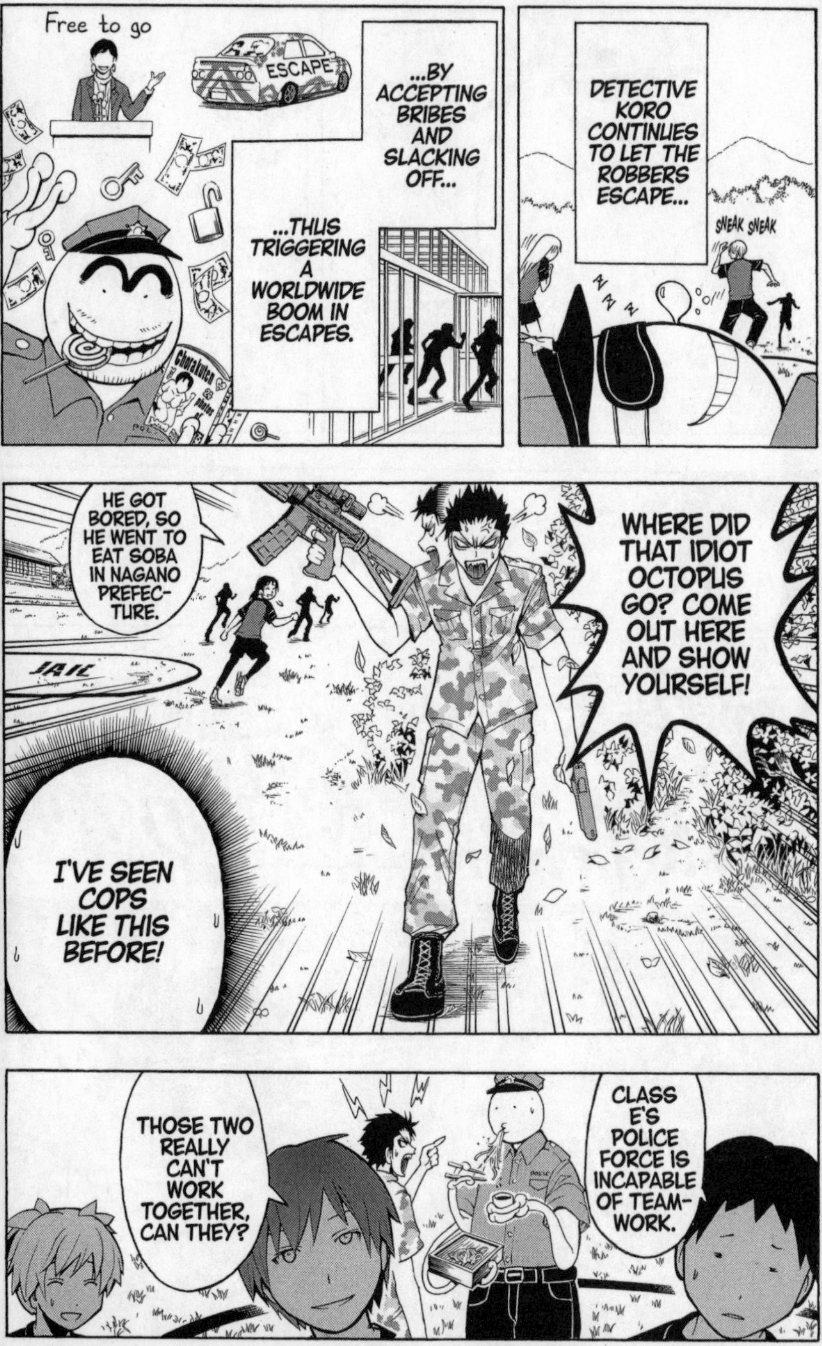
DETECTIVE KORO CONTINUES TO LET THE ROBBERS ESCAPE...
SNEAK SNEAK
...BY ACCEPTING BRIBES AND SLACKING OFF...
...THUS TRIGGERING A WORLDWIDE BOOM IN ESCAPES.
Free to go
ESCAPE
WHERE DID THAT IDIOT OCTOPUS GO? COME OUT HERE AND SHOW YOURSELF!
HE GOT BORED, SO HE WENT TO EAT SOBA IN NAGANO PREFEC-TURE.
I'VE SEEN COPS LIKE THIS BEFORE!
CLASS E'S POLICE FORCE IS INCAPABLE OF TEAM-WORK.
THOSE TWO REALLY CAN'T WORK TOGETHER, CAN THEY?

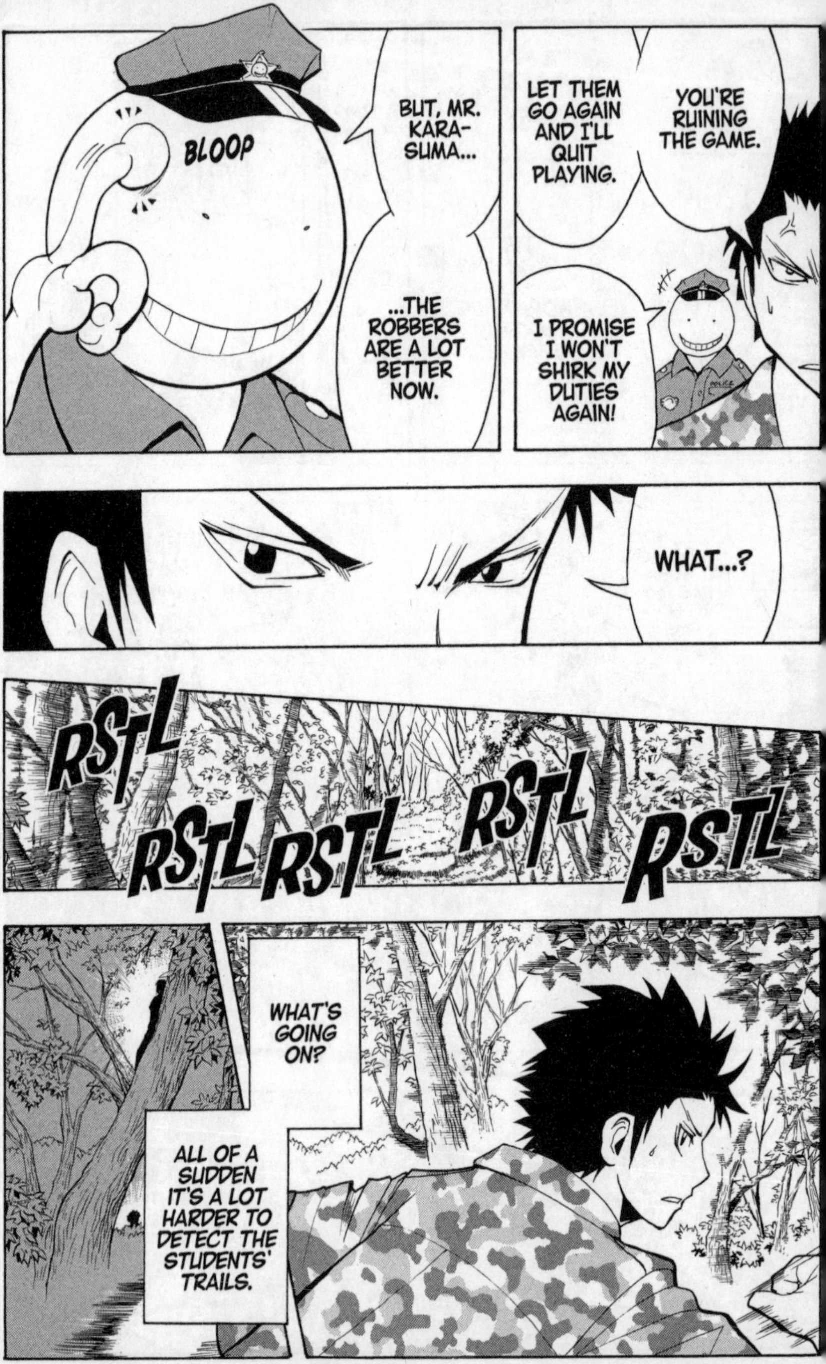
YOU'RE RUINING THE GAME.
LET THEM GO AGAIN AND I'LL QUIT PLAYING.
I PROMISE I WON'T SHIRK MY DUTIES AGAIN!
BLOOP
BUT, MR. KARA-SUMA...
...THE ROBBERS ARE A LOT BETTER NOW.
WHAT...?
RSTL
RSTL
RSTL
RSTL
RSTL
WHAT'S GOING ON?
ALL OF A SUDDEN IT'S A LOT HARDER TO DETECT THE STUDENTS' TRAILS.

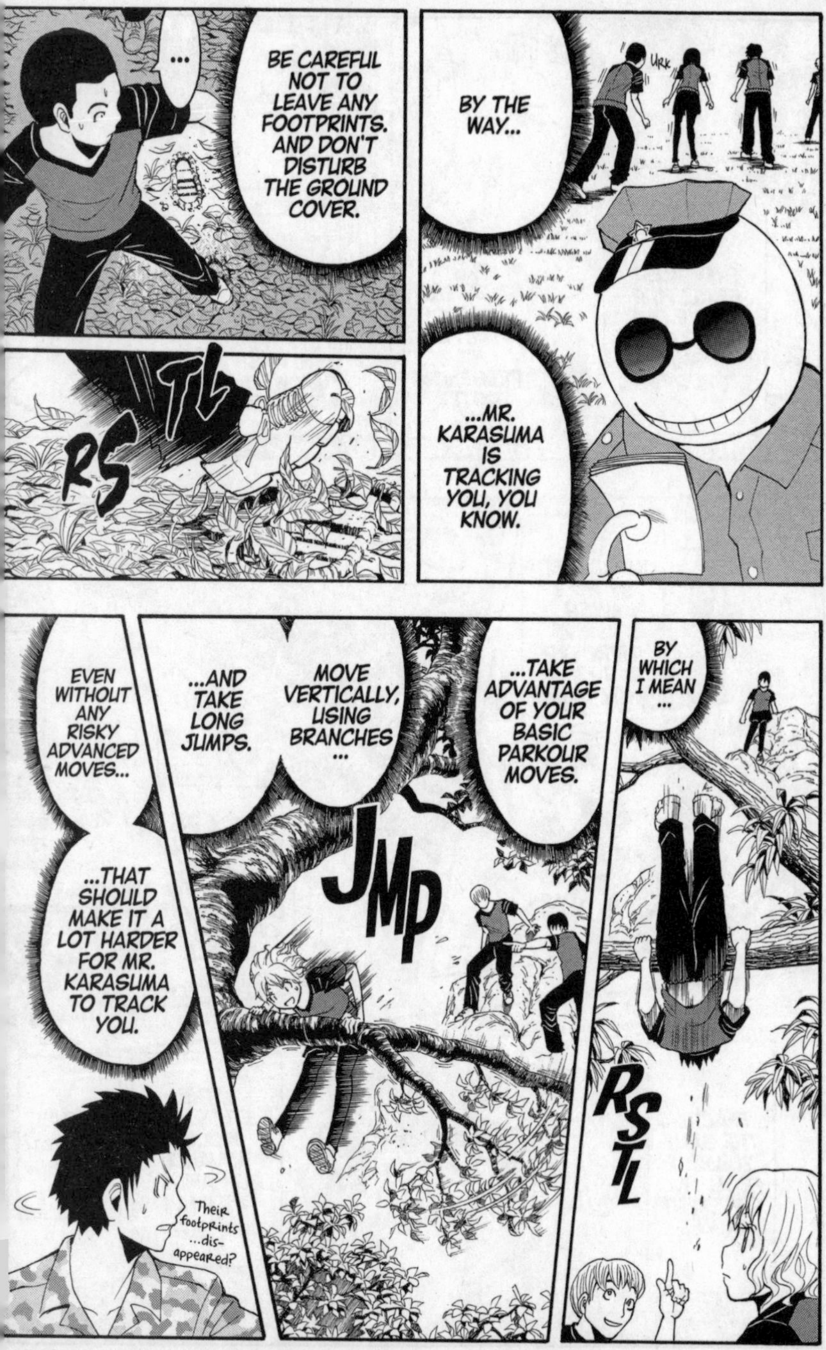
BY THE WAY...
URK
...MR. KARASUMA IS TRACKING YOU, YOU KNOW.
BE CAREFUL NOT TO LEAVE ANY FOOTPRINTS. AND DON'T DISTURB THE GROUND COVER.
...
RSTL
BY WHICH I MEAN...
RSTL
...TAKE ADVANTAGE OF YOUR BASIC PARKOUR MOVES.
MOVE VERTICALLY, USING BRANCHES...
...AND TAKE LONG JUMPS.
JMP
EVEN WITHOUT ANY RISKY ADVANCED MOVES...
...THAT SHOULD MAKE IT A LOT HARDER FOR MR. KARASUMA TO TRACK YOU.
Their footprints ...dis-appeared?

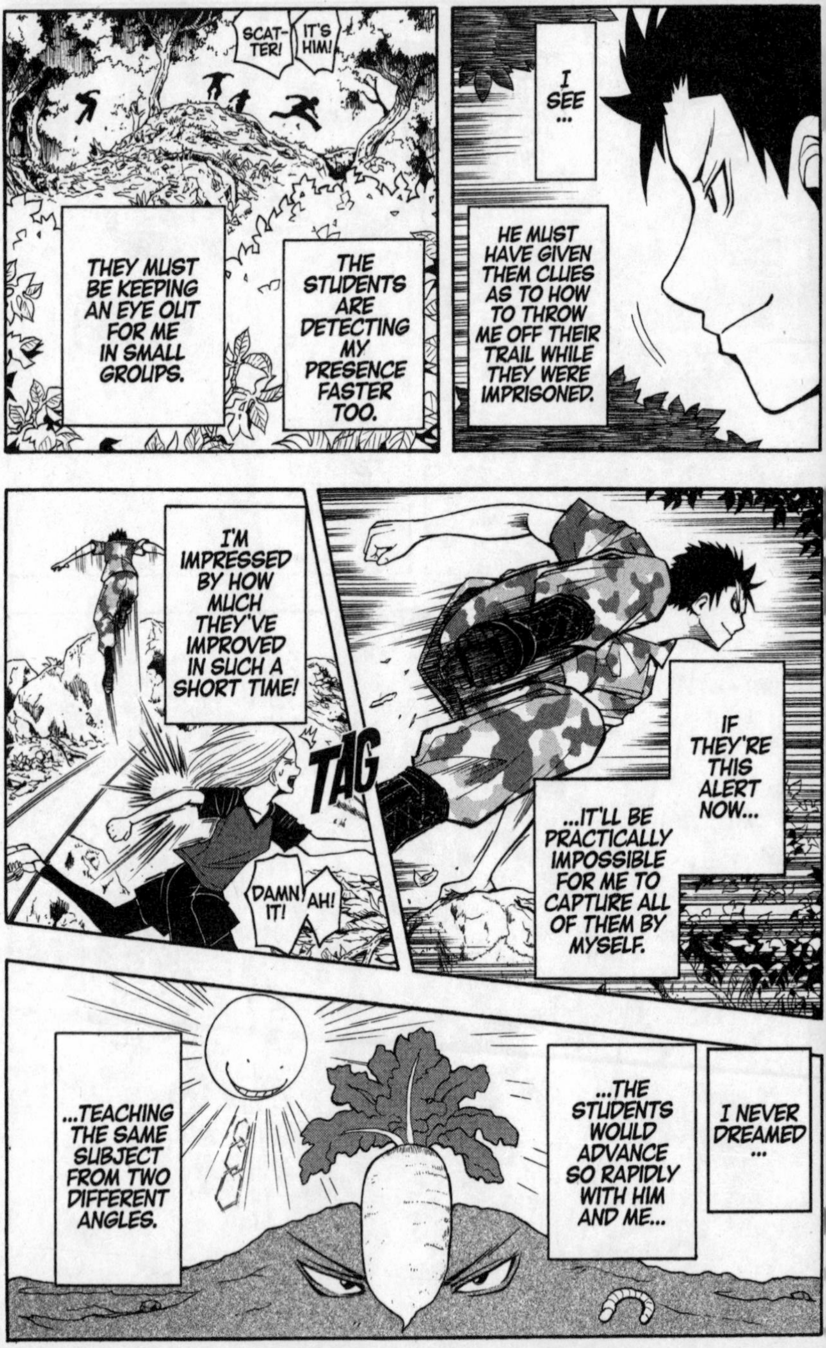
I SEE...
HE MUST HAVE GIVEN THEM CLUES AS TO HOW TO THROW ME OFF THEIR TRAIL WHILE THEY WERE IMPRISONED.
IT'S HIM!
SCAT-TER!
THE STUDENTS ARE DETECTING MY PRESENCE FASTER TOO.
THEY MUST BE KEEPING AN EYE OUT FOR ME IN SMALL GROUPS.
IF THEY'RE THIS ALERT NOW...
...IT'LL BE PRACTICALLY IMPOSSIBLE FOR ME TO CAPTURE ALL OF THEM BY MYSELF.
TAG
I'M IMPRESSED BY HOW MUCH THEY'VE IMPROVED IN SUCH A SHORT TIME!
AH!
DAMN IT!
I NEVER DREAMED...
...THE STUDENTS WOULD ADVANCE SO RAPIDLY WITH HIM AND ME...
...TEACHING THE SAME SUBJECT FROM TWO DIFFERENT ANGLES.

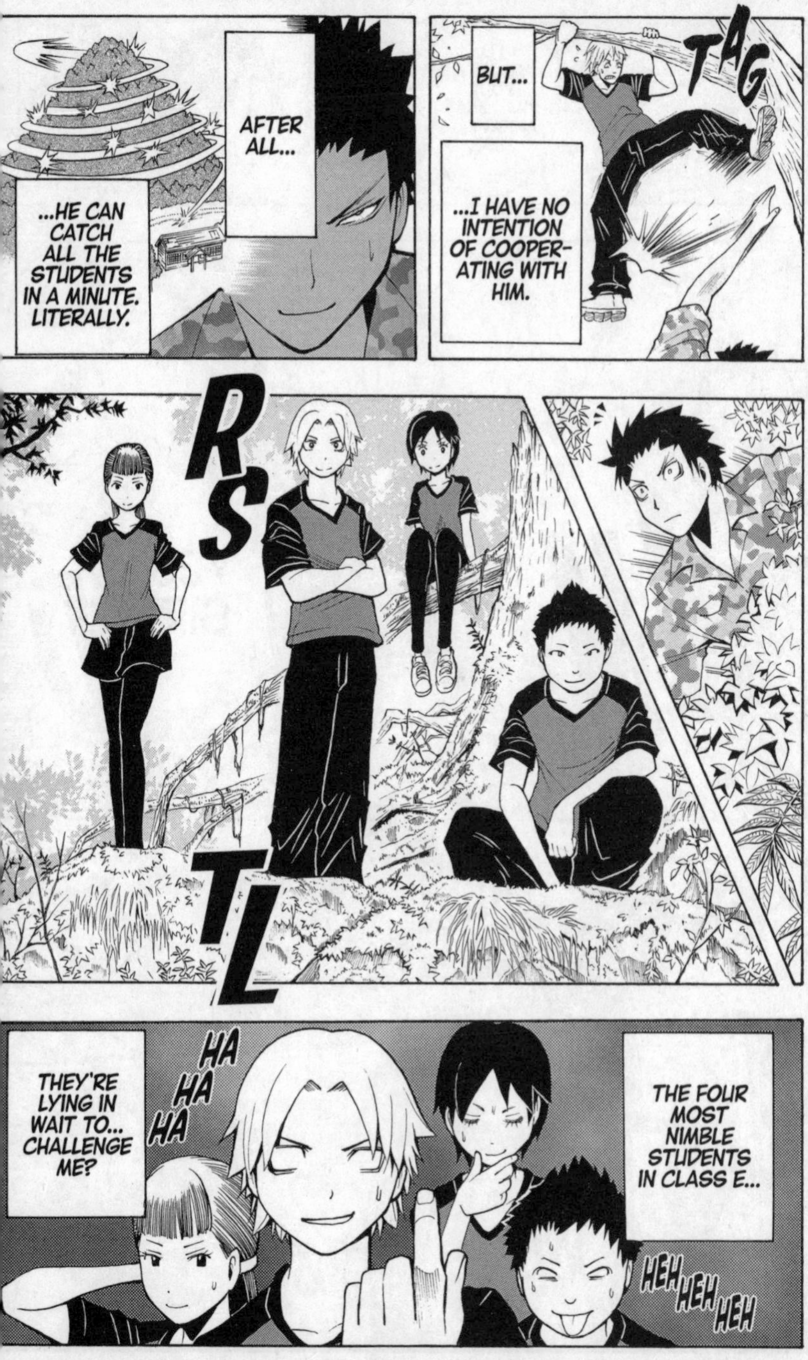
BUT...
...I HAVE NO INTENTION OF COOPERATING WITH HIM.
TAG
AFTER ALL...
...HE CAN CATCH ALL THE STUDENTS IN A MINUTE. LITERALLY.
RS
TL
THE FOUR MOST NIMBLE STUDENTS IN CLASS E...
HEH HEH HEH
HA HA HA
THEY'RE LYING IN WAIT TO... CHALLENGE ME?

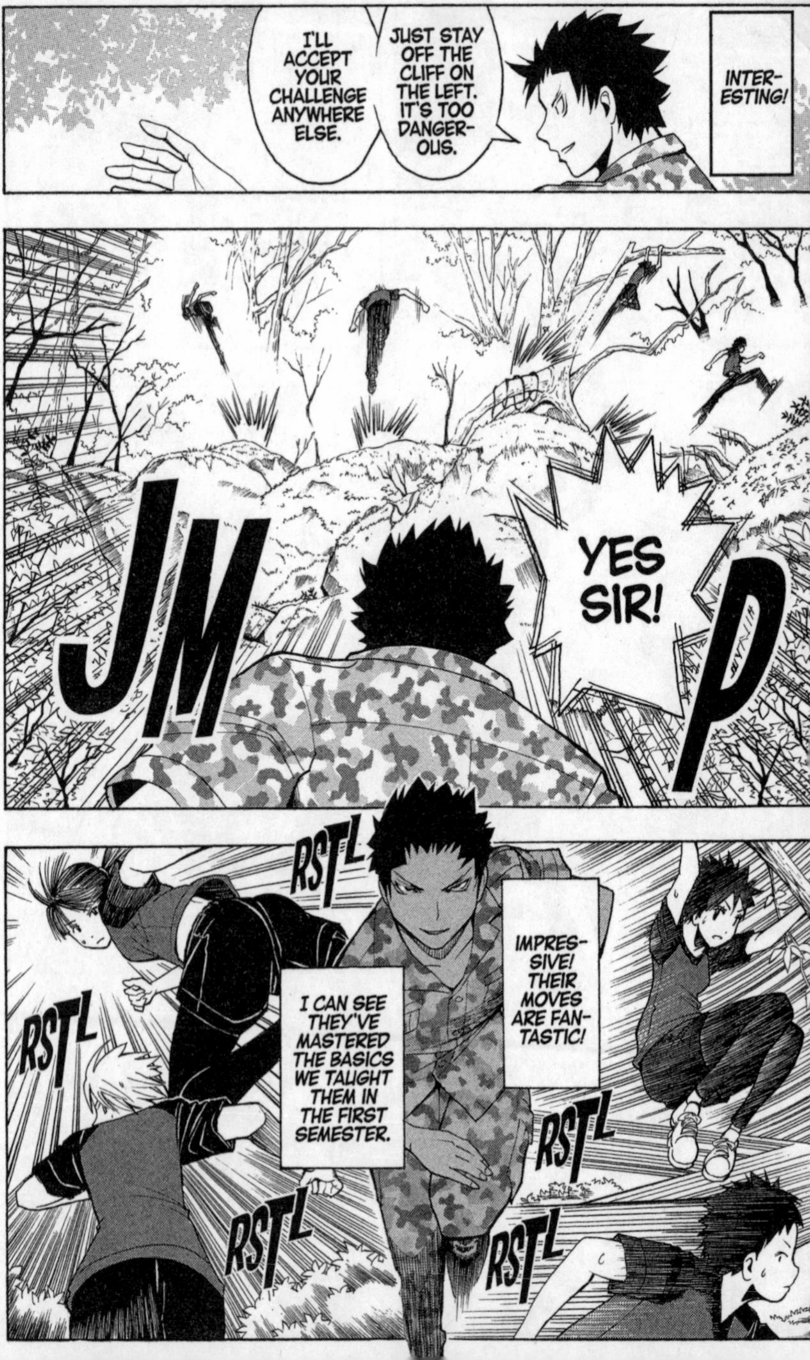
INTER-ESTING!
JUST STAY OFF THE CLIFF ON THE LEFT. IT'S TOO DANGER-OUS.
I'LL ACCEPT YOUR CHALLENGE ANYWHERE ELSE.
YES SIR!
JMP
RSTL
IMPRES-SIVE! THEIR MOVES ARE FAN-TASTIC!
I CAN SEE THEY'VE MASTERED THE BASICS WE TAUGHT THEM IN THE FIRST SEMESTER.
RSTL
RSTL
RSTL
RSTL

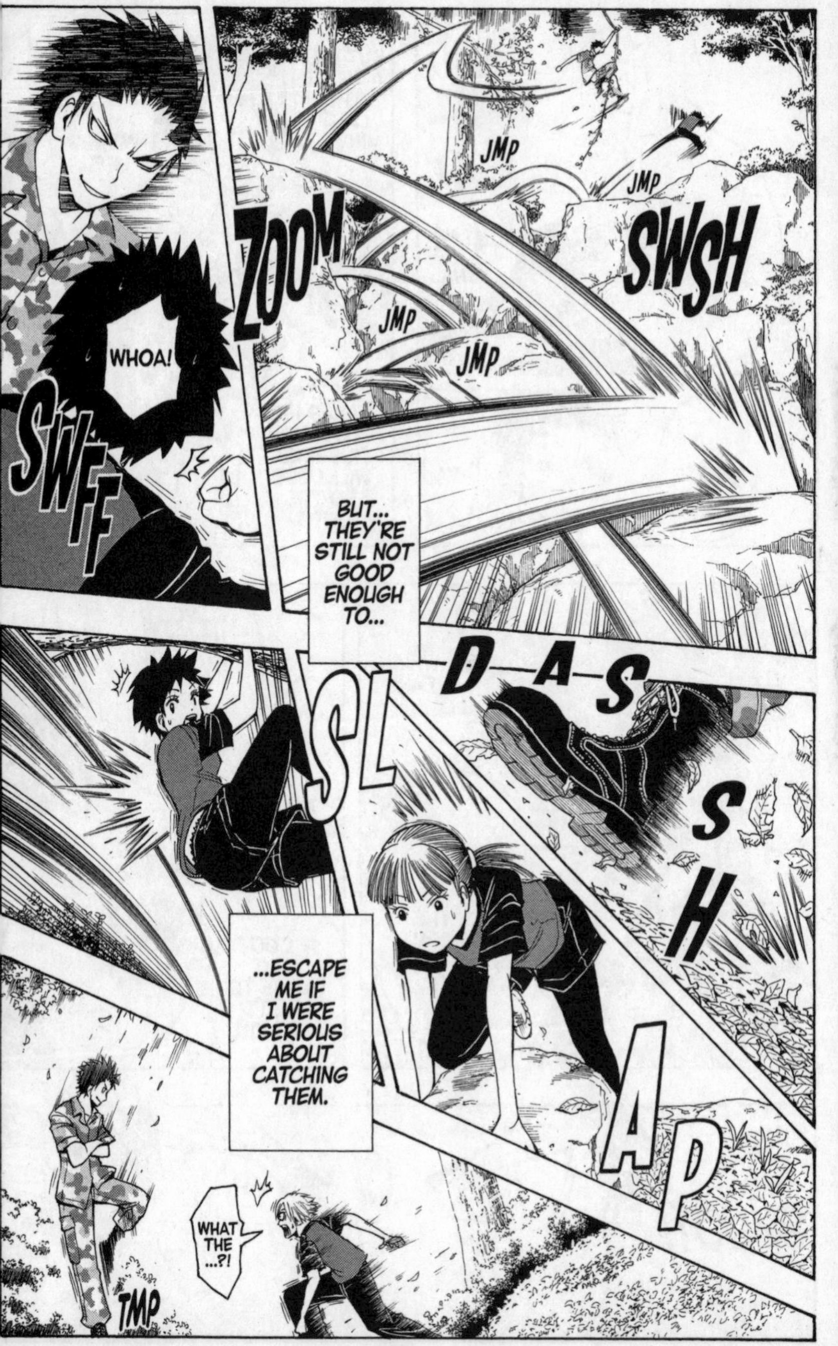
JMP
JMP
SWSH
ZOOM
JMP
JMP
WHOA!
SWFF
BUT... THEY'RE STILL NOT GOOD ENOUGH TO...
DAS
SH
SL
AP
...ESCAPE ME IF I WERE SERIOUS ABOUT CATCHING THEM.
WHAT THE ...?!
TMP

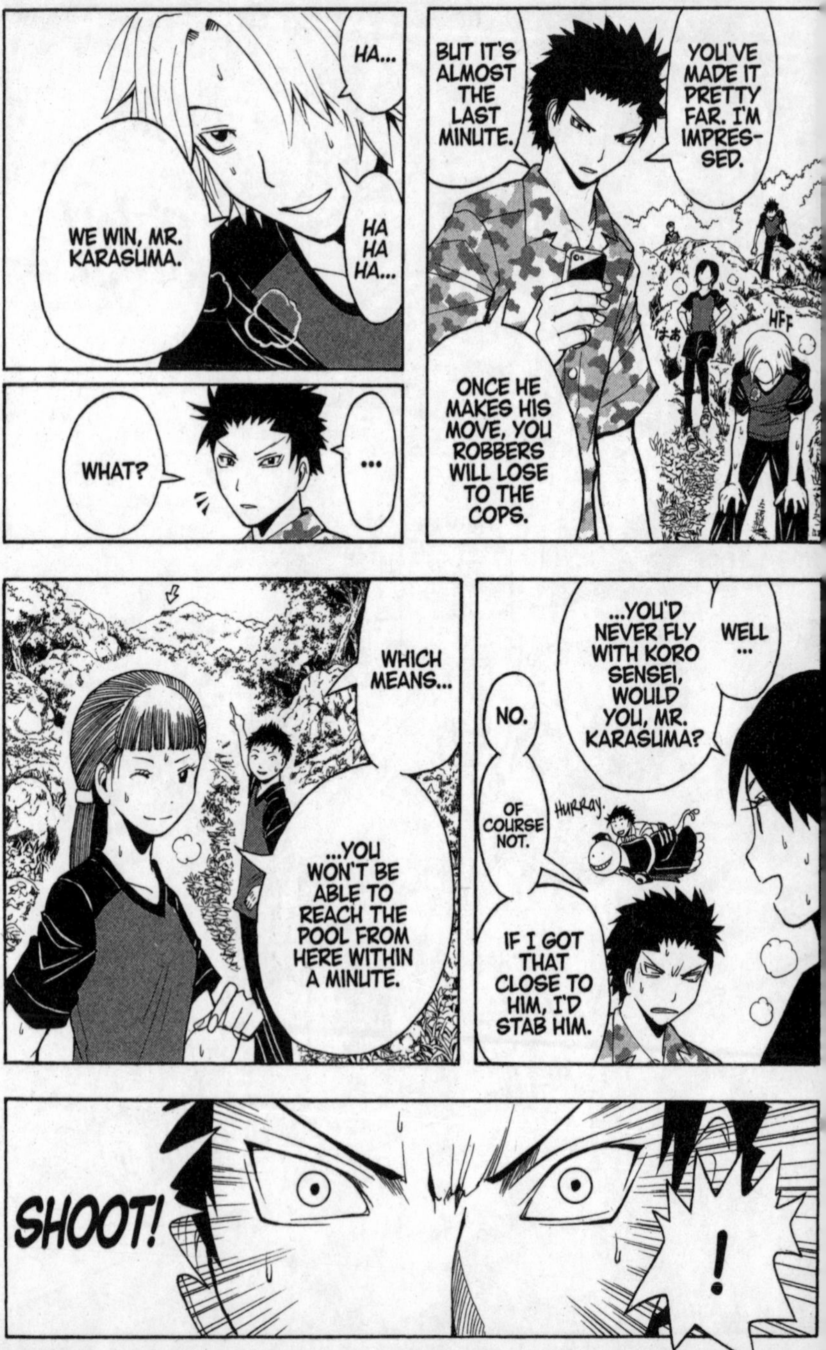
YOU'VE MADE IT PRETTY FAR. I'M IMPRESSED.
BUT IT'S ALMOST THE LAST MINUTE.
ONCE HE MAKES HIS MOVE, YOU ROBBERS WILL LOSE TO THE COPS.
HFF
はぁ
HA...
HA HA HA...
WE WIN, MR. KARASUMA.
...
WHAT?
WELL...
...YOU'D NEVER FLY WITH KORO SENSEI, WOULD YOU, MR. KARASUMA?
NO.
OF COURSE NOT.
HURRAY.
IF I GOT THAT CLOSE TO HIM, I'D STAB HIM.
WHICH MEANS...
...YOU WON'T BE ABLE TO REACH THE POOL FROM HERE WITHIN A MINUTE.
!
SHOOT!

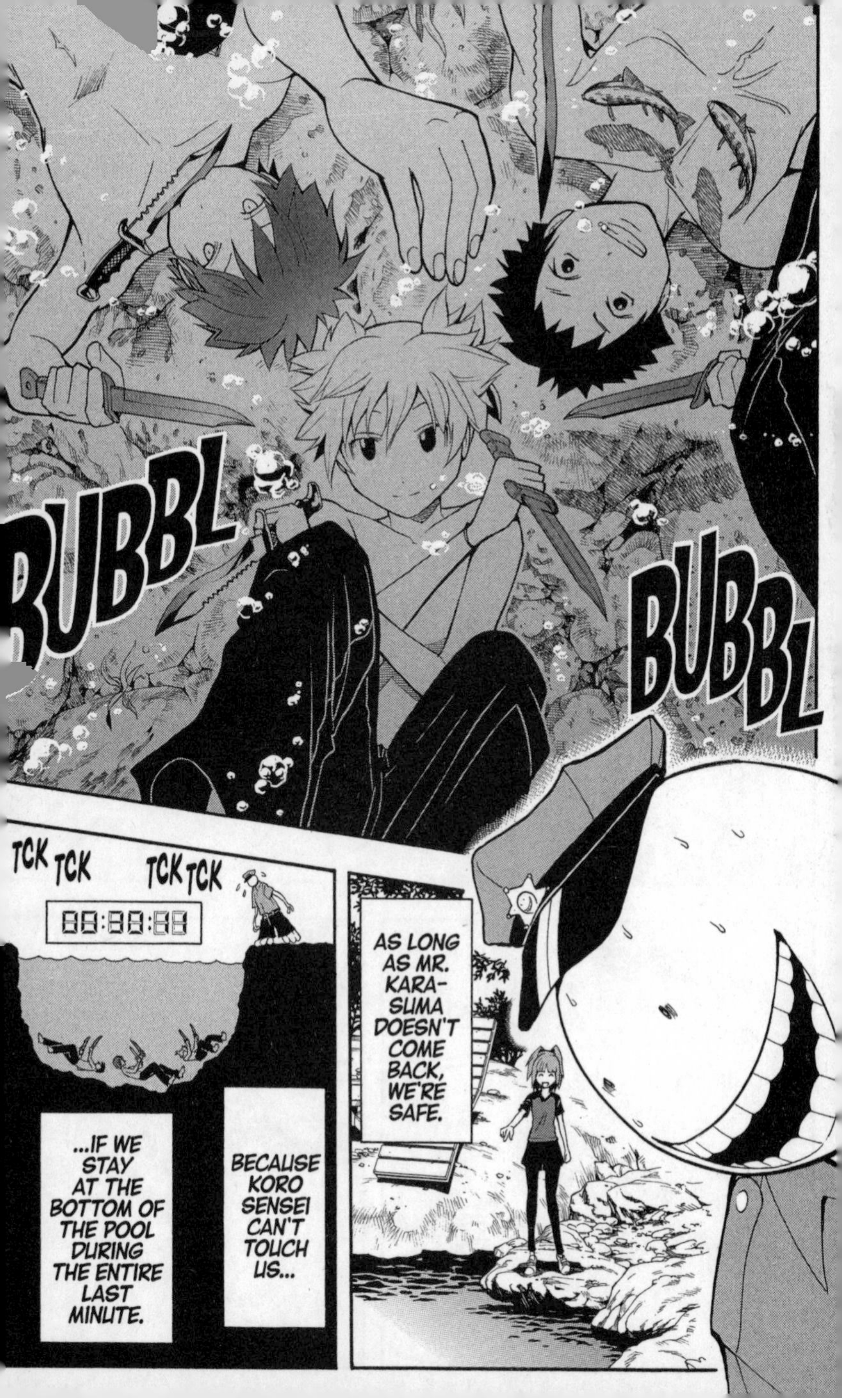
BUBBL
BUBBL
AS LONG AS MR. KARASUMA DOESN'T COME BACK, WE'RE SAFE.
TCK TCK
TCK TCK
BECAUSE KORO SENSEI CAN'T TOUCH US...
...IF WE STAY AT THE BOTTOM OF THE POOL DURING THE ENTIRE LAST MINUTE.

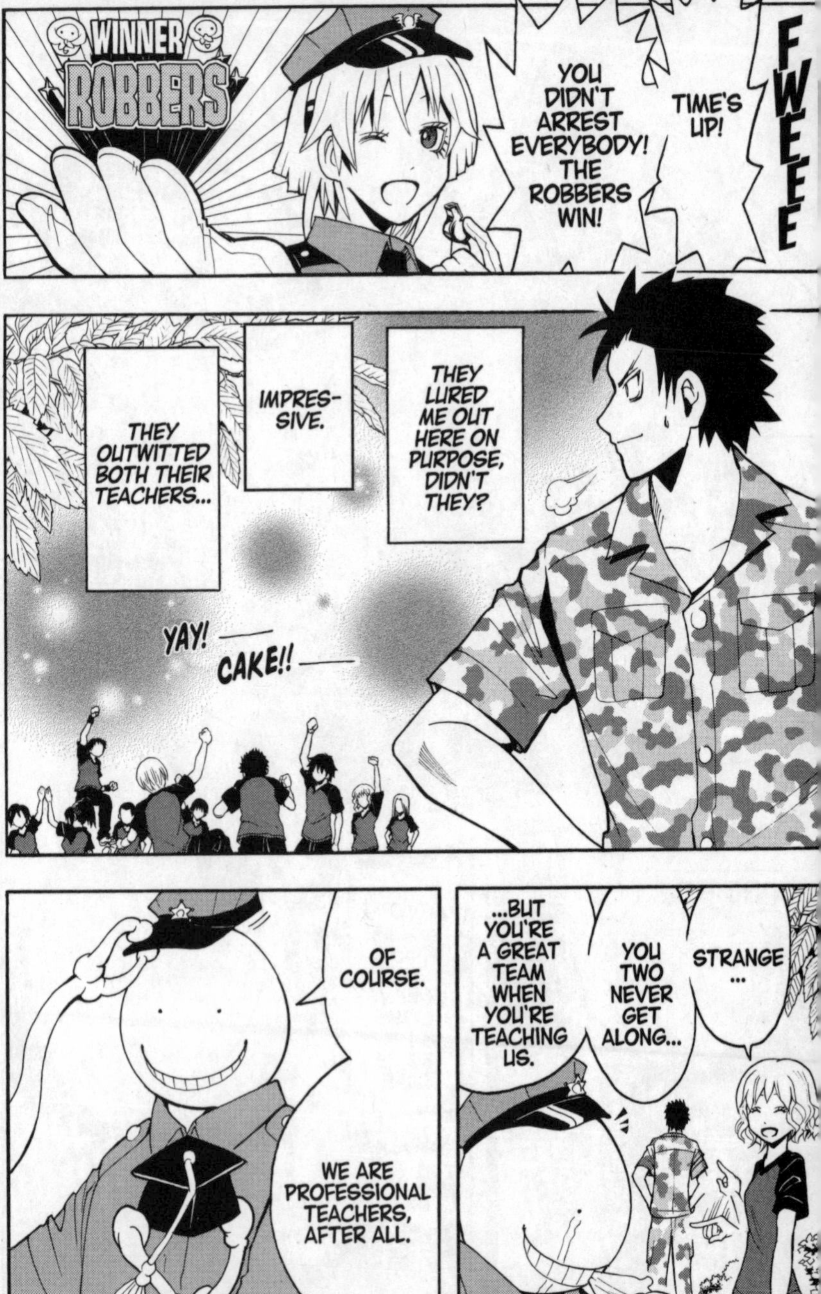
FWEEE
TIME'S UP!
YOU DIDN'T ARREST EVERYBODY! THE ROBBERS WIN!
WINNER
ROBBERS
THEY LURED ME OUT HERE ON PURPOSE, DIDN'T THEY?
IMPRES-SIVE.
THEY OUTWITTED BOTH THEIR TEACHERS...
YAY!
CAKE!!
STRANGE...
YOU TWO NEVER GET ALONG...
...BUT YOU'RE A GREAT TEAM WHEN YOU'RE TEACHING US.
OF COURSE.
WE ARE PROFESSIONAL TEACHERS, AFTER ALL.

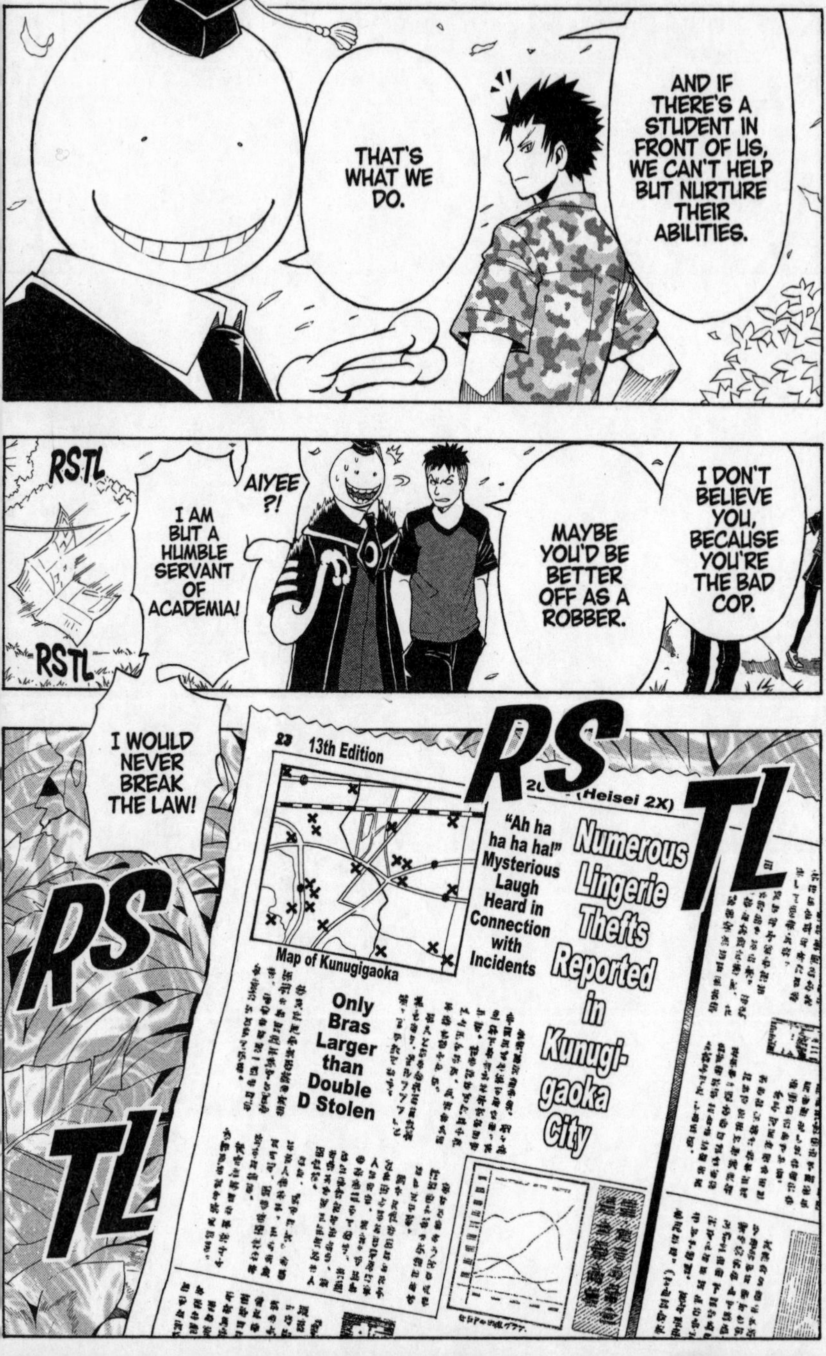
AND IF THERE'S A STUDENT IN FRONT OF US, WE CAN'T HELP BUT NURTURE THEIR ABILITIES.
THAT'S WHAT WE DO.
I DON'T BELIEVE YOU, BECAUSE YOU'RE THE BAD COP.
MAYBE YOU'D BE BETTER OFF AS A ROBBER.
AIYEE ?!
I AM BUT A HUMBLE SERVANT OF ACADEMIA!
RSTL
RSTL
RS
TL
I WOULD NEVER BREAK THE LAW!
13th Edition
(Heisei 2X)
Numerous Lingerie Thefts Reported in Kunugigaoka City
"Ah ha ha ha ha!" Mysterious Laugh Heard in Connection with Incidents
Map of Kunugigaoka
Only Bras Larger than Double D Stolen
RS
TL

The life of a police
officer is tough.

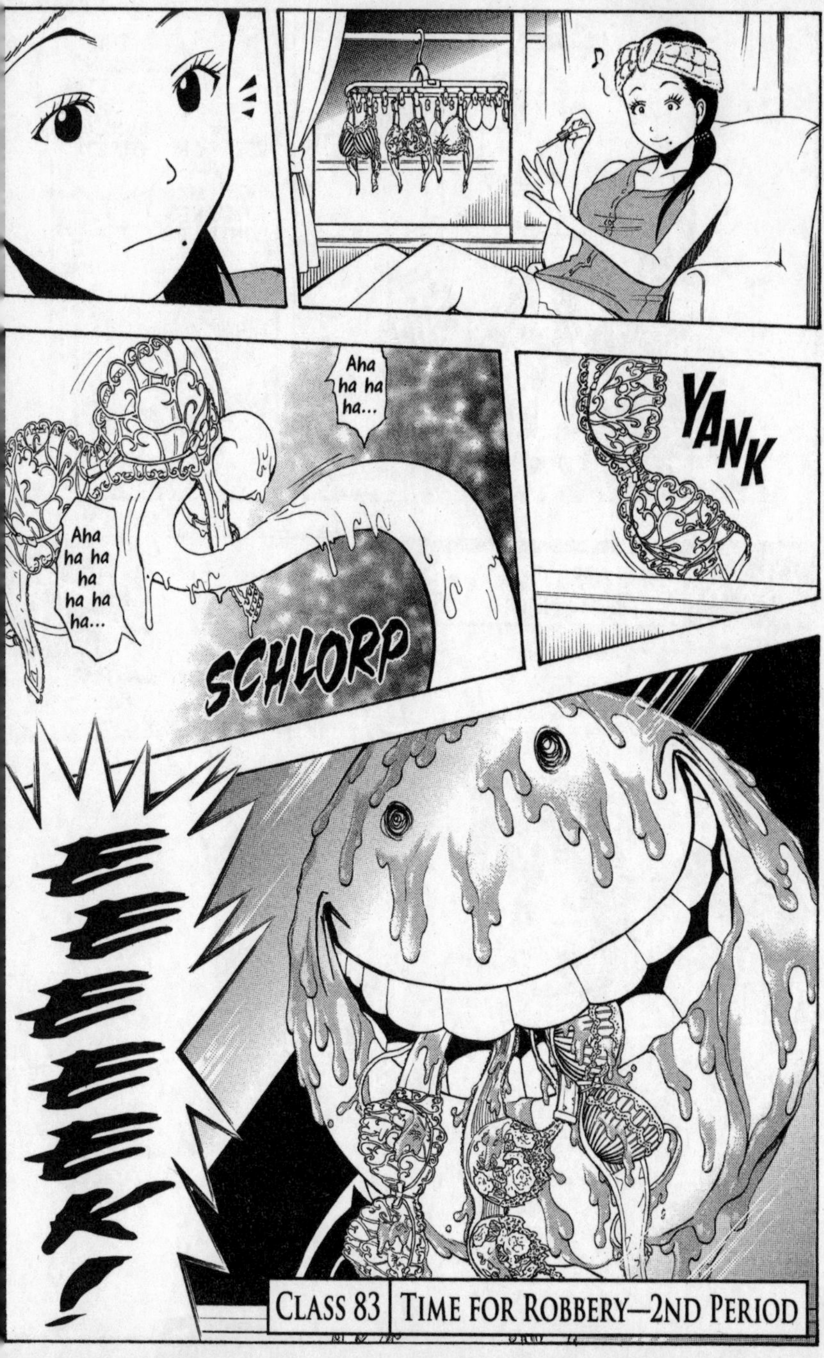
YANK
Aha ha ha ha...
Aha ha ha ha ha ha ha...
SCHLORP
EEEEEK!

Class 83 Time for Robbery—2nd Period

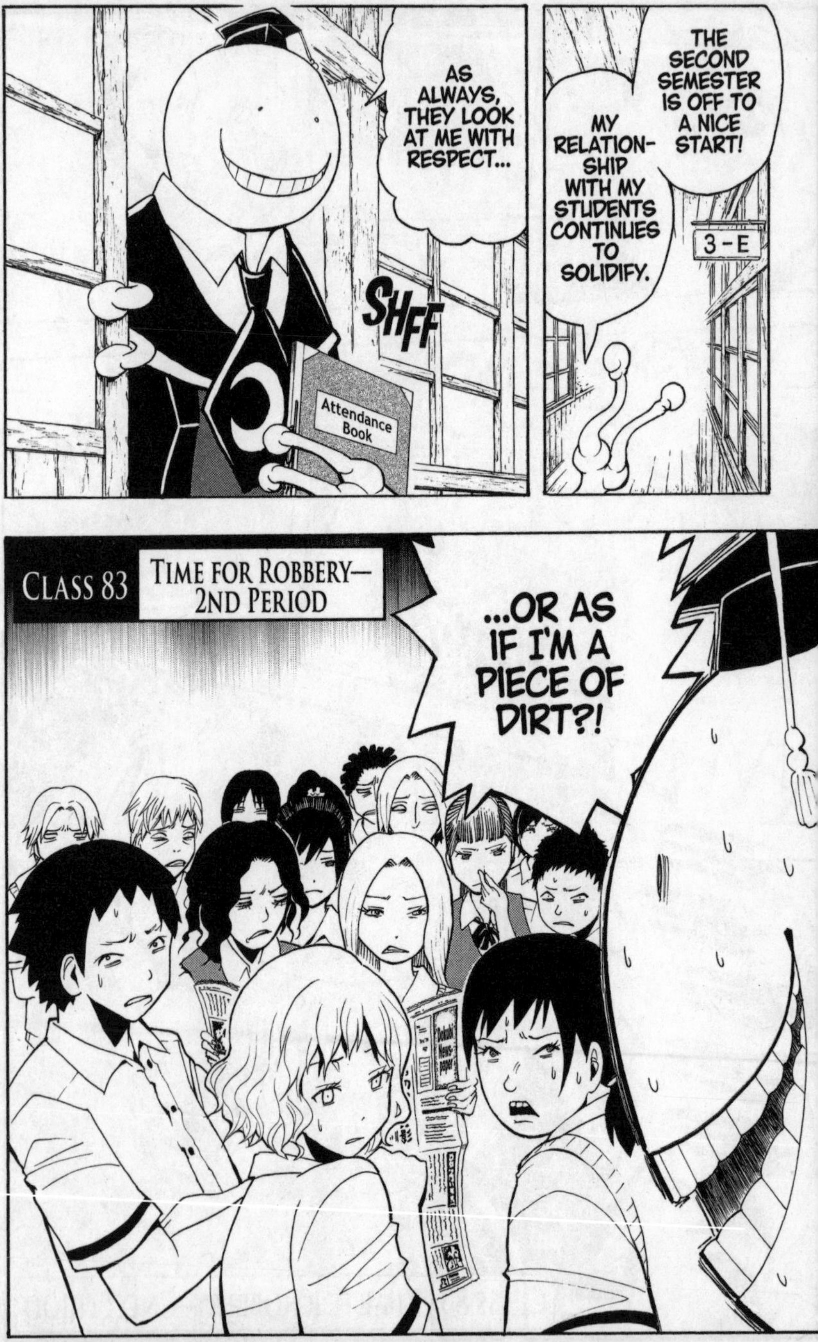
THE SECOND SEMESTER IS OFF TO A NICE START!
MY RELATIONSHIP WITH MY STUDENTS CONTINUES TO SOLIDIFY.
3-E
AS ALWAYS, THEY LOOK AT ME WITH RESPECT...
SHFF
Attendance Book
CLASS 83
TIME FOR ROBBERY—2ND PERIOD
...OR AS IF I'M A PIECE OF DIRT?!

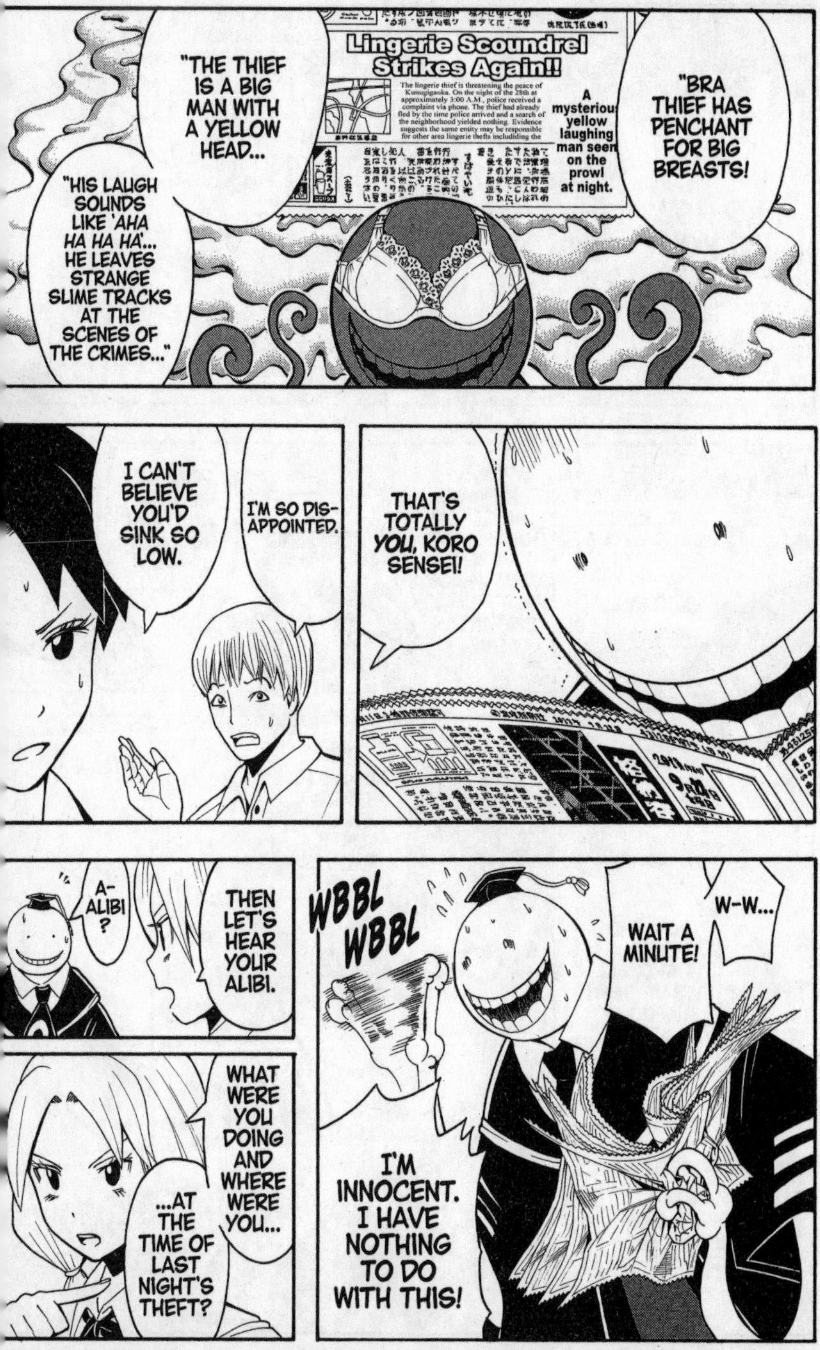
"BRA THIEF HAS PENCHANT FOR BIG BREASTS!
Lingerie Scoundrel Strikes Again!!
The lingerie thief is threatening the peace of Kunugigaoka. On the night of the 28th at approximately 3:00 A.M., police received a complaint via phone. The thief had already fled by the time police arrived and a search of the neighborhood yielded nothing. Evidence suggests the same entity may be responsible for other area lingerie thefts includiding the
A mysterious yellow laughing man seen on the prowl at night.
"THE THIEF IS A BIG MAN WITH A YELLOW HEAD...
"HIS LAUGH SOUNDS LIKE 'AHA HA HA HA'... HE LEAVES STRANGE SLIME TRACKS AT THE SCENES OF THE CRIMES..."
THAT'S TOTALLY YOU, KORO SENSEI!
I'M SO DIS-APPOINTED.
I CAN'T BELIEVE YOU'D SINK SO LOW.
W-W...
WAIT A MINUTE!
WBBL WBBL
I'M INNOCENT. I HAVE NOTHING TO DO WITH THIS!
THEN LET'S HEAR YOUR ALIBI.
A-ALIBI?
WHAT WERE YOU DOING AND WHERE WERE YOU...
...AT THE TIME OF LAST NIGHT'S THEFT?

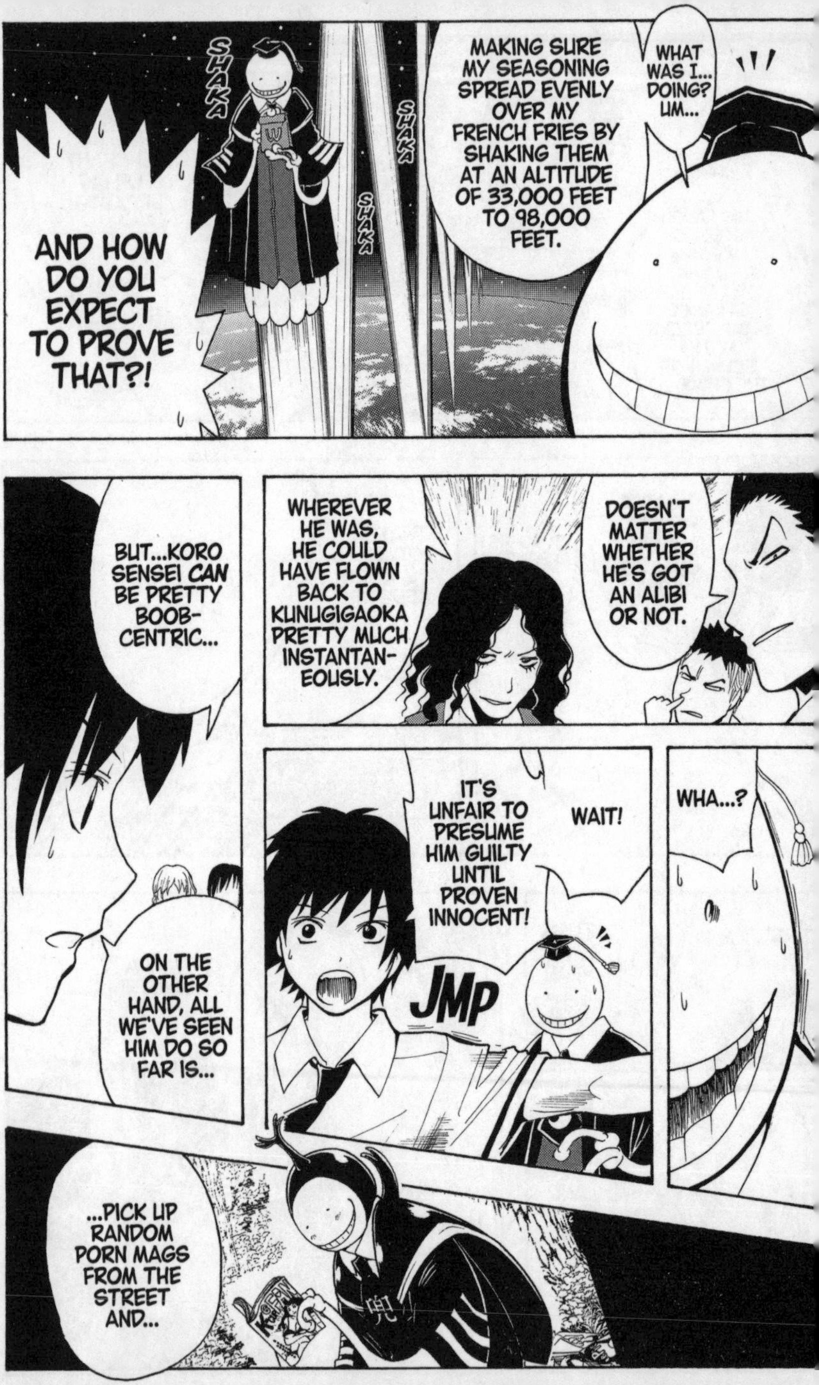
WHAT WAS I... DOING? UM...
MAKING SURE MY SEASONING SPREAD EVENLY OVER MY FRENCH FRIES BY SHAKING THEM AT AN ALTITUDE OF 33,000 FEET TO 98,000 FEET.
SHAKA
SHAKA
SHAKA
AND HOW DO YOU EXPECT TO PROVE THAT?!
DOESN'T MATTER WHETHER HE'S GOT AN ALIBI OR NOT.
WHEREVER HE WAS, HE COULD HAVE FLOWN BACK TO KUNUGIGAOKA PRETTY MUCH INSTANTANEOUSLY.
WHA...?
WAIT!
IT'S UNFAIR TO PRESUME HIM GUILTY UNTIL PROVEN INNOCENT!
JMP
BUT...KORO SENSEI CAN BE PRETTY BOOB-CENTRIC...
ON THE OTHER HAND, ALL WE'VE SEEN HIM DO SO FAR IS...
...PICK UP RANDOM PORN MAGS FROM THE STREET AND...

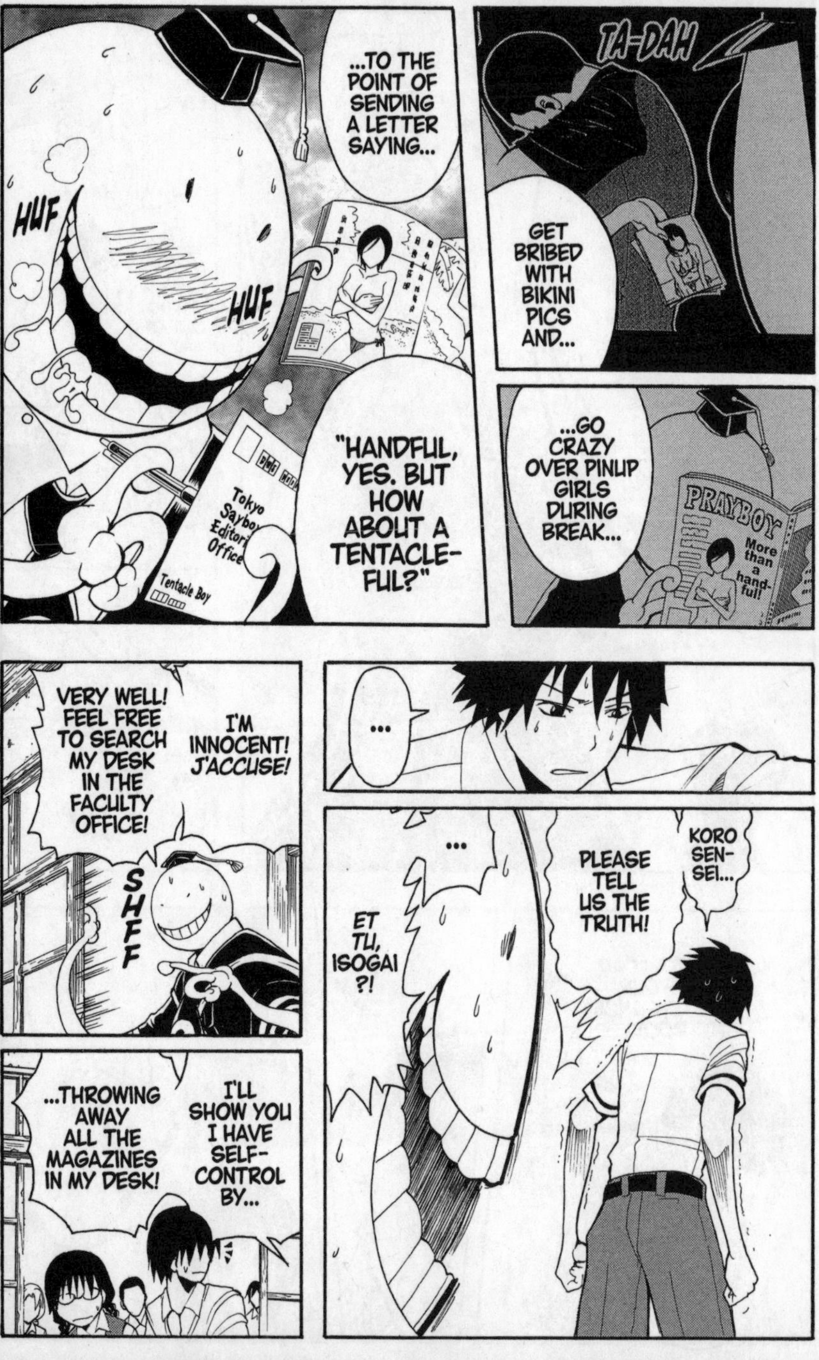
TA-DAH
GET BRIBED WITH BIKINI PICS AND...
...GO CRAZY OVER PINUP GIRLS DURING BREAK...
PRAYBOY
More than a hand-ful!
...TO THE POINT OF SENDING A LETTER SAYING...
HUF
HUF
"HANDFUL, YES. BUT HOW ABOUT A TENTACLE-FUL?"
Tokyo Sayboy Editori Office
Tentacle Boy
...
KORO SEN-SEI...
PLEASE TELL US THE TRUTH!
...
ET TU, ISOGAI ?!
I'M INNOCENT! J'ACCUSE!
VERY WELL! FEEL FREE TO SEARCH MY DESK IN THE FACULTY OFFICE!
SHFF
I'LL SHOW YOU I HAVE SELF-CONTROL BY...
...THROWING AWAY ALL THE MAGAZINES IN MY DESK!

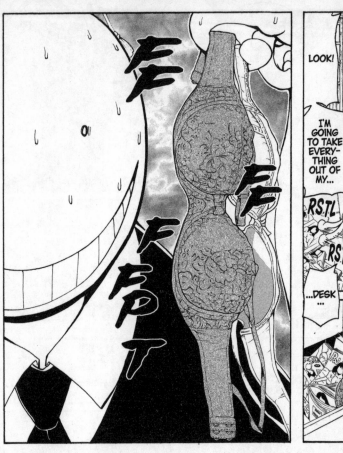

LOOK!

I'M GOING TO TAKE EVERYTHING OUT OF MY...

RSTL

RSTL

...DESK...

GRAB

GET A LOAD OF OUR ATTENDANCE BOOK!

HEY!

Attendance Book

ZIP

SERIOUSLY...?

...!

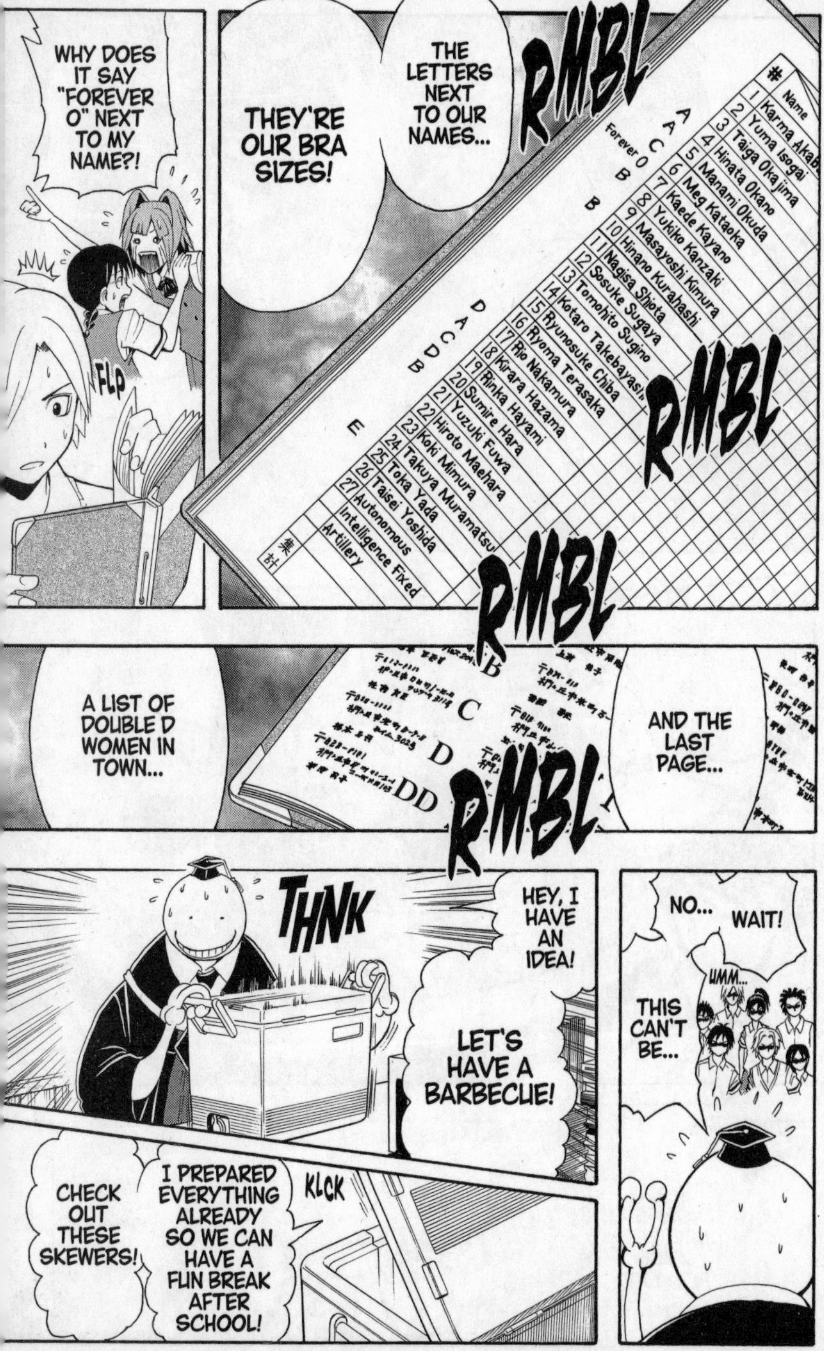
THE LETTERS NEXT TO OUR NAMES...
THEY'RE OUR BRA SIZES!
RMBL
Name
1 Karma Akaba
2 Yuma Isogai
3 Taiga Okajima
4 Hinata Okano
5 Manami Okuda
6 Meg Kataoka
7 Kaede Kayano
8 Yukiko Kanzaki
9 Masayoshi Kimura
10 Hinano Kurahashi
11 Nagisa Shiota
12 Sosuke Sugaya
13 Tomohito Sugino
14 Kotaro Takebayashi
15 Ryunosuke Chiba
16 Ryoma Terasaka
17 Rio Nakamura
18 Kirara Hazama
19 Rinka Hayami
20 Sumire Hara
21 Yuzuki Fuwa
22 Hiroto Maehara
23 Koki Mimura
24 Takuya Muramatsu
25 Toka Yada
26 Taisei Yoshida
27 Autonomous Intelligence Fixed Artillery
A
A
C
Forever 0
B
B
D
A
C
D
B
E
RMBL
RMBL
WHY DOES IT SAY "FOREVER 0" NEXT TO MY NAME?!
FLP
AND THE LAST PAGE...
RMBL
B
C
D
DD
A LIST OF DOUBLE D WOMEN IN TOWN...
NO...
WAIT!
UMM...
THIS CAN'T BE...
HEY, I HAVE AN IDEA!
THNK
LET'S HAVE A BARBECUE!
I PREPARED EVERYTHING ALREADY SO WE CAN HAVE A FUN BREAK AFTER SCHOOL!
KLCK
CHECK OUT THESE SKEWERS!

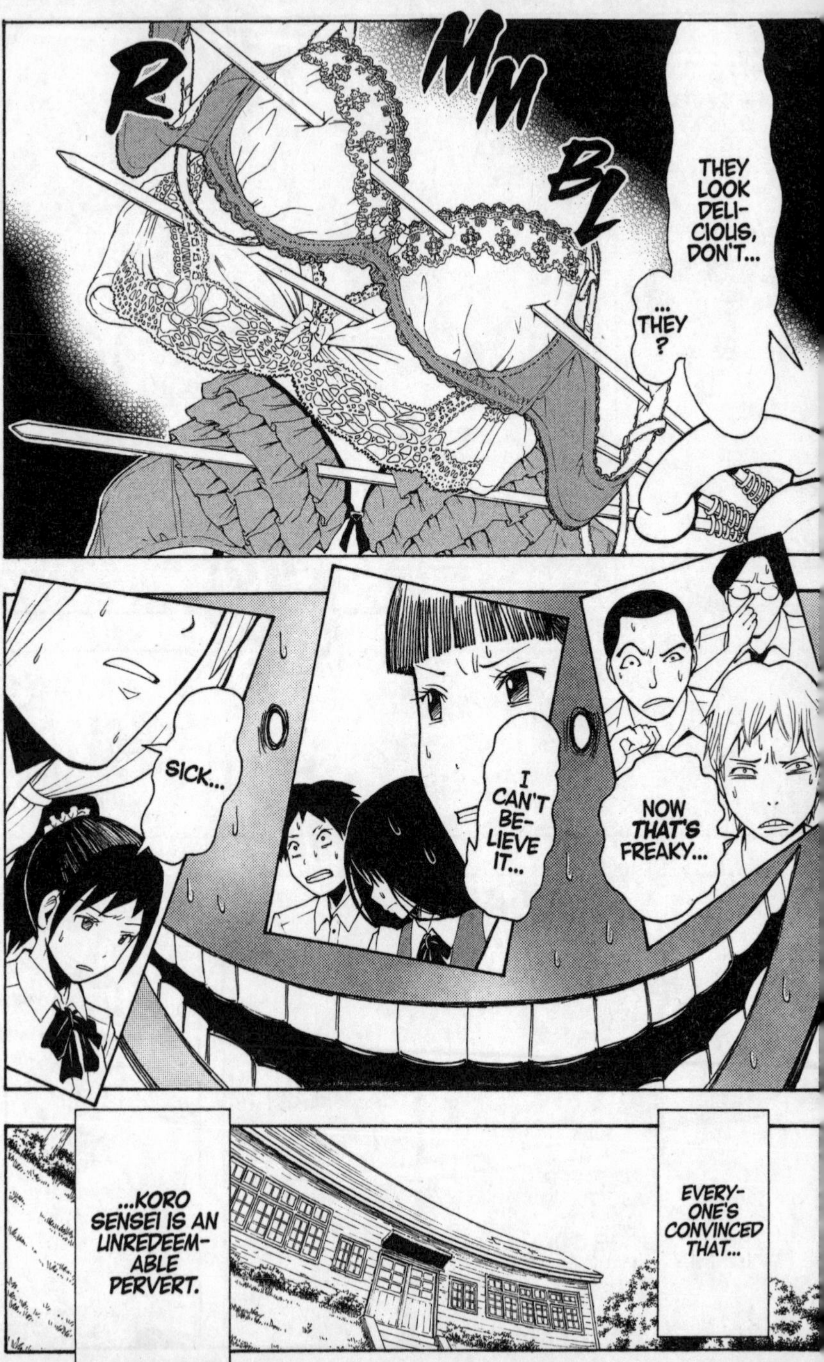
THEY LOOK DELI-CIOUS, DON'T...
...THEY?
RMMBL
NOW THAT'S FREAKY...
I CAN'T BE-LIEVE IT...
SICK...
EVERY-ONE'S CONVINCED THAT...
...KORO SENSEI IS AN UNREDEEM-ABLE PERVERT.

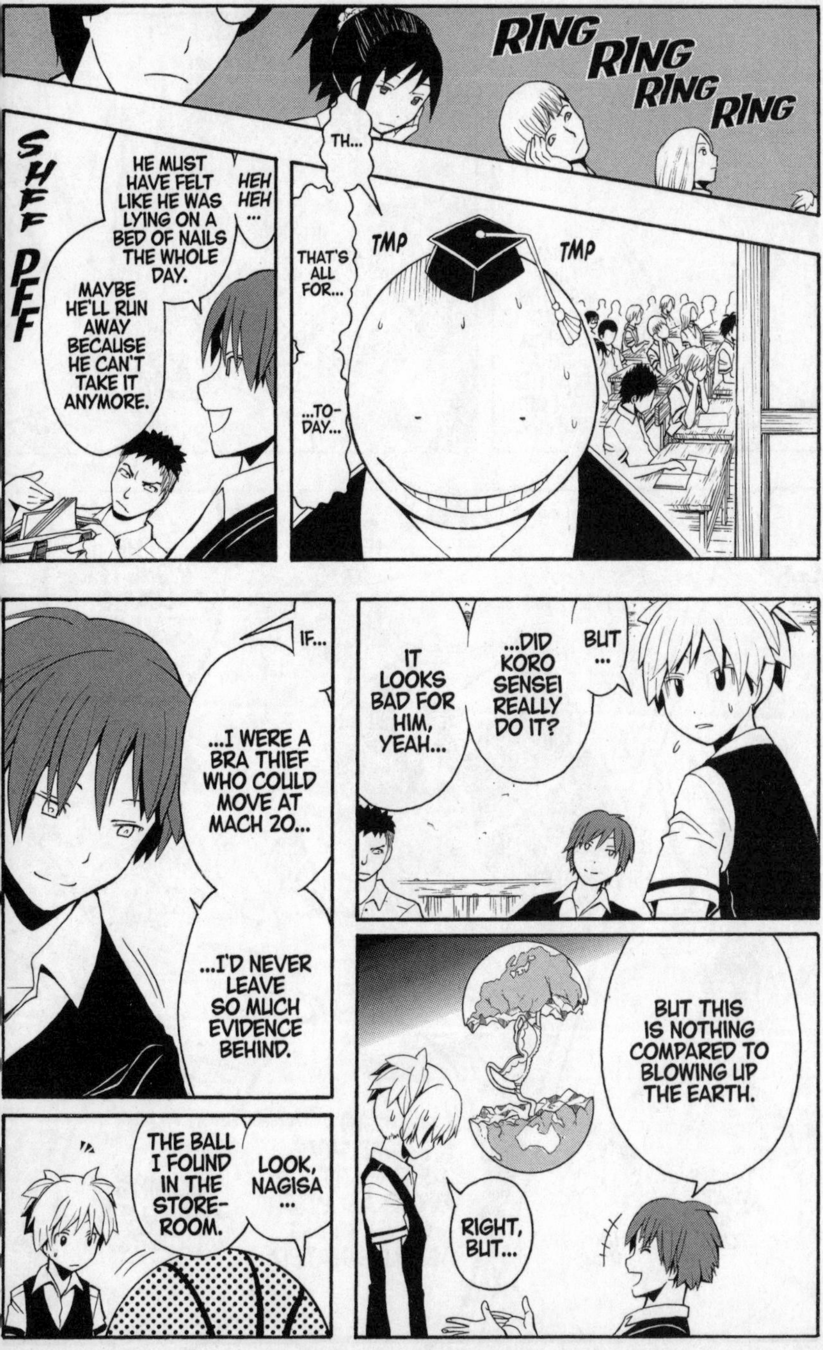
RING RING RING RING
TMP
TMP
TH...
THAT'S ALL FOR...
...TO-DAY...
SHFF
PFF
HEH HEH ...
HE MUST HAVE FELT LIKE HE WAS LYING ON A BED OF NAILS THE WHOLE DAY.
MAYBE HE'LL RUN AWAY BECAUSE HE CAN'T TAKE IT ANYMORE.
BUT ...
...DID KORO SENSEI REALLY DO IT?
IT LOOKS BAD FOR HIM, YEAH...
BUT THIS IS NOTHING COMPARED TO BLOWING UP THE EARTH.
RIGHT, BUT...
IF...
...I WERE A BRA THIEF WHO COULD MOVE AT MACH 20...
...I'D NEVER LEAVE SO MUCH EVIDENCE BEHIND.
LOOK, NAGISA ...
THE BALL I FOUND IN THE STORE-ROOM.

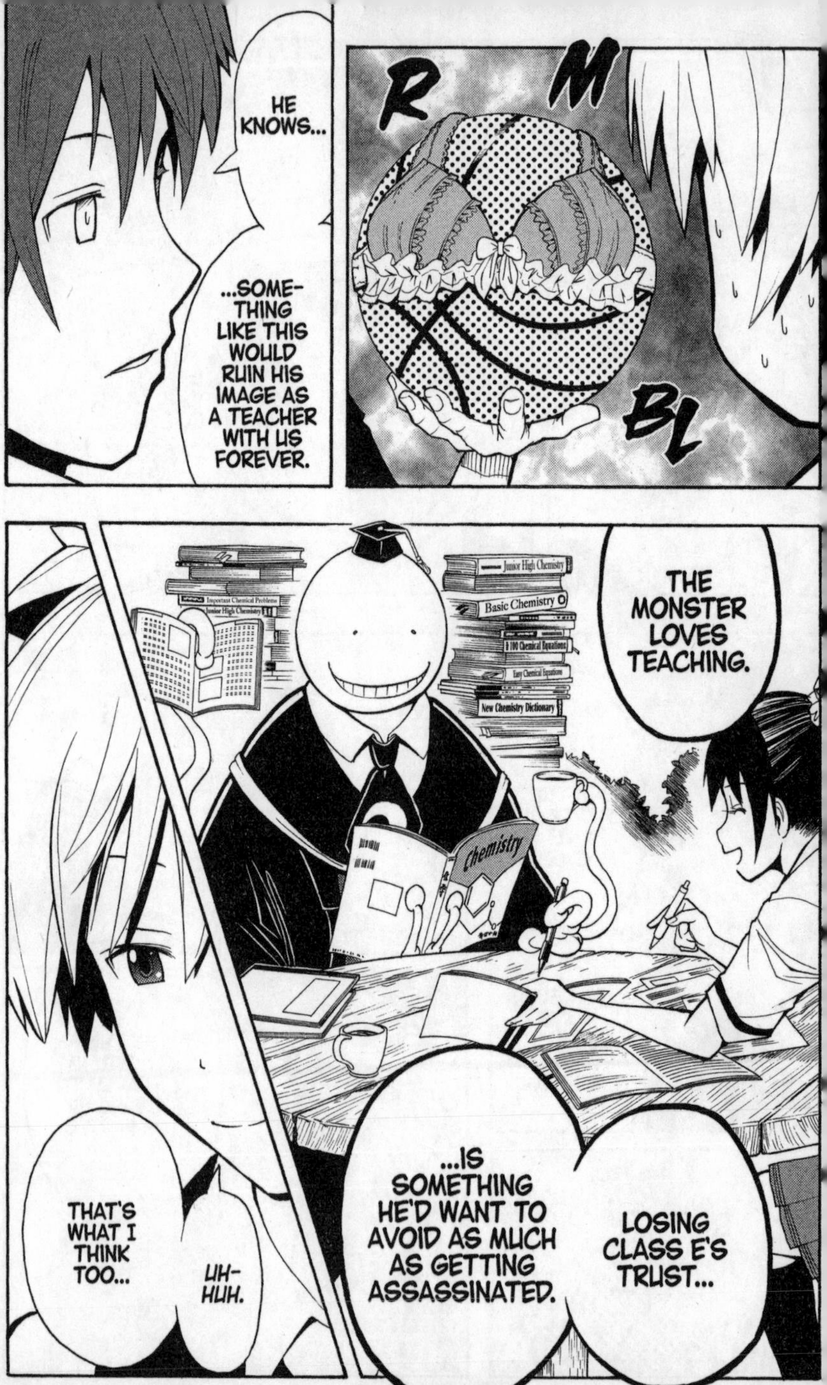
R M BL
HE KNOWS...
...SOME-THING LIKE THIS WOULD RUIN HIS IMAGE AS A TEACHER WITH US FOREVER.
THE MONSTER LOVES TEACHING.
Junior High Chemistry
Basic Chemistry
100 Chemical Equations
Easy Chemical Equations
New Chemistry Dictionary
Important Chemical Problems
Junior High Chemistry
Chemistry
LOSING CLASS E'S TRUST...
...IS SOMETHING HE'D WANT TO AVOID AS MUCH AS GETTING ASSASSINATED.
UH-HUH.
THAT'S WHAT I THINK TOO...

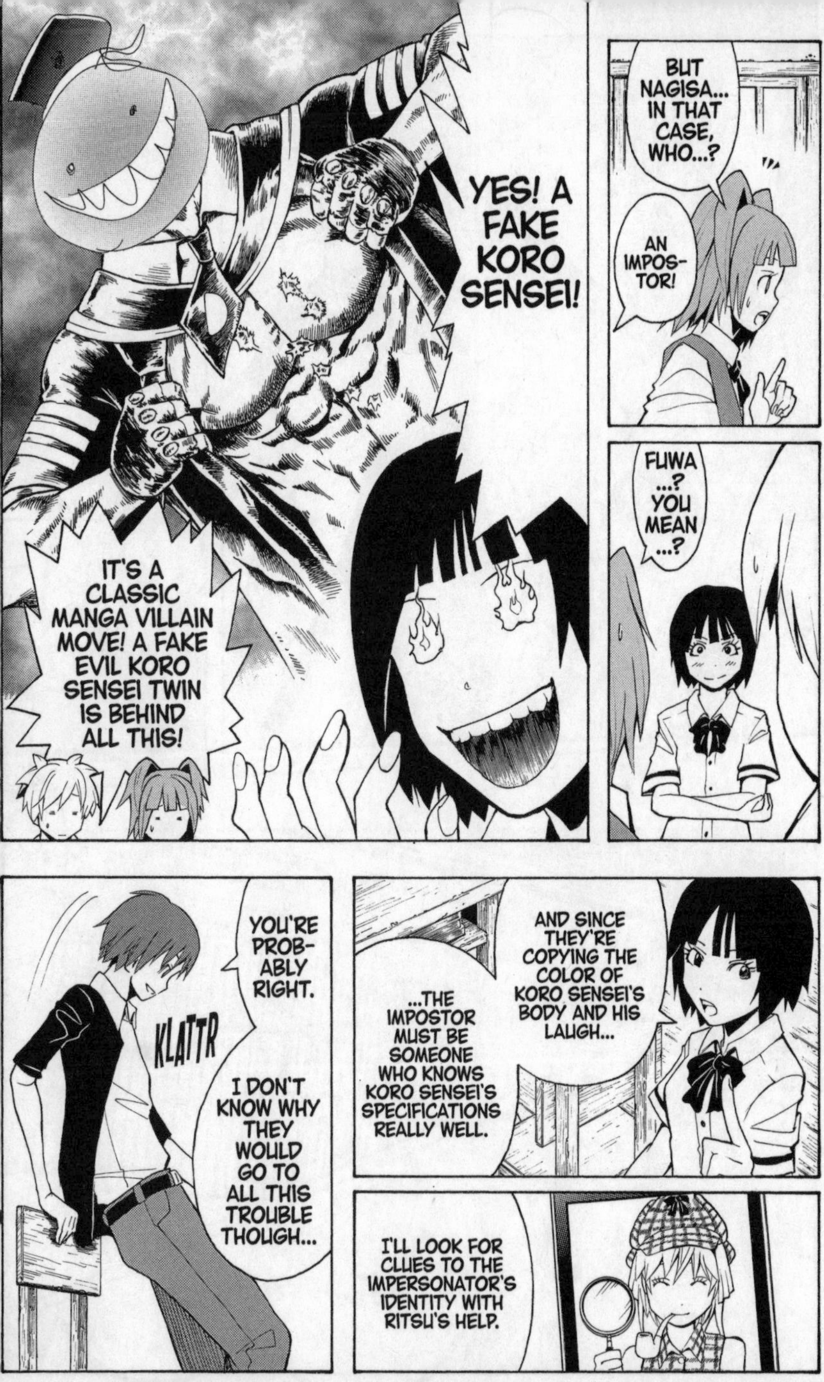
BUT NAGISA... IN THAT CASE, WHO...?
AN IMPOSTOR!
FUWA...? YOU MEAN...?
YES! A FAKE KORO SENSEI!
IT'S A CLASSIC MANGA VILLAIN MOVE! A FAKE EVIL KORO SENSEI TWIN IS BEHIND ALL THIS!
AND SINCE THEY'RE COPYING THE COLOR OF KORO SENSEI'S BODY AND HIS LAUGH...
...THE IMPOSTOR MUST BE SOMEONE WHO KNOWS KORO SENSEI'S SPECIFICATIONS REALLY WELL.
I'LL LOOK FOR CLUES TO THE IMPERSONATOR'S IDENTITY WITH RITSU'S HELP.
YOU'RE PROBABLY RIGHT.
KLATTR
I DON'T KNOW WHY THEY WOULD GO TO ALL THIS TROUBLE THOUGH...

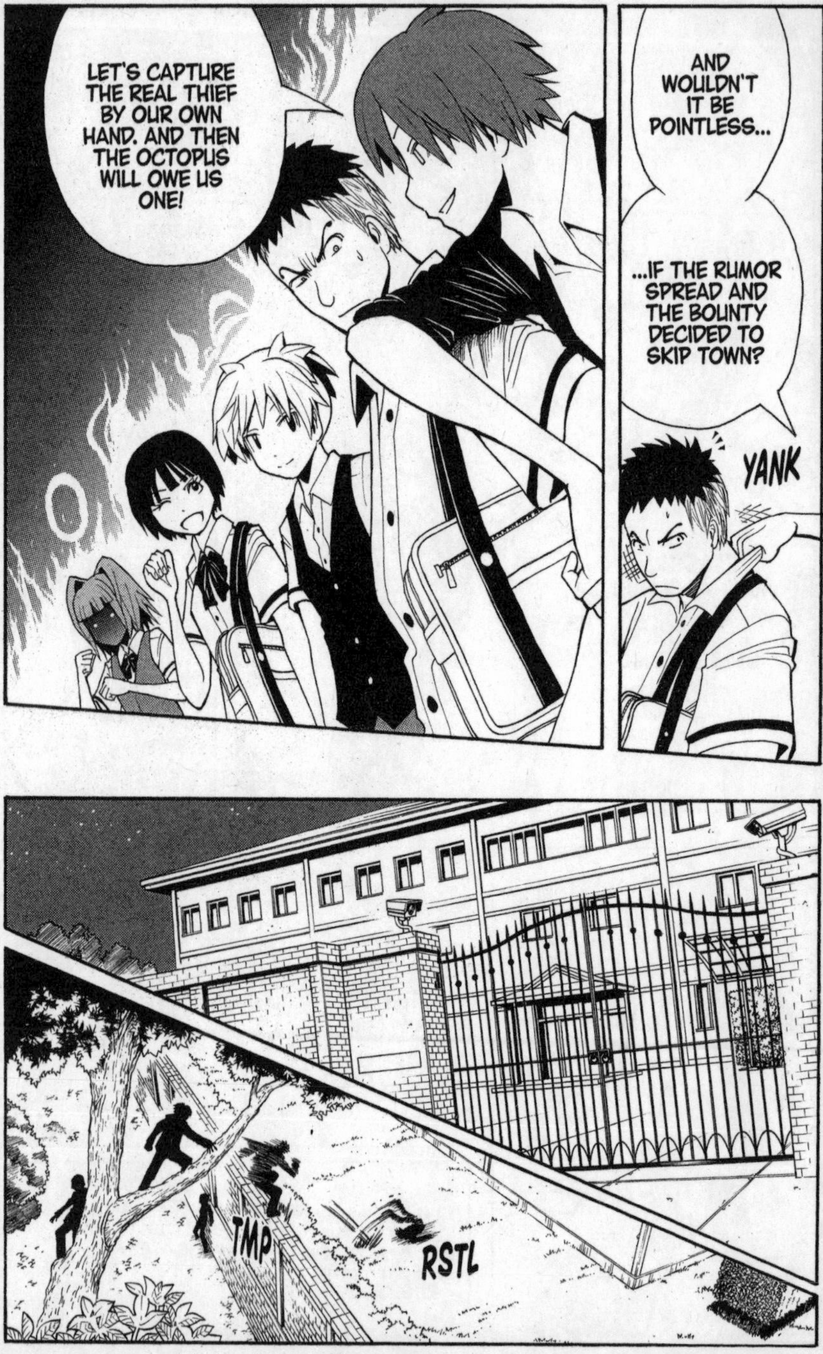
AND WOULDN'T IT BE POINTLESS...
...IF THE RUMOR SPREAD AND THE BOUNTY DECIDED TO SKIP TOWN?
YANK
LET'S CAPTURE THE REAL THIEF BY OUR OWN HAND. AND THEN THE OCTOPUS WILL OWE US ONE!
TMP
RSTL

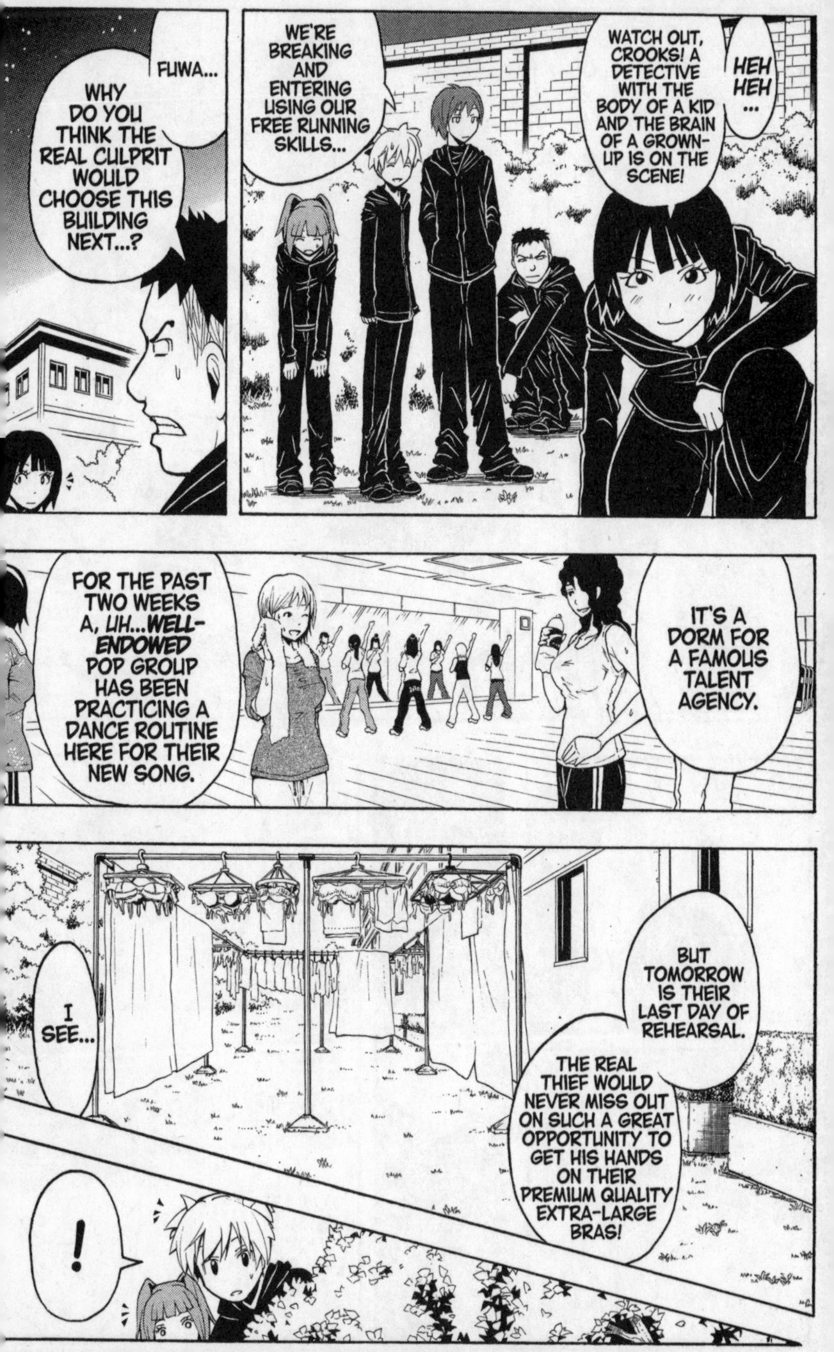
HEH HEH ...
WATCH OUT, CROOKS! A DETECTIVE WITH THE BODY OF A KID AND THE BRAIN OF A GROWN-UP IS ON THE SCENE!
WE'RE BREAKING AND ENTERING USING OUR FREE RUNNING SKILLS...
FUWA...
WHY DO YOU THINK THE REAL CULPRIT WOULD CHOOSE THIS BUILDING NEXT...?
IT'S A DORM FOR A FAMOUS TALENT AGENCY.
FOR THE PAST TWO WEEKS A, *UH...WELL-ENDOWED* POP GROUP HAS BEEN PRACTICING A DANCE ROUTINE HERE FOR THEIR NEW SONG.
BUT TOMORROW IS THEIR LAST DAY OF REHEARSAL.
THE REAL THIEF WOULD NEVER MISS OUT ON SUCH A GREAT OPPORTUNITY TO GET HIS HANDS ON THEIR PREMIUM QUALITY EXTRA-LARGE BRAS!
I SEE...
!

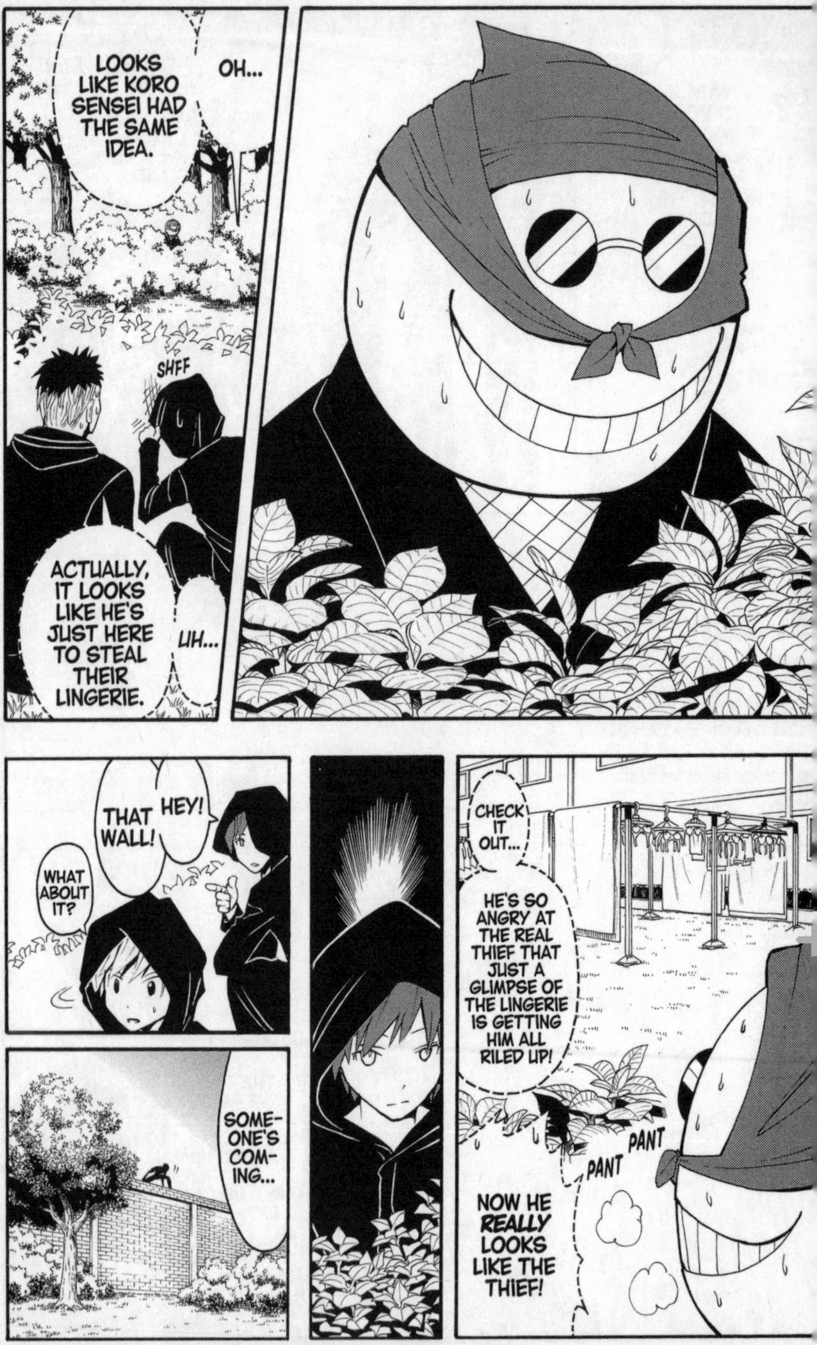
OH...
LOOKS LIKE KORO SENSEI HAD THE SAME IDEA.
SHFF
UH...
ACTUALLY, IT LOOKS LIKE HE'S JUST HERE TO STEAL THEIR LINGERIE.
CHECK IT OUT...
HE'S SO ANGRY AT THE REAL THIEF THAT JUST A GLIMPSE OF THE LINGERIE IS GETTING HIM ALL RILED UP!
PANT
PANT
NOW HE *REALLY* LOOKS LIKE THE THIEF!
HEY!
THAT WALL!
WHAT ABOUT IT?
SOME-ONE'S COM-ING...

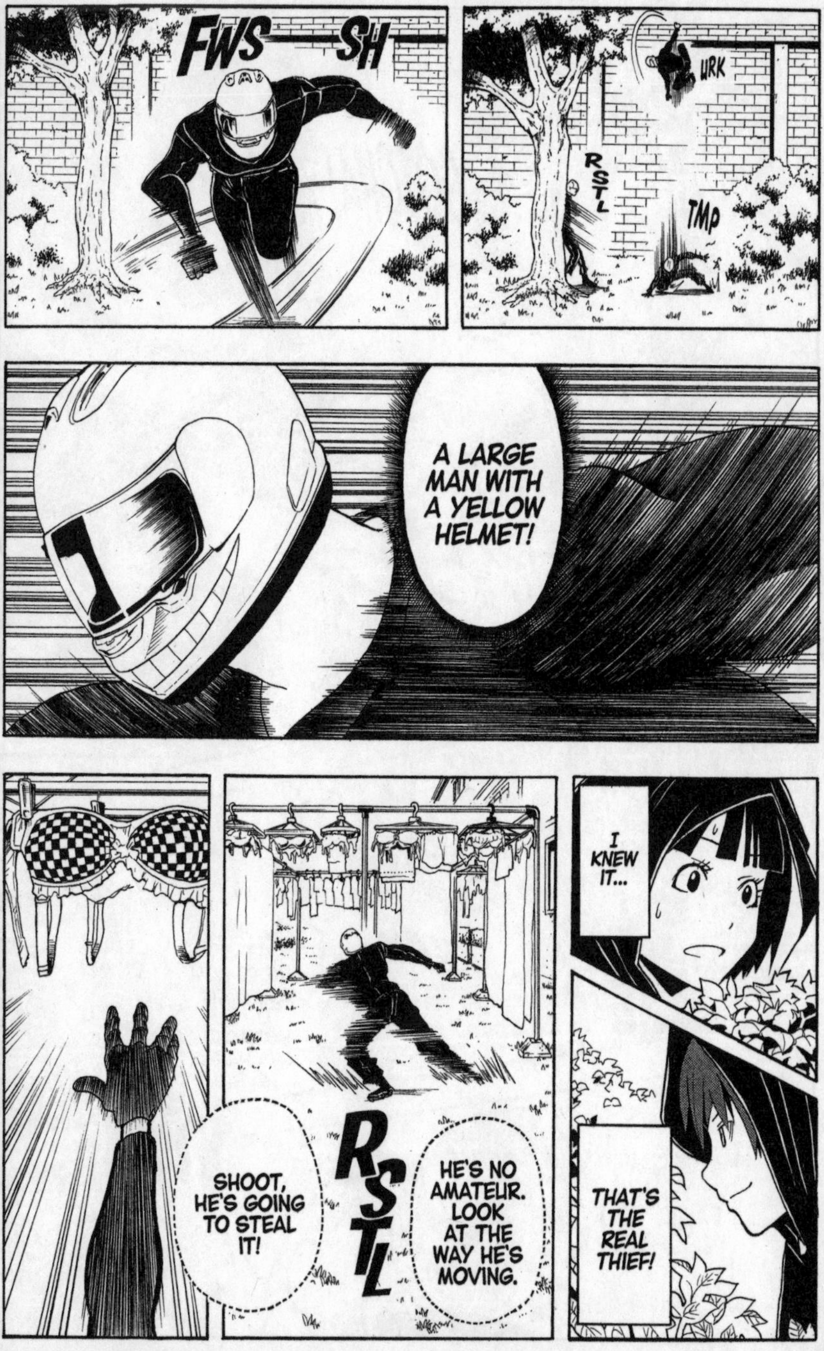
URK
RSTL
TMP
FWS—SH
A LARGE MAN WITH A YELLOW HELMET!
I KNEW IT...
THAT'S THE REAL THIEF!
HE'S NO AMATEUR. LOOK AT THE WAY HE'S MOVING.
RSTL
SHOOT, HE'S GOING TO STEAL IT!

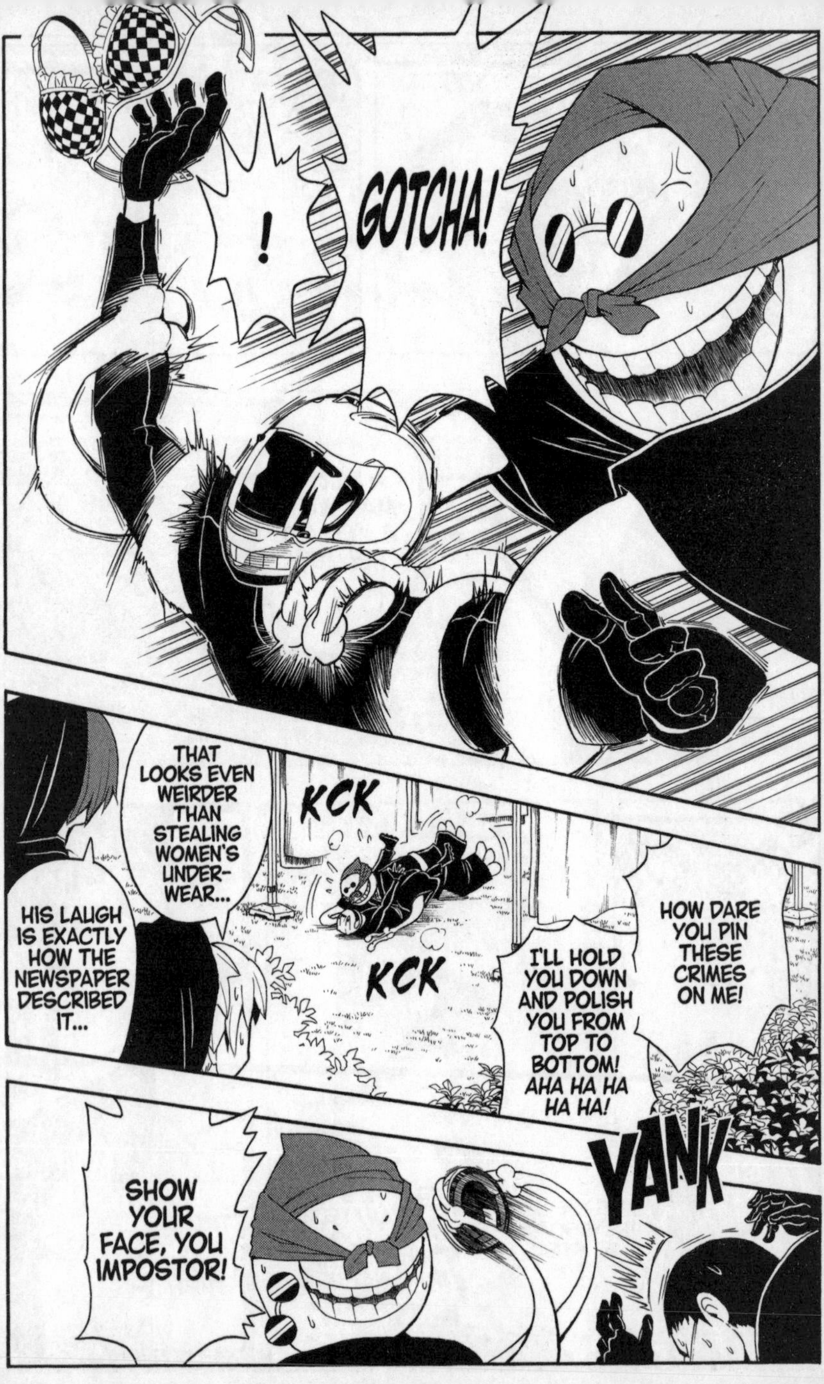
GOTCHA!
!
HOW DARE YOU PIN THESE CRIMES ON ME!
I'LL HOLD YOU DOWN AND POLISH YOU FROM TOP TO BOTTOM! AHA HA HA HA HA!
KCK
KCK
THAT LOOKS EVEN WEIRDER THAN STEALING WOMEN'S UNDER-WEAR...
HIS LAUGH IS EXACTLY HOW THE NEWSPAPER DESCRIBED IT...
YANK
SHOW YOUR FACE, YOU IMPOSTOR!

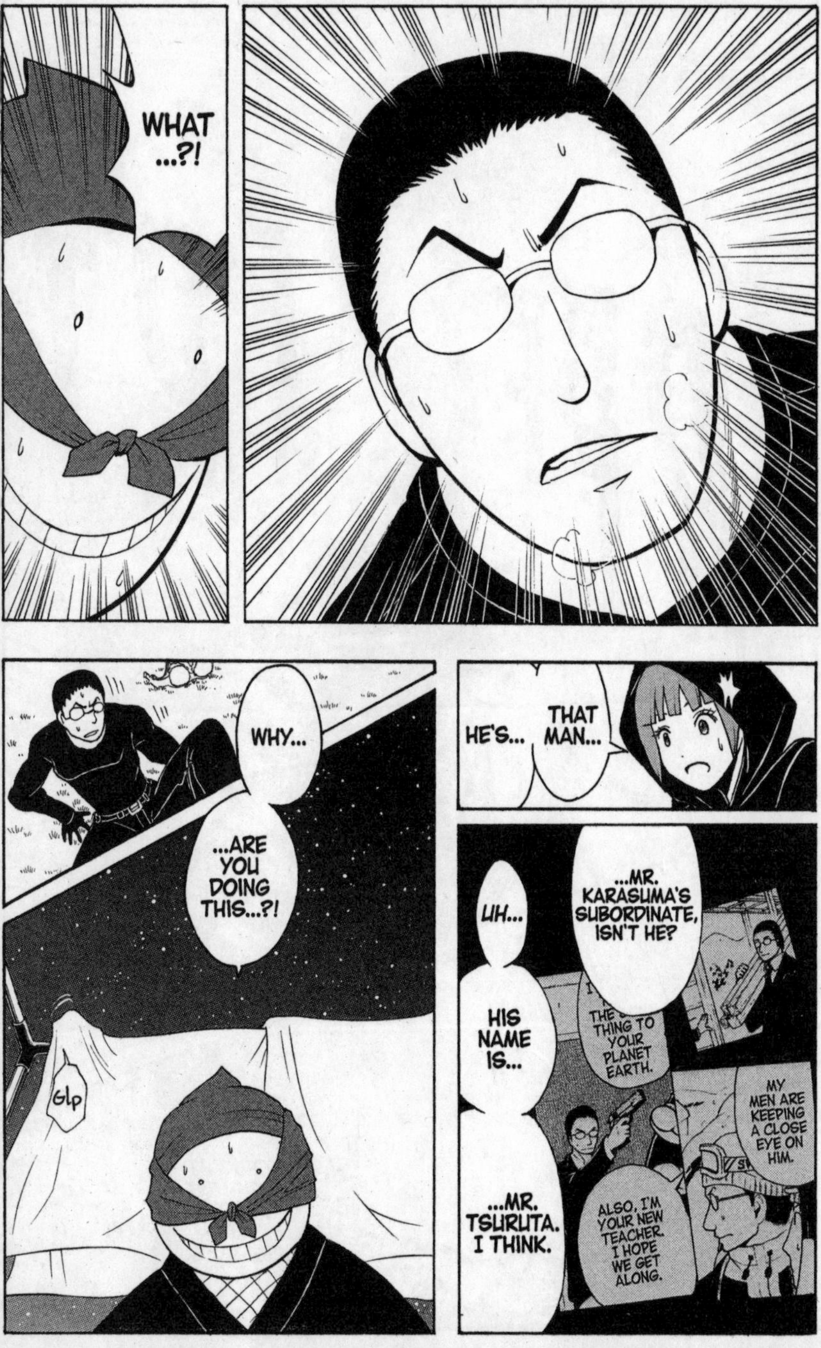
WHAT ...?!
THAT MAN...
HE'S...
...MR. KARASUMA'S SUBORDINATE, ISN'T HE?
UH...
THING TO YOUR PLANET EARTH.
MY MEN ARE KEEPING A CLOSE EYE ON HIM.
HIS NAME IS...
ALSO, I'M YOUR NEW TEACHER. I HOPE WE GET ALONG.
...MR. TSURUTA. I THINK.
WHY...
...ARE YOU DOING THIS...?!
Glp

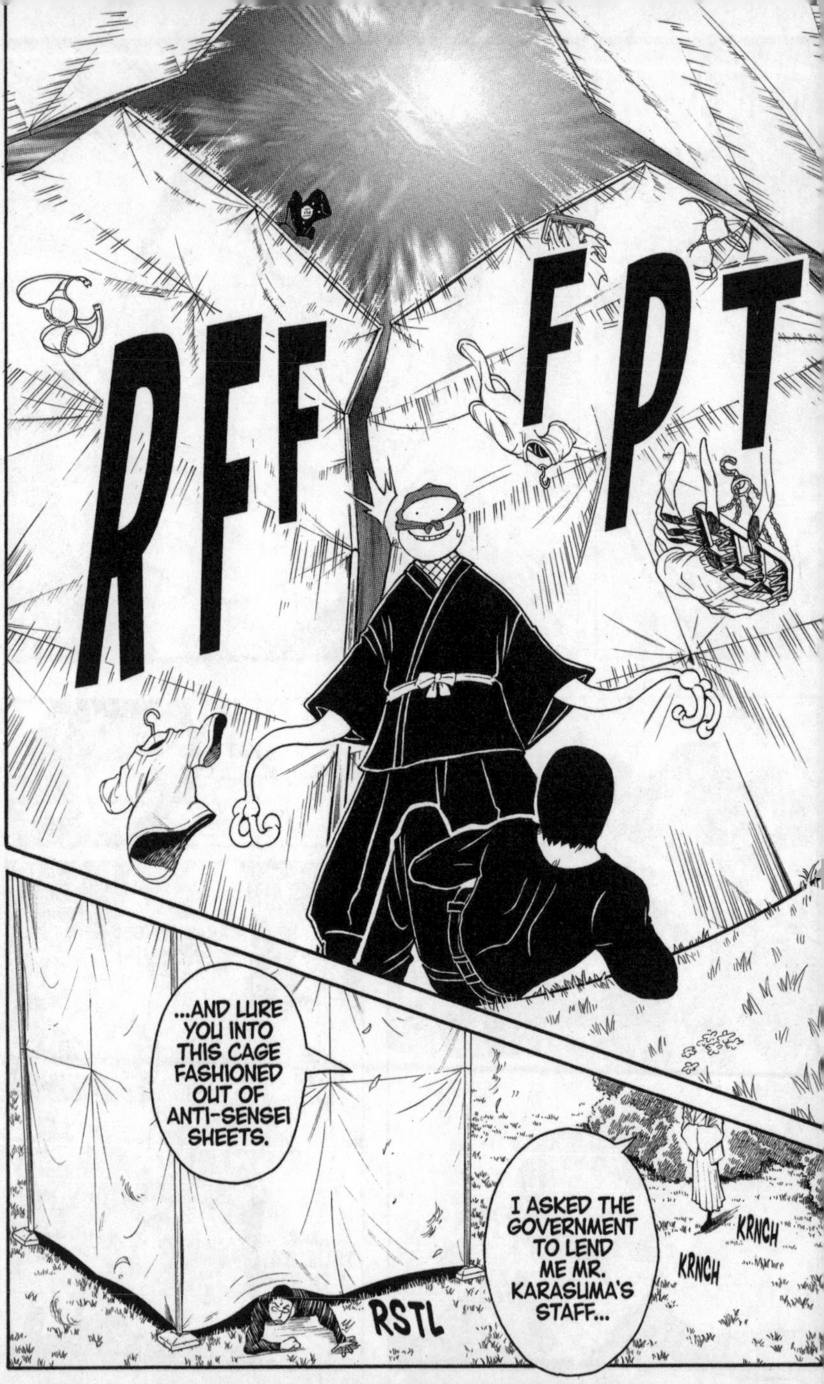
RFF
FPT
I ASKED THE GOVERNMENT TO LEND ME MR. KARASUMA'S STAFF...
KRNCH
KRNCH
...AND LURE YOU INTO THIS CAGE FASHIONED OUT OF ANTI-SENSEI SHEETS.
RSTL

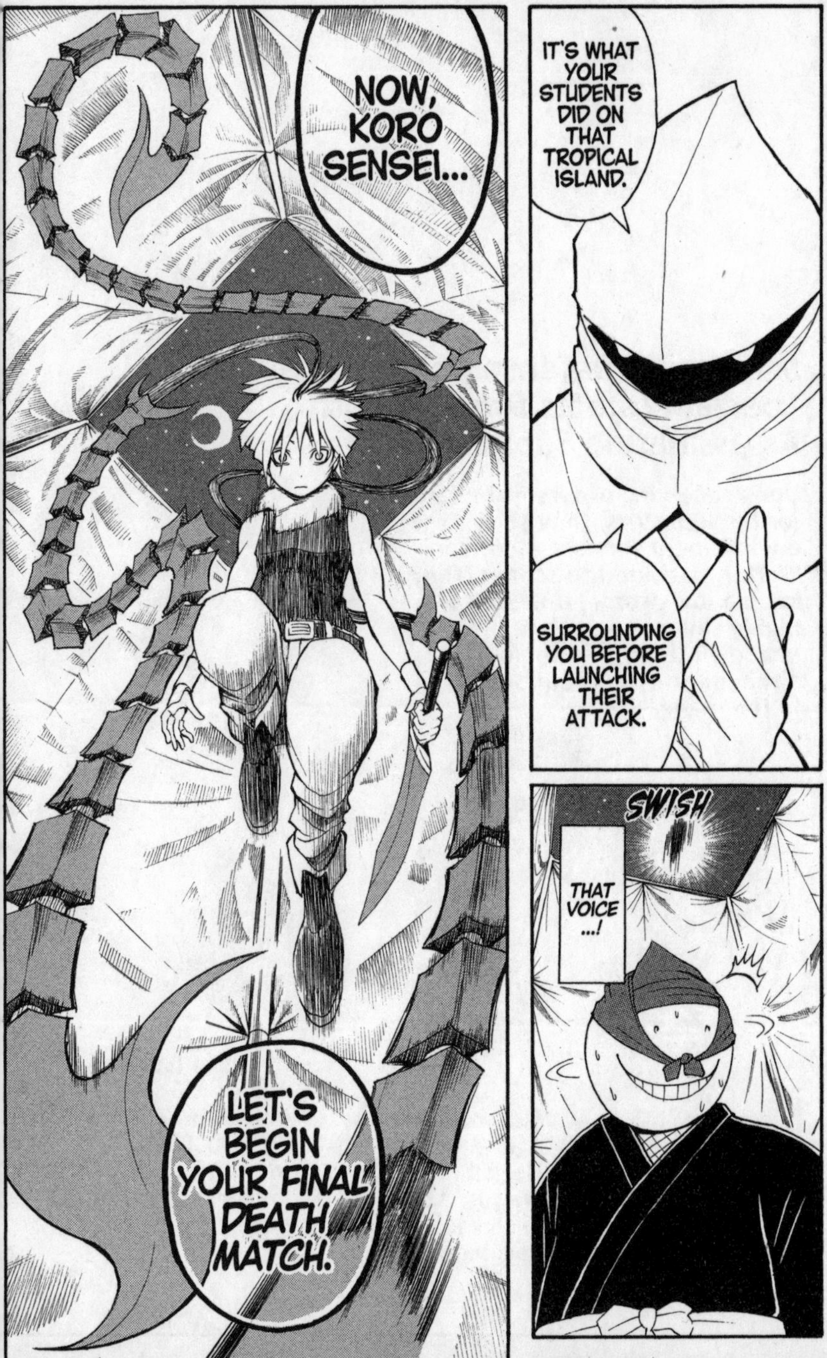
IT'S WHAT YOUR STUDENTS DID ON THAT TROPICAL ISLAND.
SURROUNDING YOU BEFORE LAUNCHING THEIR ATTACK.
SWISH
THAT VOICE ...!
NOW, KORO SENSEI...
LET'S BEGIN YOUR FINAL DEATH MATCH.

Ministry of Defense Contingency Special Projects Department: Assassination Support Team

Upon receiving orders from Karasuma (or his superiors) they set up the environment for assassinations. Working behind the scenes, they keep a low profile, but they are highly skilled operatives. There are several more of them, although they don't appear in the manga.

Kenichi Ukai
Age: 26
Height: 5' 9"
Weight: 150 lbs.
In charge of planning and design

Suzume Sonokawa
Age: 25
Height: 5' 4"
Weight: 121 lbs.
In charge of negotiations

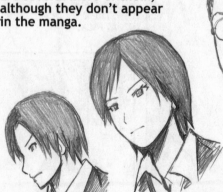

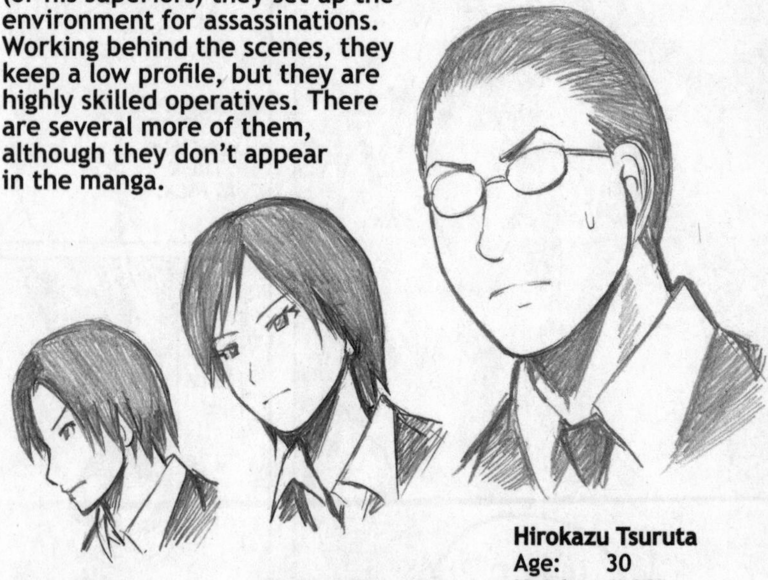

Hirokazu Tsuruta
Age: 30
Height: 6' 00"
Weight: 198 lbs.
In charge of implementing plans

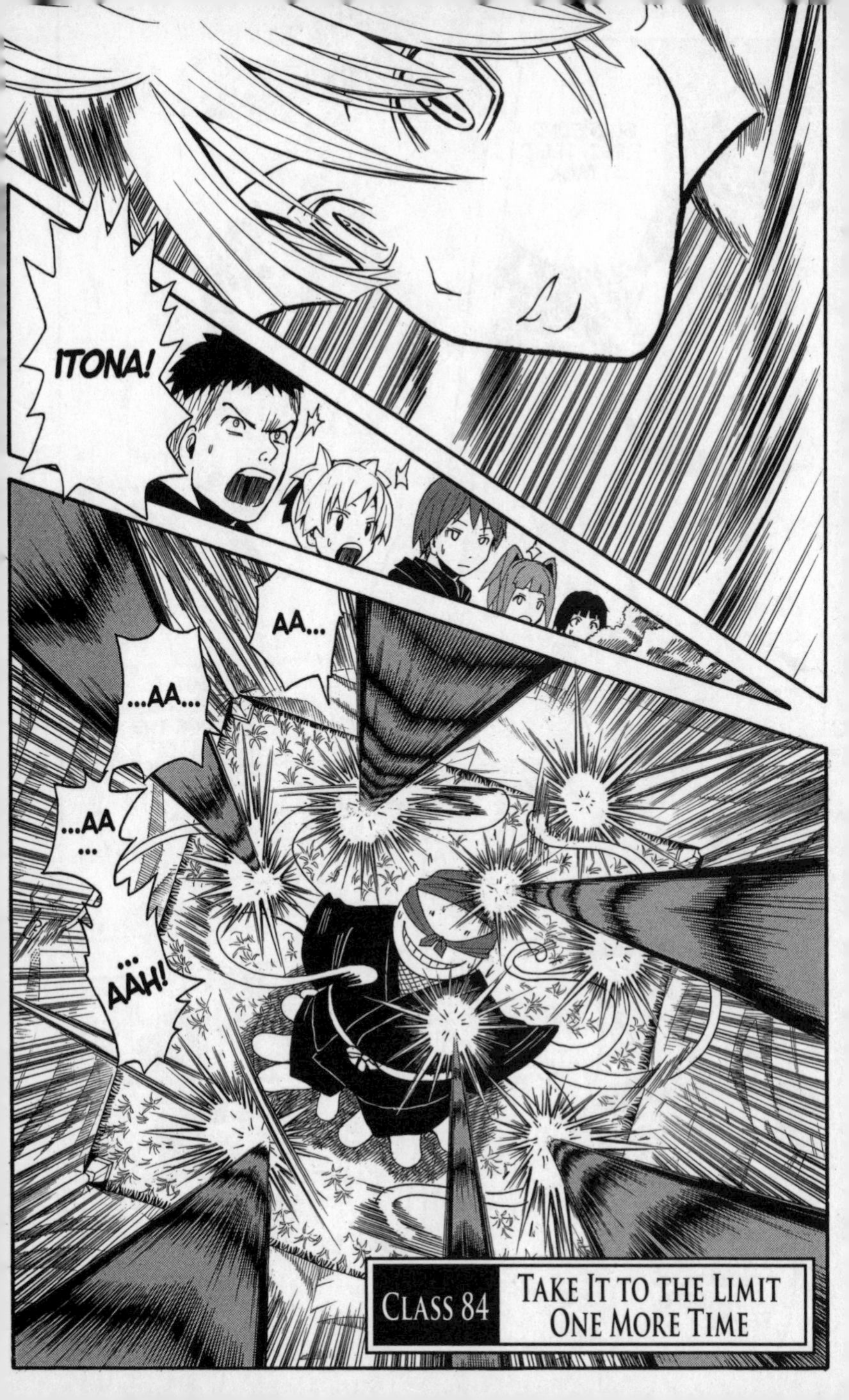
ITONA!
AA...
...AA...
...AA
...
...
AAH!

Class 84
Take It to the Limit
One More Time

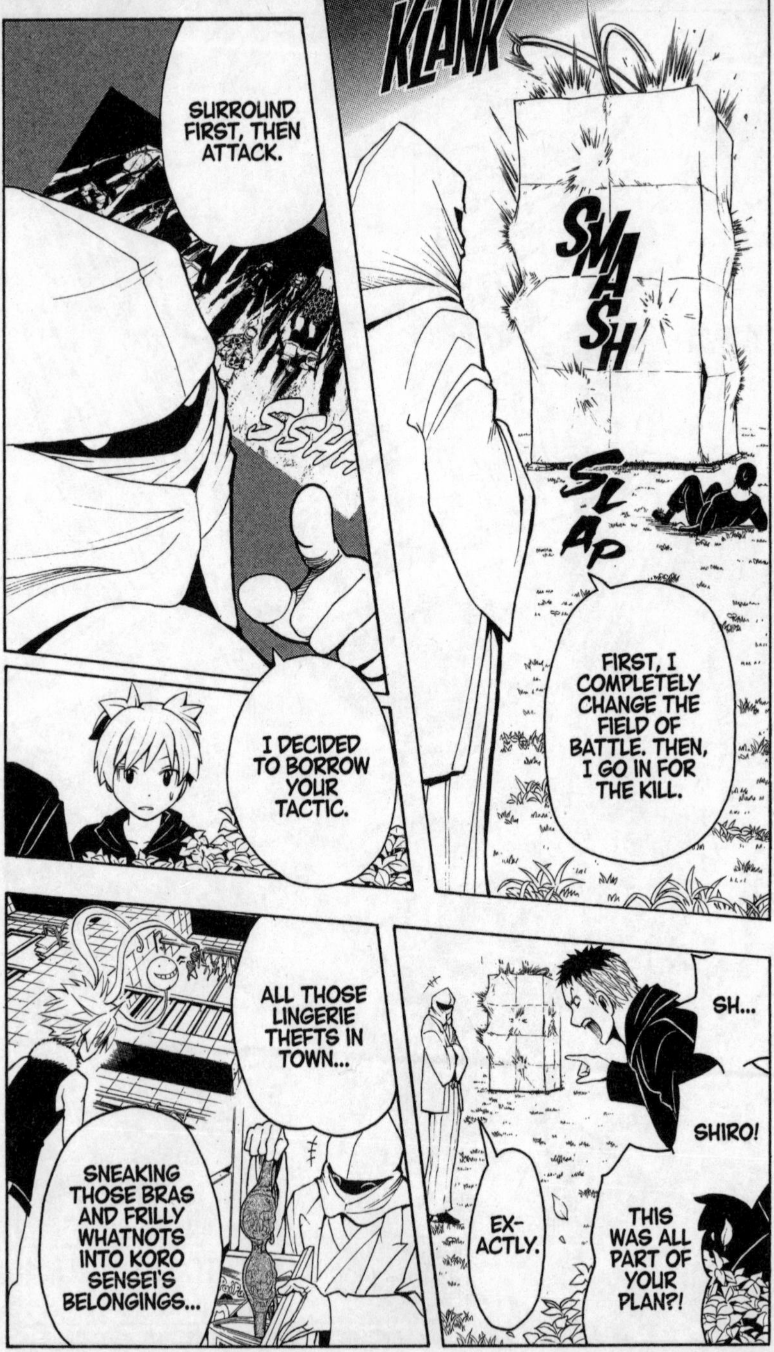
KLANK
SMASH
SLAP
FIRST, I COMPLETELY CHANGE THE FIELD OF BATTLE. THEN, I GO IN FOR THE KILL.
SURROUND FIRST, THEN ATTACK.
SSH
I DECIDED TO BORROW YOUR TACTIC.
SH...
SHIRO!
THIS WAS ALL PART OF YOUR PLAN?!
EX-ACTLY.
ALL THOSE LINGERIE THEFTS IN TOWN...
SNEAKING THOSE BRAS AND FRILLY WHATNOTS INTO KORO SENSEI'S BELONGINGS...

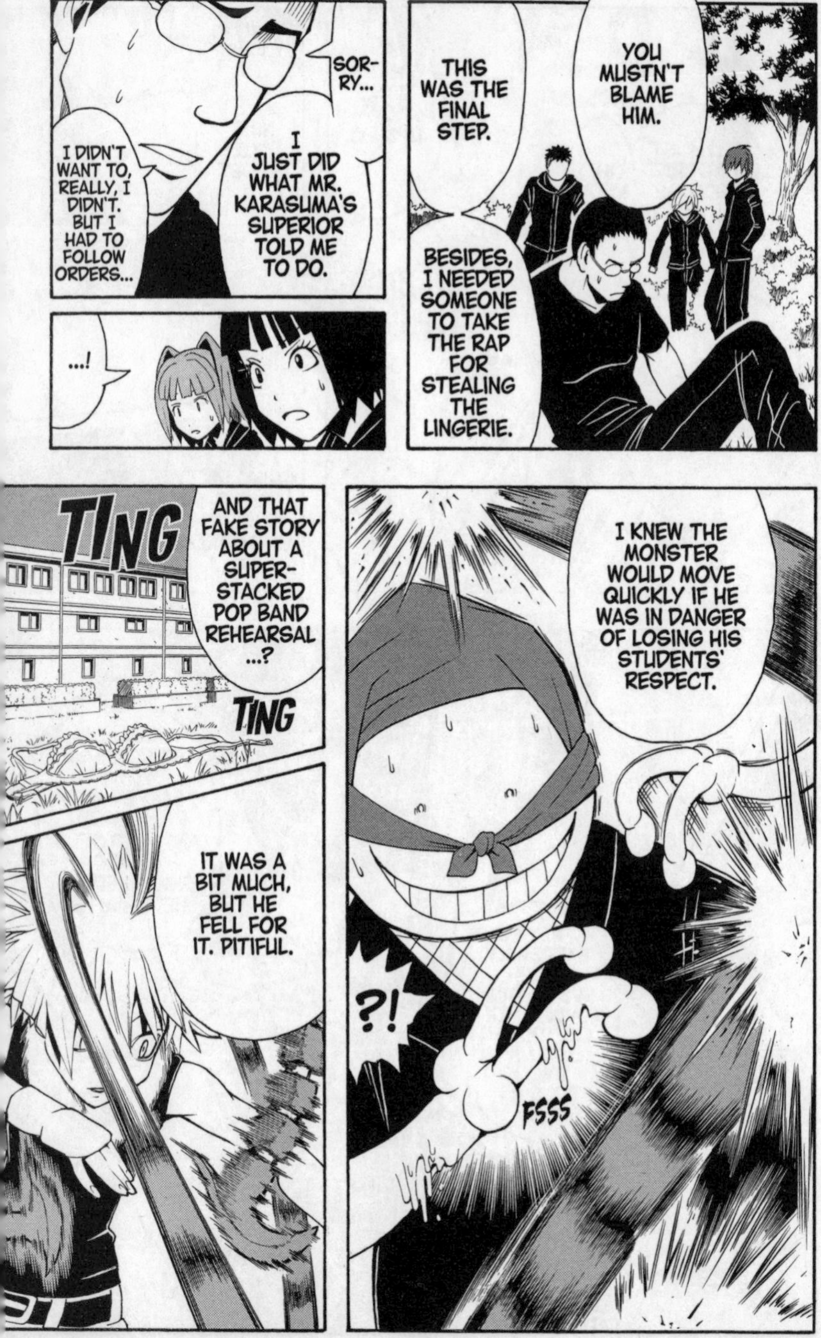
YOU MUSTN'T BLAME HIM.
THIS WAS THE FINAL STEP.
BESIDES, I NEEDED SOMEONE TO TAKE THE RAP FOR STEALING THE LINGERIE.
SOR-RY...
I JUST DID WHAT MR. KARASUMA'S SUPERIOR TOLD ME TO DO.
I DIDN'T WANT TO, REALLY, I DIDN'T. BUT I HAD TO FOLLOW ORDERS...
...!
I KNEW THE MONSTER WOULD MOVE QUICKLY IF HE WAS IN DANGER OF LOSING HIS STUDENTS' RESPECT.
?!
FSSS
AND THAT FAKE STORY ABOUT A SUPER-STACKED POP BAND REHEARSAL ...?
TING
TING
IT WAS A BIT MUCH, BUT HE FELL FOR IT. PITIFUL.

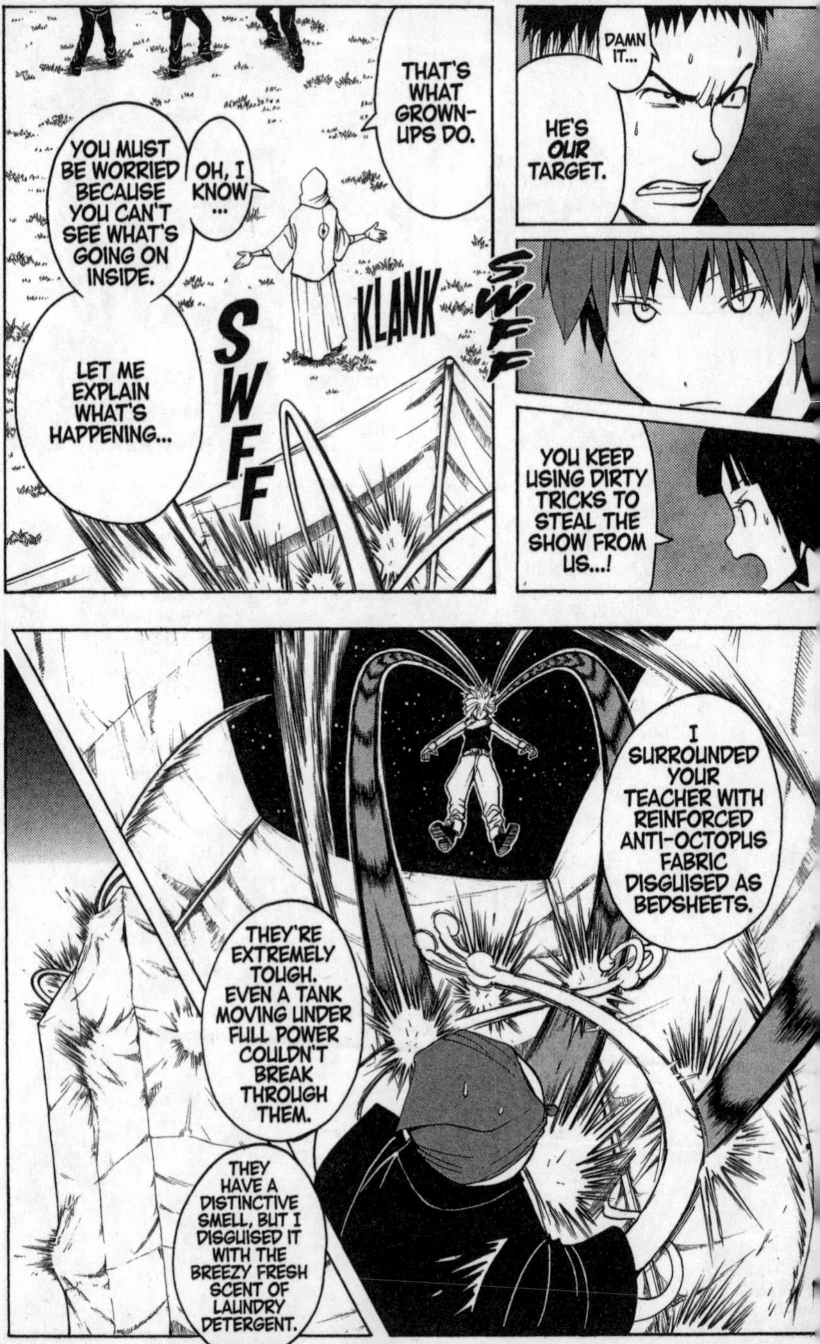
DAMN IT...
HE'S OUR TARGET.
SWFF
YOU KEEP USING DIRTY TRICKS TO STEAL THE SHOW FROM US...!
THAT'S WHAT GROWN-UPS DO.
OH, I KNOW...
YOU MUST BE WORRIED BECAUSE YOU CAN'T SEE WHAT'S GOING ON INSIDE.
LET ME EXPLAIN WHAT'S HAPPENING...
KLANK
SWFF
I SURROUNDED YOUR TEACHER WITH REINFORCED ANTI-OCTOPUS FABRIC DISGUISED AS BEDSHEETS.
THEY'RE EXTREMELY TOUGH. EVEN A TANK MOVING UNDER FULL POWER COULDN'T BREAK THROUGH THEM.
THEY HAVE A DISTINCTIVE SMELL, BUT I DISGUISED IT WITH THE BREEZY FRESH SCENT OF LAUNDRY DETERGENT.

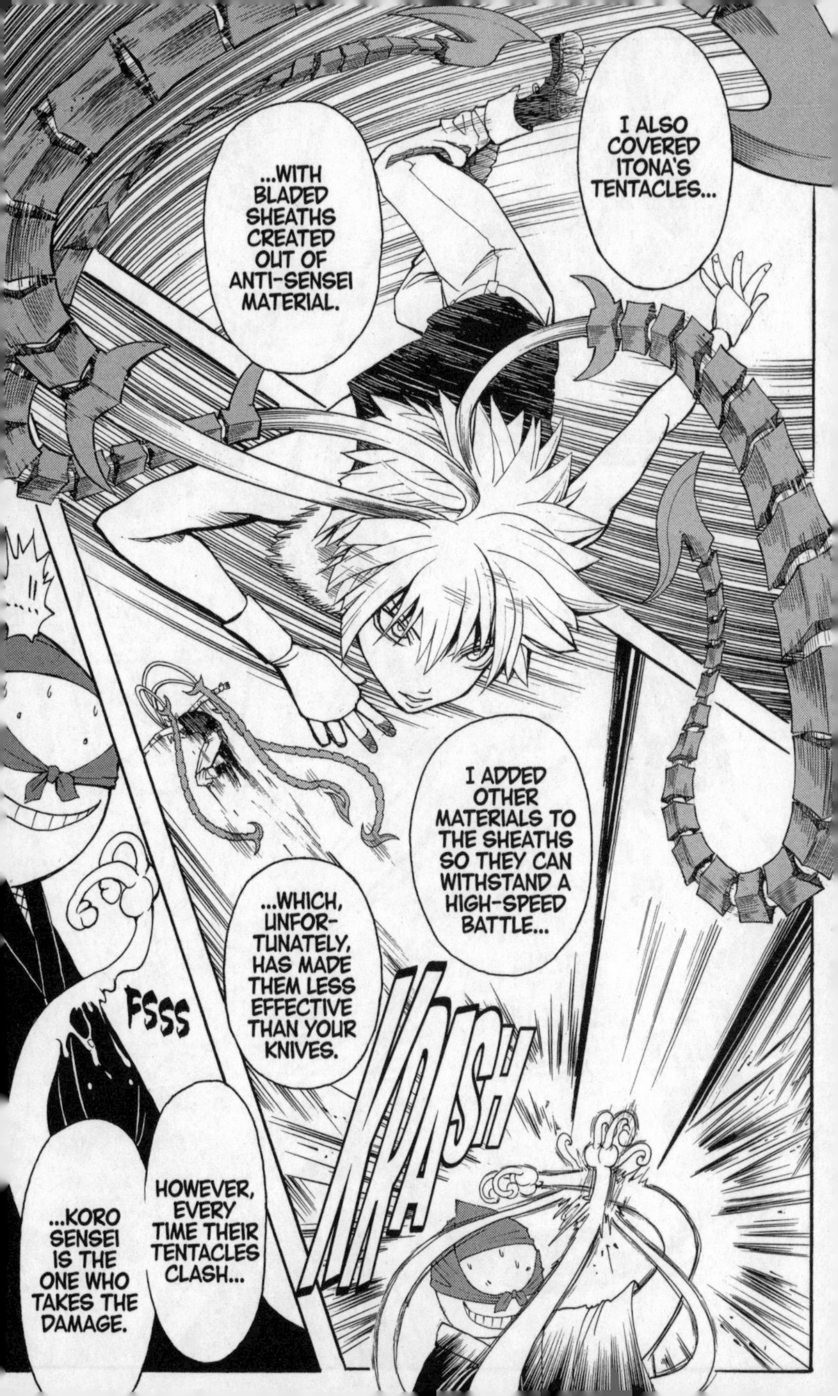
I ALSO COVERED ITONA'S TENTACLES...
...WITH BLADED SHEATHS CREATED OUT OF ANTI-SENSEI MATERIAL.
...!!
I ADDED OTHER MATERIALS TO THE SHEATHS SO THEY CAN WITHSTAND A HIGH-SPEED BATTLE...
...WHICH, UNFORTUNATELY, HAS MADE THEM LESS EFFECTIVE THAN YOUR KNIVES.
FSSS
HOWEVER, EVERY TIME THEIR TENTACLES CLASH...
...KORO SENSEI IS THE ONE WHO TAKES THE DAMAGE.

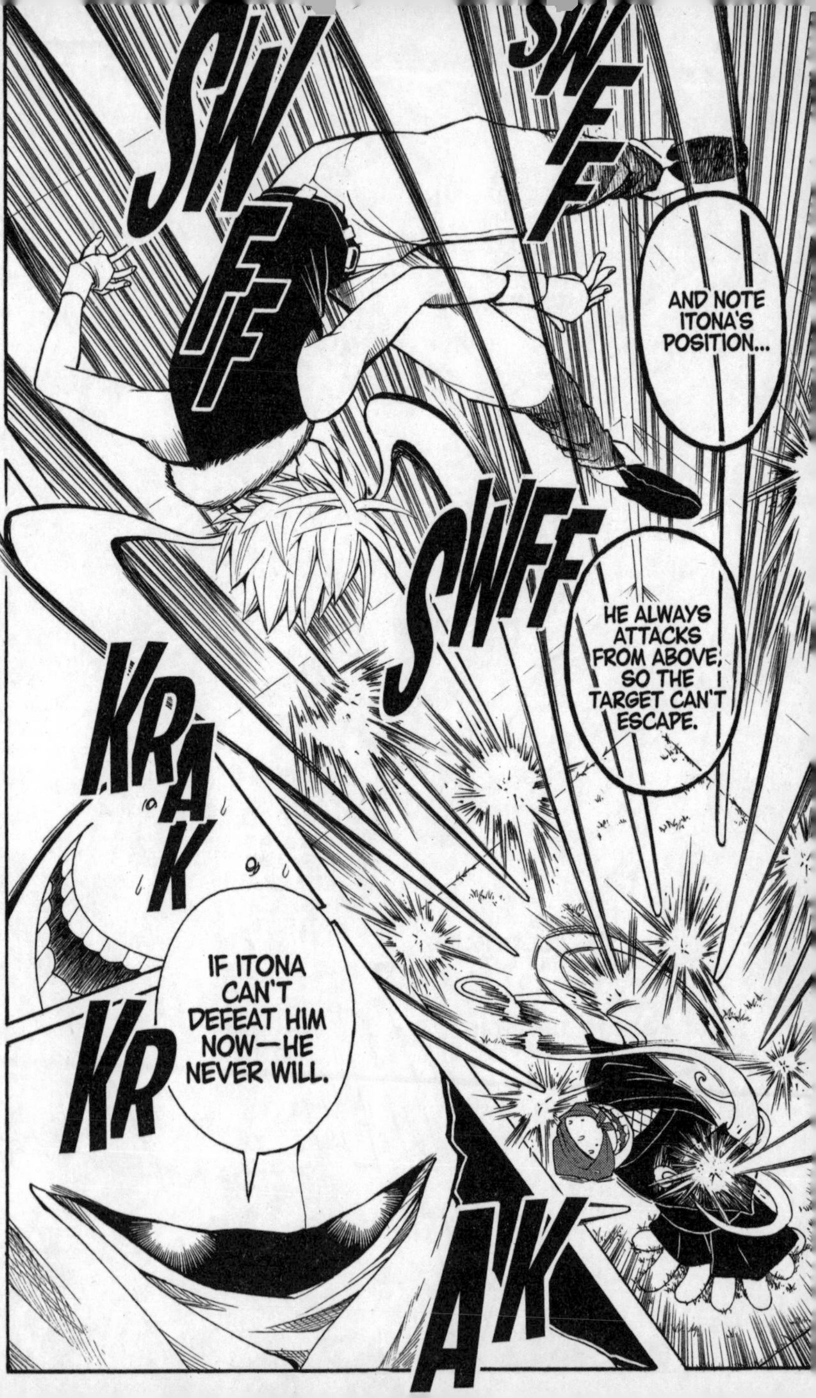
SWFF
SWFF
AND NOTE ITONA'S POSITION...
SWFF
HE ALWAYS ATTACKS FROM ABOVE, SO THE TARGET CAN'T ESCAPE.
KRAK
IF ITONA CAN'T DEFEAT HIM NOW—HE NEVER WILL.
KRAK

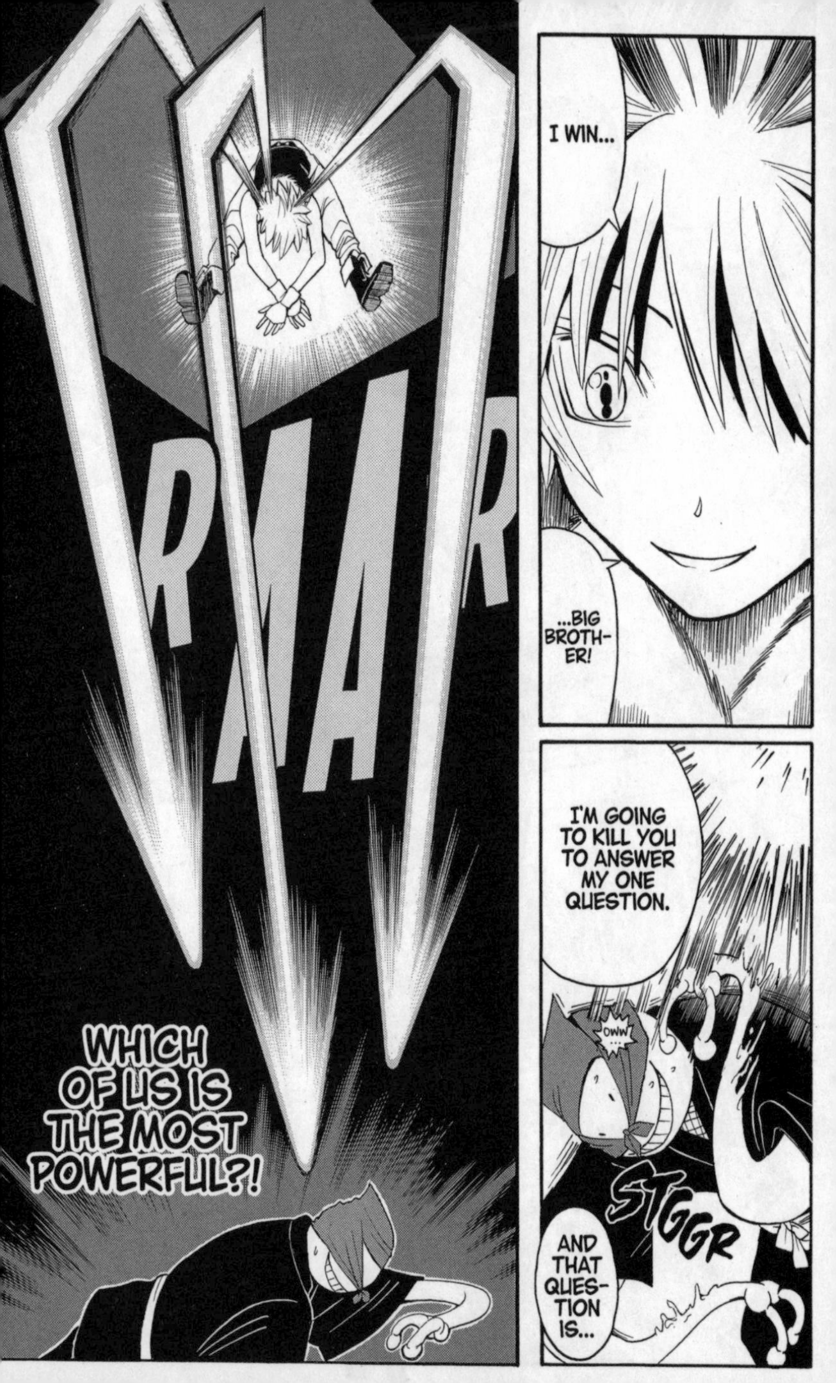
I WIN...
...BIG BROTH-ER!
I'M GOING TO KILL YOU TO ANSWER MY ONE QUESTION.
OWW...
STGGR
AND THAT QUES-TION IS...
RMAR
WHICH OF US IS THE MOST POWERFUL?!

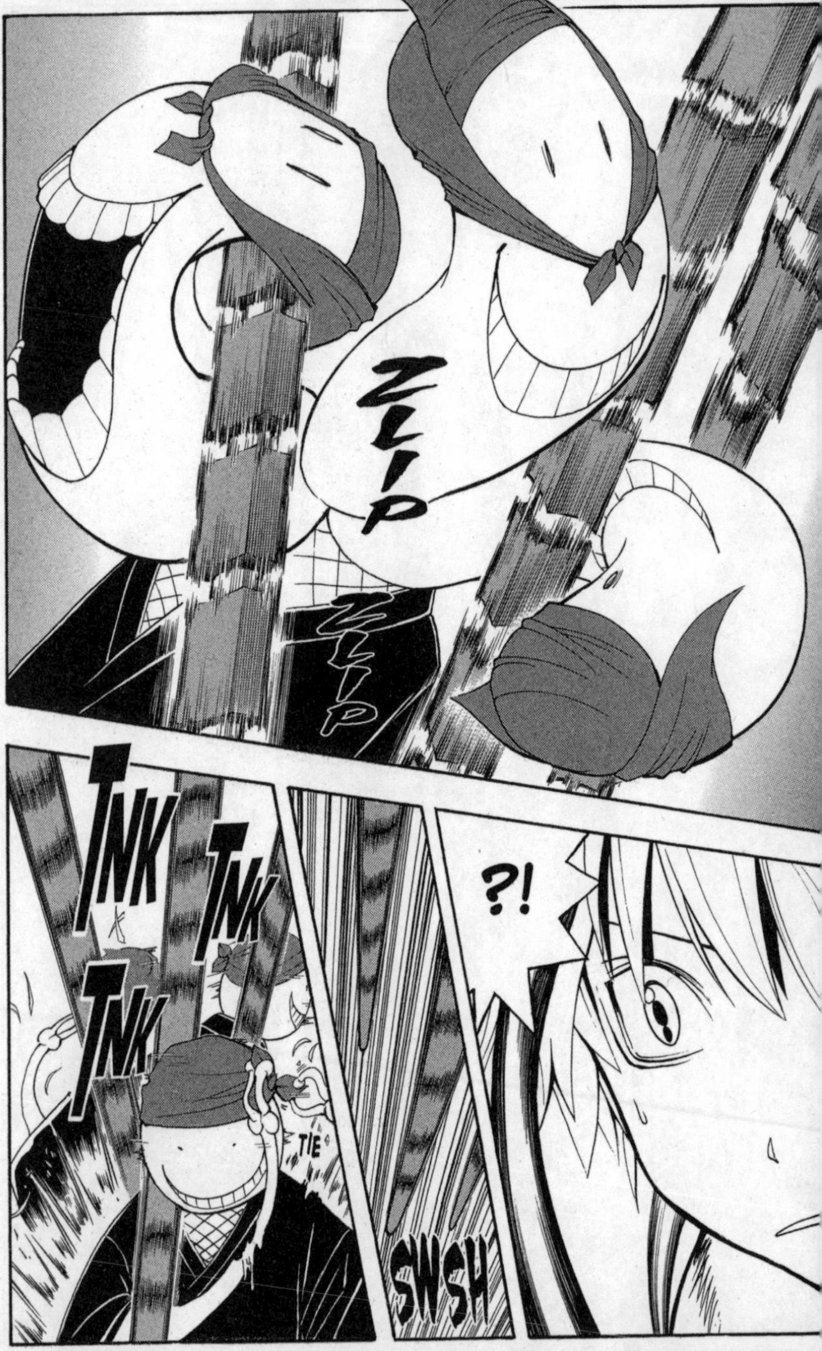
ZLIP
ZLIP
?!
SWSH
TNK
TNK
TNK
TIE

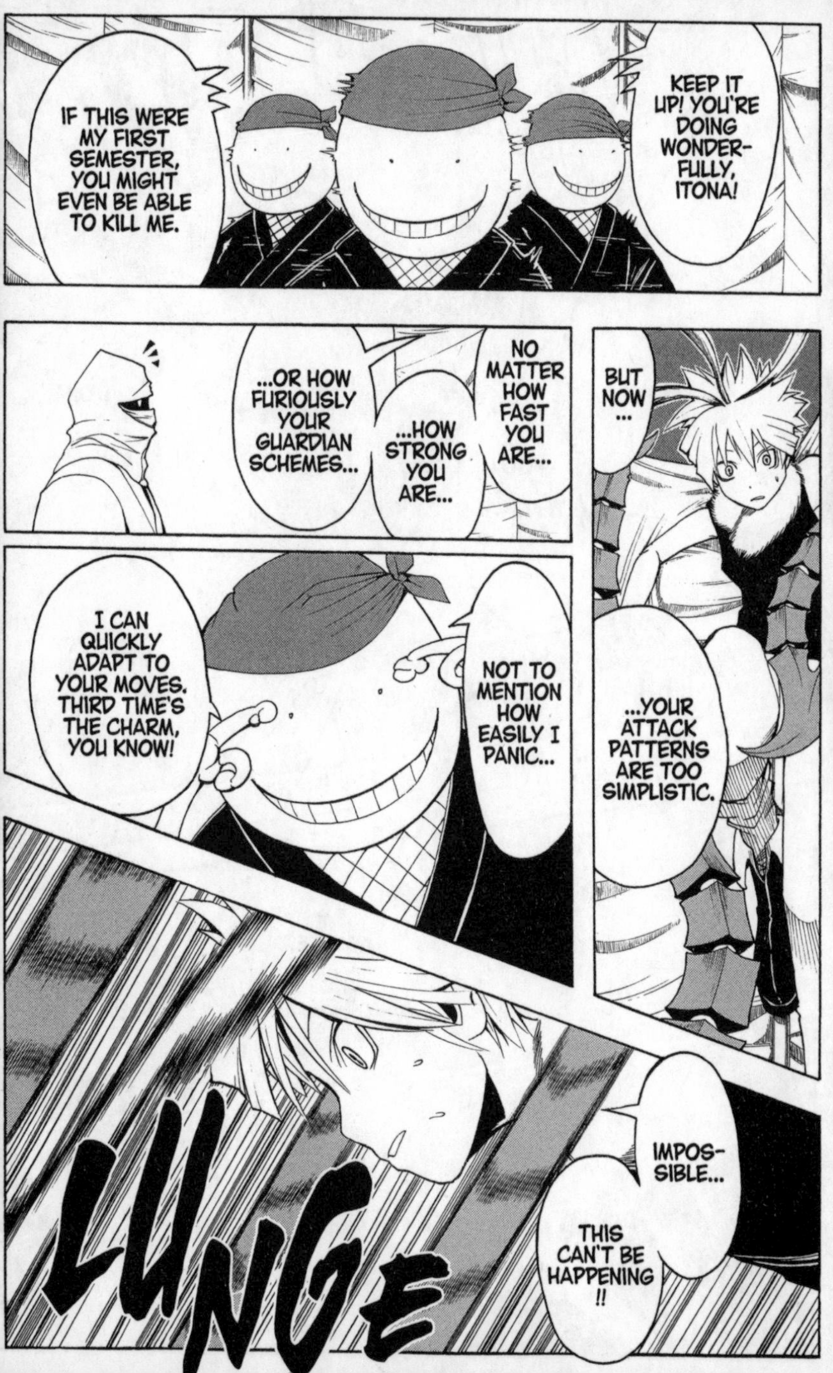
KEEP IT UP! YOU'RE DOING WONDER-FULLY, ITONA!
IF THIS WERE MY FIRST SEMESTER, YOU MIGHT EVEN BE ABLE TO KILL ME.
BUT NOW...
...YOUR ATTACK PATTERNS ARE TOO SIMPLISTIC.
NO MATTER HOW FAST YOU ARE...
...HOW STRONG YOU ARE...
...OR HOW FURIOUSLY YOUR GUARDIAN SCHEMES...
NOT TO MENTION HOW EASILY I PANIC...
I CAN QUICKLY ADAPT TO YOUR MOVES. THIRD TIME'S THE CHARM, YOU KNOW!
IMPOS-SIBLE...
THIS CAN'T BE HAPPENING !!
LUNGE

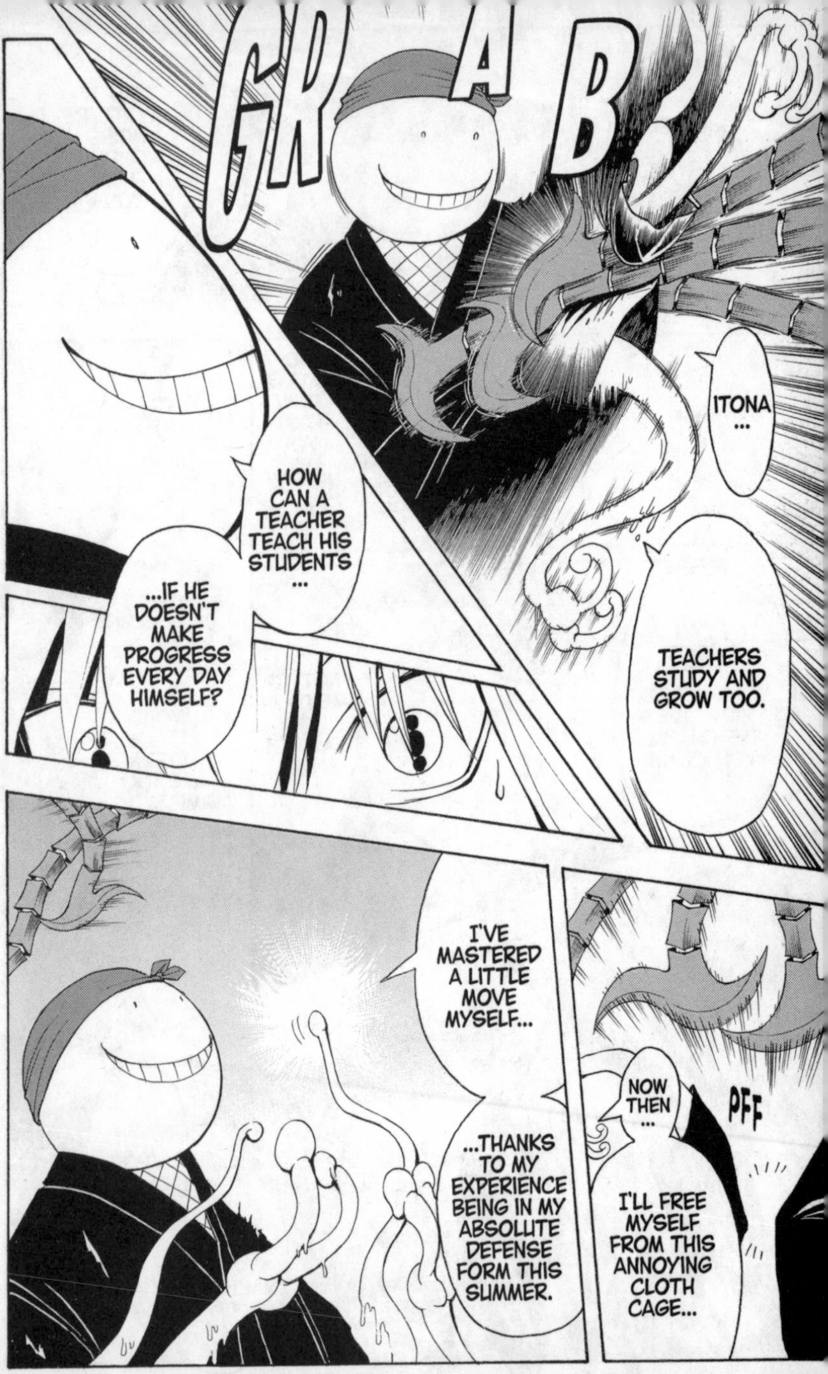
GRAB
ITONA...
TEACHERS STUDY AND GROW TOO.
HOW CAN A TEACHER TEACH HIS STUDENTS...
...IF HE DOESN'T MAKE PROGRESS EVERY DAY HIMSELF?
NOW THEN...
PFF
I'LL FREE MYSELF FROM THIS ANNOYING CLOTH CAGE...
I'VE MASTERED A LITTLE MOVE MYSELF...
...THANKS TO MY EXPERIENCE BEING IN MY ABSOLUTE DEFENSE FORM THIS SUMMER.

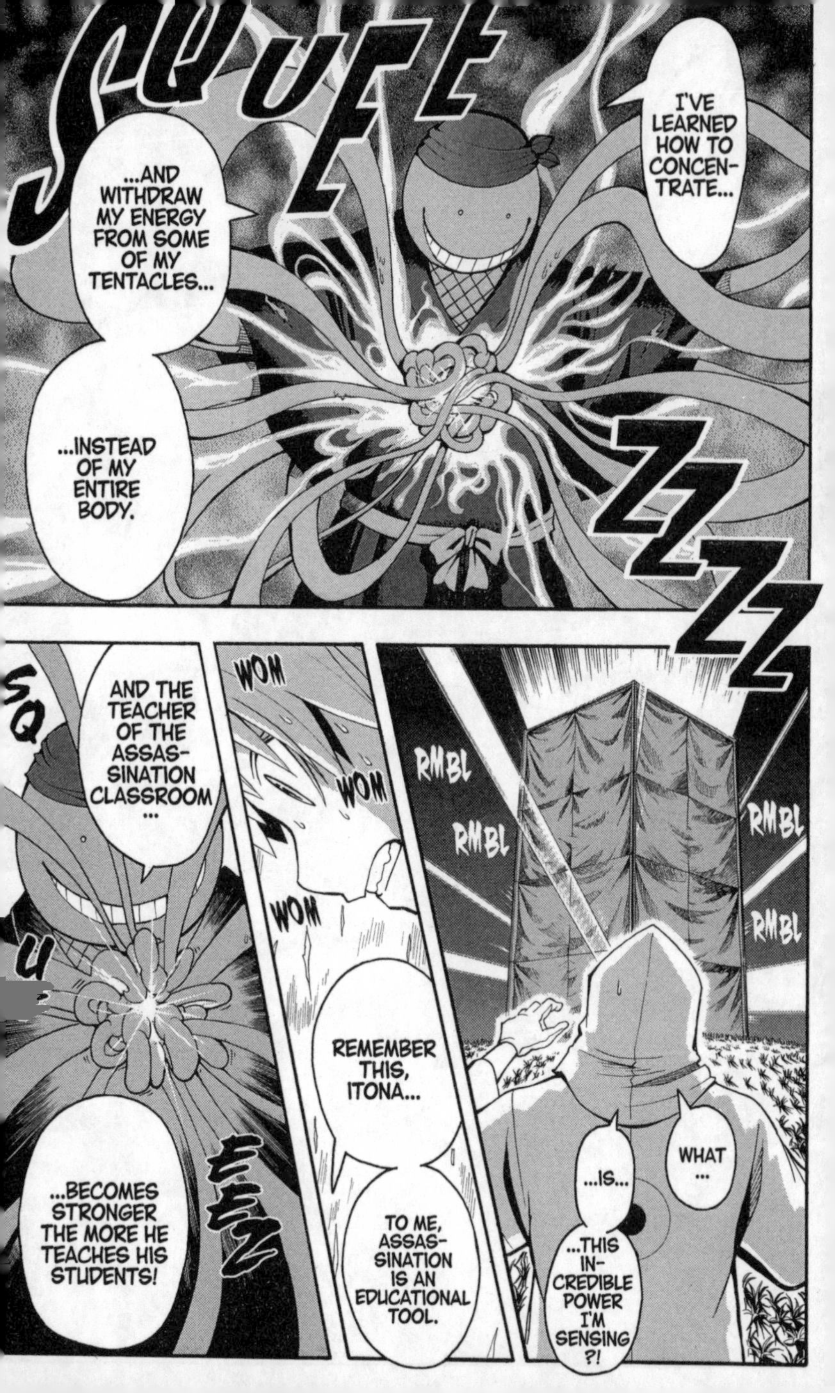
I'VE LEARNED HOW TO CONCENTRATE...
...AND WITHDRAW MY ENERGY FROM SOME OF MY TENTACLES...
...INSTEAD OF MY ENTIRE BODY.
ZZZ
RMBL
RMBL
RMBL
RMBL
WHAT...
...IS...
...THIS INCREDIBLE POWER I'M SENSING?!
WOM
WOM
WOM
REMEMBER THIS, ITONA...
TO ME, ASSASSINATION IS AN EDUCATIONAL TOOL.
AND THE TEACHER OF THE ASSASSINATION CLASSROOM...
...BECOMES STRONGER THE MORE HE TEACHES HIS STUDENTS!

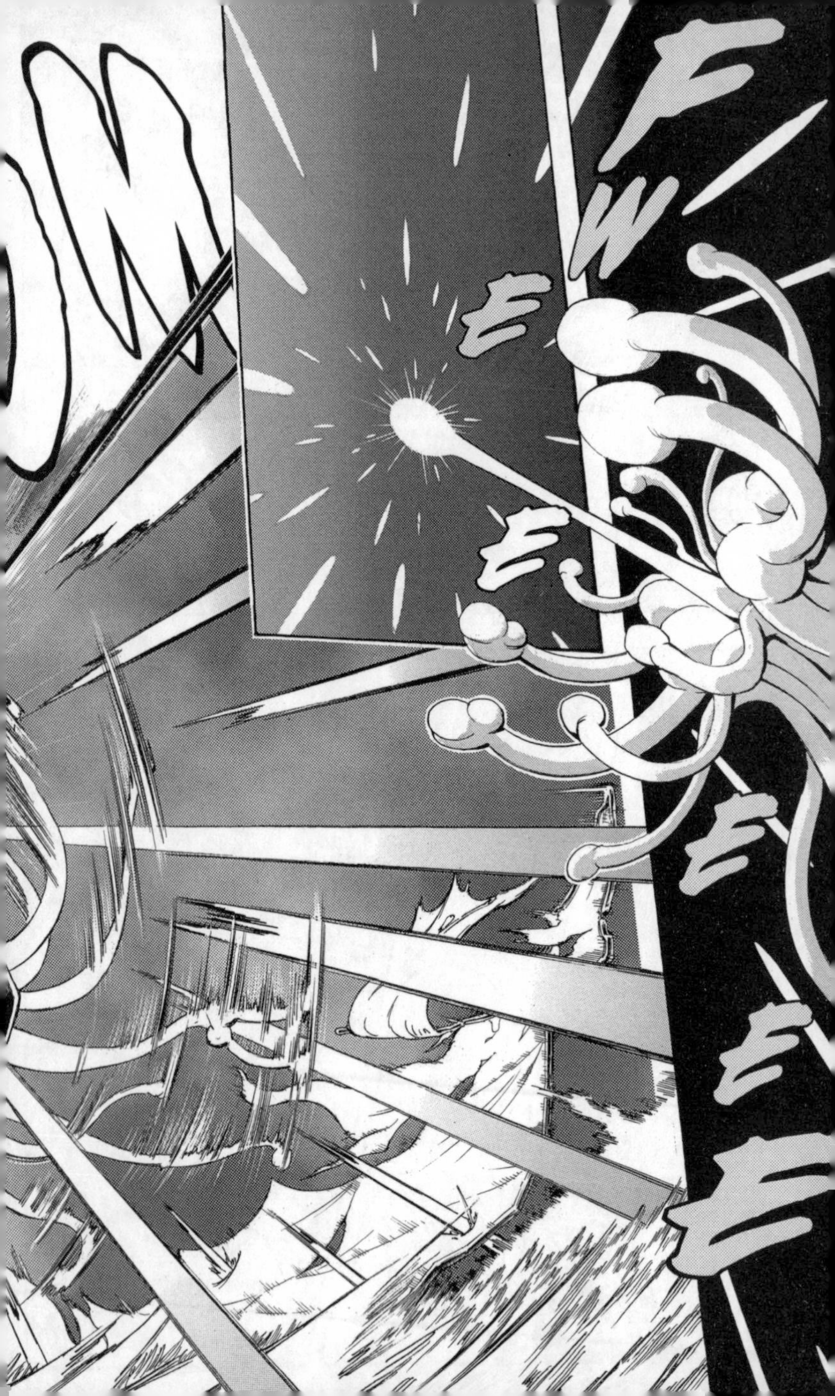
FWEEEEEE

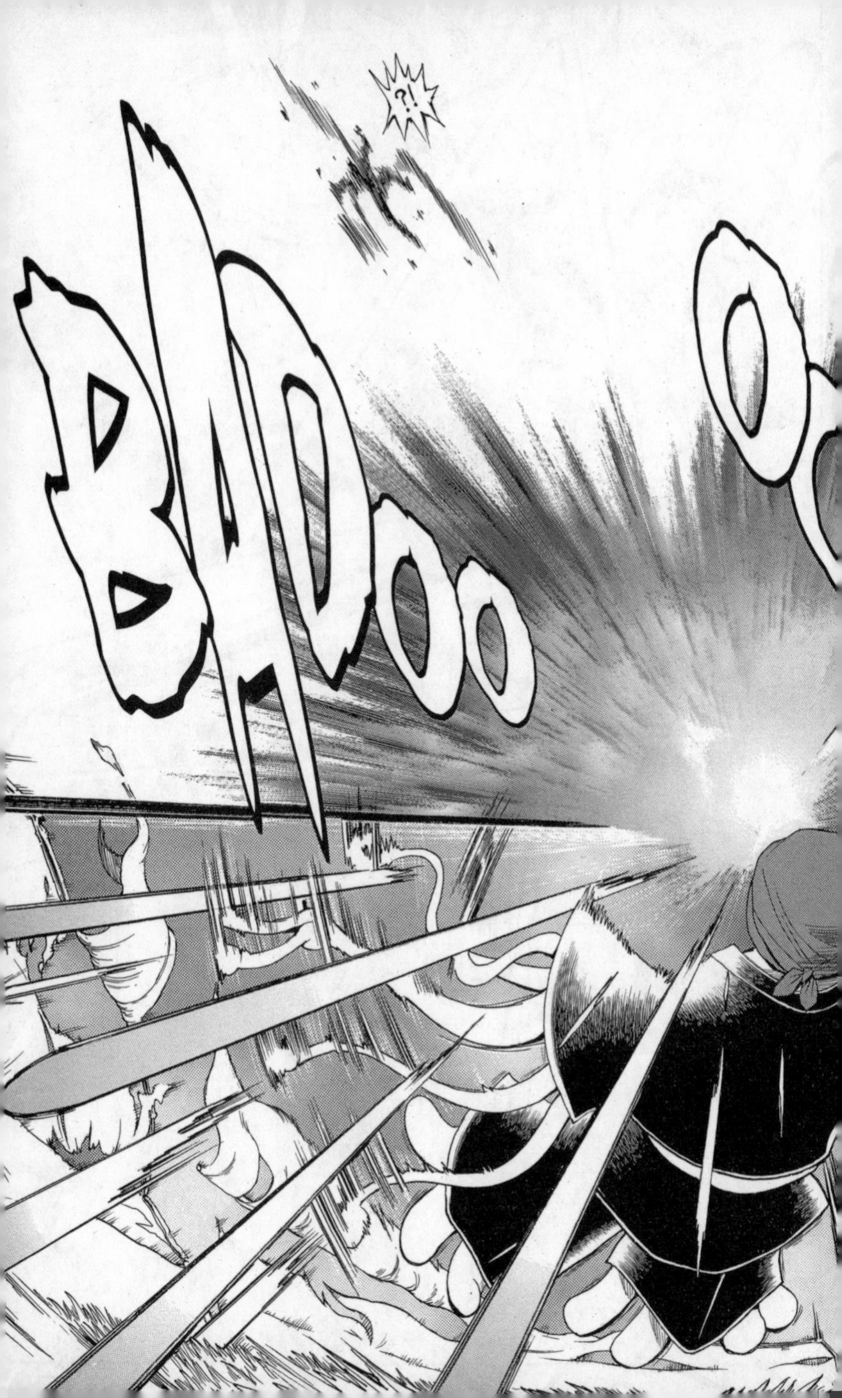
?!
BADOOOO

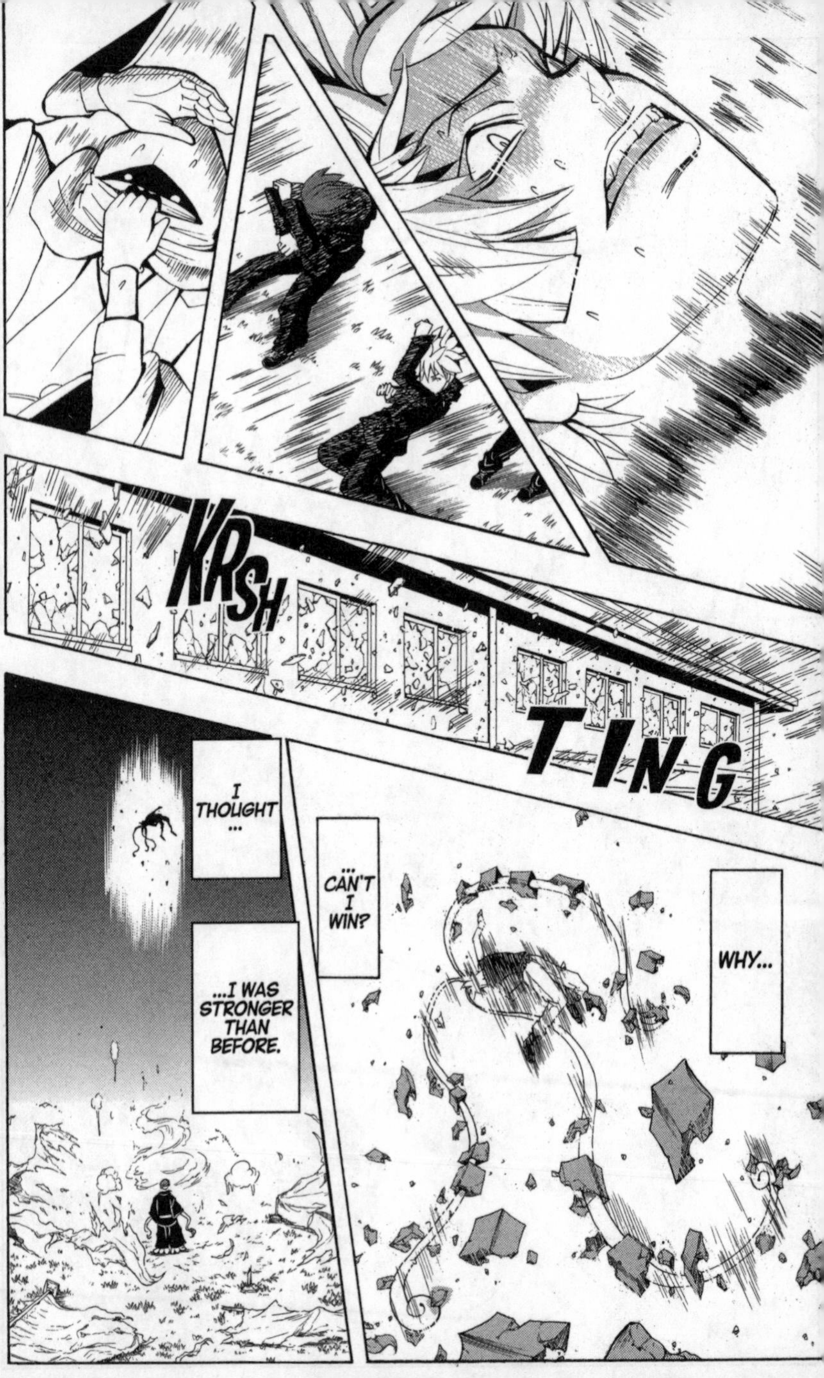
KRSH
TING
WHY...
...CAN'T I WIN?
I THOUGHT...
...I WAS STRONGER THAN BEFORE.

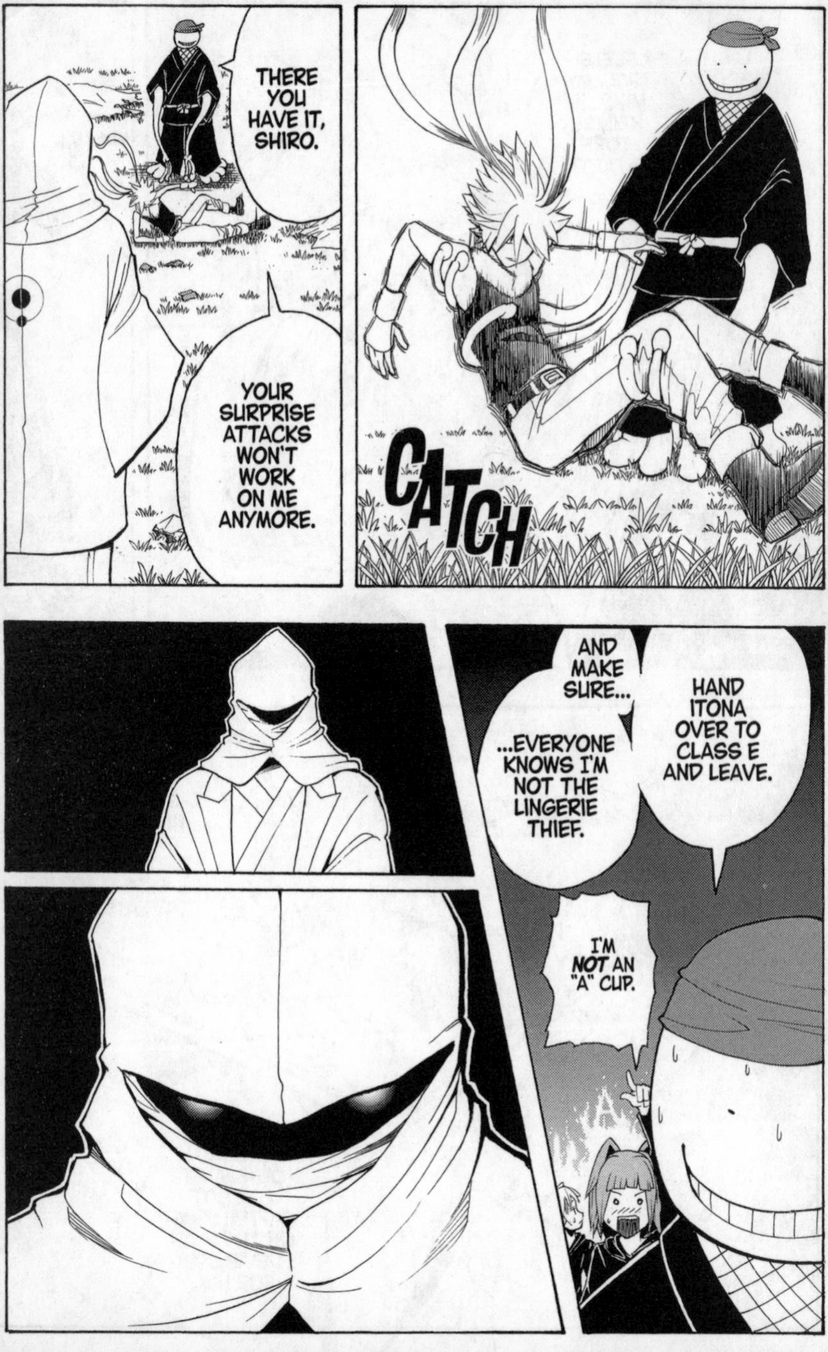
CATCH
THERE YOU HAVE IT, SHIRO.
YOUR SURPRISE ATTACKS WON'T WORK ON ME ANYMORE.
HAND ITONA OVER TO CLASS E AND LEAVE.
AND MAKE SURE...
...EVERYONE KNOWS I'M NOT THE LINGERIE THIEF.
I'M *NOT* AN "A" CUP.

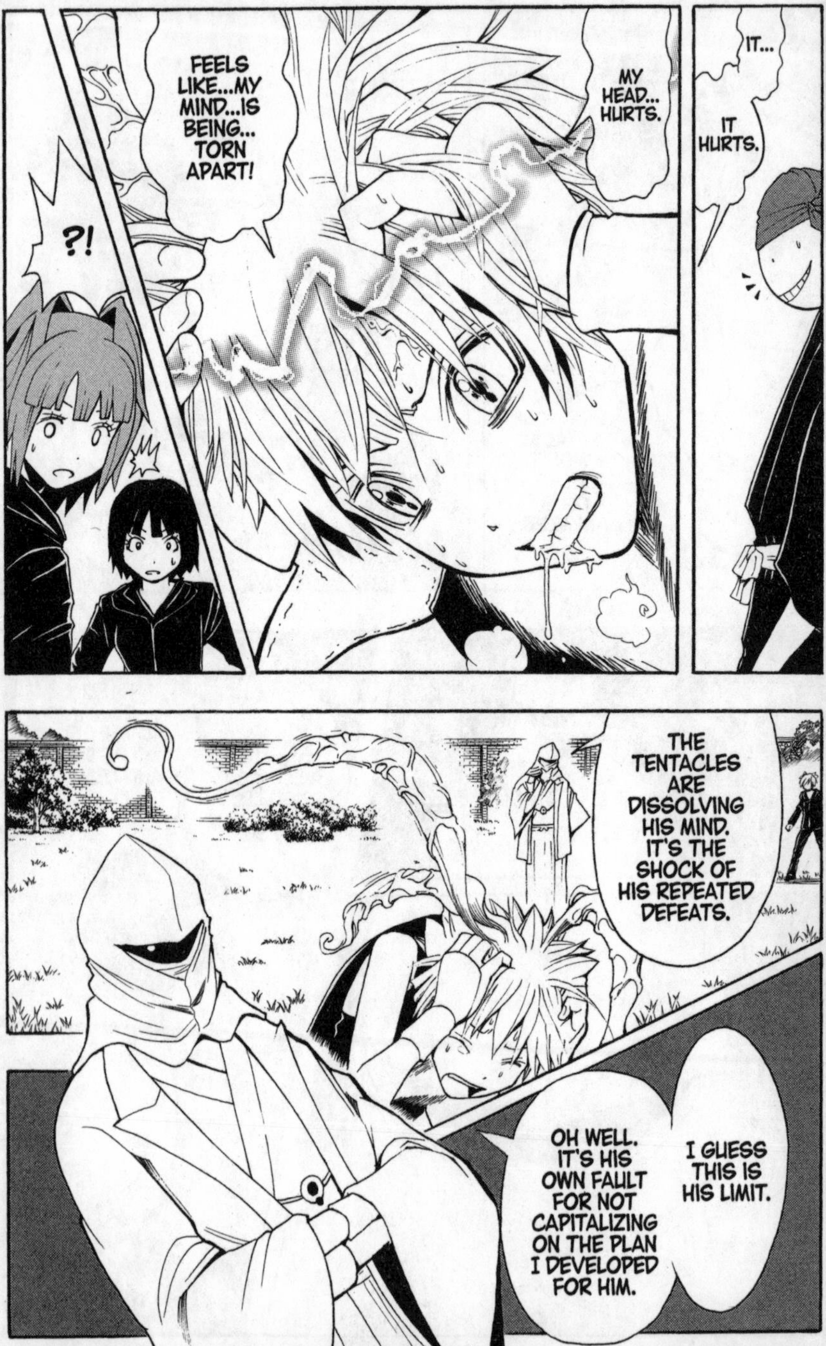
IT...
IT HURTS.
MY HEAD... HURTS.
FEELS LIKE...MY MIND...IS BEING... TORN APART!
?!
THE TENTACLES ARE DISSOLVING HIS MIND. IT'S THE SHOCK OF HIS REPEATED DEFEATS.
I GUESS THIS IS HIS LIMIT.
OH WELL. IT'S HIS OWN FAULT FOR NOT CAPITALIZING ON THE PLAN I DEVELOPED FOR HIM.

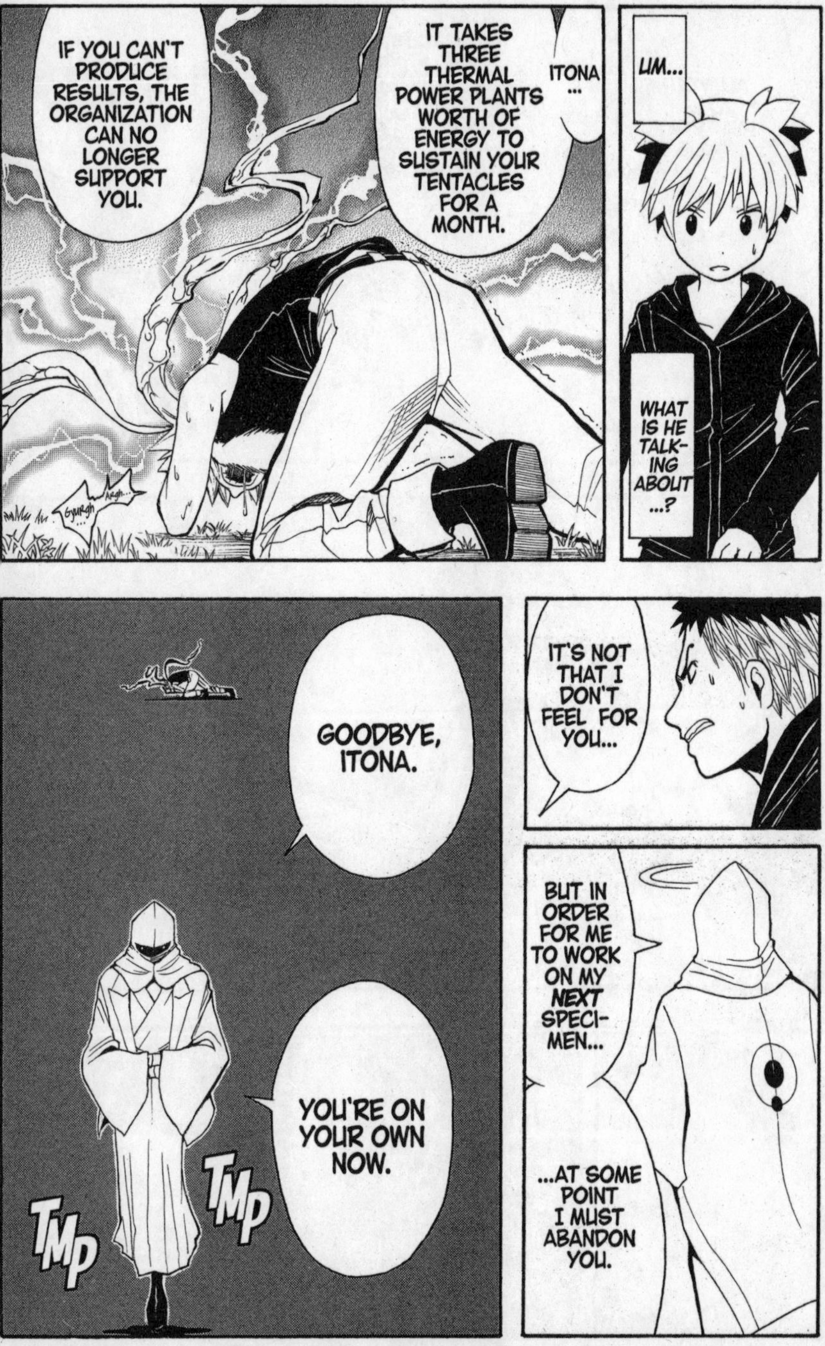
UM...
WHAT IS HE TALKING ABOUT...?
ITONA...
IT TAKES THREE THERMAL POWER PLANTS WORTH OF ENERGY TO SUSTAIN YOUR TENTACLES FOR A MONTH.
IF YOU CAN'T PRODUCE RESULTS, THE ORGANIZATION CAN NO LONGER SUPPORT YOU.
Argh...
Gyurgh...
IT'S NOT THAT I DON'T FEEL FOR YOU...
BUT IN ORDER FOR ME TO WORK ON MY NEXT SPECIMEN...
...AT SOME POINT I MUST ABANDON YOU.
GOODBYE, ITONA.
YOU'RE ON YOUR OWN NOW.
TMP
TMP

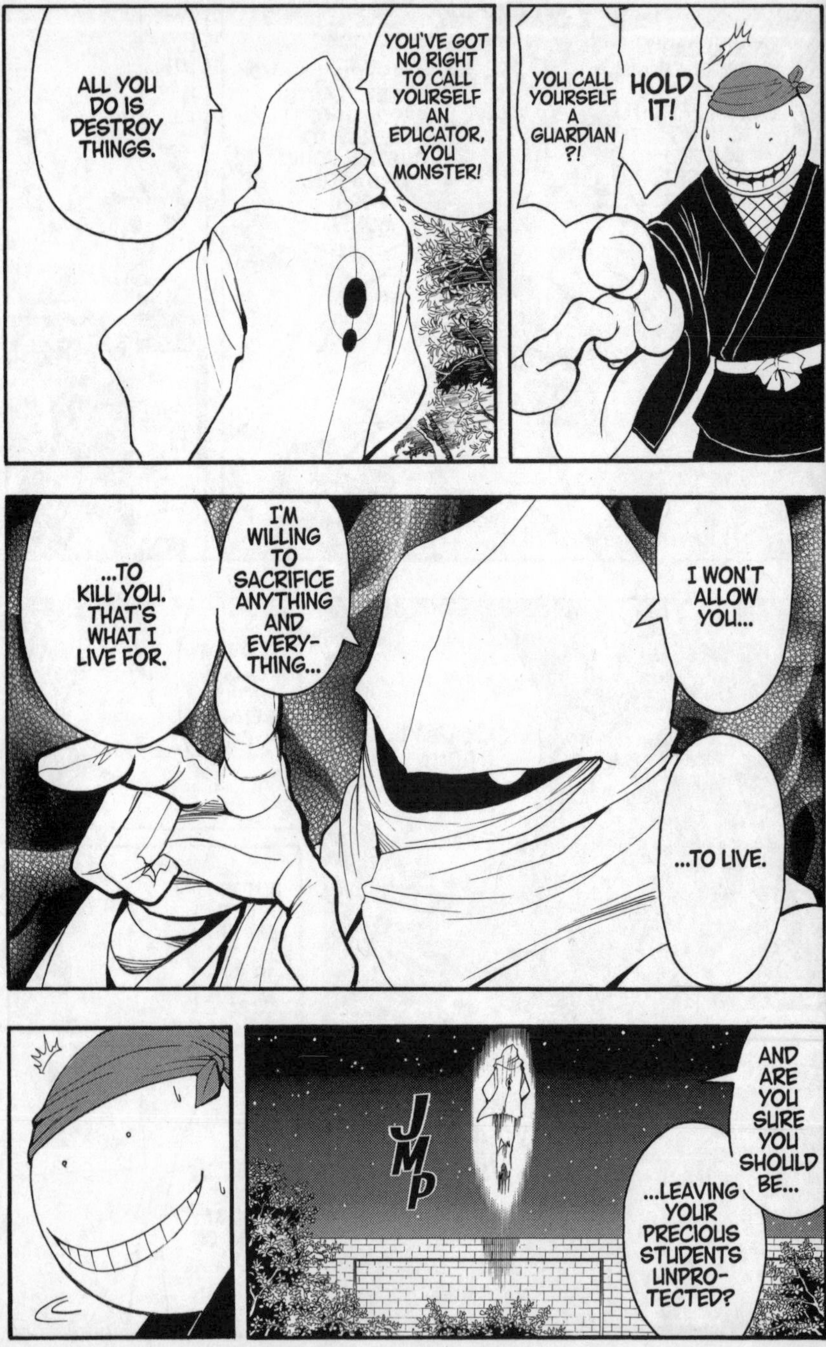
HOLD IT!
YOU CALL YOURSELF A GUARDIAN ?!
YOU'VE GOT NO RIGHT TO CALL YOURSELF AN EDUCATOR, YOU MONSTER!
ALL YOU DO IS DESTROY THINGS.
I WON'T ALLOW YOU...
...TO LIVE.
I'M WILLING TO SACRIFICE ANYTHING AND EVERY-THING...
...TO KILL YOU. THAT'S WHAT I LIVE FOR.
AND ARE YOU SURE YOU SHOULD BE...
...LEAVING YOUR PRECIOUS STUDENTS UNPRO-TECTED?
JMP

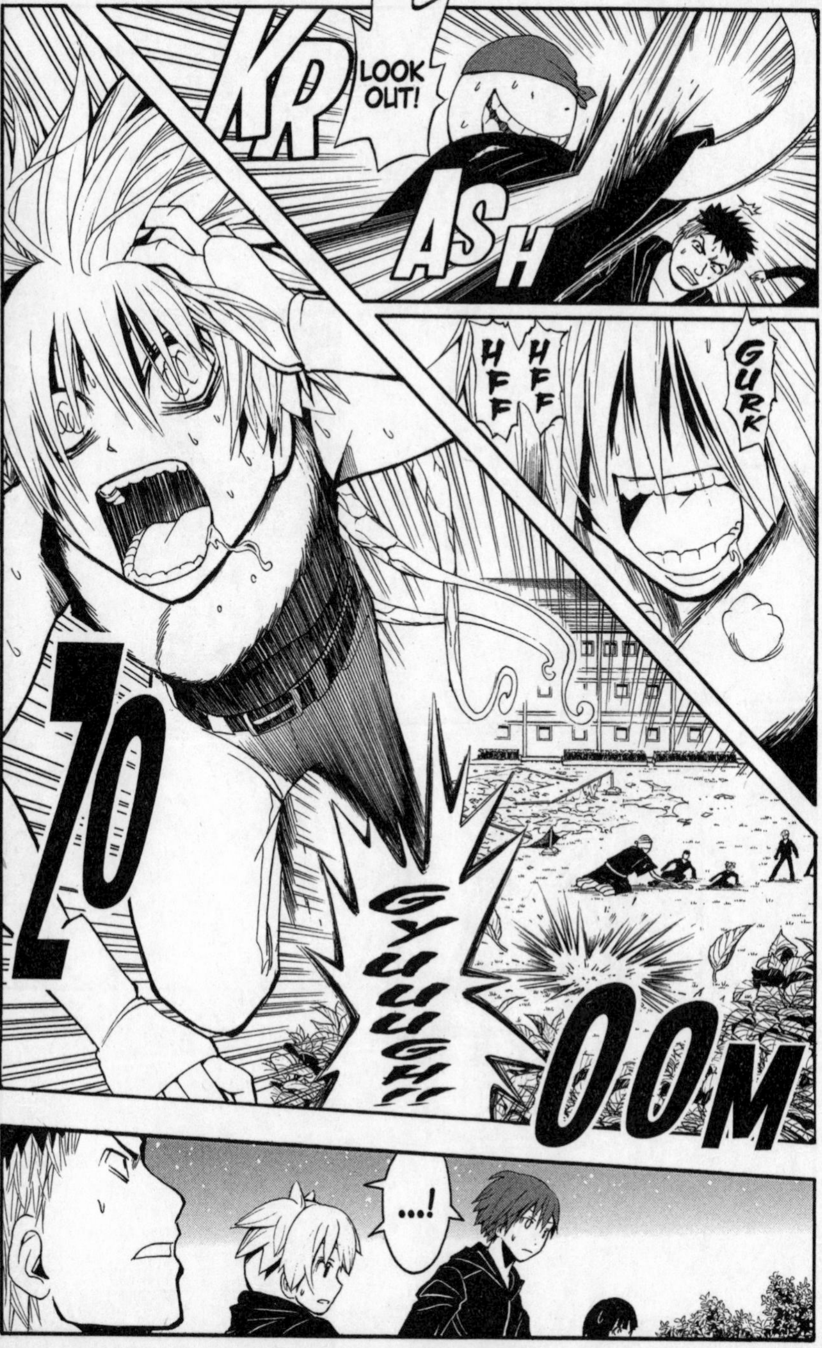
LOOK OUT!
KRASH
GURK
HFF HFF
ZOOM
GYUUUGH!!
...!

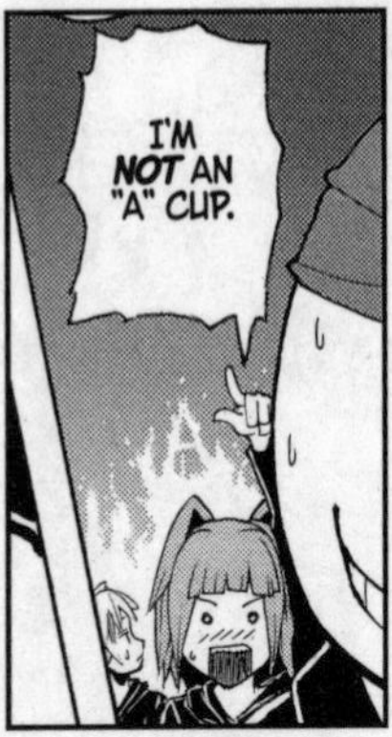
I'M **NOT** AN "A" CUP.
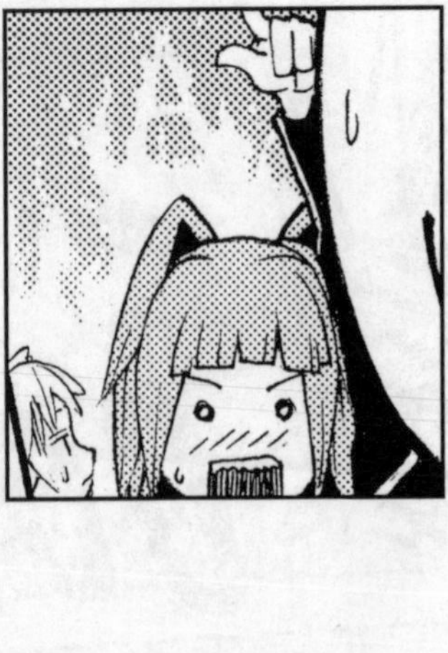

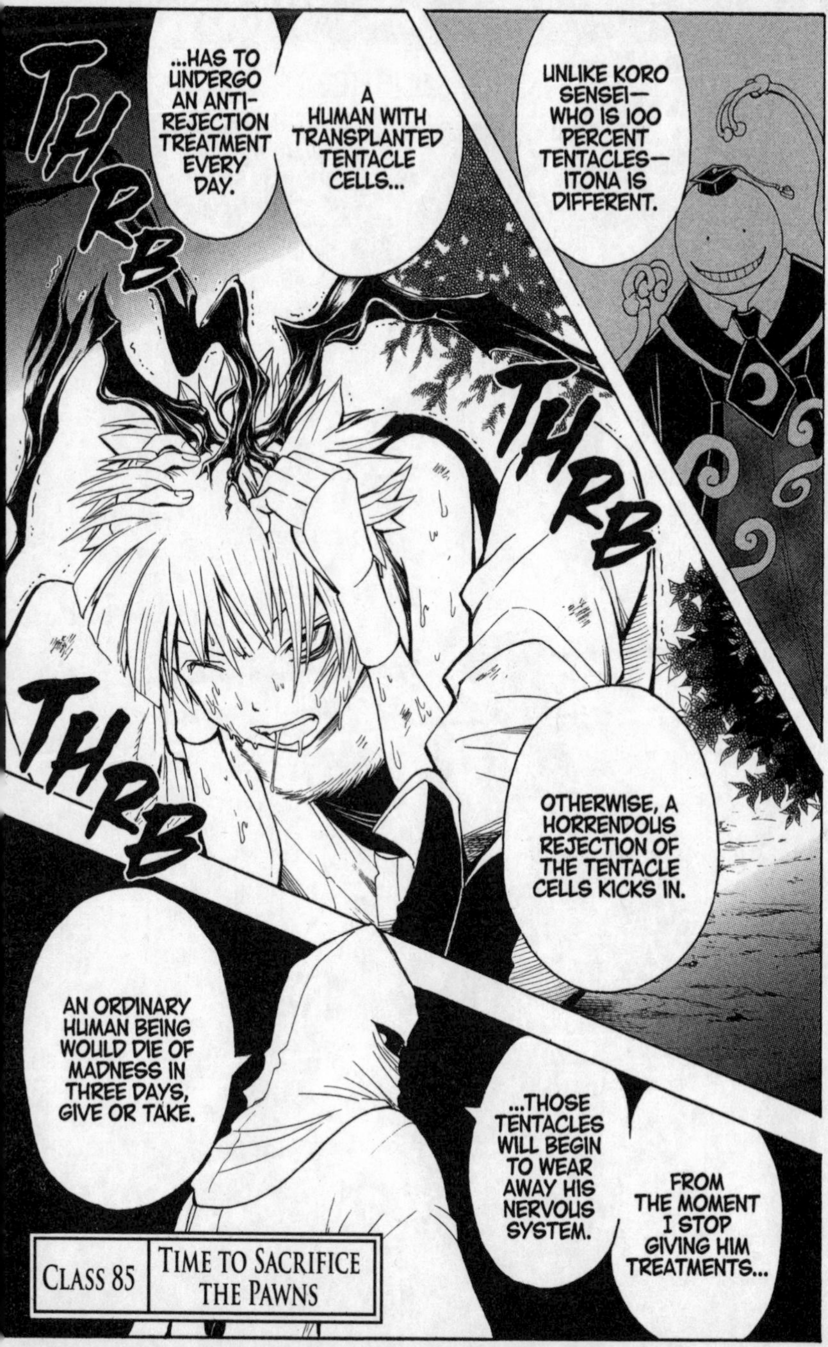
UNLIKE KORO SENSEI—WHO IS 100 PERCENT TENTACLES—ITONA IS DIFFERENT.
A HUMAN WITH TRANSPLANTED TENTACLE CELLS...
...HAS TO UNDERGO AN ANTI-REJECTION TREATMENT EVERY DAY.
THRB
THRB
THRB
OTHERWISE, A HORRENDOUS REJECTION OF THE TENTACLE CELLS KICKS IN.
FROM THE MOMENT I STOP GIVING HIM TREATMENTS...
...THOSE TENTACLES WILL BEGIN TO WEAR AWAY HIS NERVOUS SYSTEM.
AN ORDINARY HUMAN BEING WOULD DIE OF MADNESS IN THREE DAYS, GIVE OR TAKE.

Class 85 | Time to Sacrifice the Pawns

CLASS 85 TIME TO SACRIFICE THE PAWNS

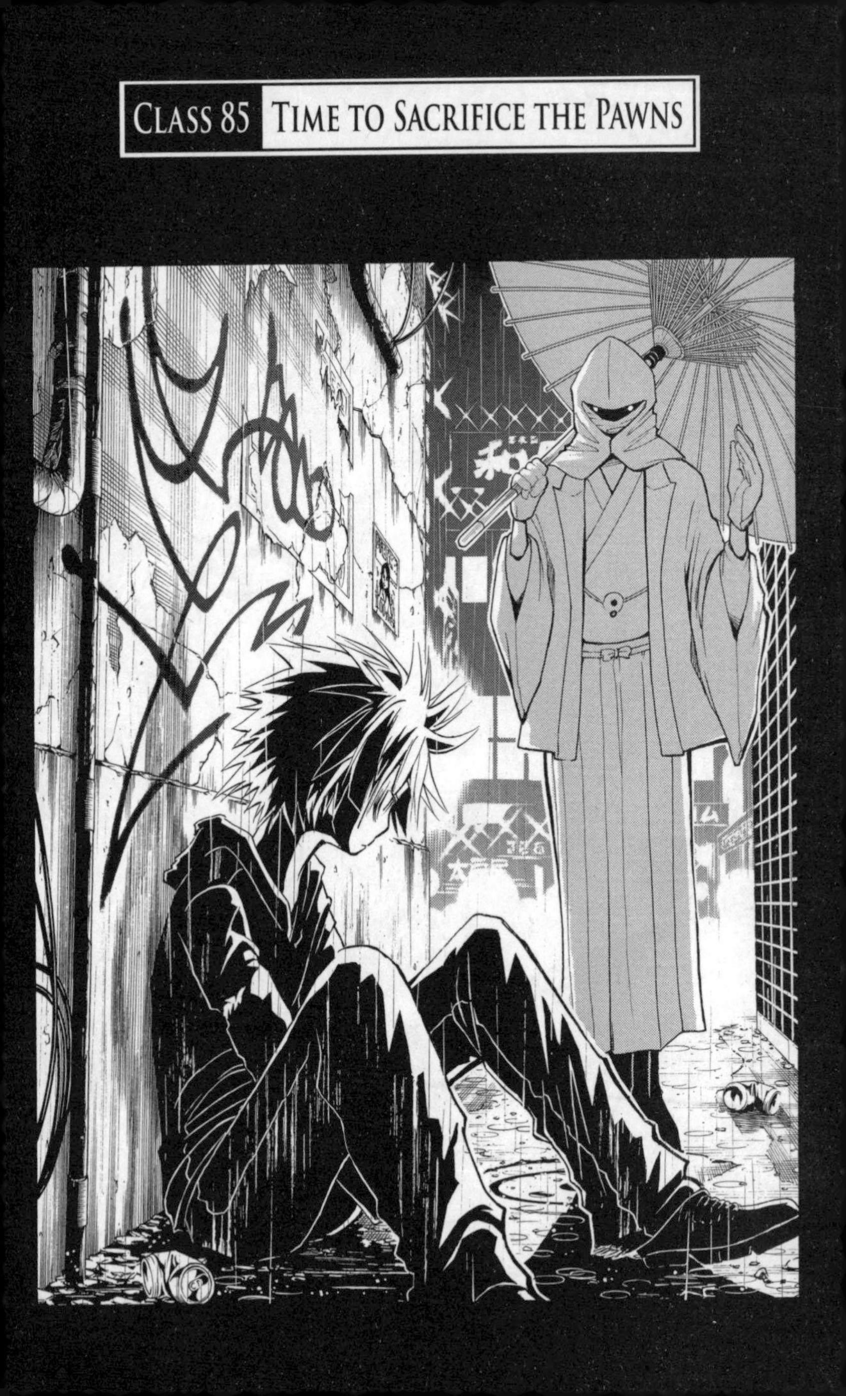

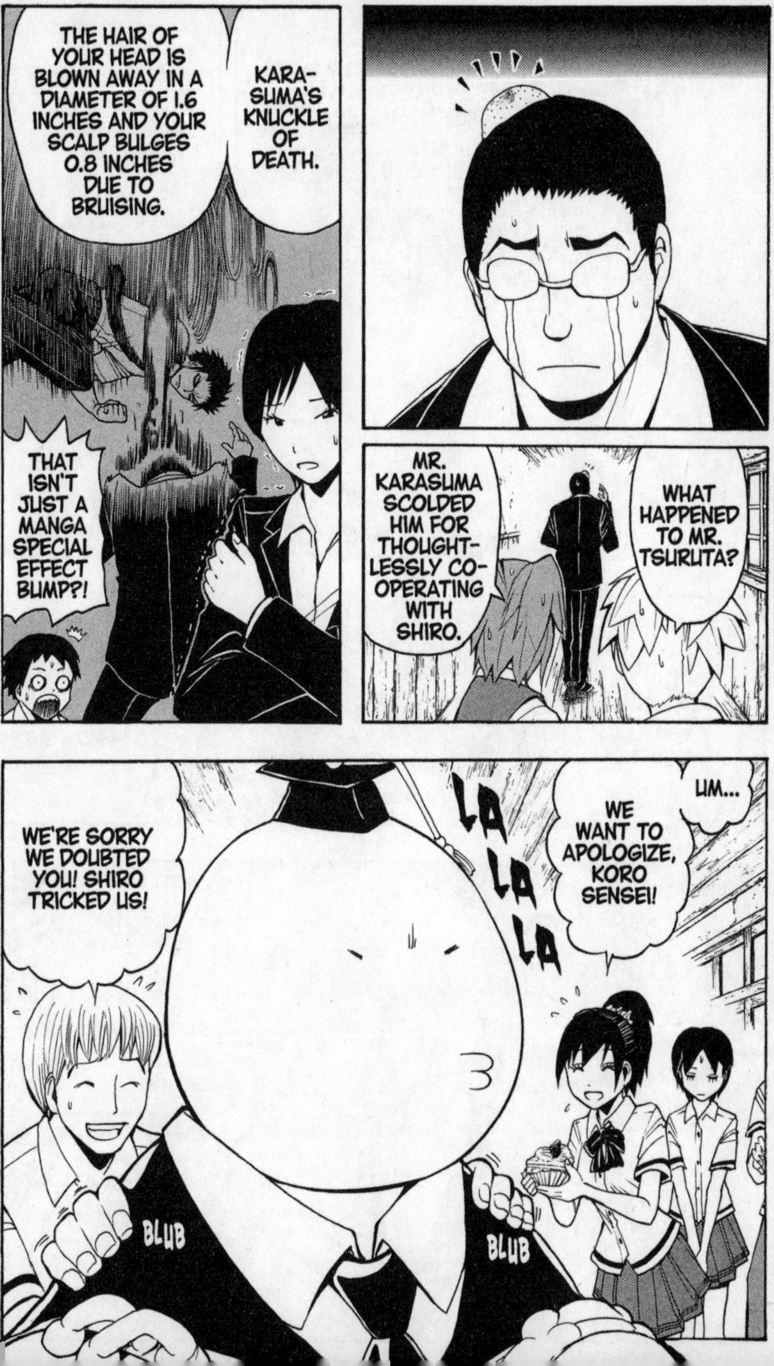
WHAT HAPPENED TO MR. TSURUTA?
MR. KARASUMA SCOLDED HIM FOR THOUGHTLESSLY CO-OPERATING WITH SHIRO.
KARA-SUMA'S KNUCKLE OF DEATH.
THE HAIR OF YOUR HEAD IS BLOWN AWAY IN A DIAMETER OF 1.6 INCHES AND YOUR SCALP BULGES 0.8 INCHES DUE TO BRUISING.
THAT ISN'T JUST A MANGA SPECIAL EFFECT BUMP?!
UM...
WE WANT TO APOLOGIZE, KORO SENSEI!
LA LA LA
WE'RE SORRY WE DOUBTED YOU! SHIRO TRICKED US!
BLUB
BLUB

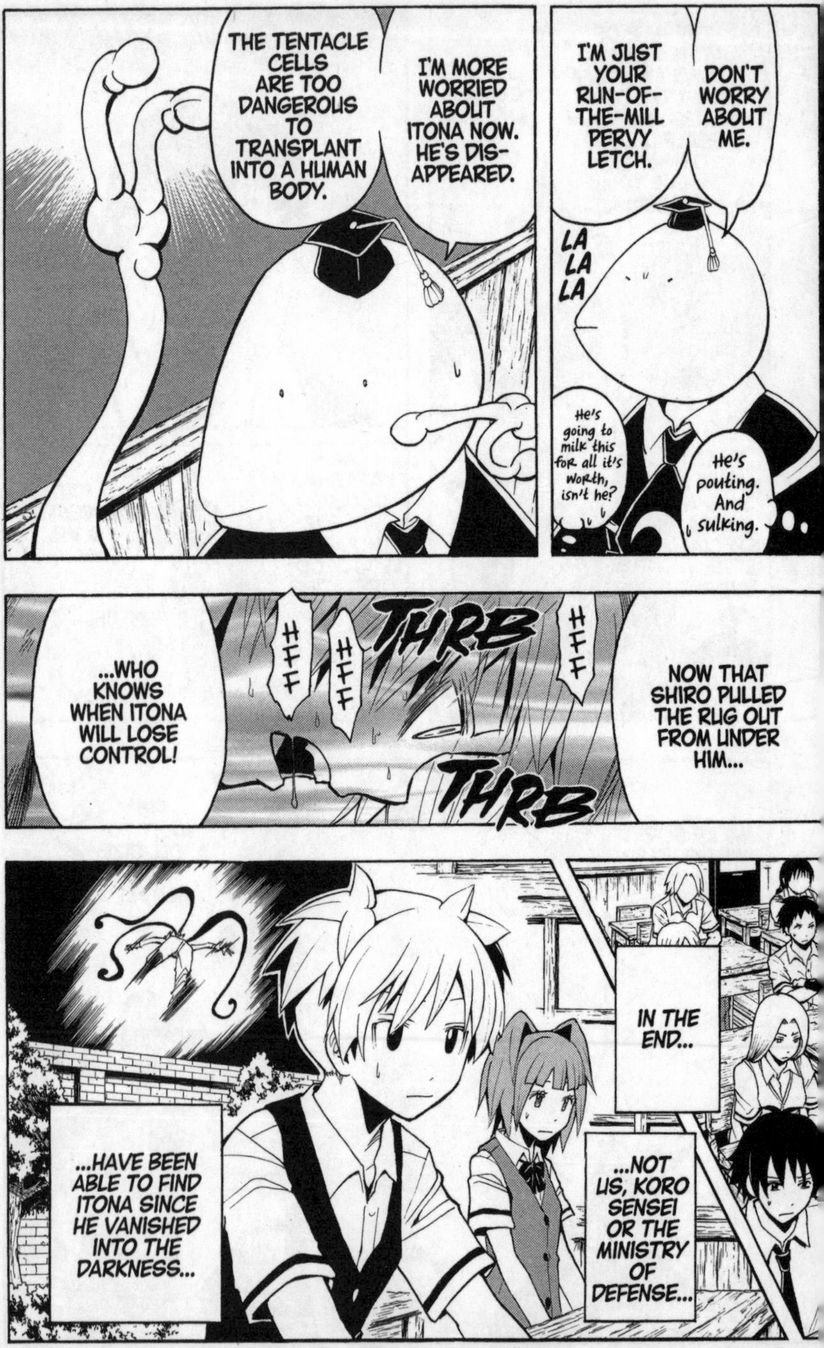
DON'T WORRY ABOUT ME.
I'M JUST YOUR RUN-OF-THE-MILL PERVY LETCH.
LA LA LA
He's pouting. And sulking.
He's going to milk this for all it's worth, isn't he?
I'M MORE WORRIED ABOUT ITONA NOW. HE'S DISAPPEARED.
THE TENTACLE CELLS ARE TOO DANGEROUS TO TRANSPLANT INTO A HUMAN BODY.
NOW THAT SHIRO PULLED THE RUG OUT FROM UNDER HIM...
HFF
THRB
HFF
THRB
...WHO KNOWS WHEN ITONA WILL LOSE CONTROL!
IN THE END...
...NOT US, KORO SENSEI OR THE MINISTRY OF DEFENSE...
...HAVE BEEN ABLE TO FIND ITONA SINCE HE VANISHED INTO THE DARKNESS...

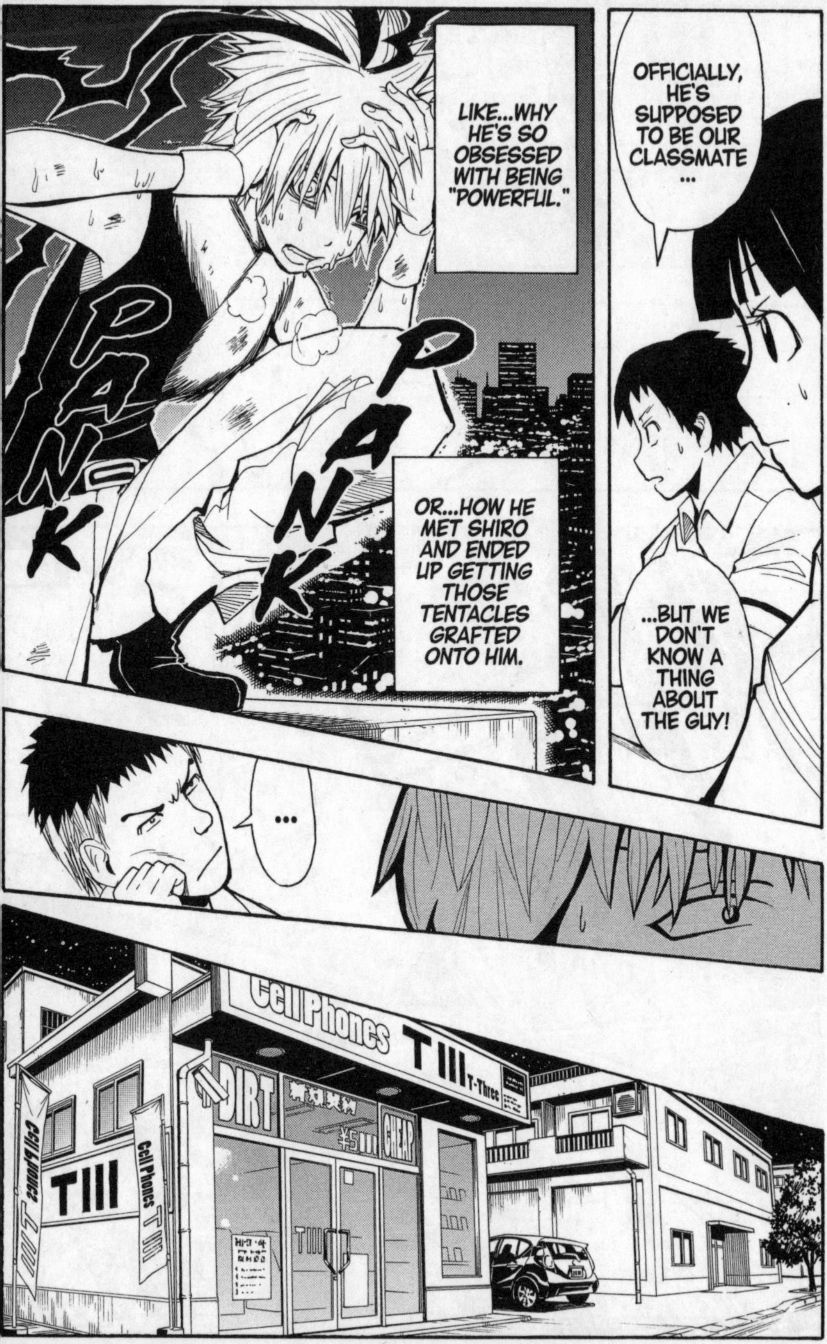
OFFICIALLY, HE'S SUPPOSED TO BE OUR CLASSMATE...
...BUT WE DON'T KNOW A THING ABOUT THE GUY!
LIKE...WHY HE'S SO OBSESSED WITH BEING "POWERFUL."
PANK
PANK
OR...HOW HE MET SHIRO AND ENDED UP GETTING THOSE TENTACLES GRAFTED ONTO HIM.
...
Cell Phones
TIII T-Three
DIRT
CHEAP
CellPhones TIII
CellPhones TIII

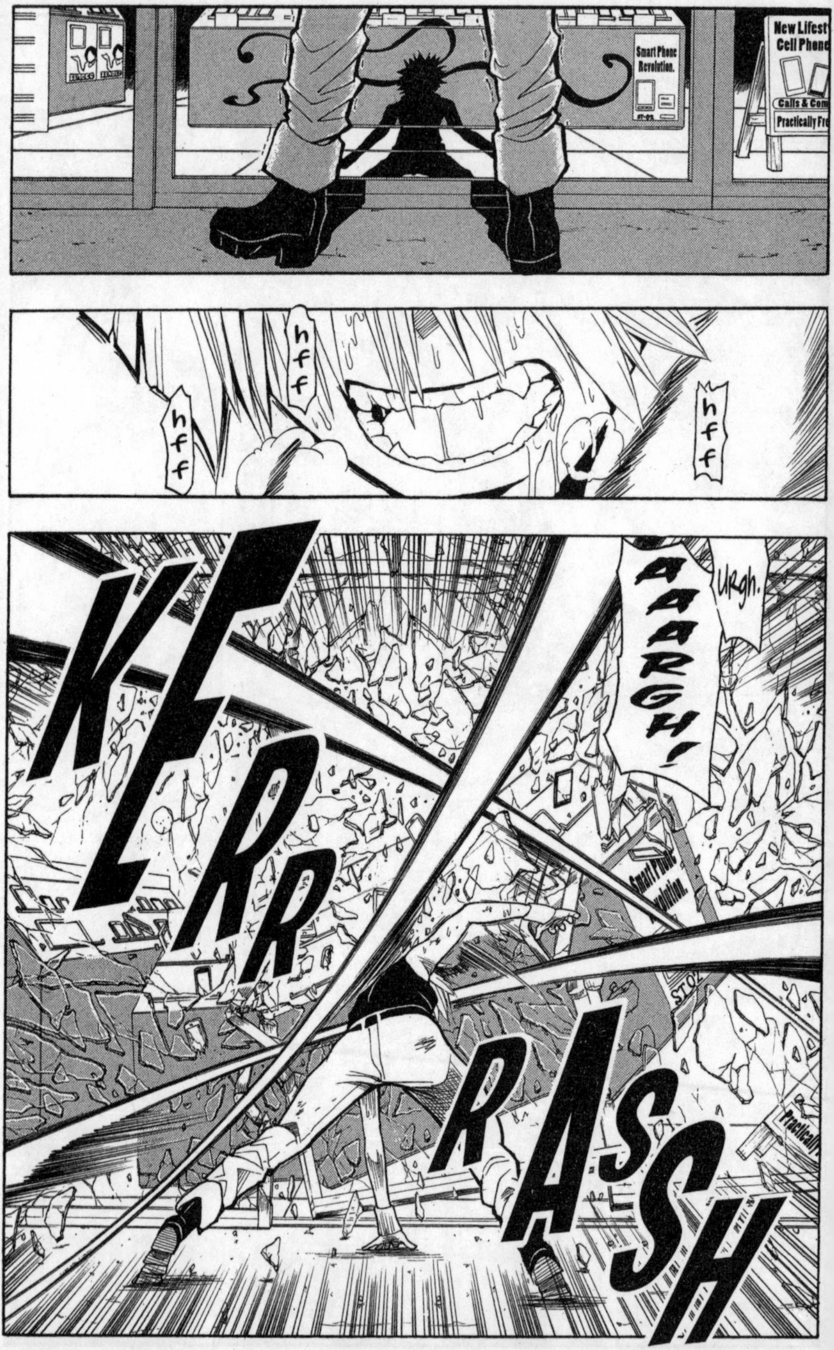
Smart Phone Revolution.
hff hff
hff hff
Urgh.
AAARGH!
KLRR
RASH

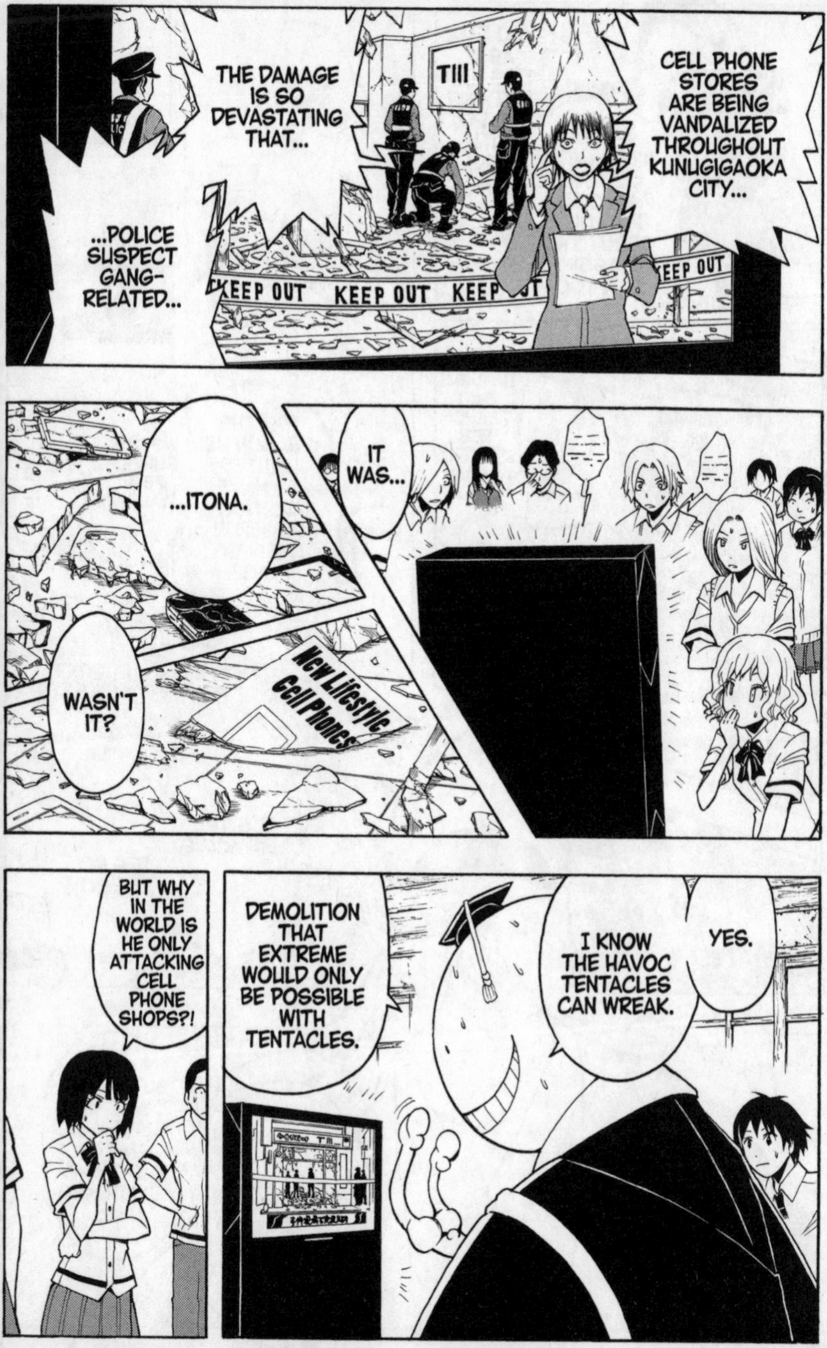
CELL PHONE STORES ARE BEING VANDALIZED THROUGHOUT KUNUGIGAOKA CITY...
TIII
THE DAMAGE IS SO DEVASTATING THAT...
KEEP OUT
KEEP OUT KEEP OUT KEEP
...POLICE SUSPECT GANG-RELATED...
IT WAS...
...ITONA.
New Lifestyle Cell Phones
WASN'T IT?
YES.
I KNOW THE HAVOC TENTACLES CAN WREAK.
DEMOLITION THAT EXTREME WOULD ONLY BE POSSIBLE WITH TENTACLES.
BUT WHY IN THE WORLD IS HE ONLY ATTACKING CELL PHONE SHOPS?!

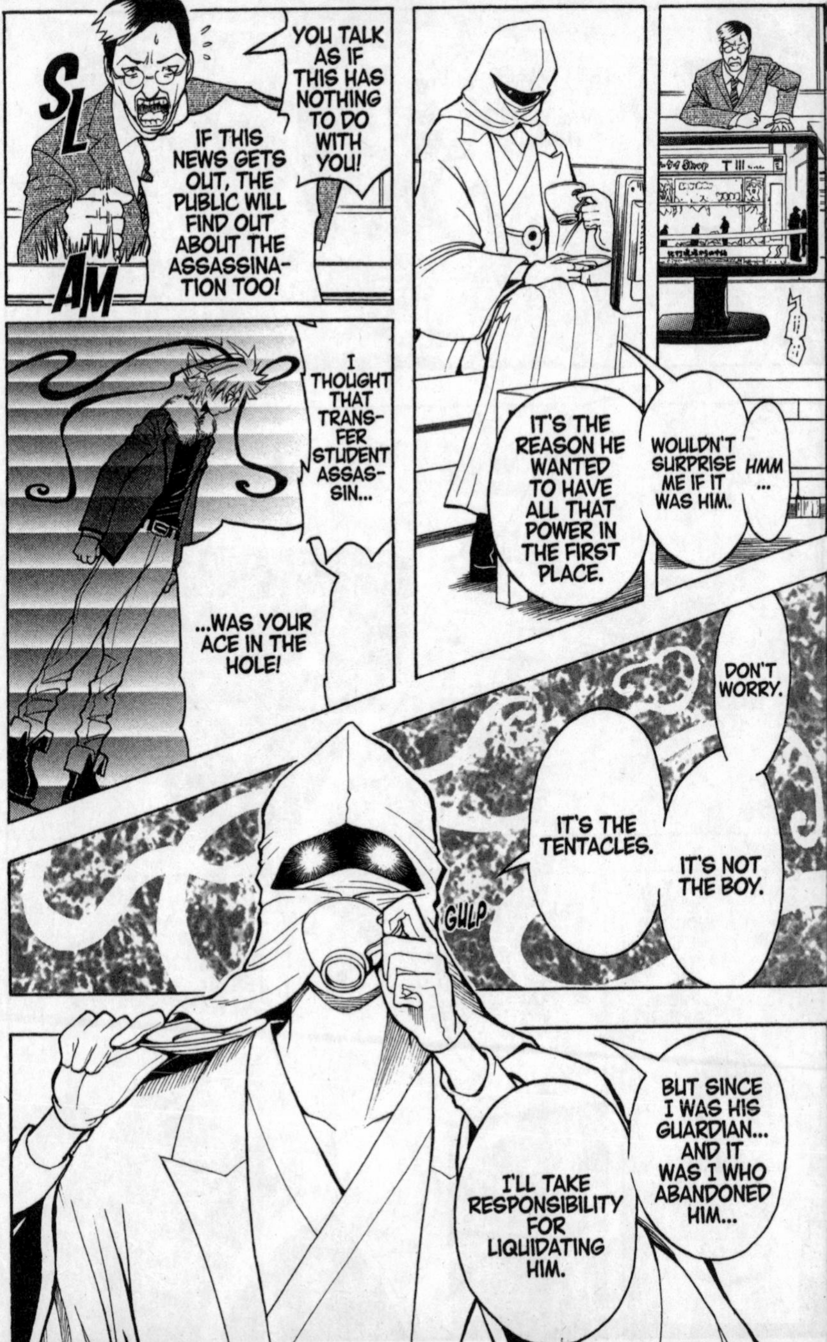
HMM...
WOULDN'T SURPRISE ME IF IT WAS HIM.
IT'S THE REASON HE WANTED TO HAVE ALL THAT POWER IN THE FIRST PLACE.
YOU TALK AS IF THIS HAS NOTHING TO DO WITH YOU!
IF THIS NEWS GETS OUT, THE PUBLIC WILL FIND OUT ABOUT THE ASSASSINATION TOO!
SLAM
I THOUGHT THAT TRANSFER STUDENT ASSASSIN...
...WAS YOUR ACE IN THE HOLE!
DON'T WORRY.
IT'S NOT THE BOY.
IT'S THE TENTACLES.
GULP
BUT SINCE I WAS HIS GUARDIAN... AND IT WAS I WHO ABANDONED HIM...
I'LL TAKE RESPONSIBILITY FOR LIQUIDATING HIM.

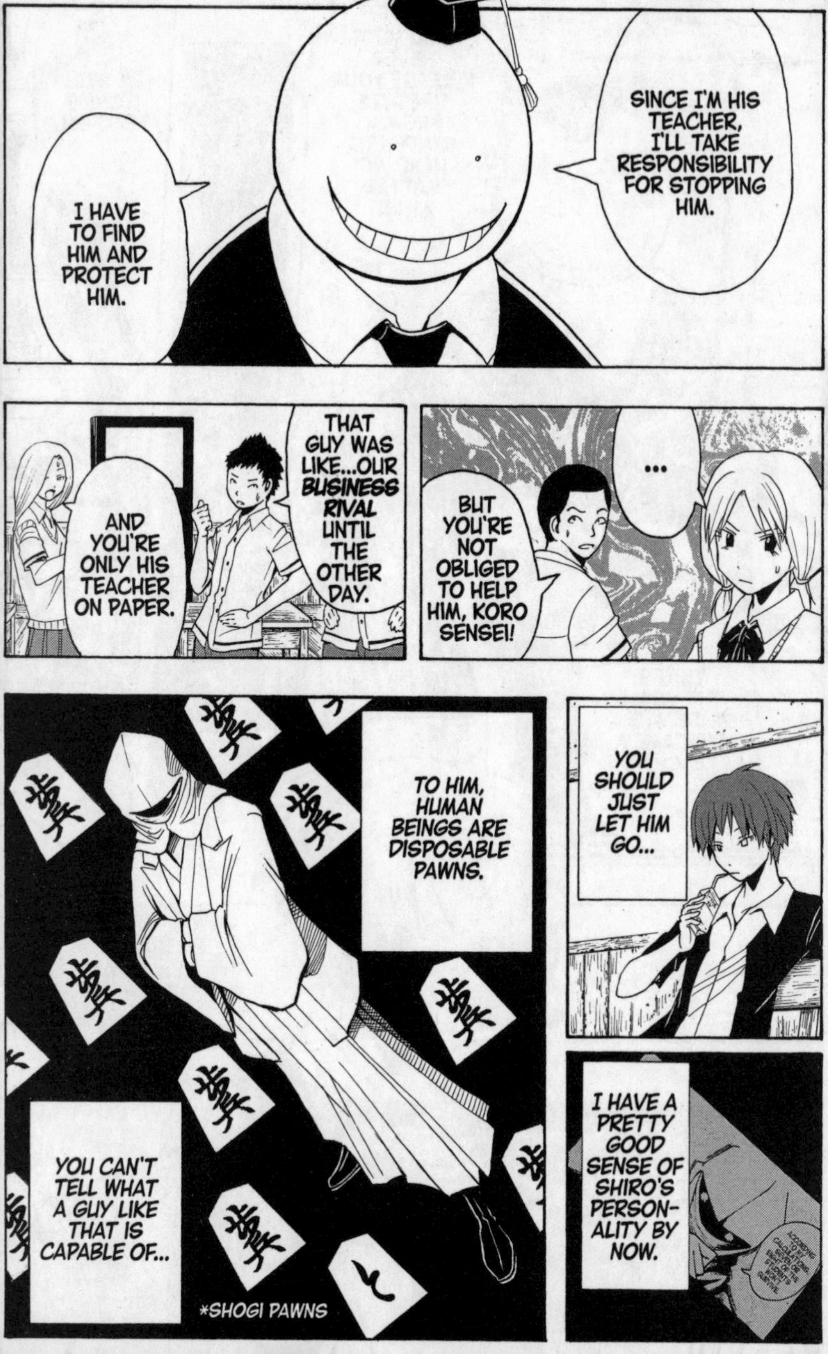

SINCE I'M HIS TEACHER, I'LL TAKE RESPONSIBILITY FOR STOPPING HIM.
I HAVE TO FIND HIM AND PROTECT HIM.
...
BUT YOU'RE NOT OBLIGED TO HELP HIM, KORO SENSEI!
THAT GUY WAS LIKE...OUR *BUSINESS RIVAL* UNTIL THE OTHER DAY.
AND YOU'RE ONLY HIS TEACHER ON PAPER.
YOU SHOULD JUST LET HIM GO...
I HAVE A PRETTY GOOD SENSE OF SHIRO'S PERSONALITY BY NOW.
ACCORDING TO MY CALCULATIONS, SEVEN OR EIGHT OF THE STUDENTS WON'T SURVIVE
TO HIM, HUMAN BEINGS ARE DISPOSABLE PAWNS.
YOU CAN'T TELL WHAT A GUY LIKE THAT IS CAPABLE OF...
*SHOGI PAWNS

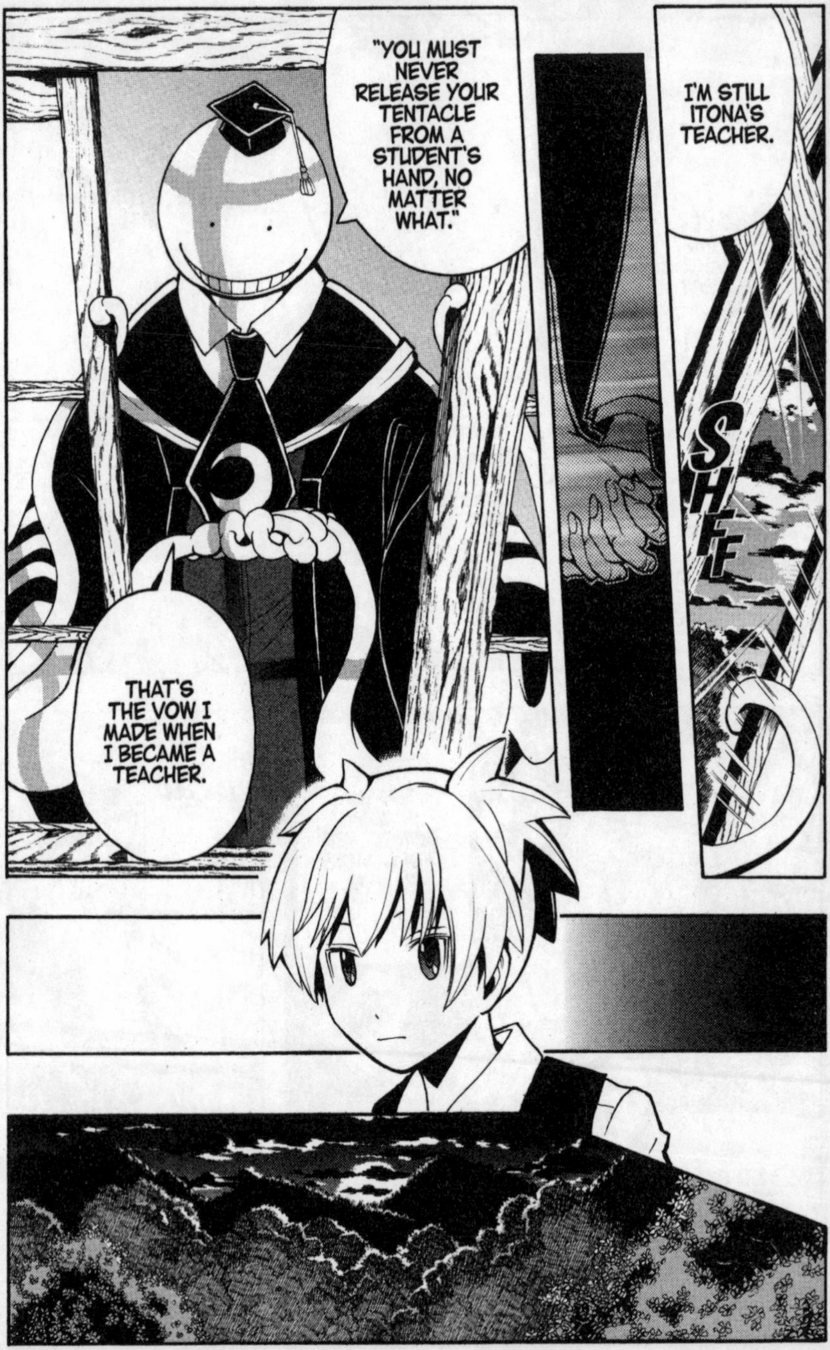
I'M STILL ITONA'S TEACHER.
SHFF
"YOU MUST NEVER RELEASE YOUR TENTACLE FROM A STUDENT'S HAND, NO MATTER WHAT."
THAT'S THE VOW I MADE WHEN I BECAME A TEACHER.

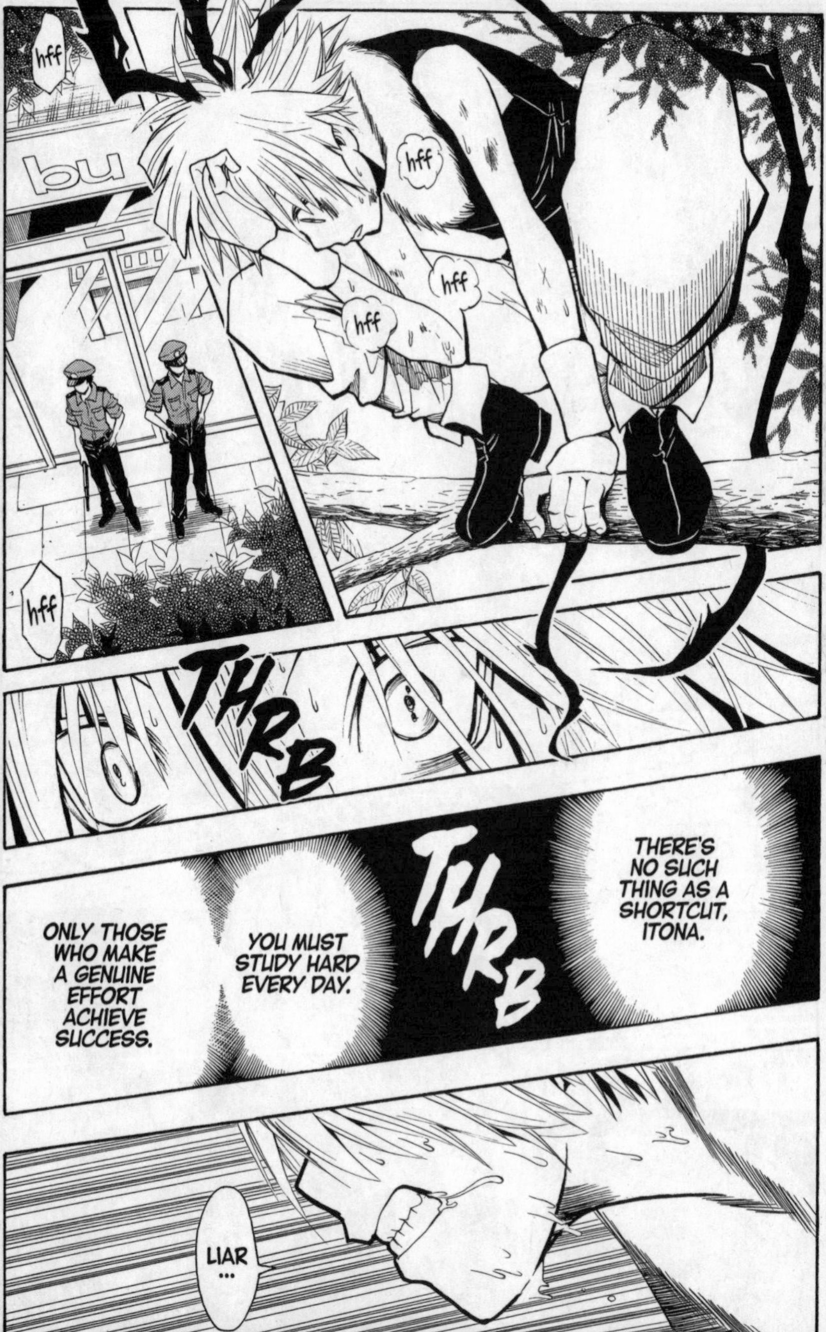
hff
hff
hff
hff
hff
THRB
THERE'S NO SUCH THING AS A SHORTCUT, ITONA.
THRB
YOU MUST STUDY HARD EVERY DAY.
ONLY THOSE WHO MAKE A GENUINE EFFORT ACHIEVE SUCCESS.
LIAR...

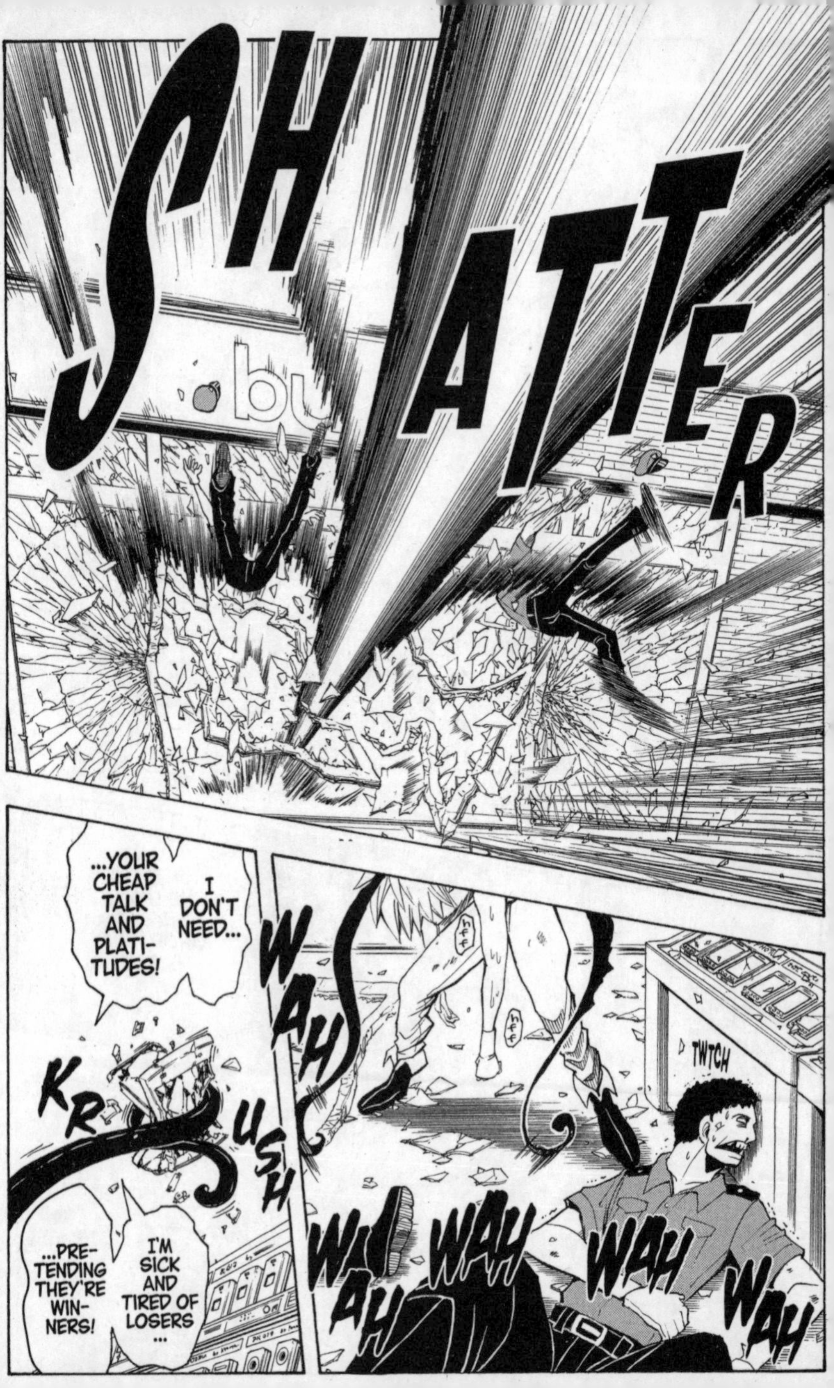
SHATTER
hff
hff
WAH
WAH
TWTCH
WAH WAH WAH WAH WAH WAH
I DON'T NEED...
...YOUR CHEAP TALK AND PLATITUDES!
KRUSH
I'M SICK AND TIRED OF LOSERS...
...PRETENDING THEY'RE WINNERS!

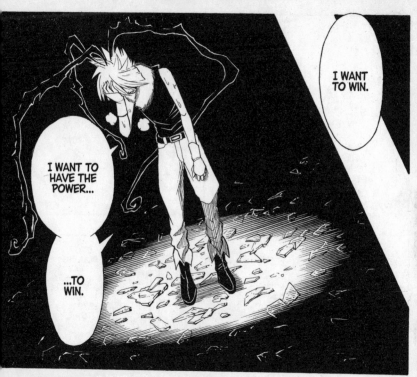

I WANT TO WIN.

I WANT TO HAVE THE POWER...

...TO WIN.

KRNCH

KRNCH

...I'M GETTING TO SEE YOUR HUMAN SIDE, ITONA.

FIN-ALLY...

KRNCH

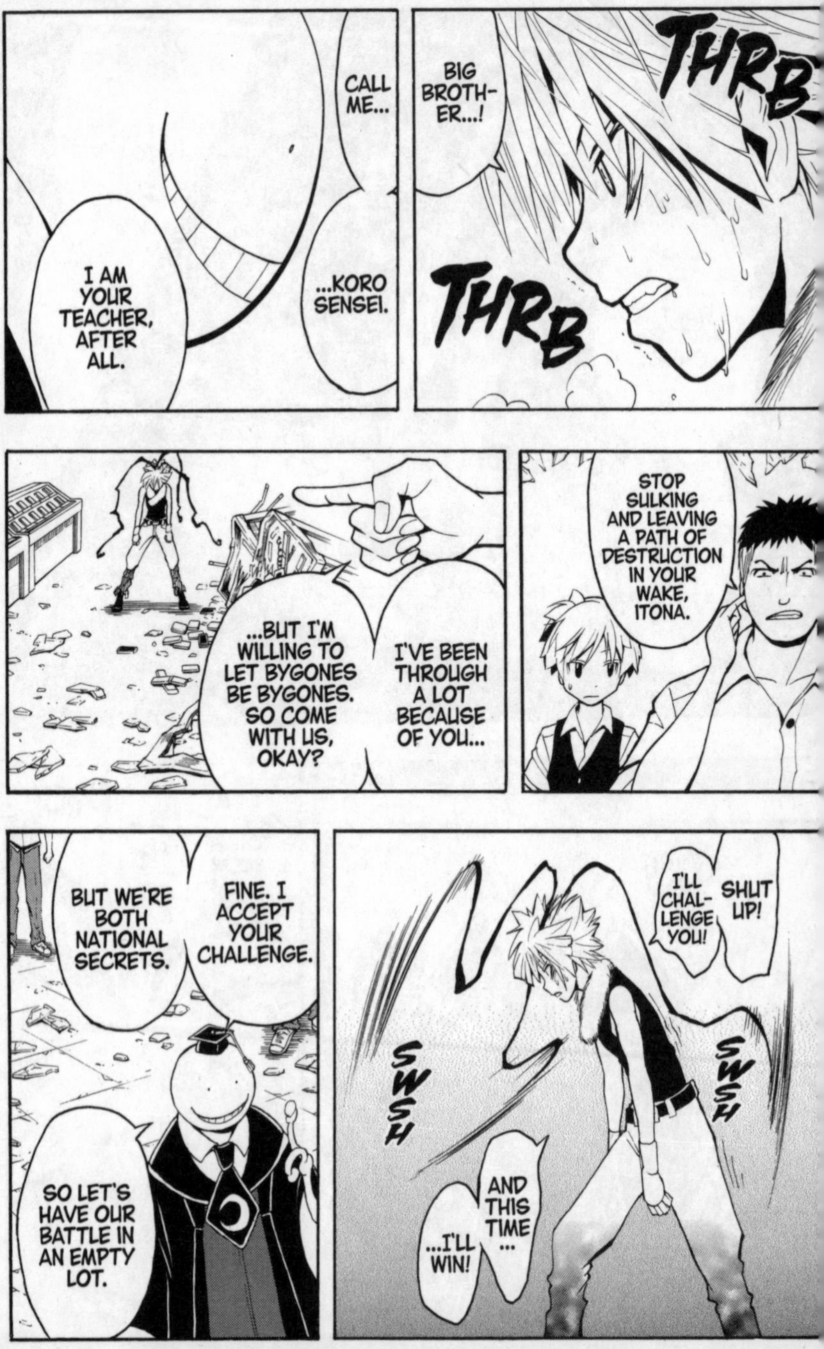
BIG BROTH-ER...!
THRB
THRB
CALL ME...
...KORO SENSEI.
I AM YOUR TEACHER, AFTER ALL.
STOP SULKING AND LEAVING A PATH OF DESTRUCTION IN YOUR WAKE, ITONA.
I'VE BEEN THROUGH A LOT BECAUSE OF YOU...
...BUT I'M WILLING TO LET BYGONES BE BYGONES. SO COME WITH US, OKAY?
SHUT UP!
I'LL CHAL-LENGE YOU!
SWSH
SWSH
AND THIS TIME...
...I'LL WIN!
FINE. I ACCEPT YOUR CHALLENGE.
BUT WE'RE BOTH NATIONAL SECRETS.
SO LET'S HAVE OUR BATTLE IN AN EMPTY LOT.

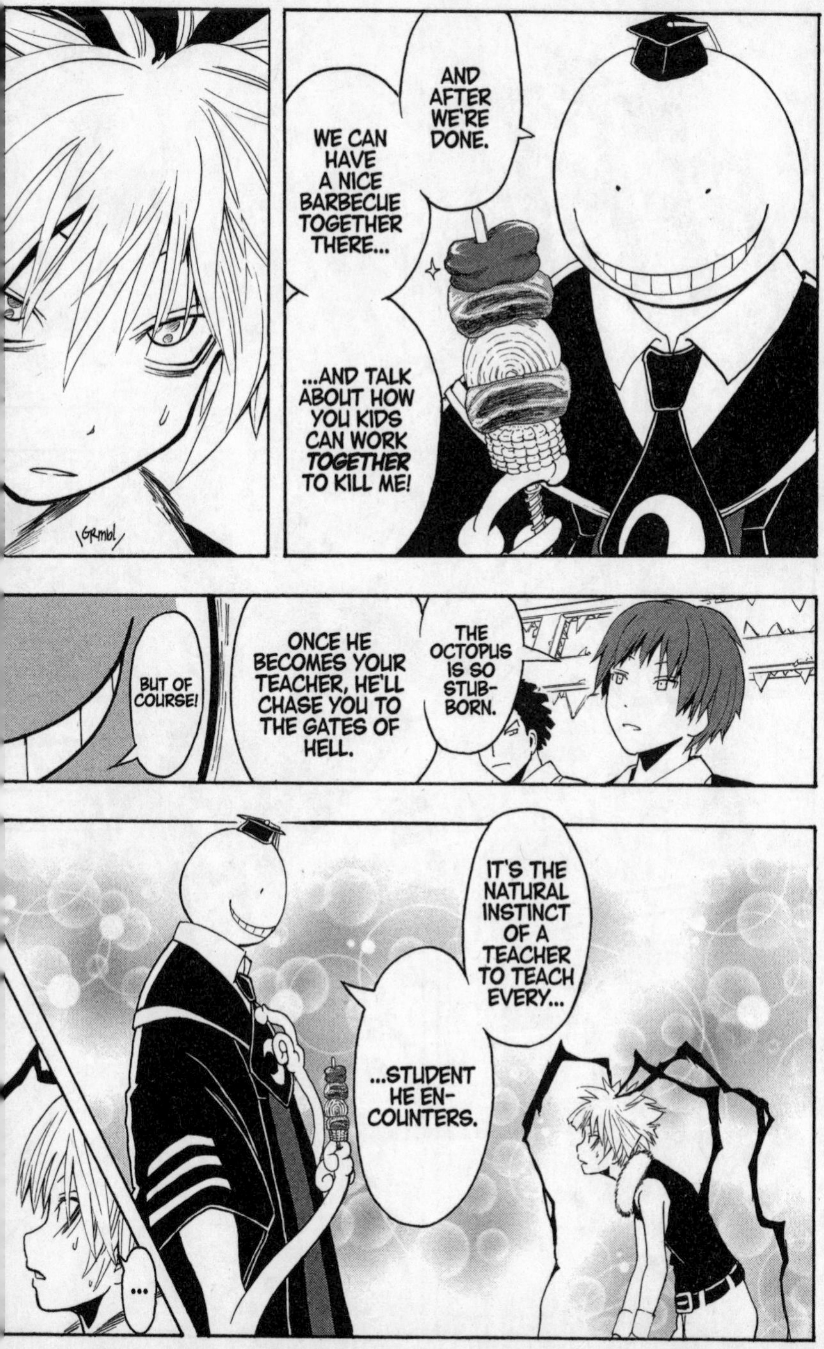
AND AFTER WE'RE DONE.
WE CAN HAVE A NICE BARBECUE TOGETHER THERE...
...AND TALK ABOUT HOW YOU KIDS CAN WORK *TOGETHER* TO KILL ME!
GRMBL
THE OCTOPUS IS SO STUB-BORN.
ONCE HE BECOMES YOUR TEACHER, HE'LL CHASE YOU TO THE GATES OF HELL.
BUT OF COURSE!
IT'S THE NATURAL INSTINCT OF A TEACHER TO TEACH EVERY...
...STUDENT HE EN-COUNTERS.
...

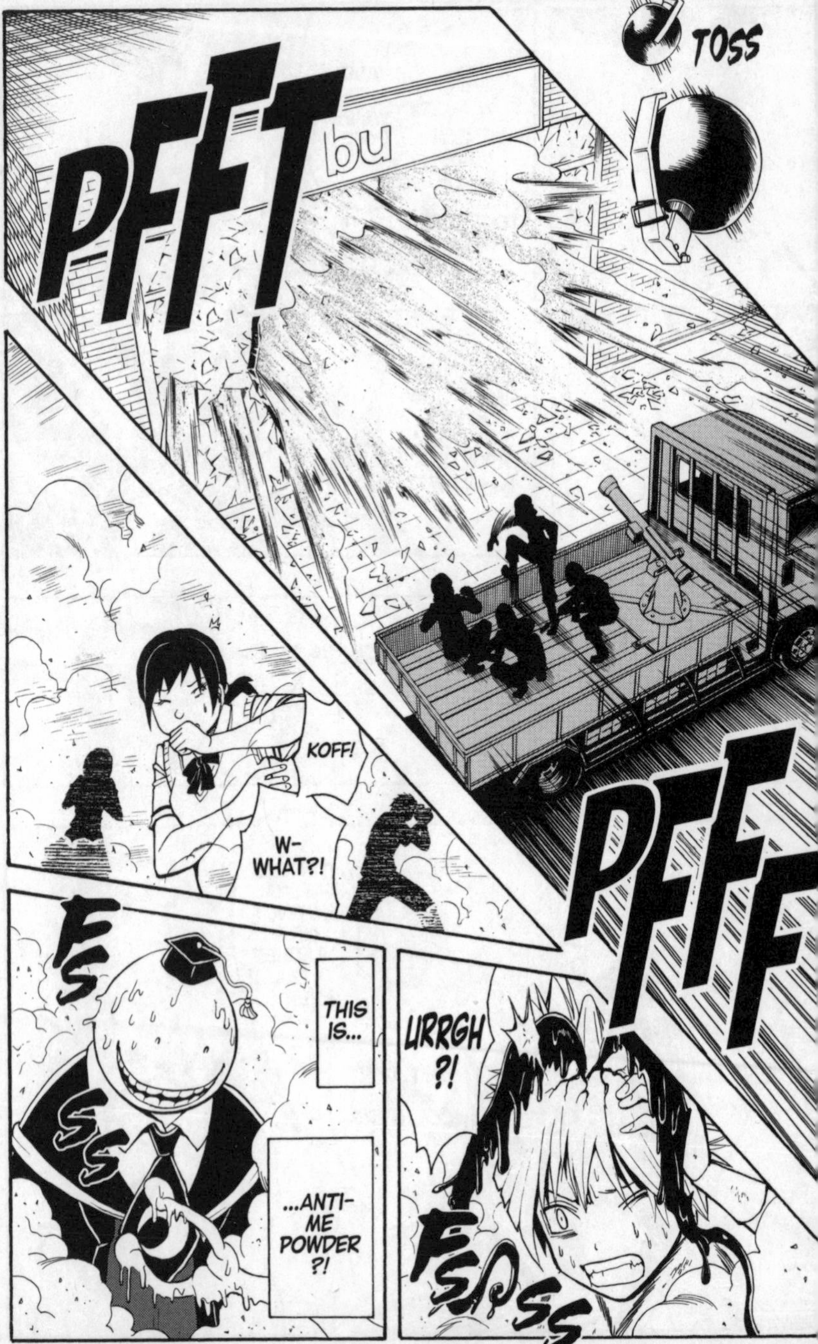
TOSS
PFFT
bu
PFFF
KOFF!
W-WHAT?!
URRGH ?!
FSSSS
FS
THIS IS...
...ANTI-ME POWDER ?!
SS

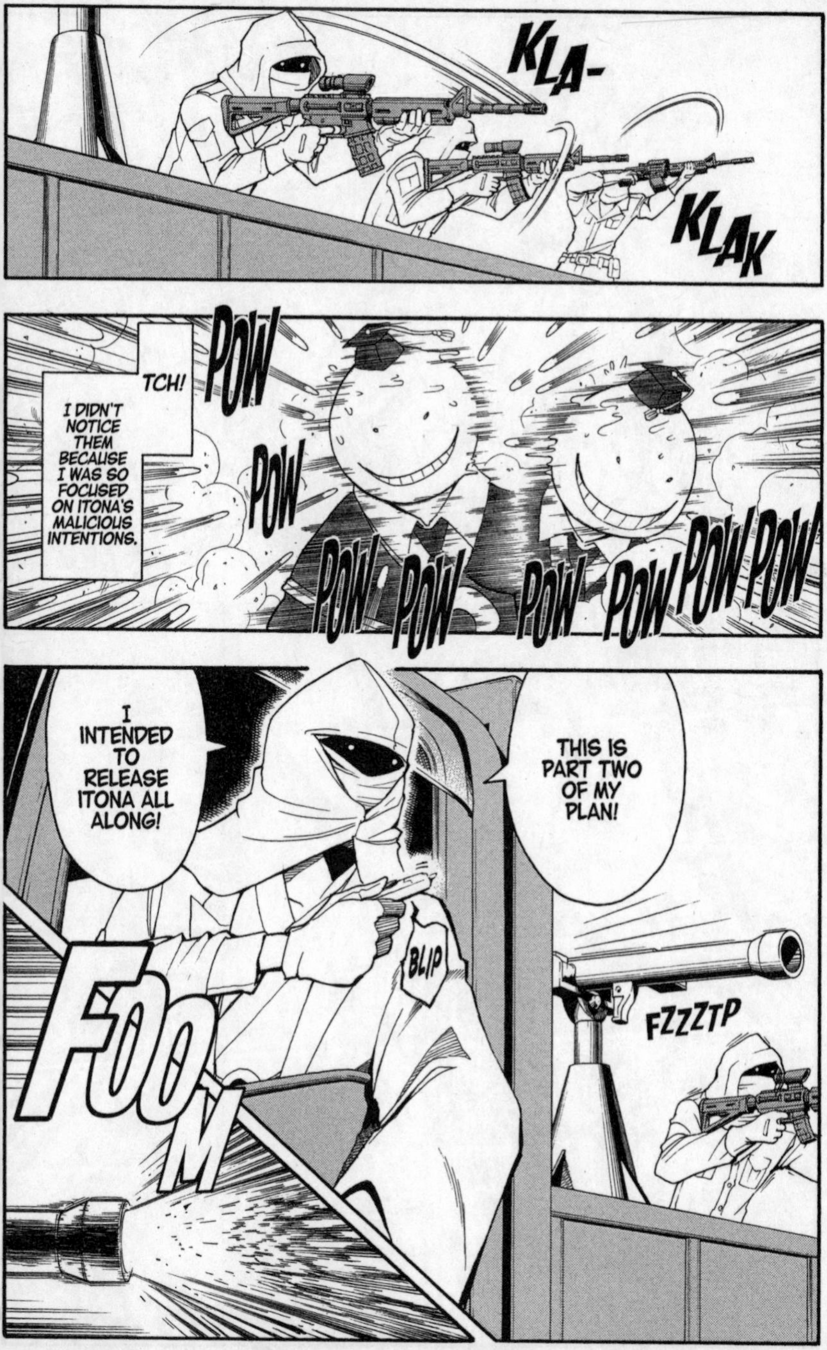
KLA-
KLAK
POW POW
POW POW
POW
POW
POW
POW
POW
TCH!
I DIDN'T NOTICE THEM BECAUSE I WAS SO FOCUSED ON ITONA'S MALICIOUS INTENTIONS.
THIS IS PART TWO OF MY PLAN!
I INTENDED TO RELEASE ITONA ALL ALONG!
FZZZTP
BLIP
FOOM

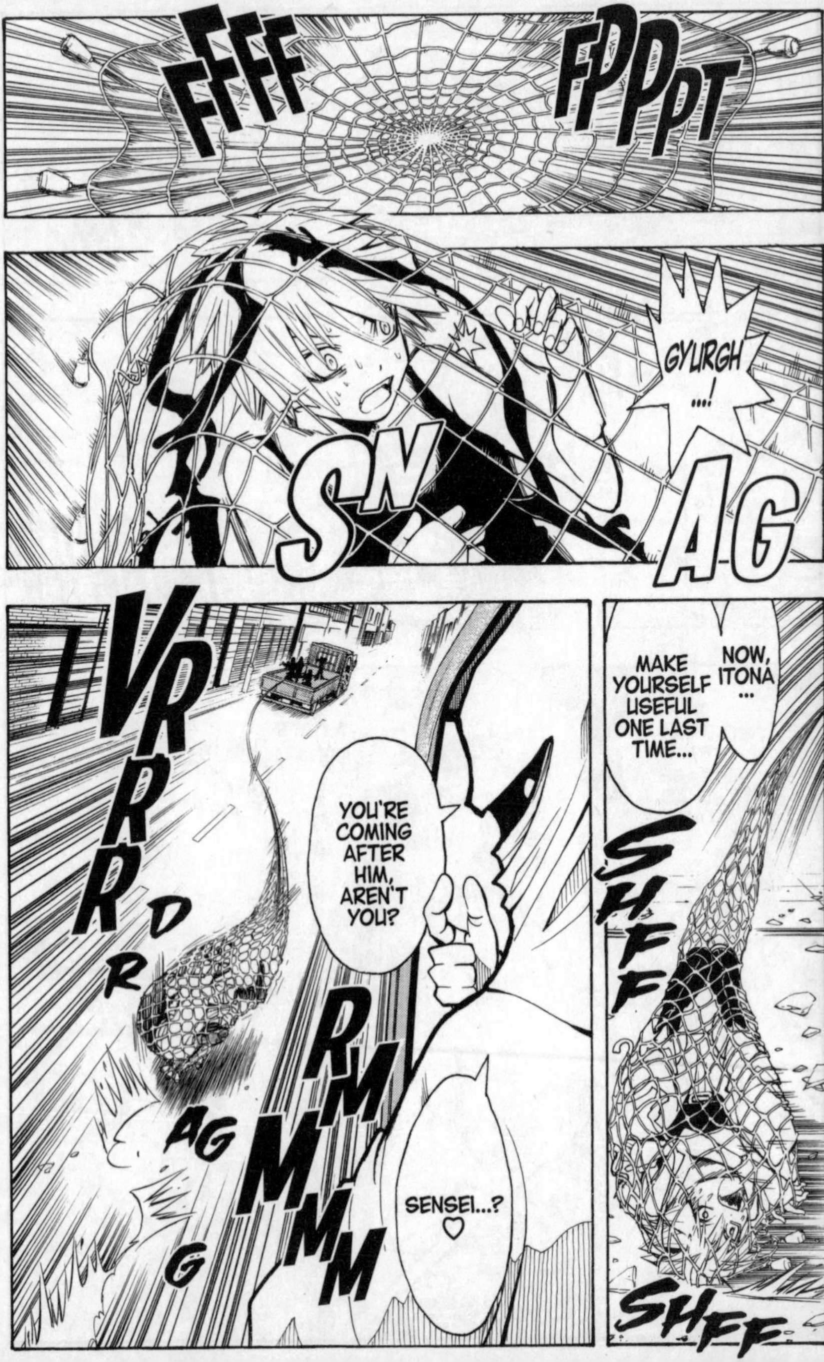
FFFF
FPPPT
GYURGH ...!
SNAG
NOW, ITONA...
MAKE YOURSELF USEFUL ONE LAST TIME...
SHFF
SHFF
TVRRRR
DRAG
G
RMMMMM
YOU'RE COMING AFTER HIM, AREN'T YOU?
SENSEI...? ♡

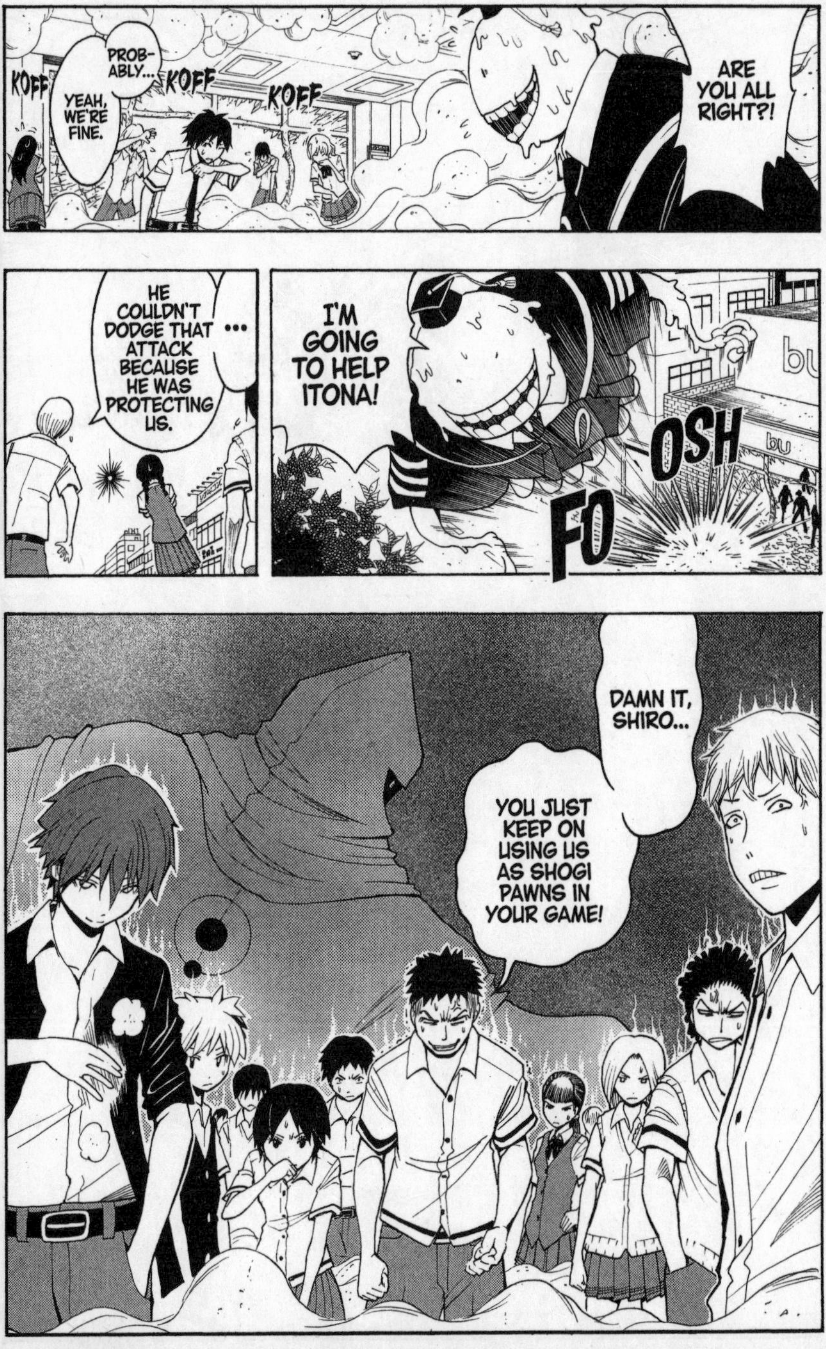
ARE YOU ALL RIGHT?!
KOFF
PROB-
ABLY...
KOFF
YEAH, WE'RE FINE.
KOFF
I'M GOING TO HELP ITONA!
FO
OSH
...
HE COULDN'T DODGE THAT ATTACK BECAUSE HE WAS PROTECTING US.
DAMN IT, SHIRO...
YOU JUST KEEP ON USING US AS SHOGI PAWNS IN YOUR GAME!

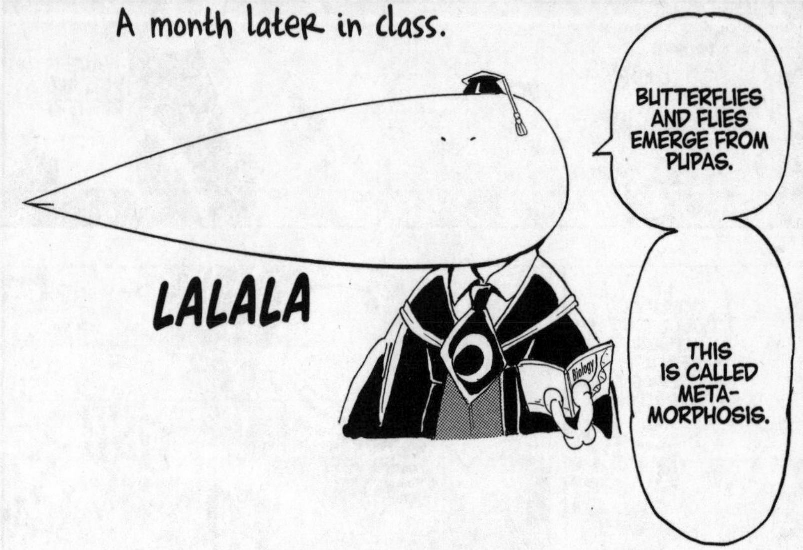
A month later in class.
BUTTERFLIES AND FLIES EMERGE FROM PUPAS.
THIS IS CALLED META-MORPHOSIS.
LALALA
Biology

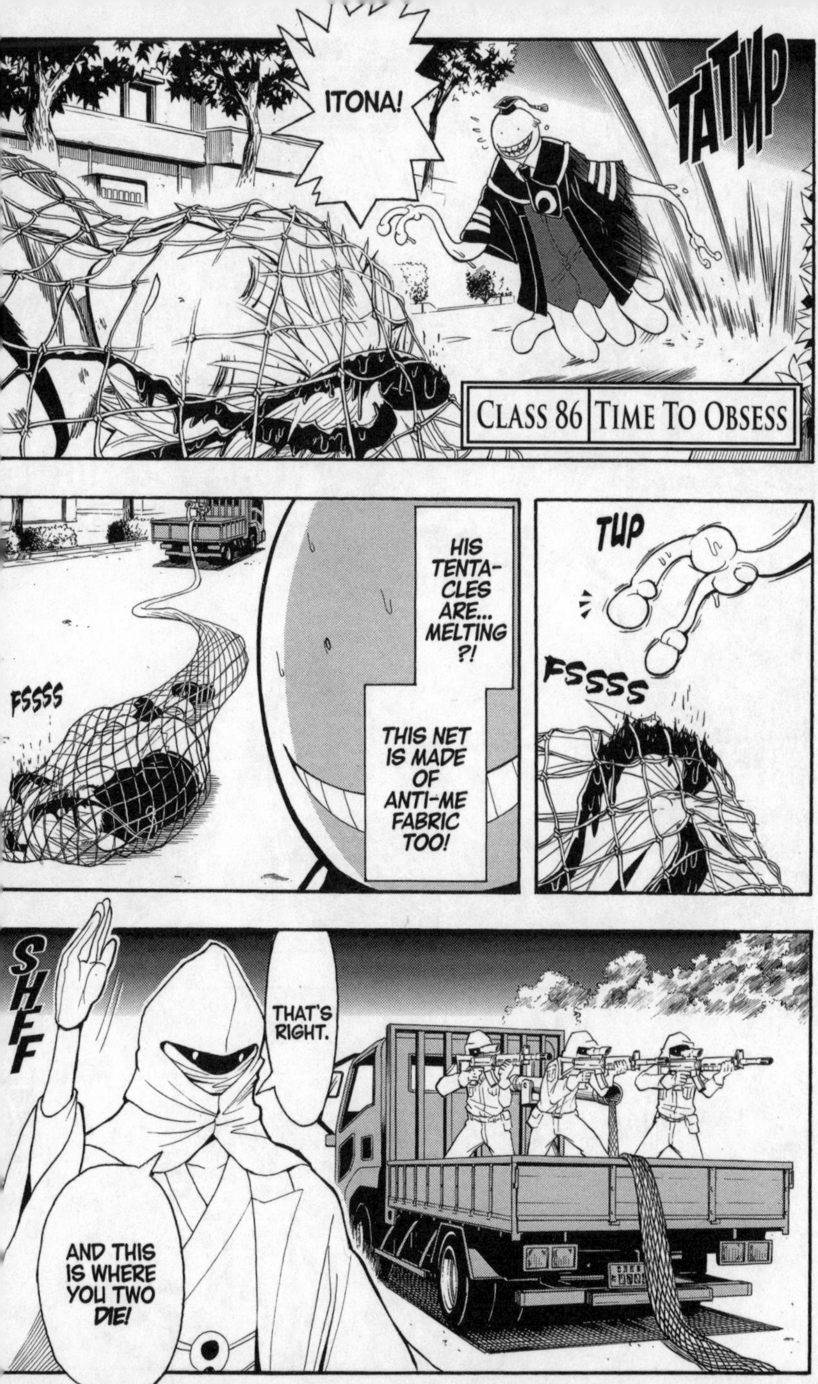
TATMP
ITONA!
CLASS 86 TIME TO OBSESS
TUP
FSSSS
HIS TENTACLES ARE... MELTING?!
THIS NET IS MADE OF ANTI-ME FABRIC TOO!
FSSSS
THAT'S RIGHT.
SHFF
AND THIS IS WHERE YOU TWO DIE!

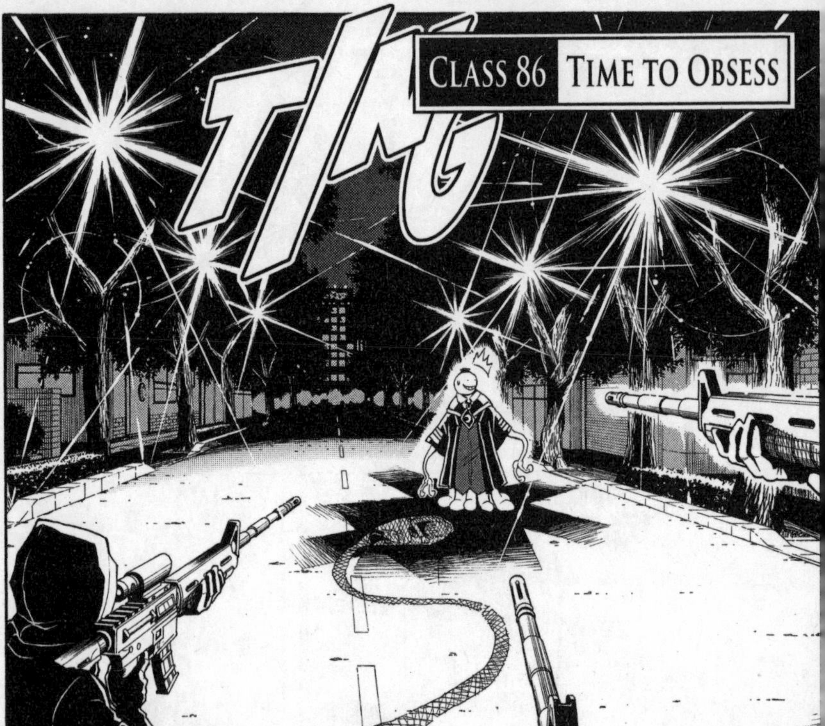
CLASS 86 TIME TO OBSESS
TING

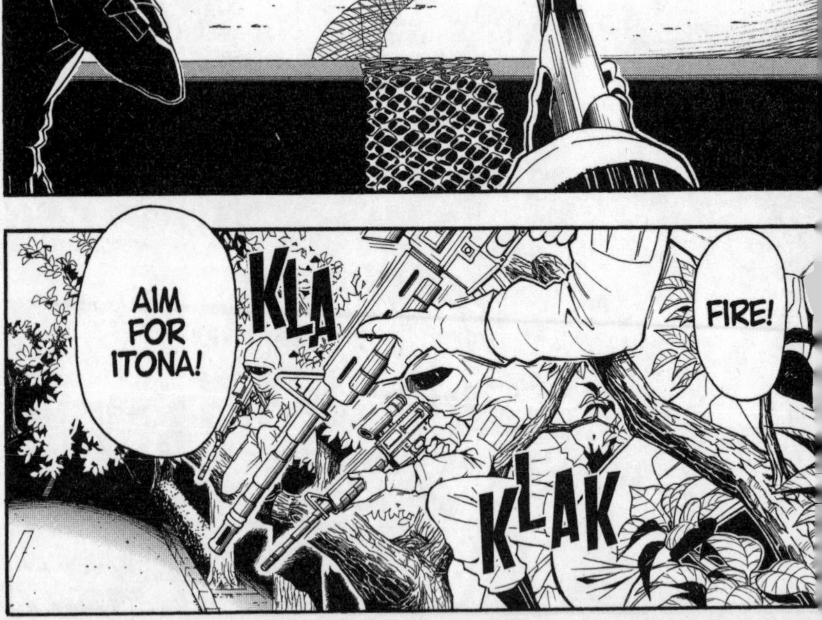
FIRE!
KLA
AIM FOR ITONA!
KLAK

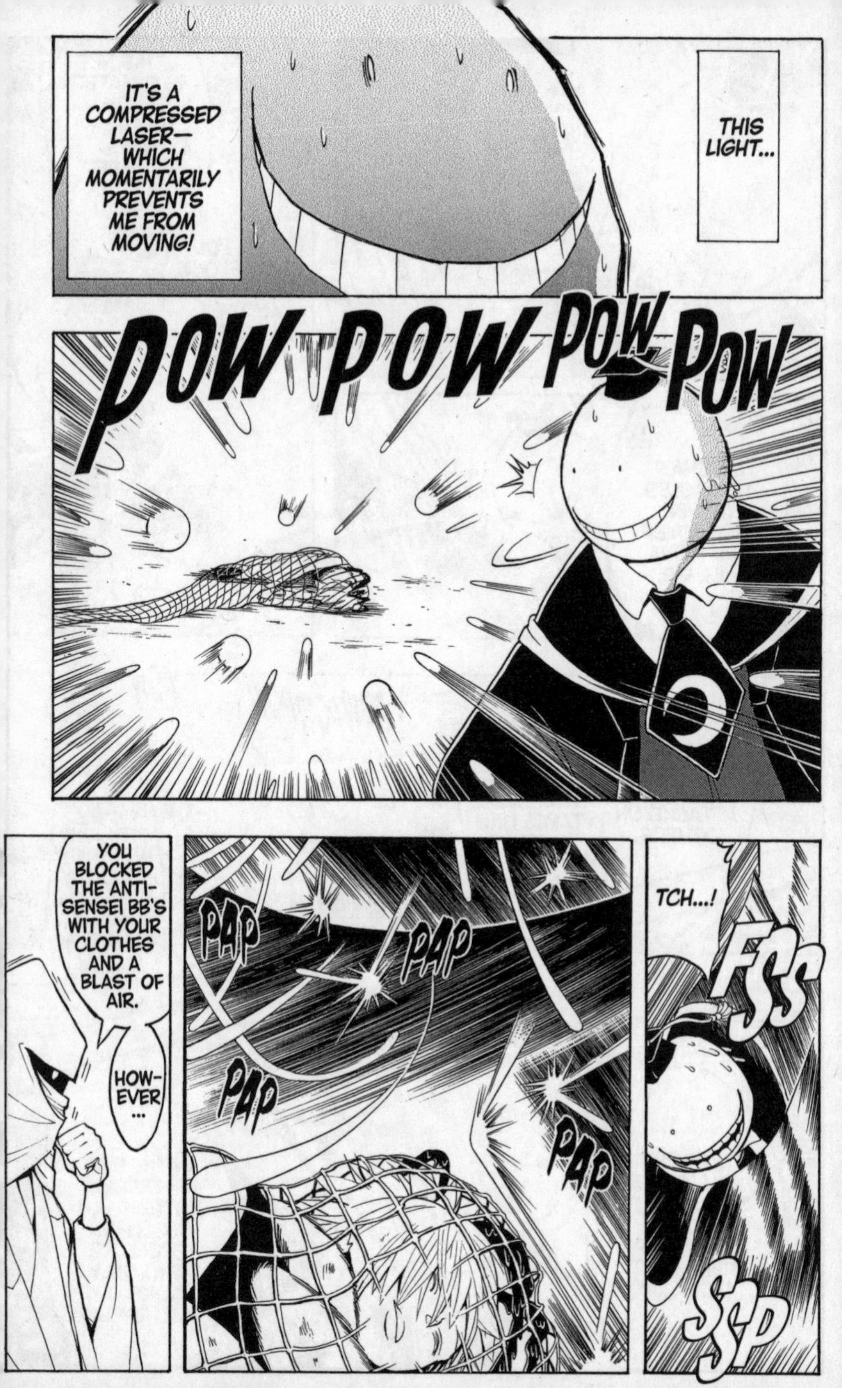
THIS LIGHT...
IT'S A COMPRESSED LASER—WHICH MOMENTARILY PREVENTS ME FROM MOVING!
POW POW POW POW
TCH...!
FSS
SSP
PAP
PAP
PAP
PAP
YOU BLOCKED THE ANTI-SENSEI BB'S WITH YOUR CLOTHES AND A BLAST OF AIR.
HOW-EVER...

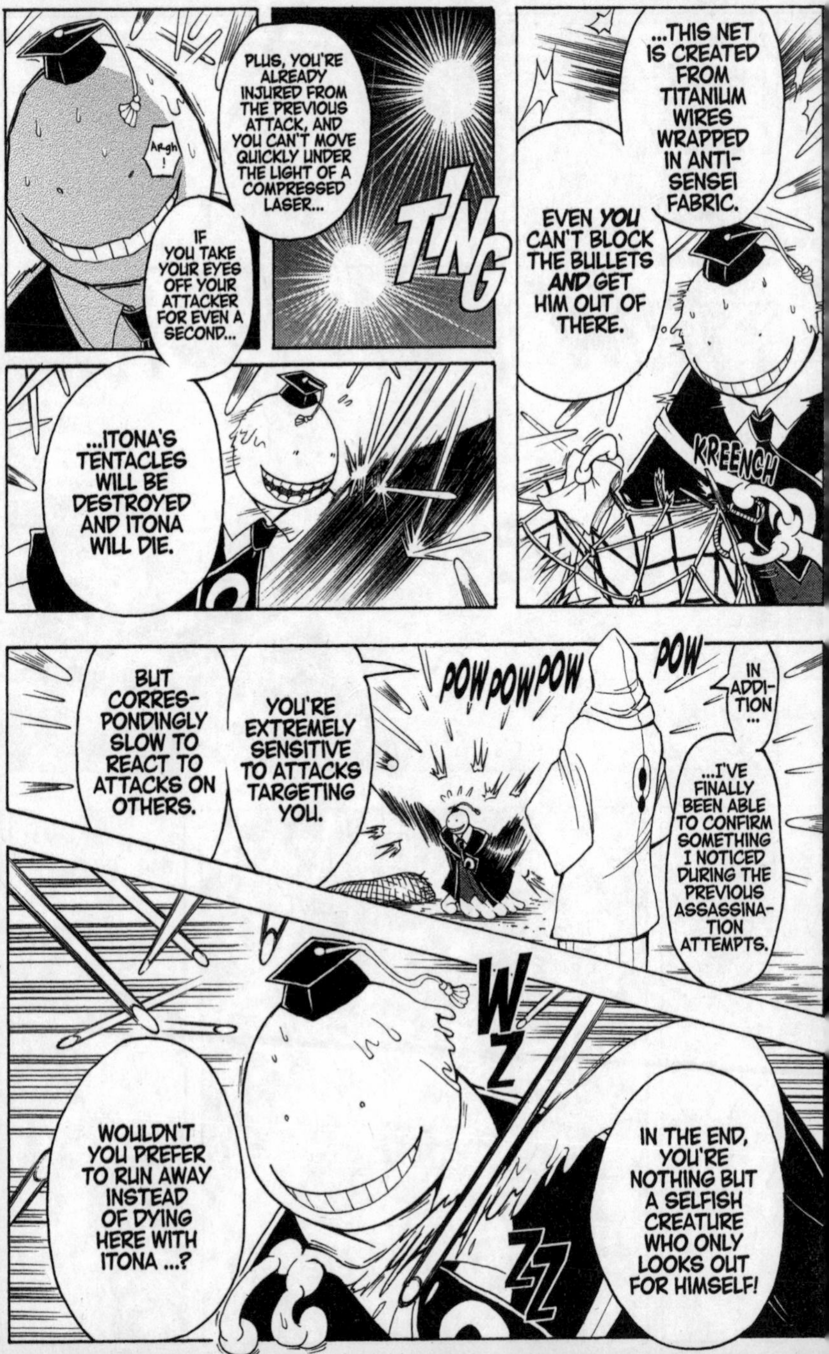
...THIS NET IS CREATED FROM TITANIUM WIRES WRAPPED IN ANTI-SENSEI FABRIC.
EVEN YOU CAN'T BLOCK THE BULLETS AND GET HIM OUT OF THERE.
KREENCH
TING
PLUS, YOU'RE ALREADY INJURED FROM THE PREVIOUS ATTACK, AND YOU CAN'T MOVE QUICKLY UNDER THE LIGHT OF A COMPRESSED LASER...
Argh!
IF YOU TAKE YOUR EYES OFF YOUR ATTACKER FOR EVEN A SECOND...
...ITONA'S TENTACLES WILL BE DESTROYED AND ITONA WILL DIE.
POW
IN ADDITION...
...I'VE FINALLY BEEN ABLE TO CONFIRM SOMETHING I NOTICED DURING THE PREVIOUS ASSASSINATION ATTEMPTS.
POWPOWPOW
YOU'RE EXTREMELY SENSITIVE TO ATTACKS TARGETING YOU.
BUT CORRESPONDINGLY SLOW TO REACT TO ATTACKS ON OTHERS.
WZ
IN THE END, YOU'RE NOTHING BUT A SELFISH CREATURE WHO ONLY LOOKS OUT FOR HIMSELF!
ZZ
WOULDN'T YOU PREFER TO RUN AWAY INSTEAD OF DYING HERE WITH ITONA ...?

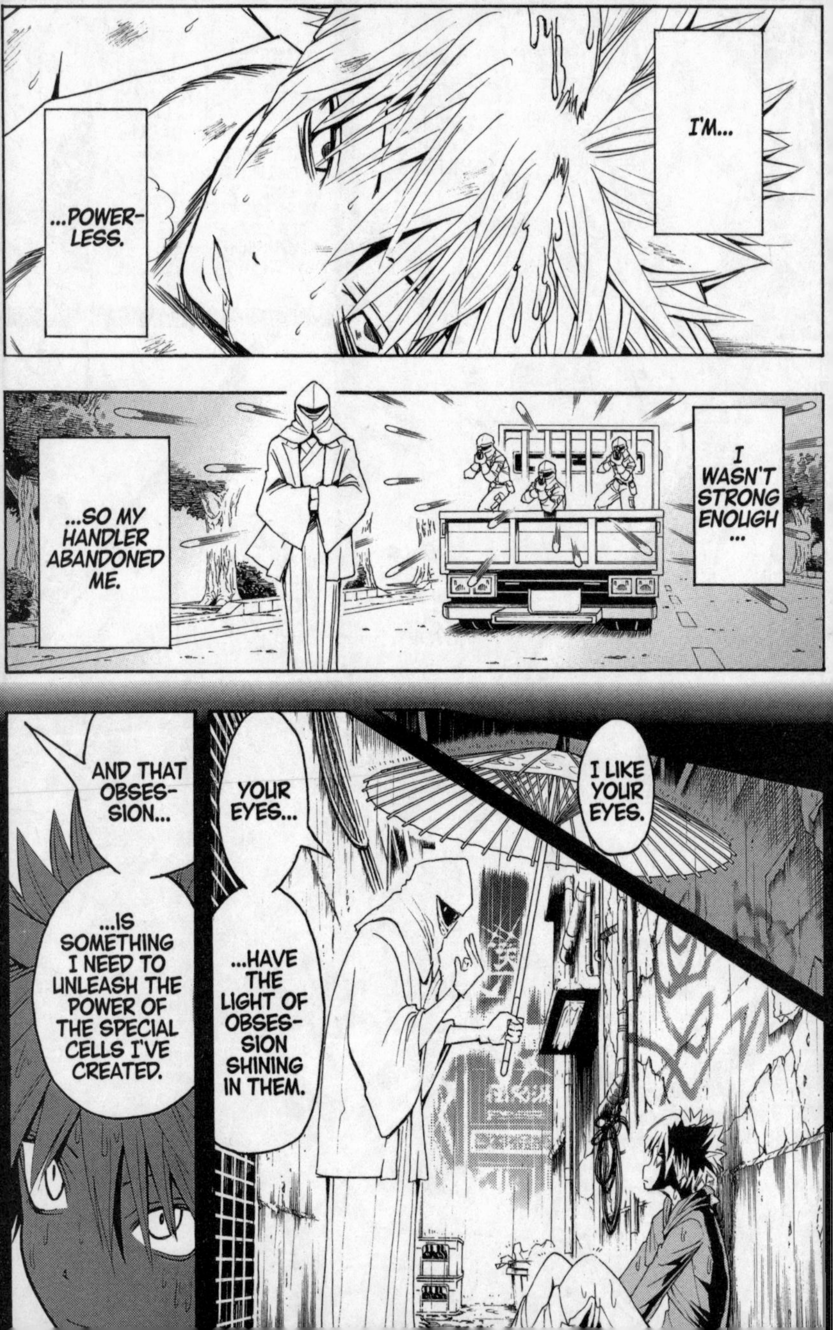
I'M...
...POWER-LESS.
I WASN'T STRONG ENOUGH...
...SO MY HANDLER ABANDONED ME.
I LIKE YOUR EYES.
YOUR EYES...
...HAVE THE LIGHT OF OBSES-SION SHINING IN THEM.
AND THAT OBSES-SION...
...IS SOMETHING I NEED TO UNLEASH THE POWER OF THE SPECIAL CELLS I'VE CREATED.

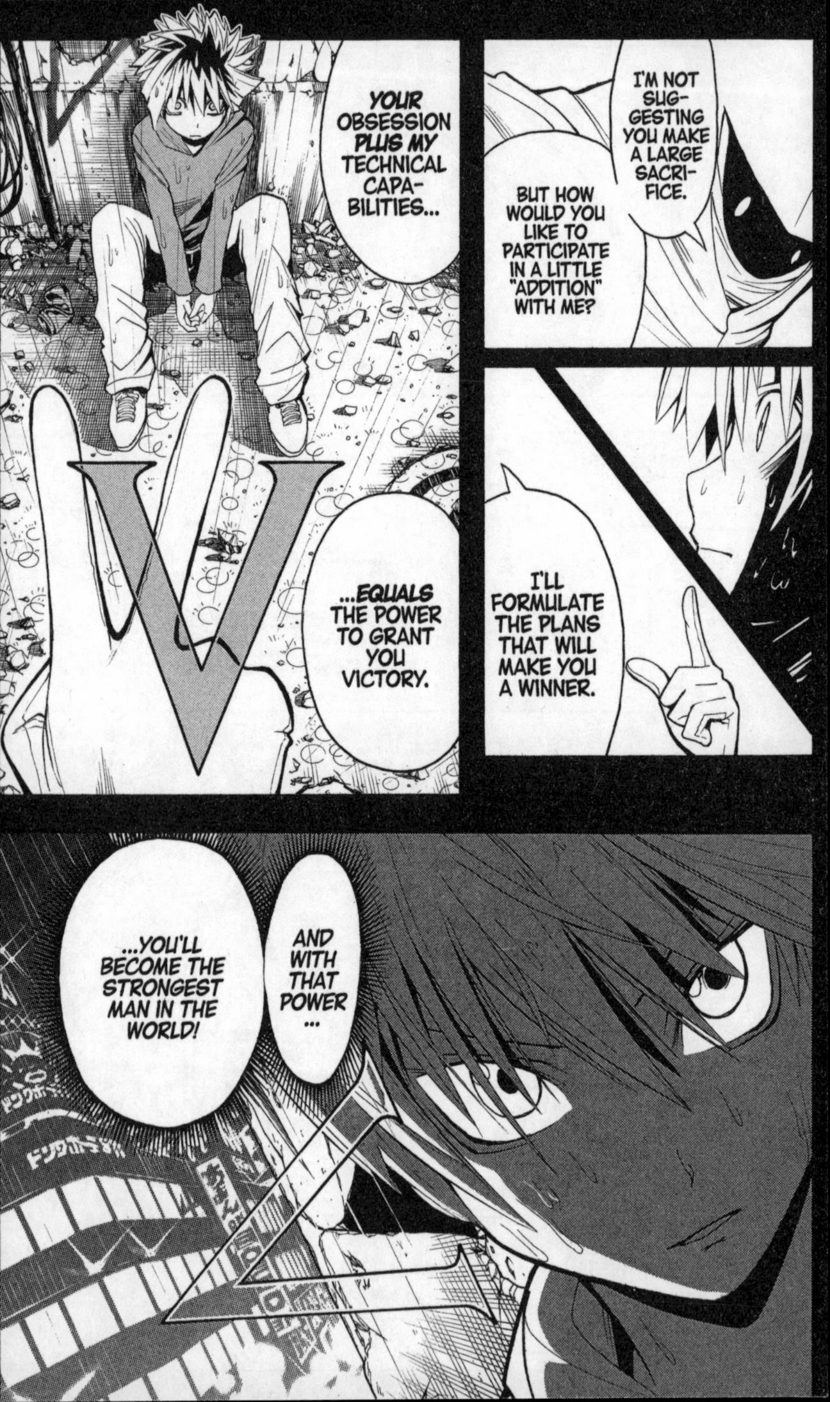
I'M NOT SUGGESTING YOU MAKE A LARGE SACRIFICE.
BUT HOW WOULD YOU LIKE TO PARTICIPATE IN A LITTLE "ADDITION" WITH ME?
I'LL FORMULATE THE PLANS THAT WILL MAKE YOU A WINNER.
YOUR OBSESSION *PLUS MY* TECHNICAL CAPABILITIES...
...*EQUALS* THE POWER TO GRANT YOU VICTORY.
AND WITH THAT POWER...
...YOU'LL BECOME THE STRONGEST MAN IN THE WORLD!

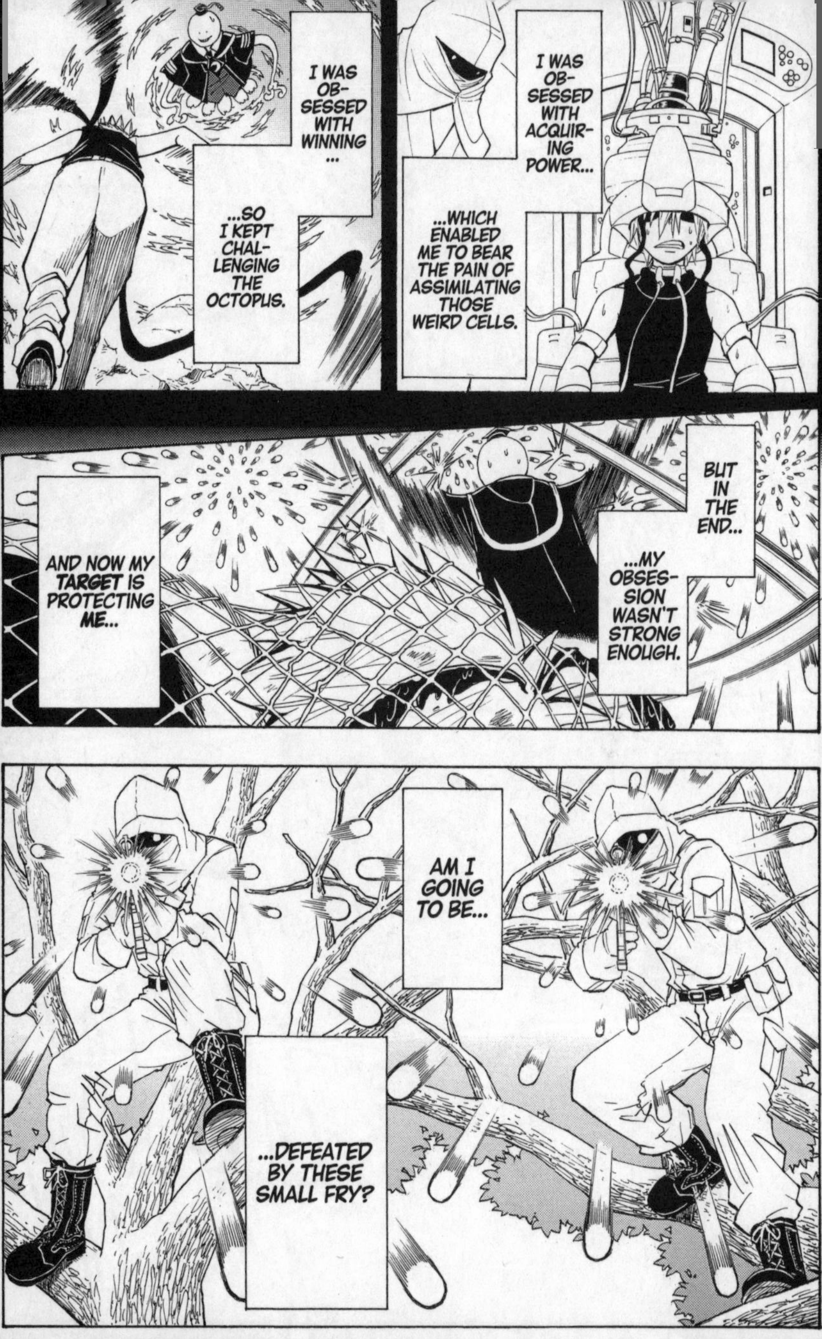
I WAS OBSESSED WITH ACQUIRING POWER...
...WHICH ENABLED ME TO BEAR THE PAIN OF ASSIMILATING THOSE WEIRD CELLS.
I WAS OBSESSED WITH WINNING...
...SO I KEPT CHALLENGING THE OCTOPUS.
BUT IN THE END...
...MY OBSESSION WASN'T STRONG ENOUGH.
AND NOW MY TARGET IS PROTECTING ME...
AM I GOING TO BE...
...DEFEATED BY THESE SMALL FRY?

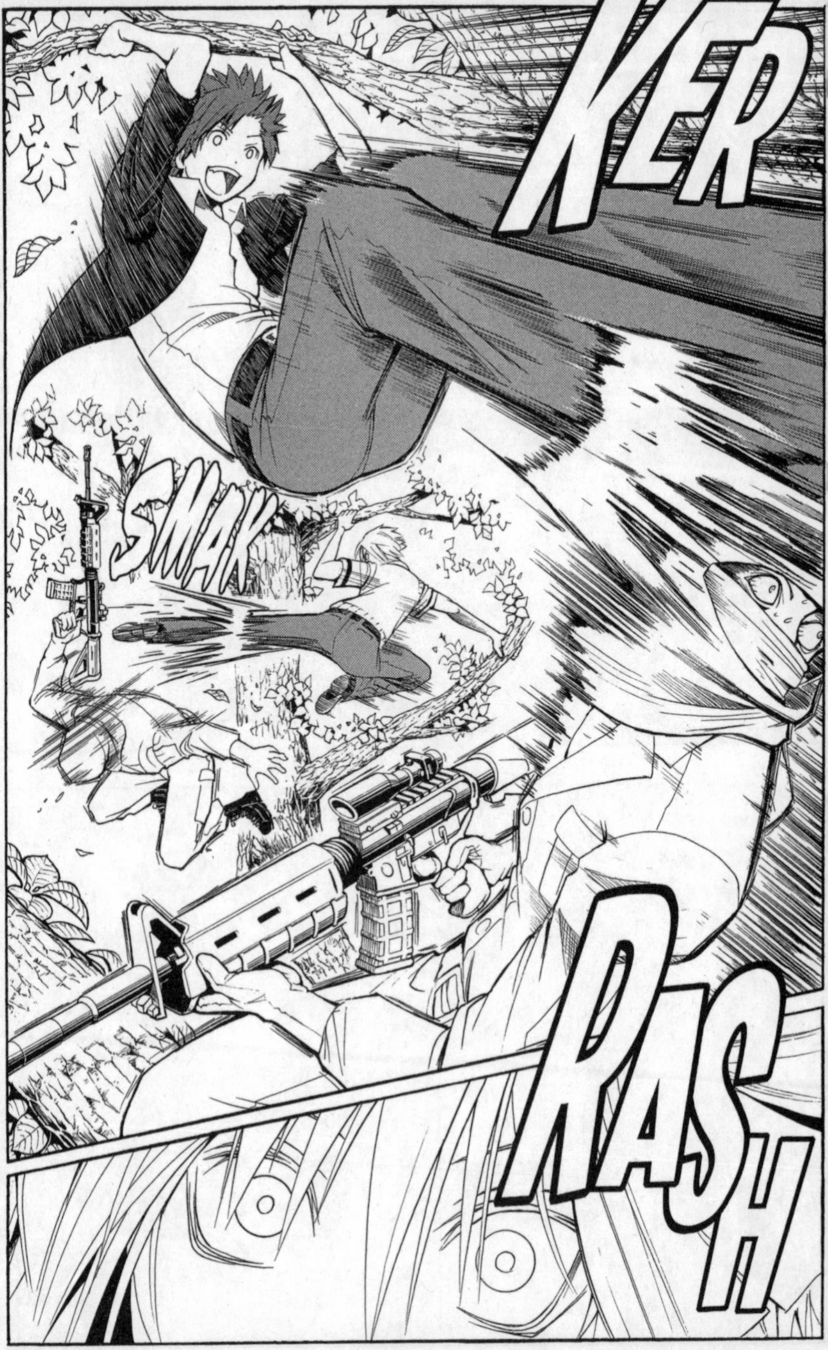
KER
SMAK
RASH

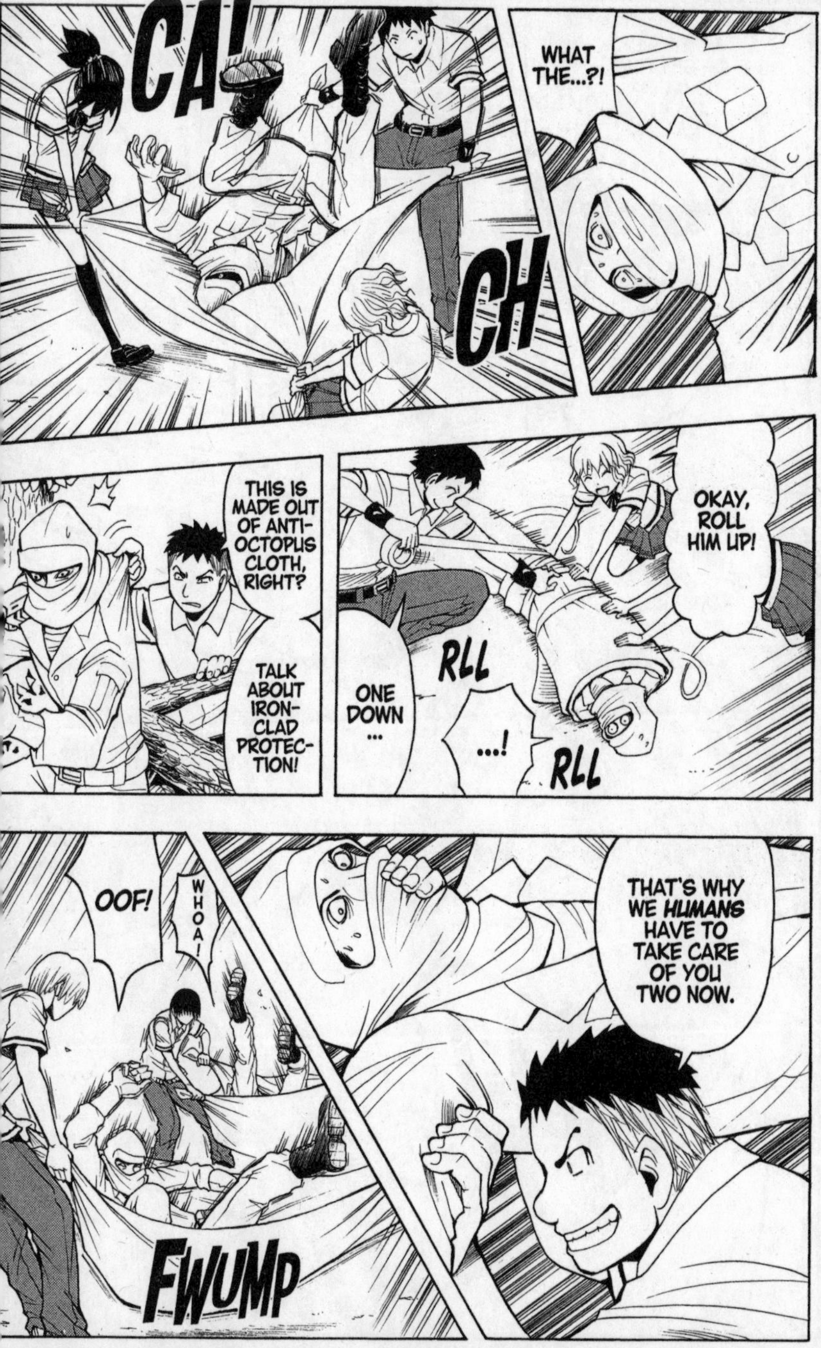
WHAT THE...?!
CAT
CH
OKAY, ROLL HIM UP!
RLL
ONE DOWN ...
...!
RLL
THIS IS MADE OUT OF ANTI-OCTOPUS CLOTH, RIGHT?
TALK ABOUT IRON-CLAD PROTECTION!
THAT'S WHY WE *HUMANS* HAVE TO TAKE CARE OF YOU TWO NOW.
WHOA!
OOF!
FWUMP

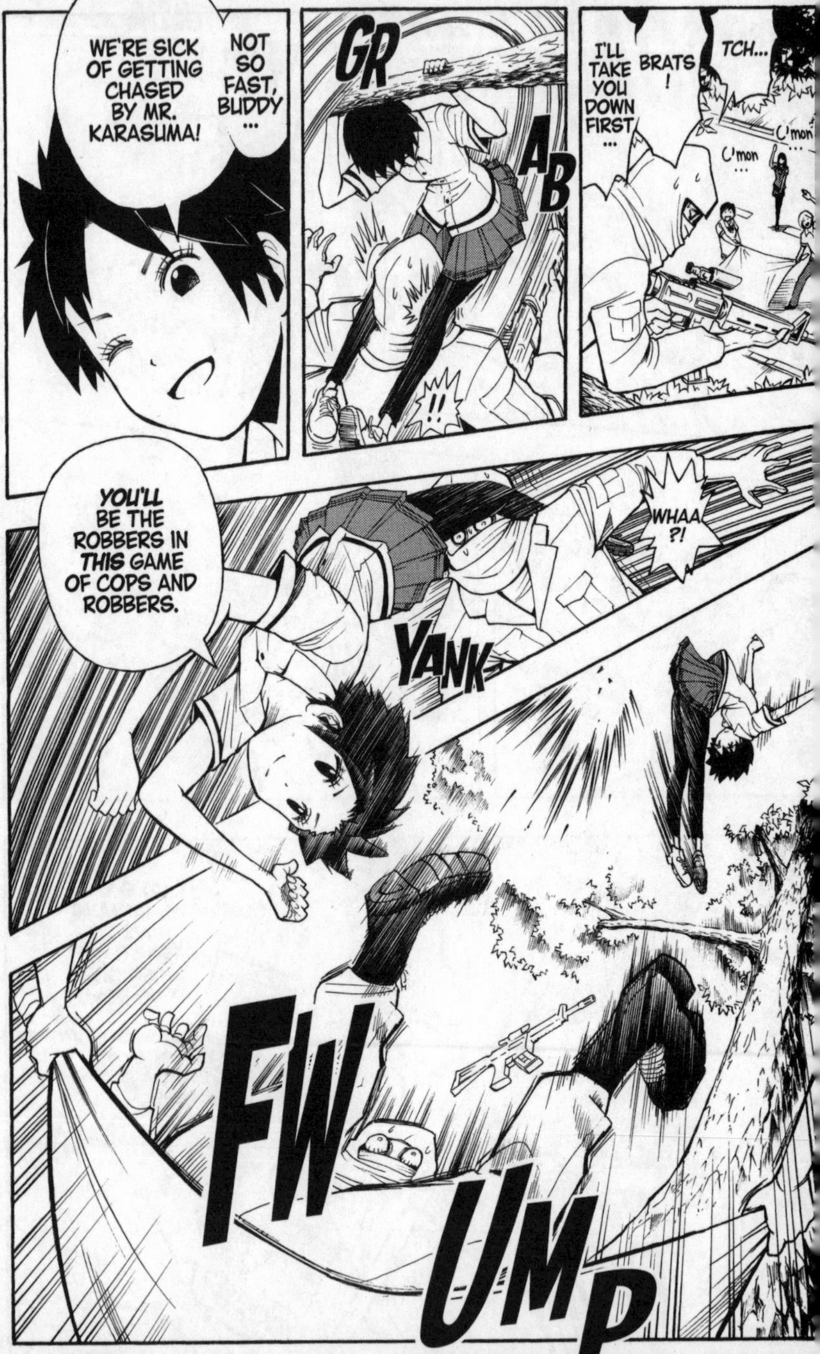
TCH...
BRATS!
I'LL TAKE YOU DOWN FIRST...
C'mon...
C'mon...
GRAB
!!
NOT SO FAST, BUDDY...
WE'RE SICK OF GETTING CHASED BY MR. KARASUMA!
WHAA?!
YANK
YOU'LL BE THE ROBBERS IN THIS GAME OF COPS AND ROBBERS.
FWUMP

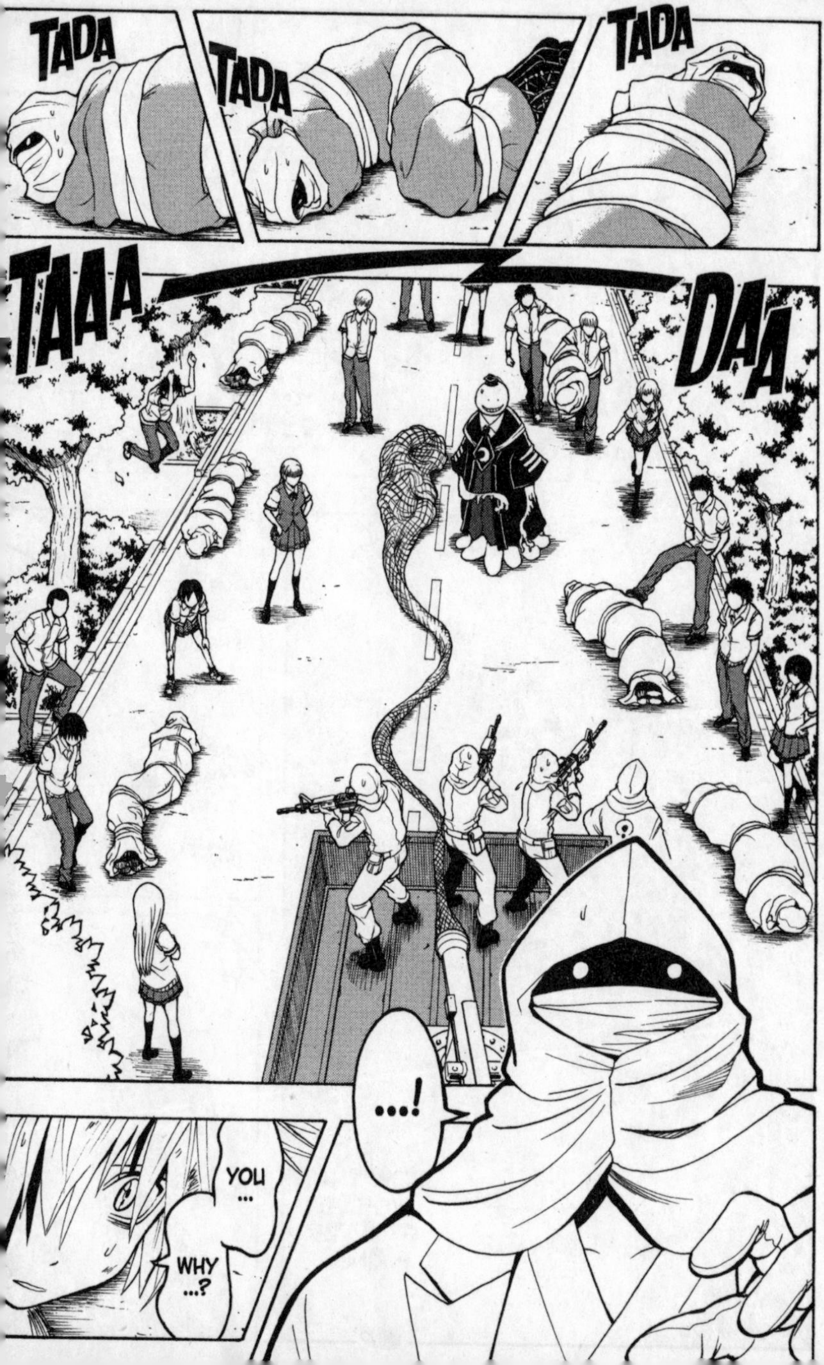
TADA
TADA
TADA
TAAA
DAA
...!
YOU ...
WHY ...?

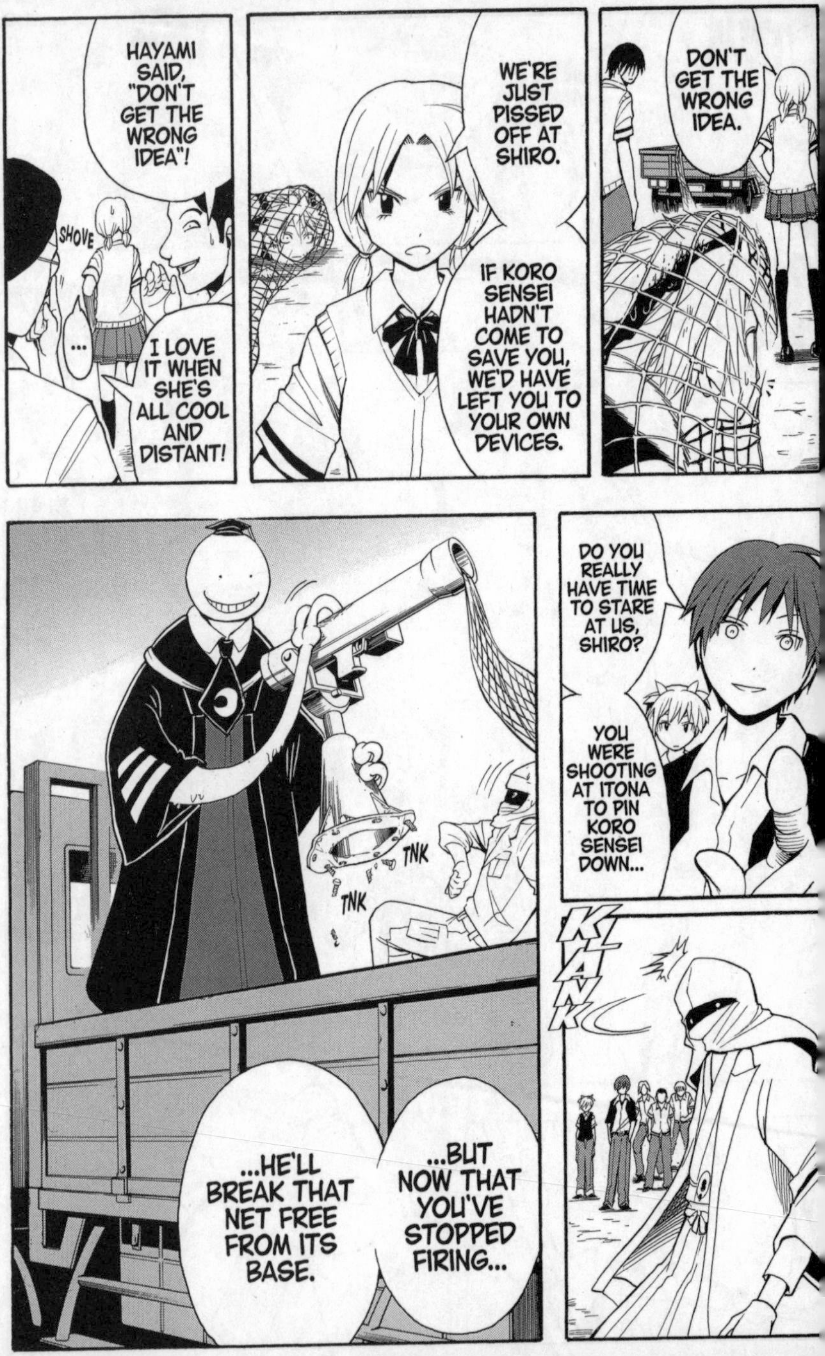
DON'T GET THE WRONG IDEA.
WE'RE JUST PISSED OFF AT SHIRO.
IF KORO SENSEI HADN'T COME TO SAVE YOU, WE'D HAVE LEFT YOU TO YOUR OWN DEVICES.
HAYAMI SAID, "DON'T GET THE WRONG IDEA"!
SHOVE
...
I LOVE IT WHEN SHE'S ALL COOL AND DISTANT!
DO YOU REALLY HAVE TIME TO STARE AT US, SHIRO?
YOU WERE SHOOTING AT ITONA TO PIN KORO SENSEI DOWN...
KLANK
TNK
TNK
...BUT NOW THAT YOU'VE STOPPED FIRING...
...HE'LL BREAK THAT NET FREE FROM ITS BASE.

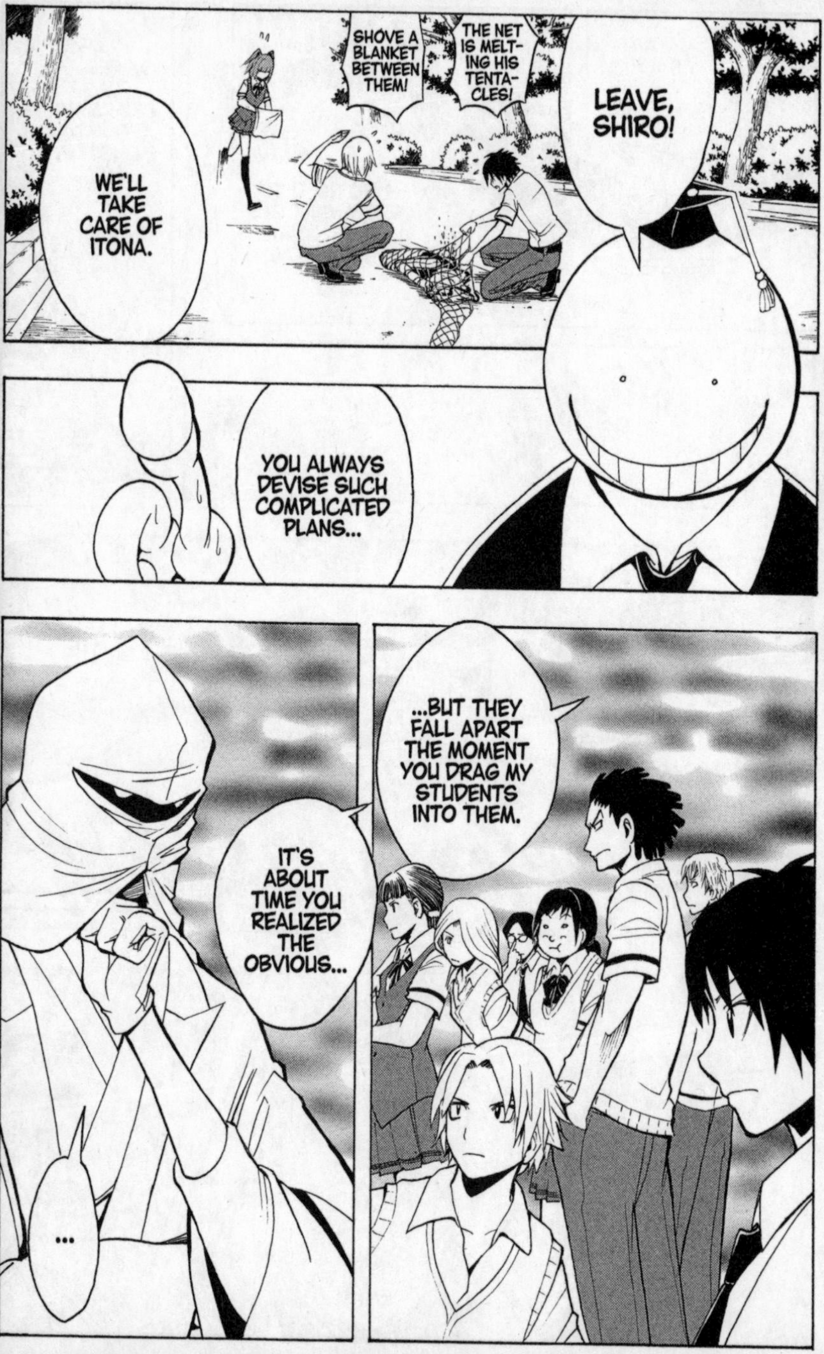
LEAVE, SHIRO!
THE NET IS MELTING HIS TENTACLES!
SHOVE A BLANKET BETWEEN THEM!
WE'LL TAKE CARE OF ITONA.
YOU ALWAYS DEVISE SUCH COMPLICATED PLANS...
...BUT THEY FALL APART THE MOMENT YOU DRAG MY STUDENTS INTO THEM.
IT'S ABOUT TIME YOU REALIZED THE OBVIOUS...
...

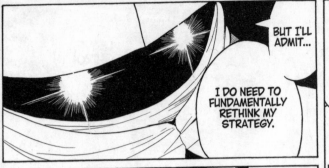

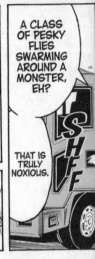

A CLASS OF PESKY FLIES SWARMING AROUND A MONSTER, EH?
SHFF
THAT IS TRULY NOXIOUS.
BUT I'LL ADMIT...
I DO NEED TO FUNDAMENTALLY RETHINK MY STRATEGY.
...
KEEP THE BOY.
HE ONLY HAS A COUPLE OF DAYS LEFT IN HIM ANYWAY.
ENJOY HIS COMPANY FOR THE TIME HE HAS LEFT!
VRMMMMM
FWUMP

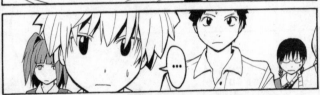

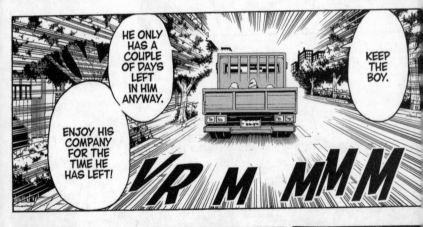

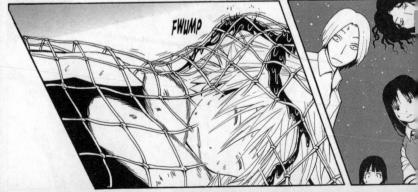

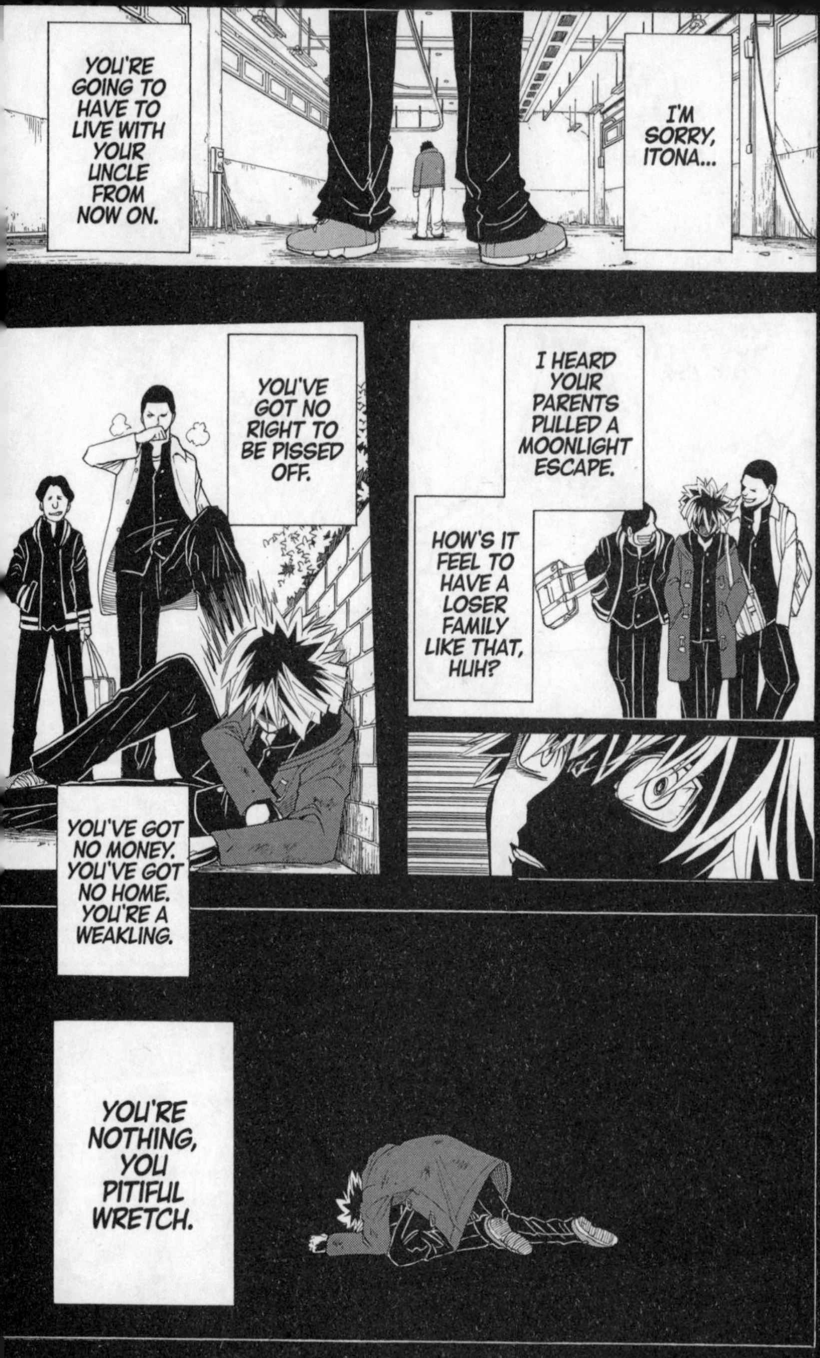
I'M SORRY, ITONA...
YOU'RE GOING TO HAVE TO LIVE WITH YOUR UNCLE FROM NOW ON.
I HEARD YOUR PARENTS PULLED A MOONLIGHT ESCAPE.
HOW'S IT FEEL TO HAVE A LOSER FAMILY LIKE THAT, HUH?
YOU'VE GOT NO RIGHT TO BE PISSED OFF.
YOU'VE GOT NO MONEY. YOU'VE GOT NO HOME. YOU'RE A WEAKLING.
YOU'RE NOTHING, YOU PITIFUL WRETCH.

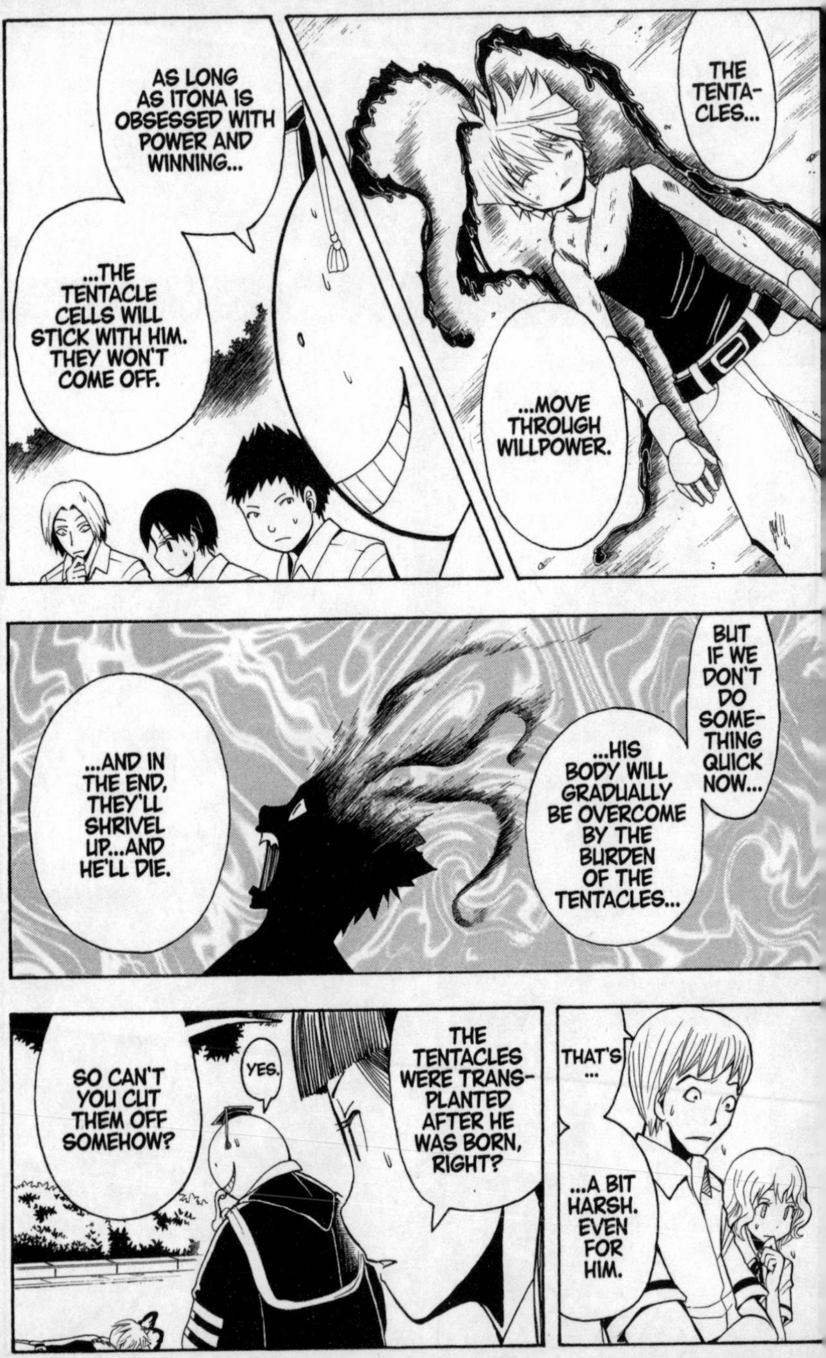
THE TENTACLES...
...MOVE THROUGH WILLPOWER.
AS LONG AS ITONA IS OBSESSED WITH POWER AND WINNING...
...THE TENTACLE CELLS WILL STICK WITH HIM. THEY WON'T COME OFF.
BUT IF WE DON'T DO SOMETHING QUICK NOW...
...HIS BODY WILL GRADUALLY BE OVERCOME BY THE BURDEN OF THE TENTACLES...
...AND IN THE END, THEY'LL SHRIVEL UP...AND HE'LL DIE.
THAT'S...
...A BIT HARSH. EVEN FOR HIM.
THE TENTACLES WERE TRANSPLANTED AFTER HE WAS BORN, RIGHT?
YES.
SO CAN'T YOU CUT THEM OFF SOMEHOW?

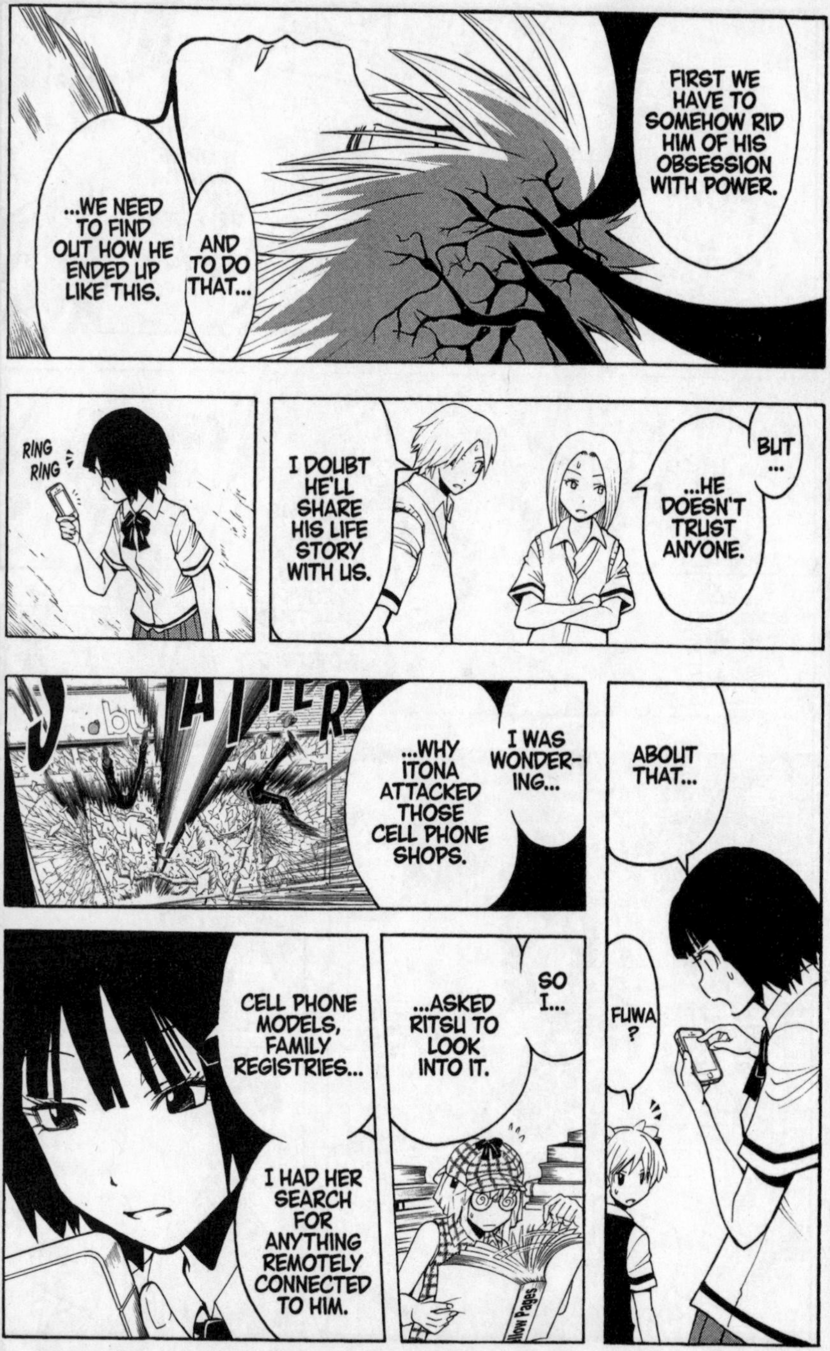
FIRST WE HAVE TO SOMEHOW RID HIM OF HIS OBSESSION WITH POWER.
AND TO DO THAT...
...WE NEED TO FIND OUT HOW HE ENDED UP LIKE THIS.
BUT...
...HE DOESN'T TRUST ANYONE.
I DOUBT HE'LL SHARE HIS LIFE STORY WITH US.
RING RING
ABOUT THAT...
FUWA?
I WAS WONDERING...
...WHY ITONA ATTACKED THOSE CELL PHONE SHOPS.
SO I...
...ASKED RITSU TO LOOK INTO IT.
CELL PHONE MODELS, FAMILY REGISTRIES...
I HAD HER SEARCH FOR ANYTHING REMOTELY CONNECTED TO HIM.

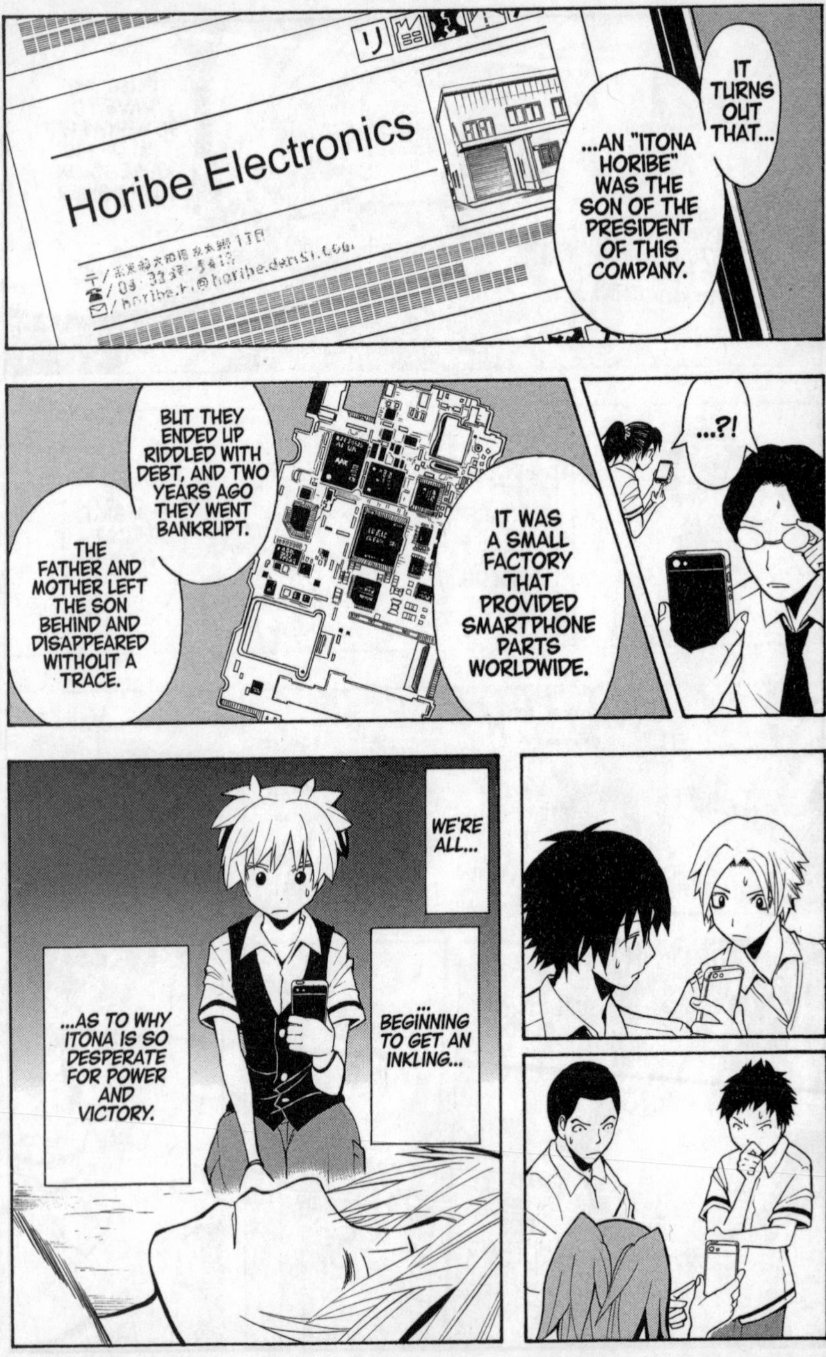
Horibe Electronics
IT TURNS OUT THAT...
...AN "ITONA HORIBE" WAS THE SON OF THE PRESIDENT OF THIS COMPANY.
...?!
IT WAS A SMALL FACTORY THAT PROVIDED SMARTPHONE PARTS WORLDWIDE.
BUT THEY ENDED UP RIDDLED WITH DEBT, AND TWO YEARS AGO THEY WENT BANKRUPT.
THE FATHER AND MOTHER LEFT THE SON BEHIND AND DISAPPEARED WITHOUT A TRACE.
WE'RE ALL...
...BEGINNING TO GET AN INKLING...
...AS TO WHY ITONA IS SO DESPERATE FOR POWER AND VICTORY.

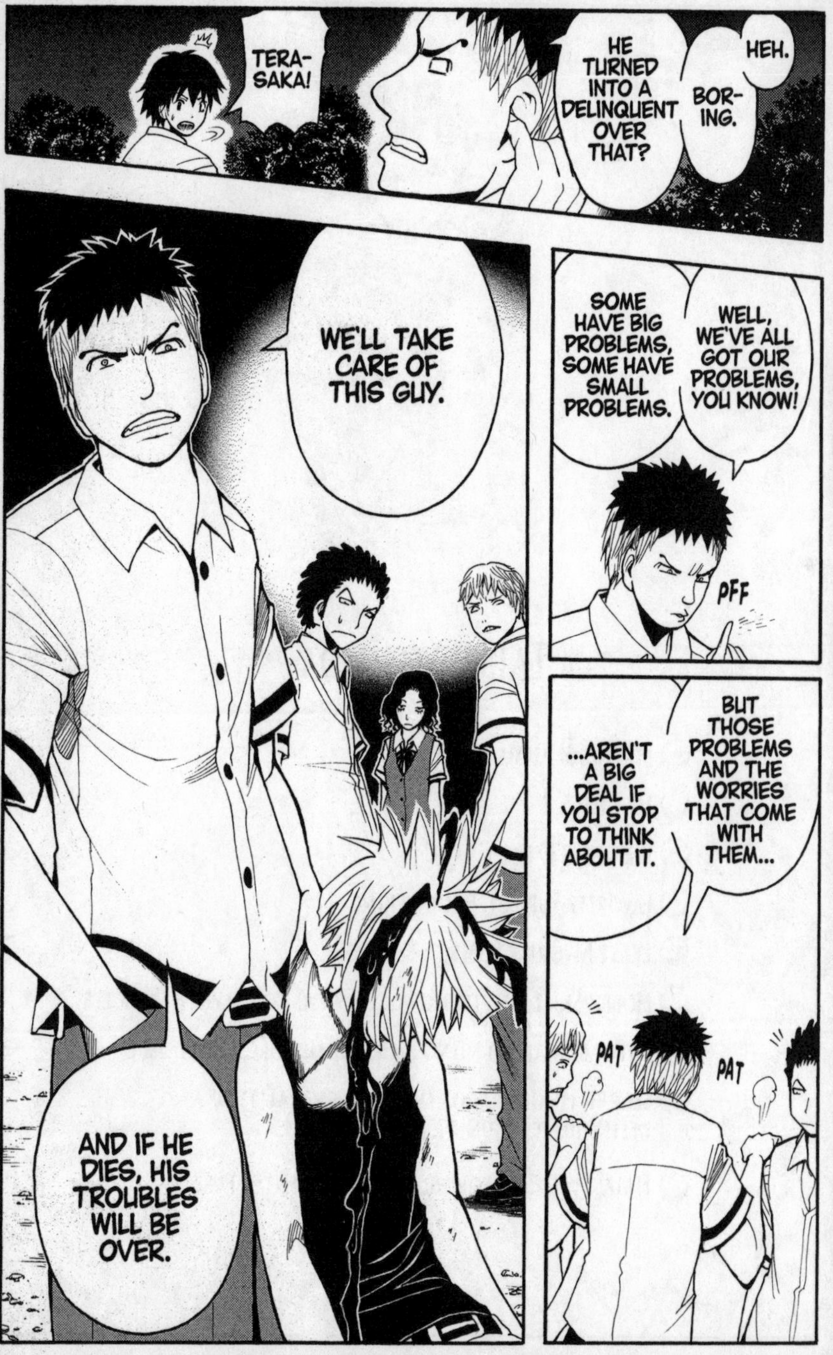
HEH.
BOR-ING.
HE TURNED INTO A DELINQUENT OVER THAT?
TERA-SAKA!
WELL, WE'VE ALL GOT OUR PROBLEMS, YOU KNOW!
SOME HAVE BIG PROBLEMS, SOME HAVE SMALL PROBLEMS.
PFF
BUT THOSE PROBLEMS AND THE WORRIES THAT COME WITH THEM...
...AREN'T A BIG DEAL IF YOU STOP TO THINK ABOUT IT.
PAT
PAT
WE'LL TAKE CARE OF THIS GUY.
AND IF HE DIES, HIS TROUBLES WILL BE OVER.

E-26 TAISEI YOSHIDA

- 🙂 BIRTHDAY: AUGUST 19
- 🙂 HEIGHT: 5' 8"
- 🙂 WEIGHT: 139 LBS.
- 🙂 FAVORITE SUBJECT: ENGINEERING
- 🙂 LEAST FAVORITE SUBJECT: ENGLISH
- 🙂 HOBBY/SKILL: ANYTHING MECHANICAL TO DO WITH VEHICLES
- 🙂 FUTURE GOAL: TO BRING BACK THE MOTORCYCLE BOOM
- 🙂 SECRET: HE ONLY TOOK ON THE PERSONALITY OF A DELINQUENT IN JUNIOR HIGH SCHOOL
- 🙂 HAIRSTYLE PLAN FOR HIGH SCHOOL: CENTER PART

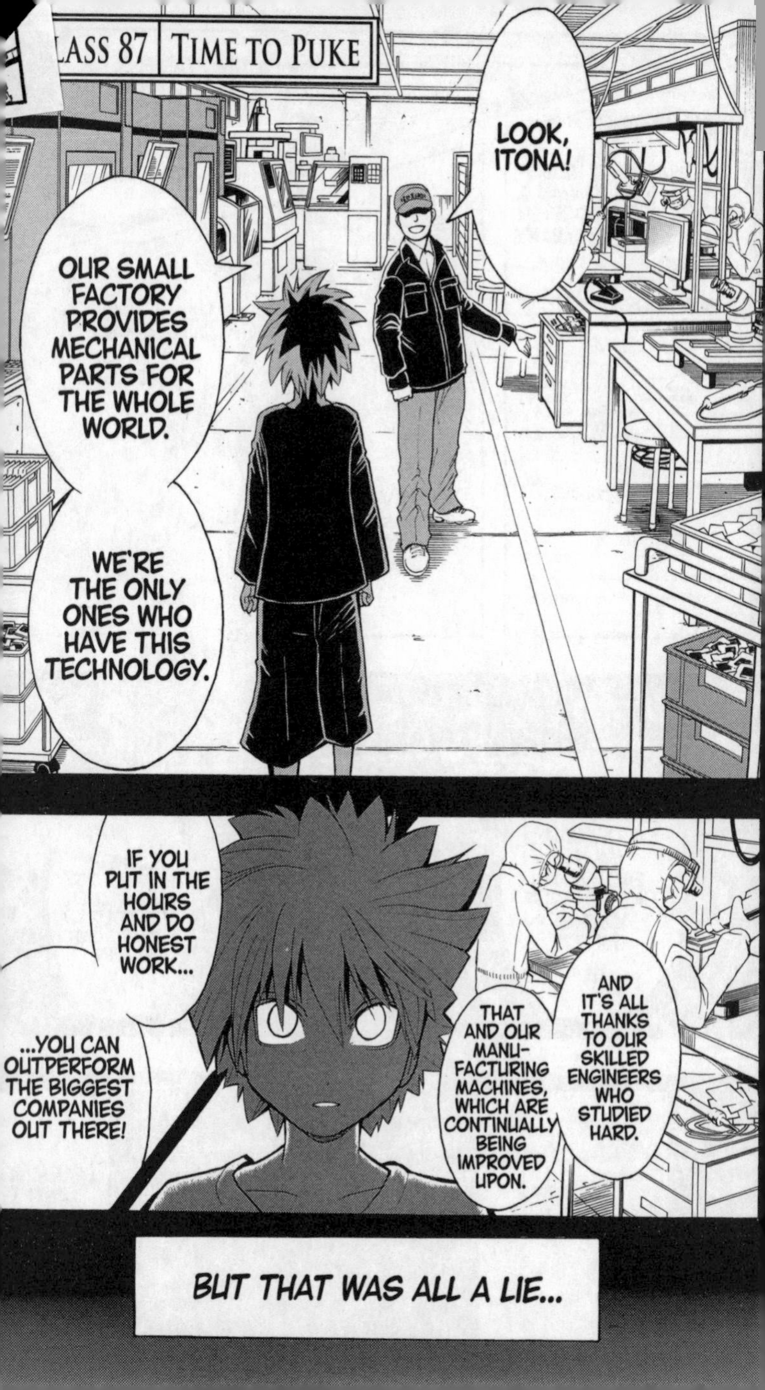
CLASS 87 TIME TO PUKE
LOOK, ITONA!
OUR SMALL FACTORY PROVIDES MECHANICAL PARTS FOR THE WHOLE WORLD.
WE'RE THE ONLY ONES WHO HAVE THIS TECHNOLOGY.
AND IT'S ALL THANKS TO OUR SKILLED ENGINEERS WHO STUDIED HARD.
THAT AND OUR MANU-FACTURING MACHINES, WHICH ARE CONTINUALLY BEING IMPROVED UPON.
IF YOU PUT IN THE HOURS AND DO HONEST WORK...
...YOU CAN OUTPERFORM THE BIGGEST COMPANIES OUT THERE!
BUT THAT WAS ALL A LIE...

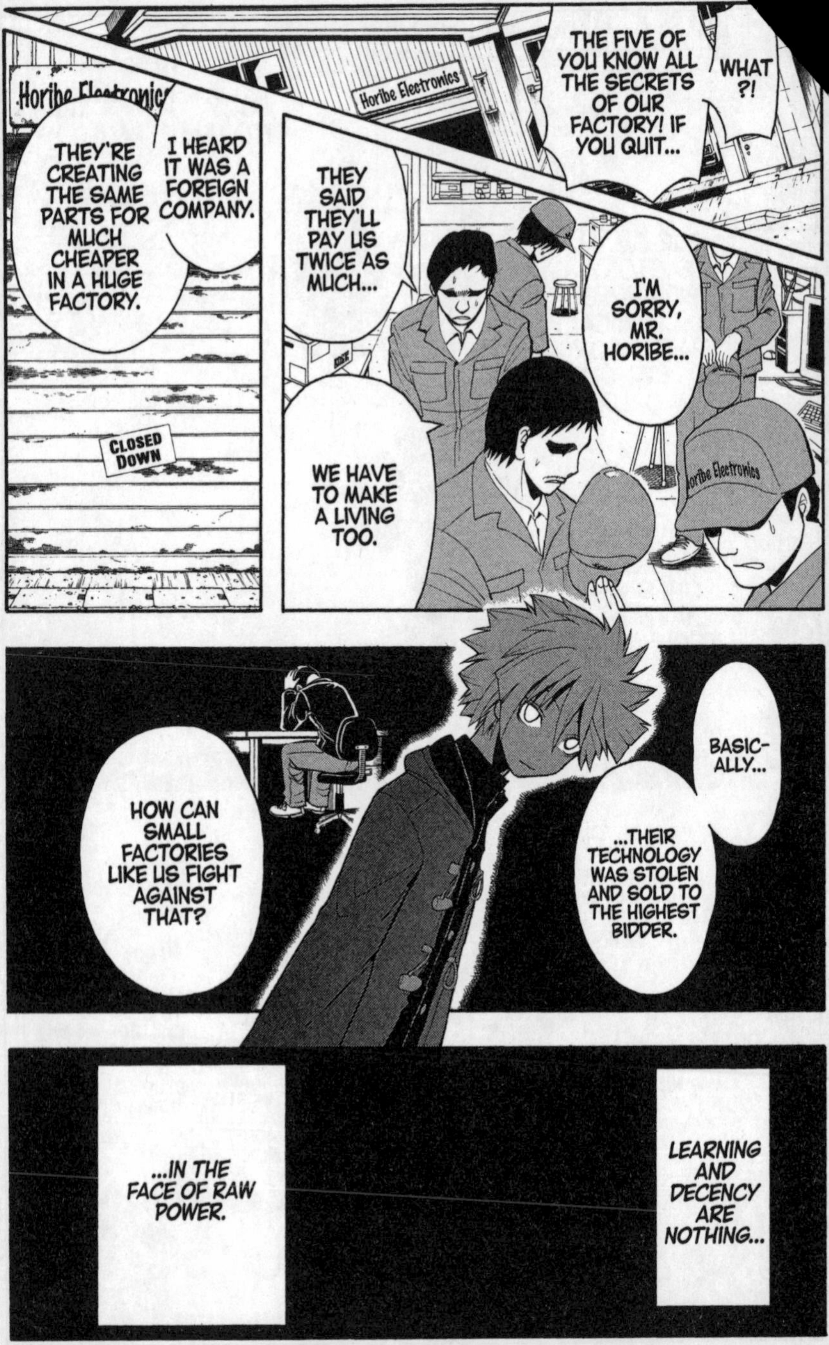

WHAT?!
THE FIVE OF YOU KNOW ALL THE SECRETS OF OUR FACTORY! IF YOU QUIT...
Horibe Electronics
I'M SORRY, MR. HORIBE...
THEY SAID THEY'LL PAY US TWICE AS MUCH...
WE HAVE TO MAKE A LIVING TOO.
Horibe Electronics
I HEARD IT WAS A FOREIGN COMPANY.
THEY'RE CREATING THE SAME PARTS FOR MUCH CHEAPER IN A HUGE FACTORY.
CLOSED DOWN
BASIC-ALLY...
...THEIR TECHNOLOGY WAS STOLEN AND SOLD TO THE HIGHEST BIDDER.
HOW CAN SMALL FACTORIES LIKE US FIGHT AGAINST THAT?
LEARNING AND DECENCY ARE NOTHING...
...IN THE FACE OF RAW POWER.

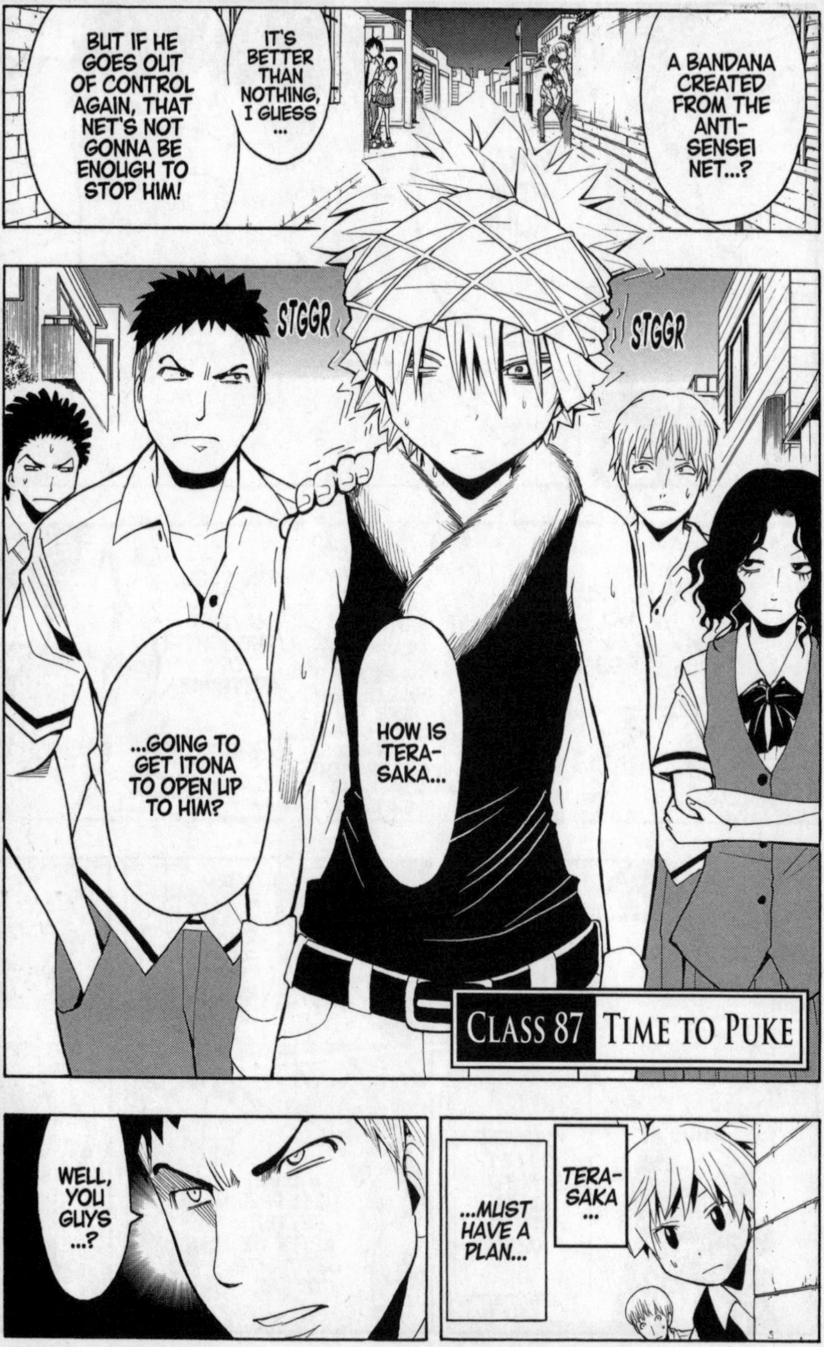
A BANDANA CREATED FROM THE ANTI-SENSEI NET...?
IT'S BETTER THAN NOTHING, I GUESS ...
BUT IF HE GOES OUT OF CONTROL AGAIN, THAT NET'S NOT GONNA BE ENOUGH TO STOP HIM!
STGGR
STGGR
HOW IS TERA-SAKA...
...GOING TO GET ITONA TO OPEN UP TO HIM?
CLASS 87 TIME TO PUKE
TERA-SAKA ...
...MUST HAVE A PLAN...
WELL, YOU GUYS ...?

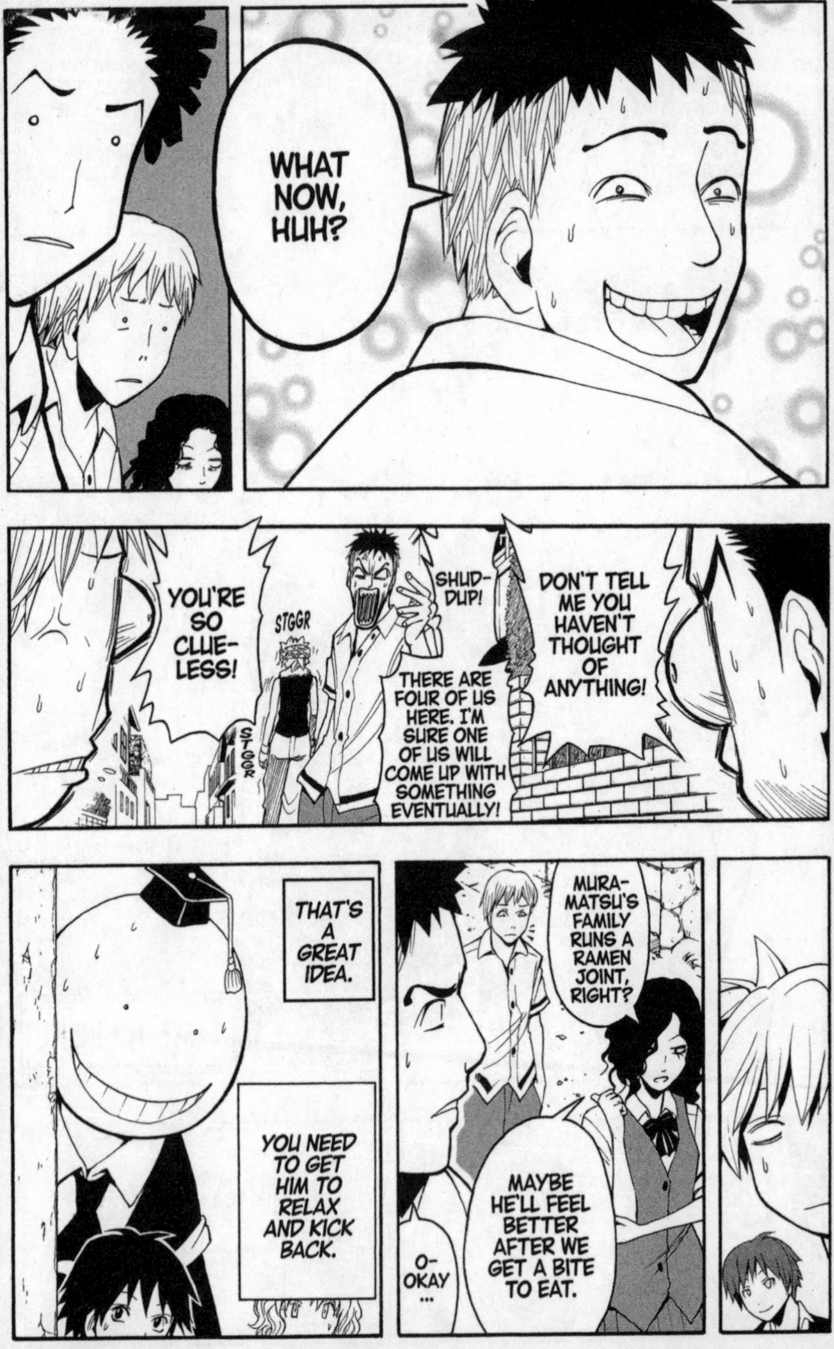
WHAT NOW, HUH?
DON'T TELL ME YOU HAVEN'T THOUGHT OF ANYTHING!
SHUD-DUP!
THERE ARE FOUR OF US HERE. I'M SURE ONE OF US WILL COME UP WITH SOMETHING EVENTUALLY!
YOU'RE SO CLUE-LESS!
STGGR
STGGR
MURA-MATSU'S FAMILY RUNS A RAMEN JOINT, RIGHT?
MAYBE HE'LL FEEL BETTER AFTER WE GET A BITE TO EAT.
O-OKAY...
THAT'S A GREAT IDEA.
YOU NEED TO GET HIM TO RELAX AND KICK BACK.

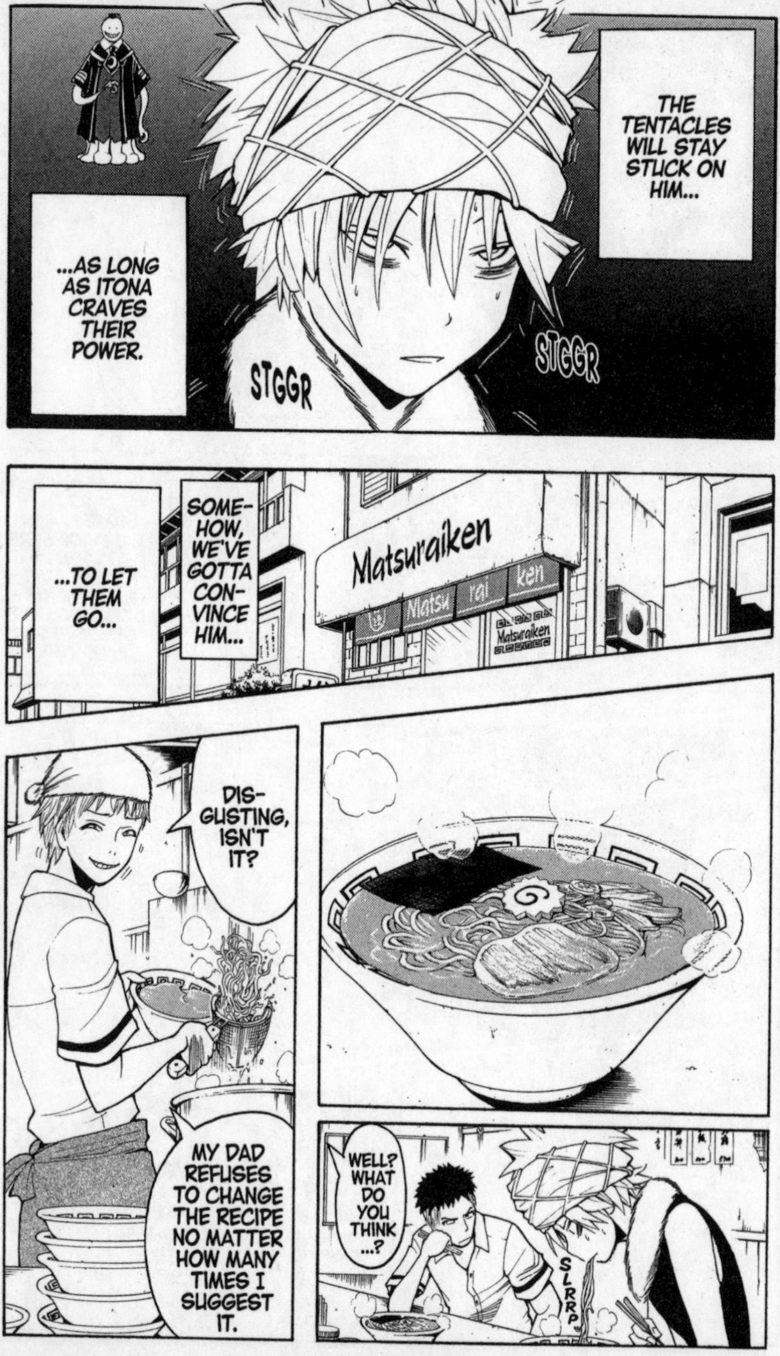
THE TENTACLES WILL STAY STUCK ON HIM...
...AS LONG AS ITONA CRAVES THEIR POWER.
STGGR
STGGR
SOME-HOW, WE'VE GOTTA CON-VINCE HIM...
...TO LET THEM GO...
Matsuraiken
Matsu rai ken
Matsuraiken
WELL? WHAT DO YOU THINK...?
SLRRP
DIS-GUSTING, ISN'T IT?
MY DAD REFUSES TO CHANGE THE RECIPE NO MATTER HOW MANY TIMES I SUGGEST IT.

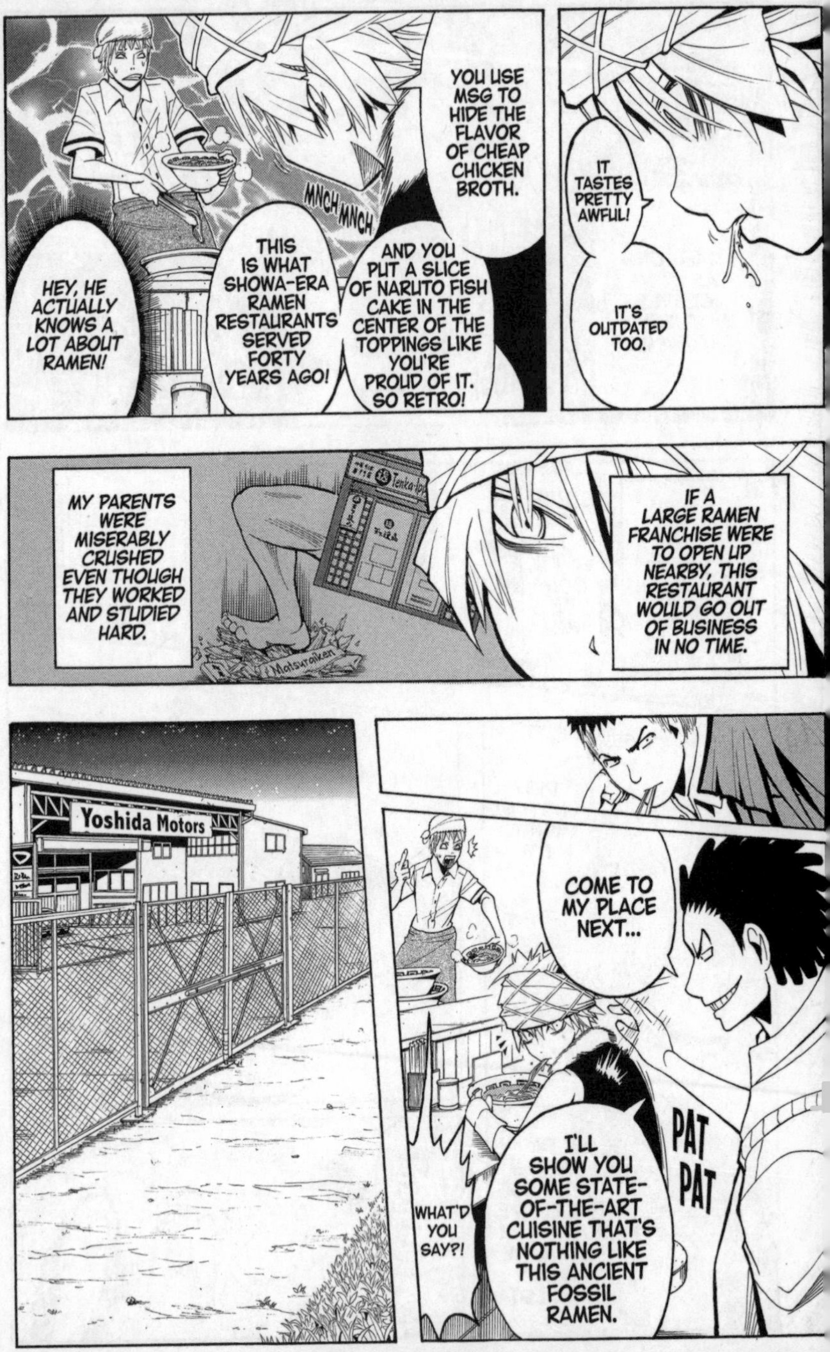

IT TASTES PRETTY AWFUL!
IT'S OUTDATED TOO.
YOU USE MSG TO HIDE THE FLAVOR OF CHEAP CHICKEN BROTH.
MNCH MNCH
AND YOU PUT A SLICE OF NARUTO FISH CAKE IN THE CENTER OF THE TOPPINGS LIKE YOU'RE PROUD OF IT. SO RETRO!
THIS IS WHAT SHOWA-ERA RAMEN RESTAURANTS SERVED FORTY YEARS AGO!
HEY, HE ACTUALLY KNOWS A LOT ABOUT RAMEN!
IF A LARGE RAMEN FRANCHISE WERE TO OPEN UP NEARBY, THIS RESTAURANT WOULD GO OUT OF BUSINESS IN NO TIME.
MY PARENTS WERE MISERABLY CRUSHED EVEN THOUGH THEY WORKED AND STUDIED HARD.
Matsuraiken
COME TO MY PLACE NEXT...
PAT PAT
I'LL SHOW YOU SOME STATE-OF-THE-ART CUISINE THAT'S NOTHING LIKE THIS ANCIENT FOSSIL RAMEN.
WHAT'D YOU SAY?!
Yoshida Motors

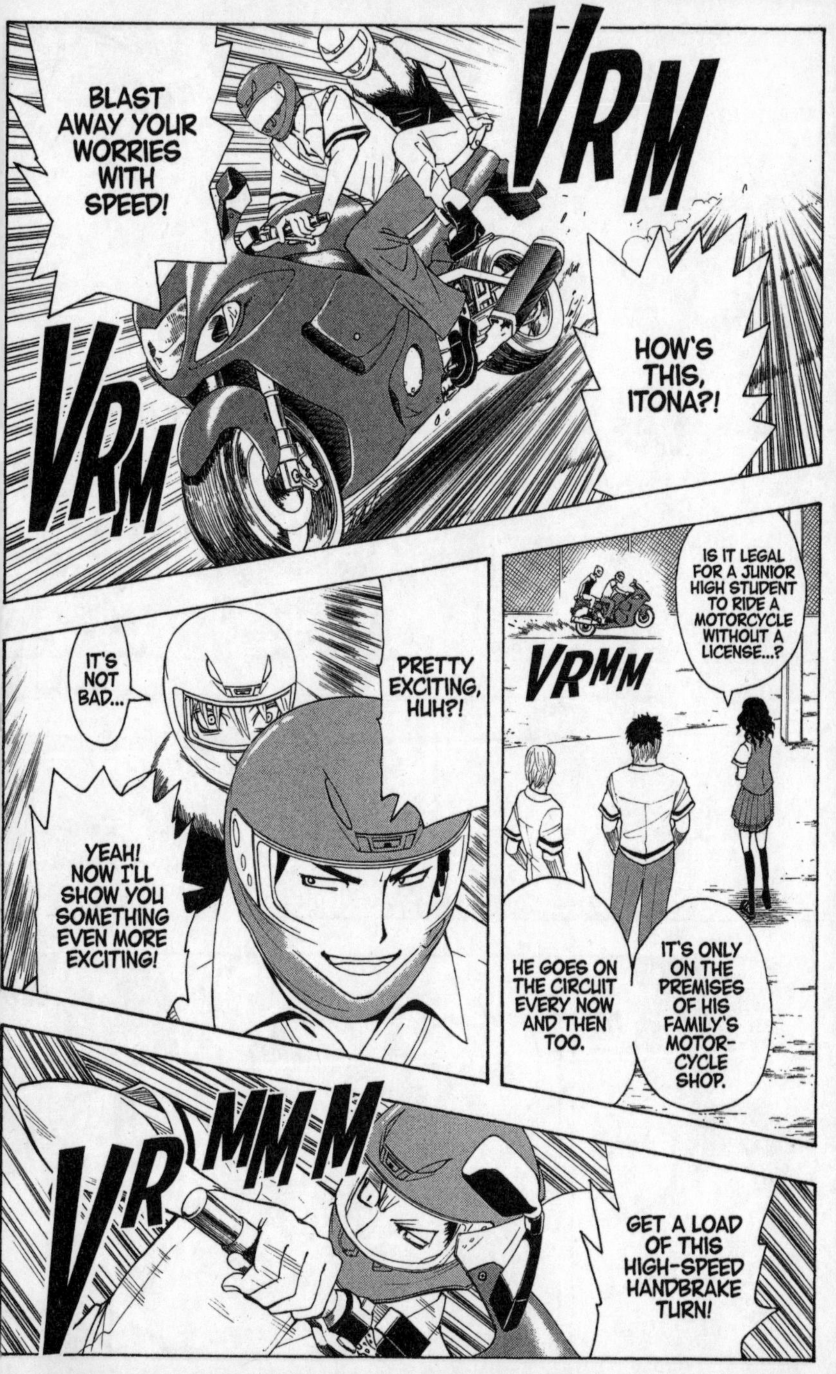
VRM
BLAST AWAY YOUR WORRIES WITH SPEED!
HOW'S THIS, ITONA?!
VRM
IS IT LEGAL FOR A JUNIOR HIGH STUDENT TO RIDE A MOTORCYCLE WITHOUT A LICENSE...?
VRMM
IT'S ONLY ON THE PREMISES OF HIS FAMILY'S MOTOR-CYCLE SHOP.
HE GOES ON THE CIRCUIT EVERY NOW AND THEN TOO.
PRETTY EXCITING, HUH?!
IT'S NOT BAD...
YEAH! NOW I'LL SHOW YOU SOMETHING EVEN MORE EXCITING!
VRMMMM
GET A LOAD OF THIS HIGH-SPEED HANDBRAKE TURN!

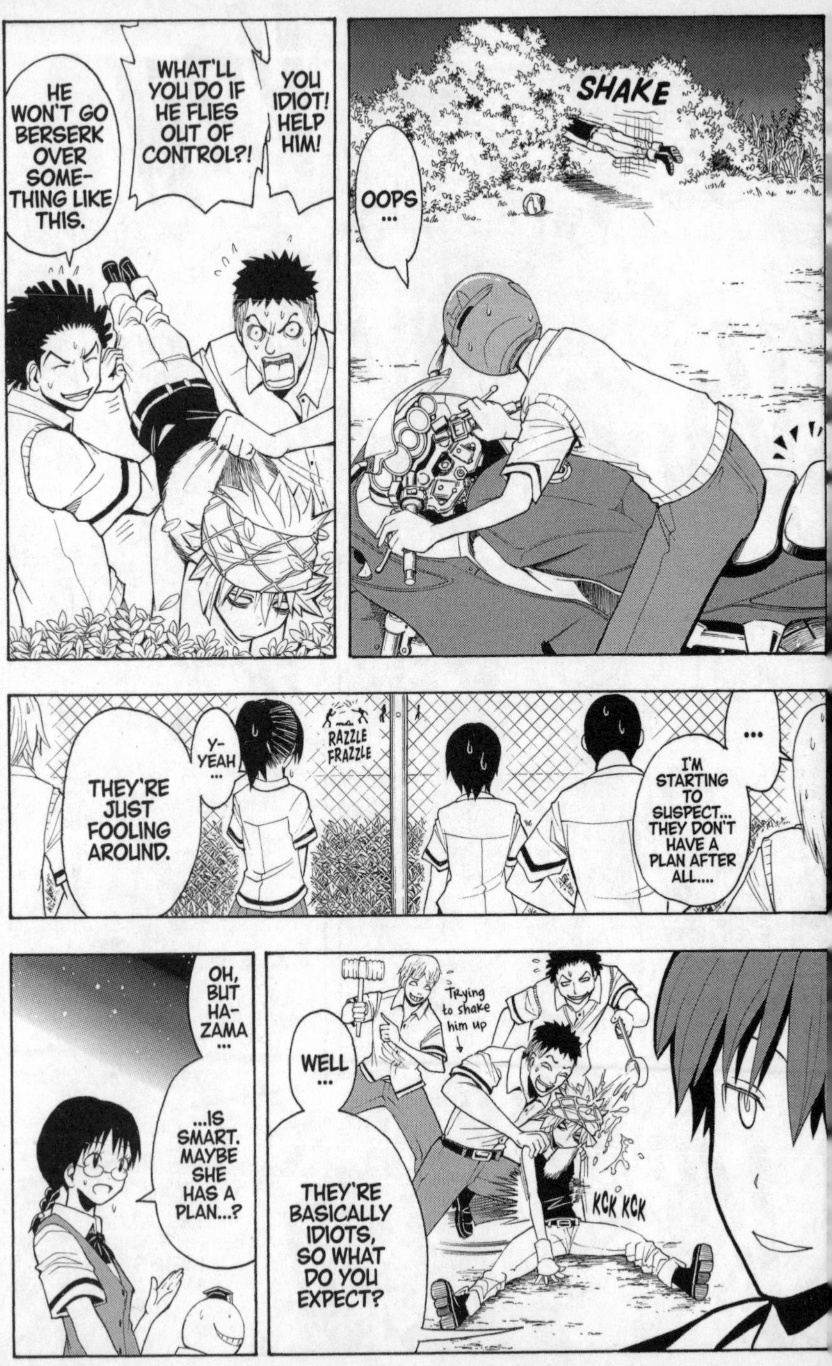
SHAKE
OOPS...
YOU IDIOT! HELP HIM!
WHAT'LL YOU DO IF HE FLIES OUT OF CONTROL?!
HE WON'T GO BERSERK OVER SOMETHING LIKE THIS.
...
I'M STARTING TO SUSPECT... THEY DON'T HAVE A PLAN AFTER ALL....
RAZZLE FRAZZLE
Y-YEAH...
THEY'RE JUST FOOLING AROUND.
Trying to shake him up
WELL...
THEY'RE BASICALLY IDIOTS, SO WHAT DO YOU EXPECT?
KCK KCK
OH, BUT HAZAMA...
...IS SMART. MAYBE SHE HAS A PLAN...?

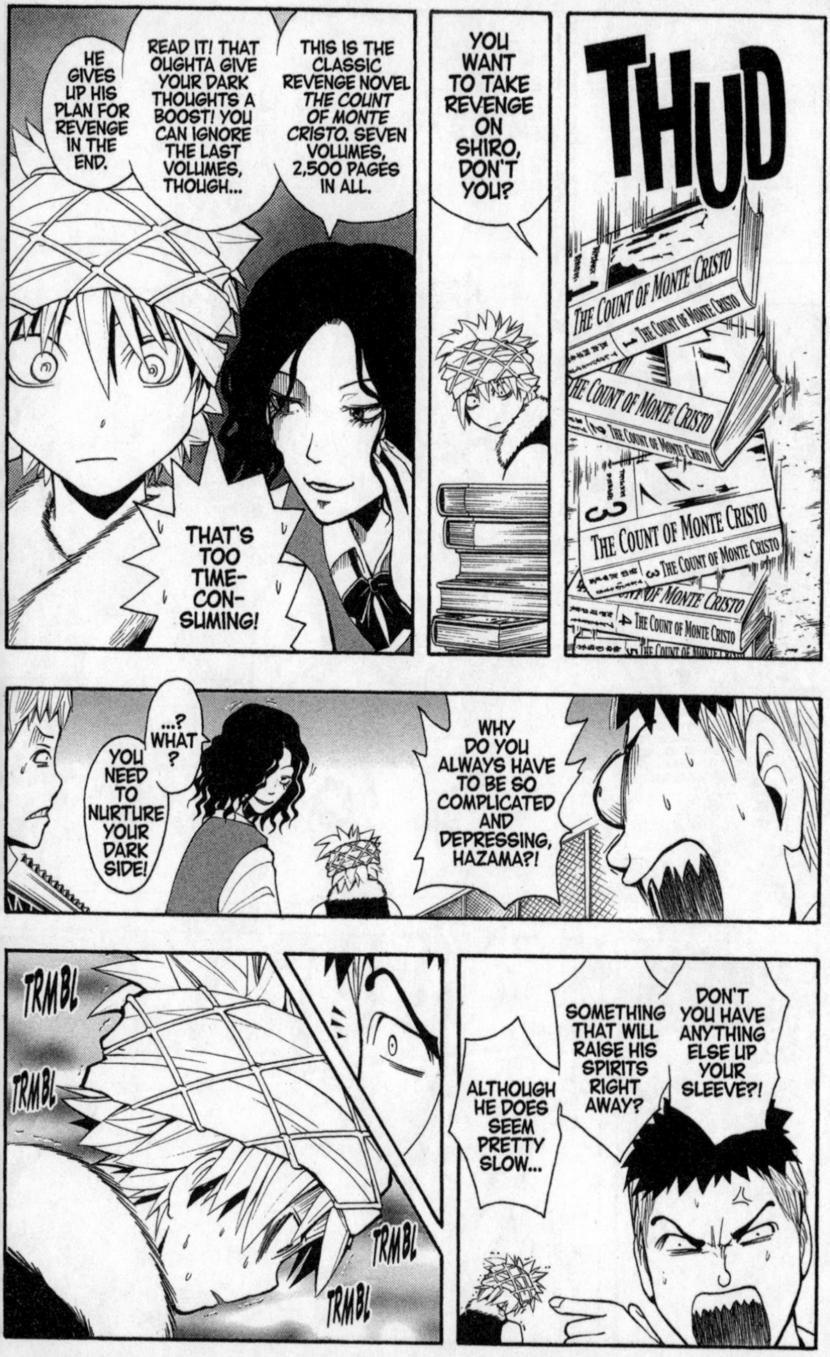
THUD
THE COUNT OF MONTE CRISTO
1 THE COUNT OF MONTE CRISTO
THE COUNT OF MONTE CRISTO
THE COUNT OF MONTE CRISTO
THE COUNT OF MONTE CRISTO
3 THE COUNT OF MONTE CRISTO
OF MONTE CRISTO
4 THE COUNT OF MONTE CRISTO
YOU WANT TO TAKE REVENGE ON SHIRO, DON'T YOU?
THIS IS THE CLASSIC REVENGE NOVEL *THE COUNT OF MONTE CRISTO*. SEVEN VOLUMES, 2,500 PAGES IN ALL.
READ IT! THAT OUGHTA GIVE YOUR DARK THOUGHTS A BOOST! YOU CAN IGNORE THE LAST VOLUMES, THOUGH...
HE GIVES UP HIS PLAN FOR REVENGE IN THE END.
THAT'S TOO TIME-CONSUMING!
WHY DO YOU ALWAYS HAVE TO BE SO COMPLICATED AND DEPRESSING, HAZAMA?!
...? WHAT?
YOU NEED TO NURTURE YOUR DARK SIDE!
DON'T YOU HAVE ANYTHING ELSE UP YOUR SLEEVE?!
SOMETHING THAT WILL RAISE HIS SPIRITS RIGHT AWAY?
ALTHOUGH HE DOES SEEM PRETTY SLOW...
TRMBL
TRMBL
TRMBL
TRMBL

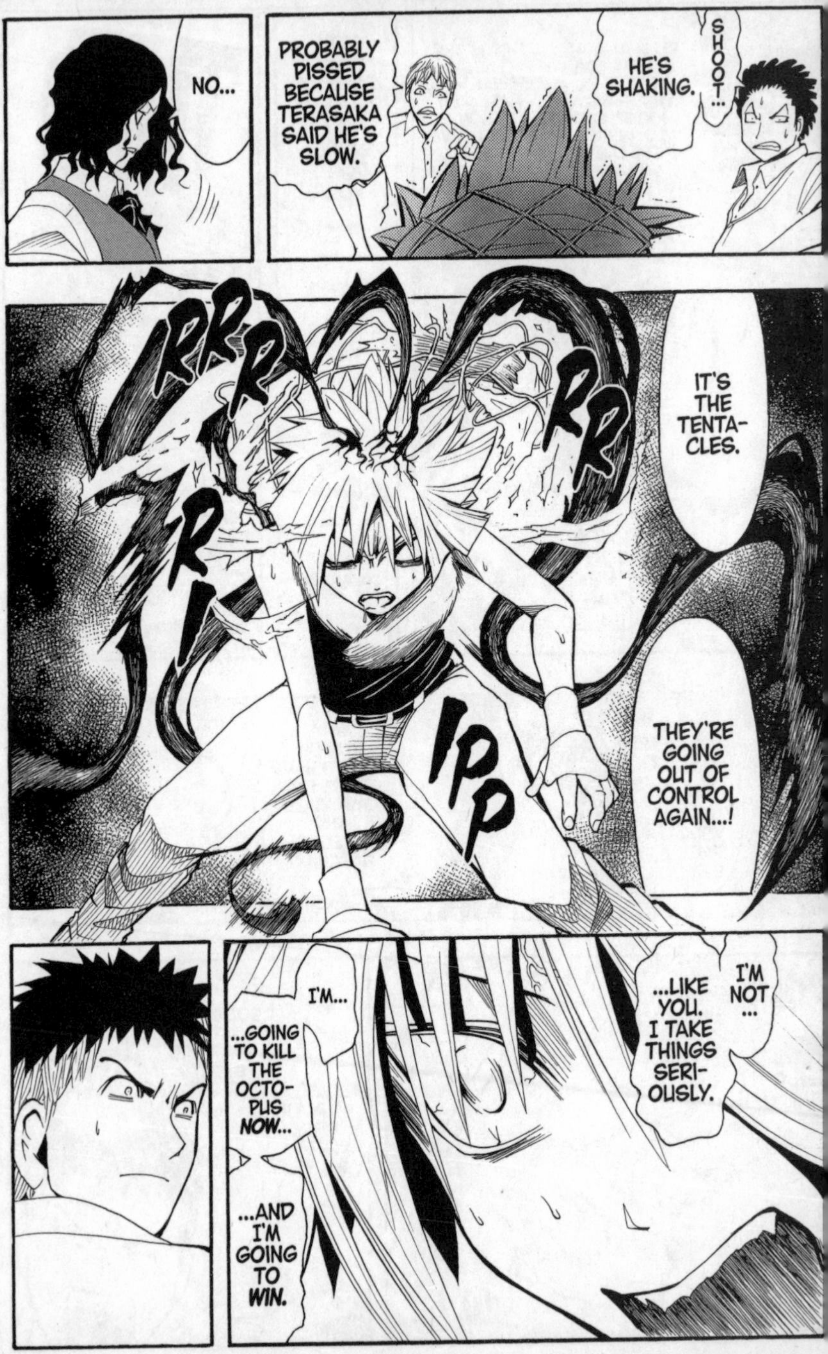
SHOOT...
HE'S SHAKING.
PROBABLY PISSED BECAUSE TERASAKA SAID HE'S SLOW.
NO...
IT'S THE TENTA-CLES.
THEY'RE GOING OUT OF CONTROL AGAIN...!
RRRRRIPP
I'M NOT...
...LIKE YOU. I TAKE THINGS SERI-OUSLY.
I'M...
...GOING TO KILL THE OCTO-PUS *NOW*...
...AND I'M GOING TO *WIN.*

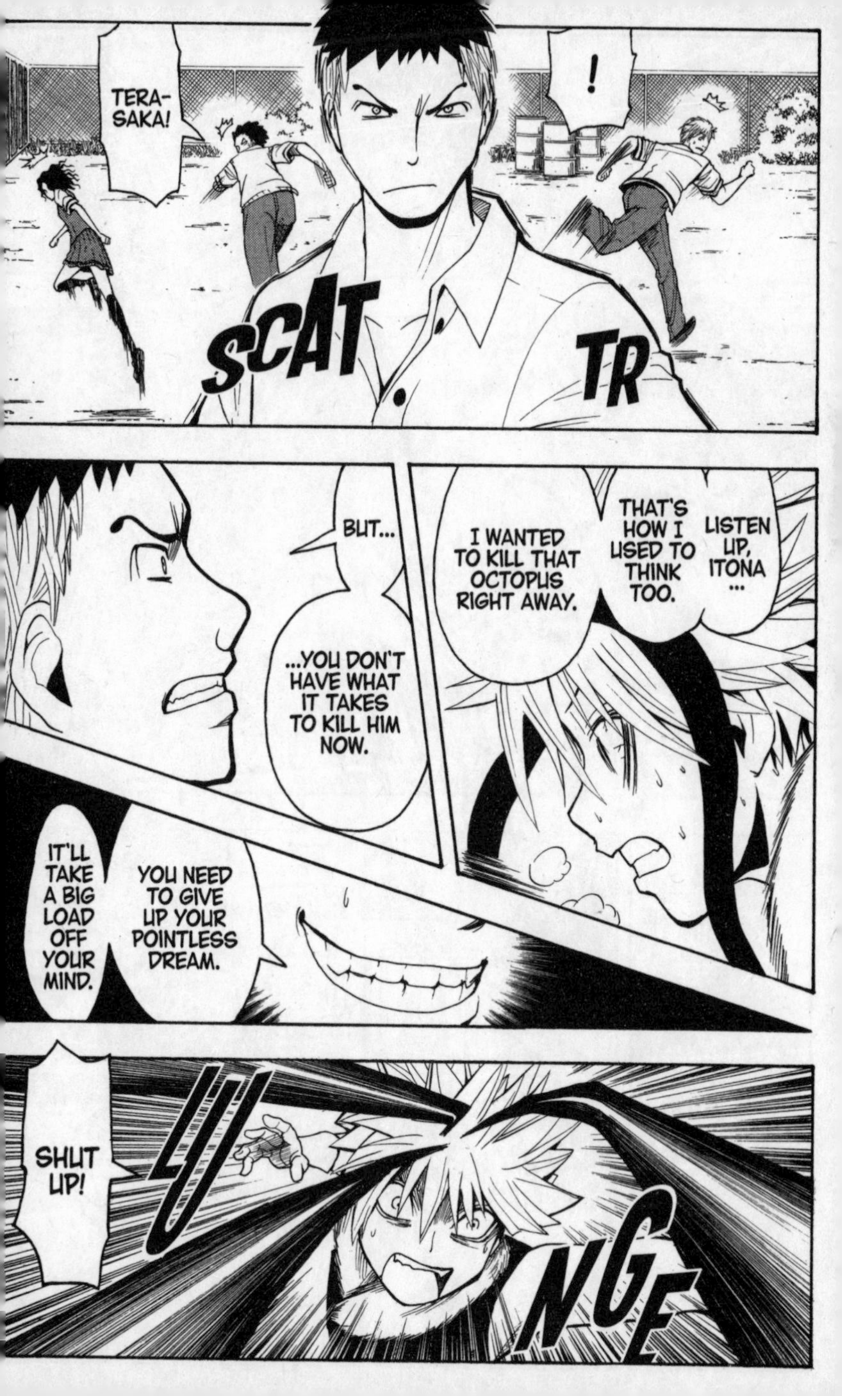
!
TERA-SAKA!
SCAT
TR
LISTEN UP, ITONA...
THAT'S HOW I USED TO THINK TOO.
I WANTED TO KILL THAT OCTOPUS RIGHT AWAY.
BUT...
...YOU DON'T HAVE WHAT IT TAKES TO KILL HIM NOW.
YOU NEED TO GIVE UP YOUR POINTLESS DREAM.
IT'LL TAKE A BIG LOAD OFF YOUR MIND.
SHUT UP!
LU
NGE

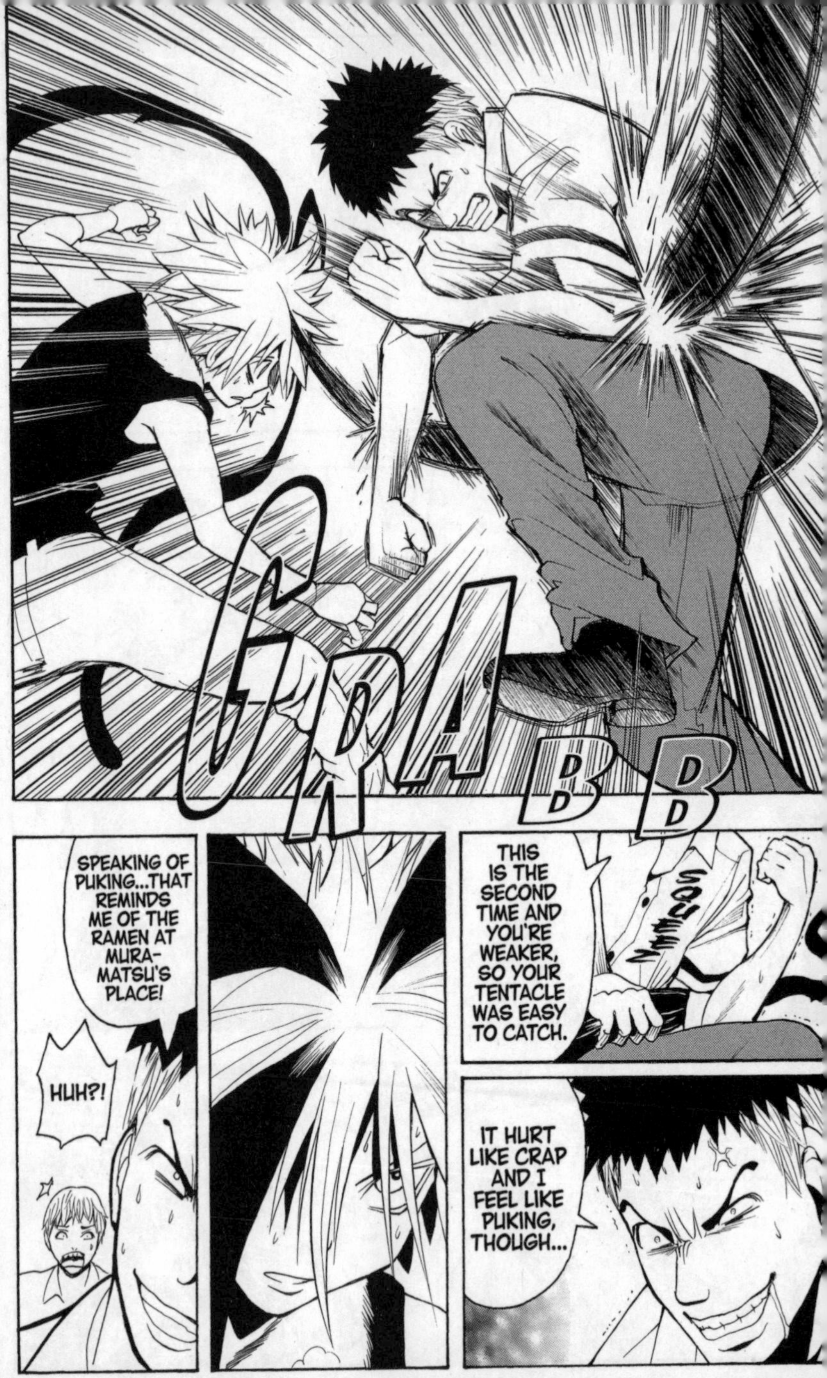
GRABBB
SQUEEEN
THIS IS THE SECOND TIME AND YOU'RE WEAKER, SO YOUR TENTACLE WAS EASY TO CATCH.
IT HURT LIKE CRAP AND I FEEL LIKE PUKING, THOUGH...
SPEAKING OF PUKING...THAT REMINDS ME OF THE RAMEN AT MURA-MATSU'S PLACE!
HUH?!

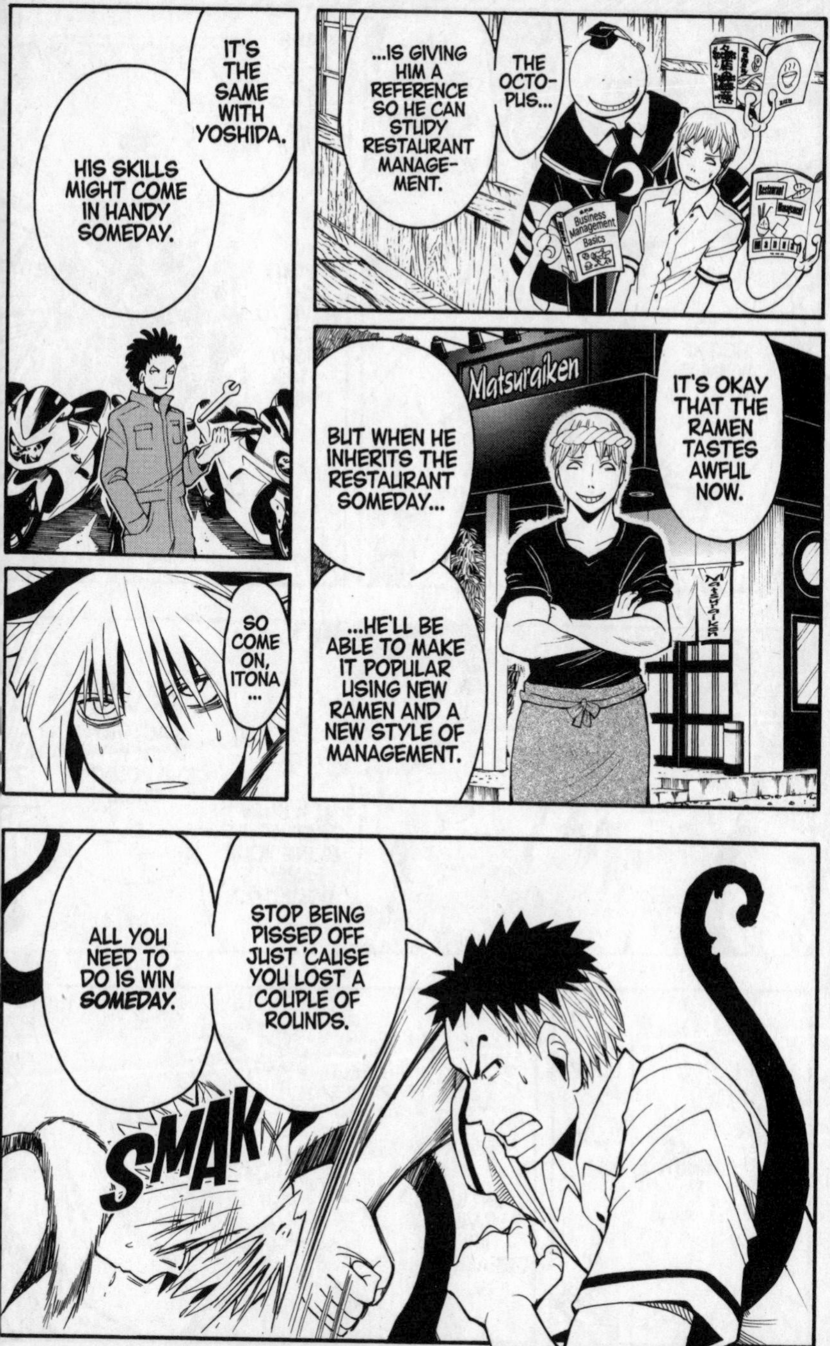
THE OCTO-PUS...
...IS GIVING HIM A REFERENCE SO HE CAN STUDY RESTAURANT MANAGE-MENT.
Business Management Basics
Restaurant Management
IT'S OKAY THAT THE RAMEN TASTES AWFUL NOW.
Matsuraiken
BUT WHEN HE INHERITS THE RESTAURANT SOMEDAY...
...HE'LL BE ABLE TO MAKE IT POPULAR USING NEW RAMEN AND A NEW STYLE OF MANAGEMENT.
Matsuraiken
IT'S THE SAME WITH YOSHIDA.
HIS SKILLS MIGHT COME IN HANDY SOMEDAY.
SO COME ON, ITONA...
STOP BEING PISSED OFF JUST 'CAUSE YOU LOST A COUPLE OF ROUNDS.
ALL YOU NEED TO DO IS WIN *SOMEDAY*.
SMAK

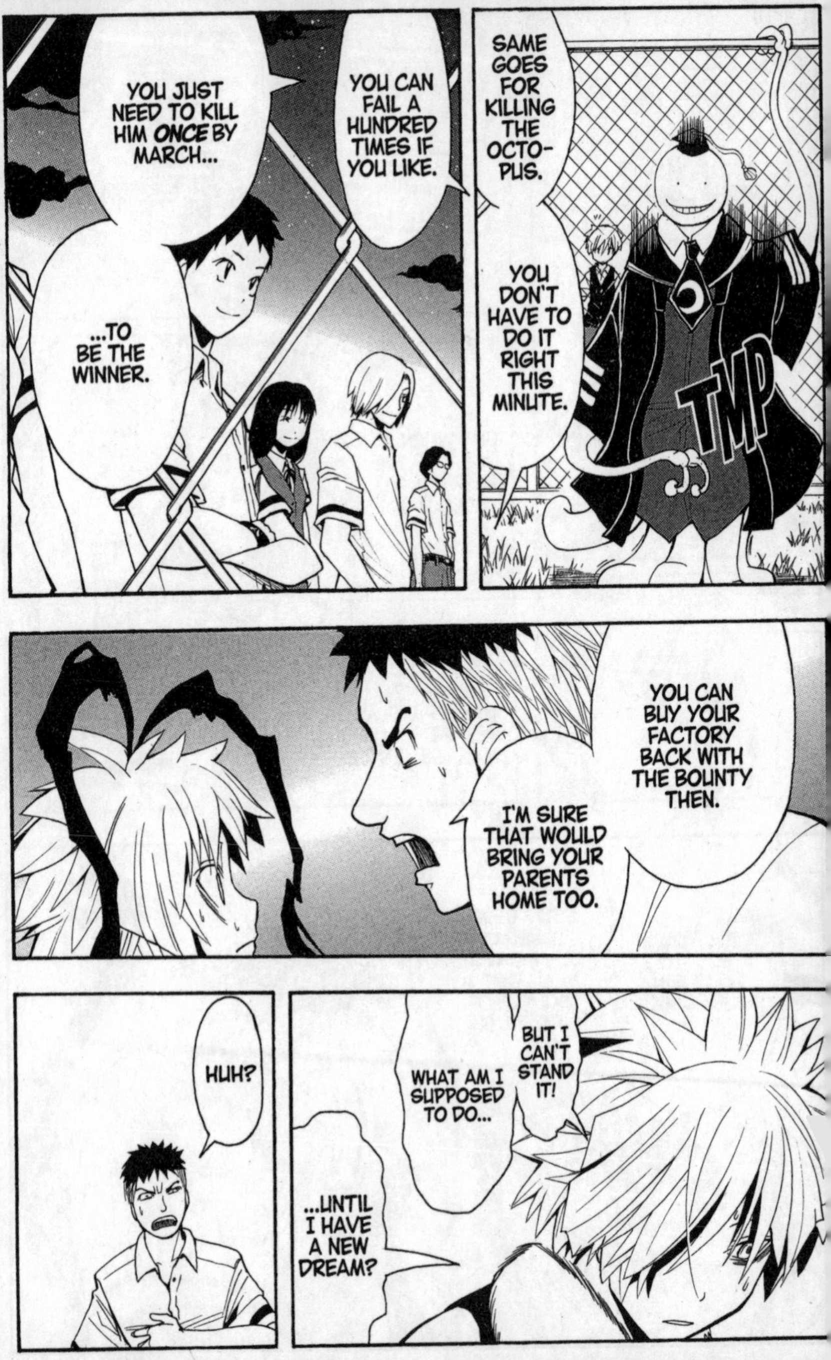
SAME GOES FOR KILLING THE OCTO-PUS.
YOU DON'T HAVE TO DO IT RIGHT THIS MINUTE.
TMP
YOU CAN FAIL A HUNDRED TIMES IF YOU LIKE.
YOU JUST NEED TO KILL HIM ONCE BY MARCH...
...TO BE THE WINNER.
YOU CAN BUY YOUR FACTORY BACK WITH THE BOUNTY THEN.
I'M SURE THAT WOULD BRING YOUR PARENTS HOME TOO.
BUT I CAN'T STAND IT!
WHAT AM I SUPPOSED TO DO...
...UNTIL I HAVE A NEW DREAM?
HUH?

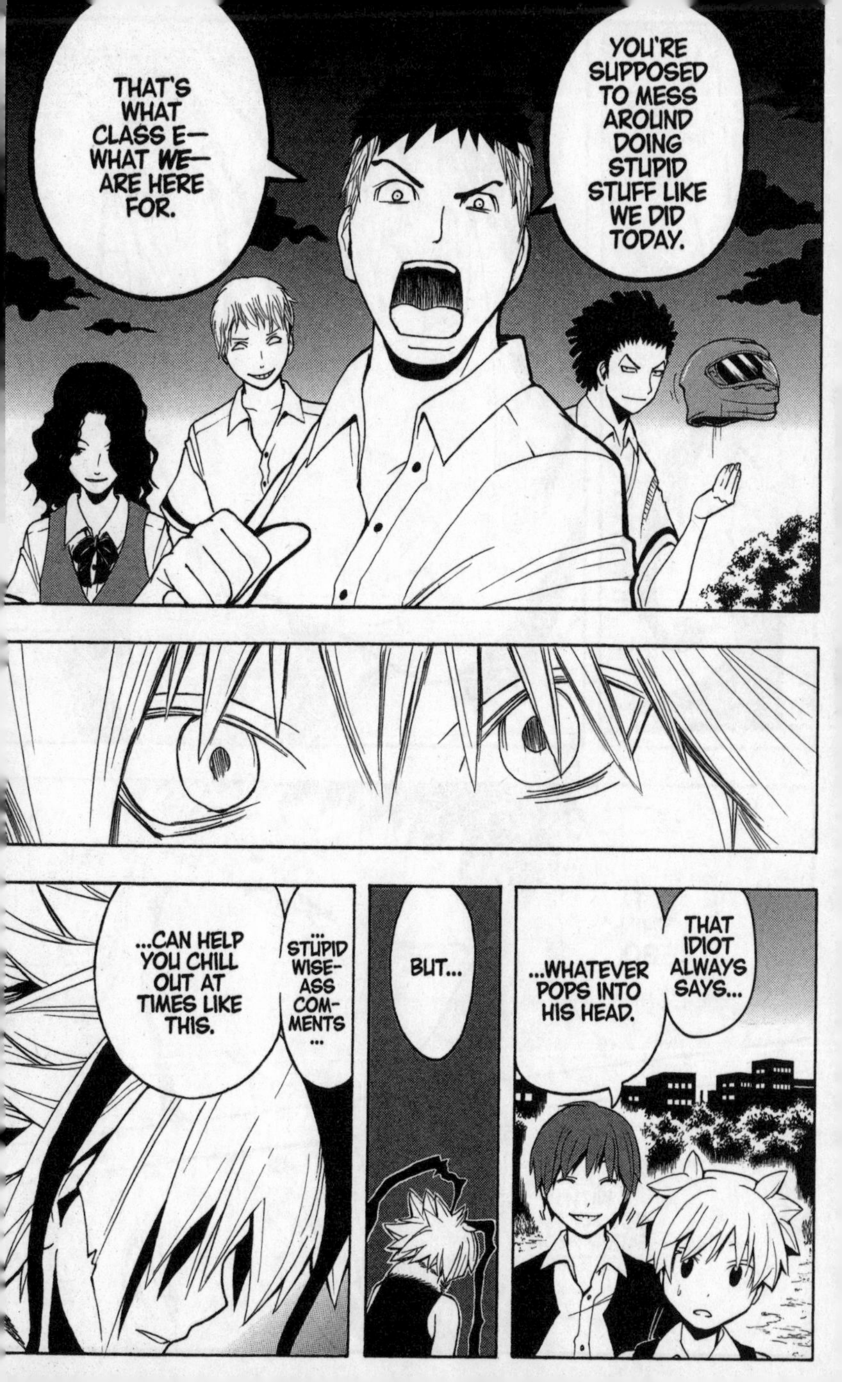
YOU'RE SUPPOSED TO MESS AROUND DOING STUPID STUFF LIKE WE DID TODAY.
THAT'S WHAT CLASS E— WHAT WE— ARE HERE FOR.
THAT IDIOT ALWAYS SAYS...
...WHATEVER POPS INTO HIS HEAD.
BUT...
...STUPID WISE-ASS COMMENTS...
...CAN HELP YOU CHILL OUT AT TIMES LIKE THIS.

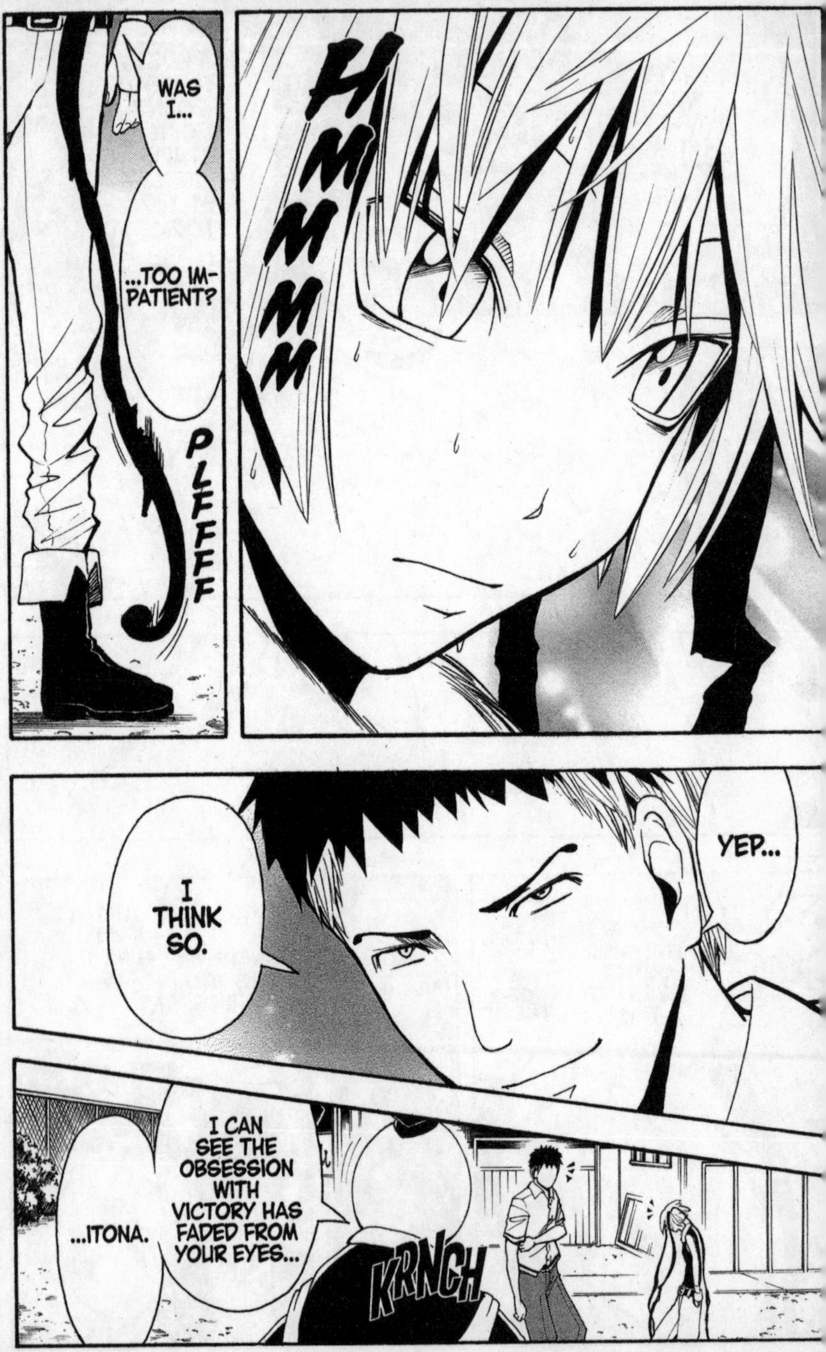
HMMMMMM
WAS I...
...TOO IM-PATIENT?
PLFFFFF
YEP...
I THINK SO.
I CAN SEE THE OBSESSION WITH VICTORY HAS FADED FROM YOUR EYES...
...ITONA.
KRNCH

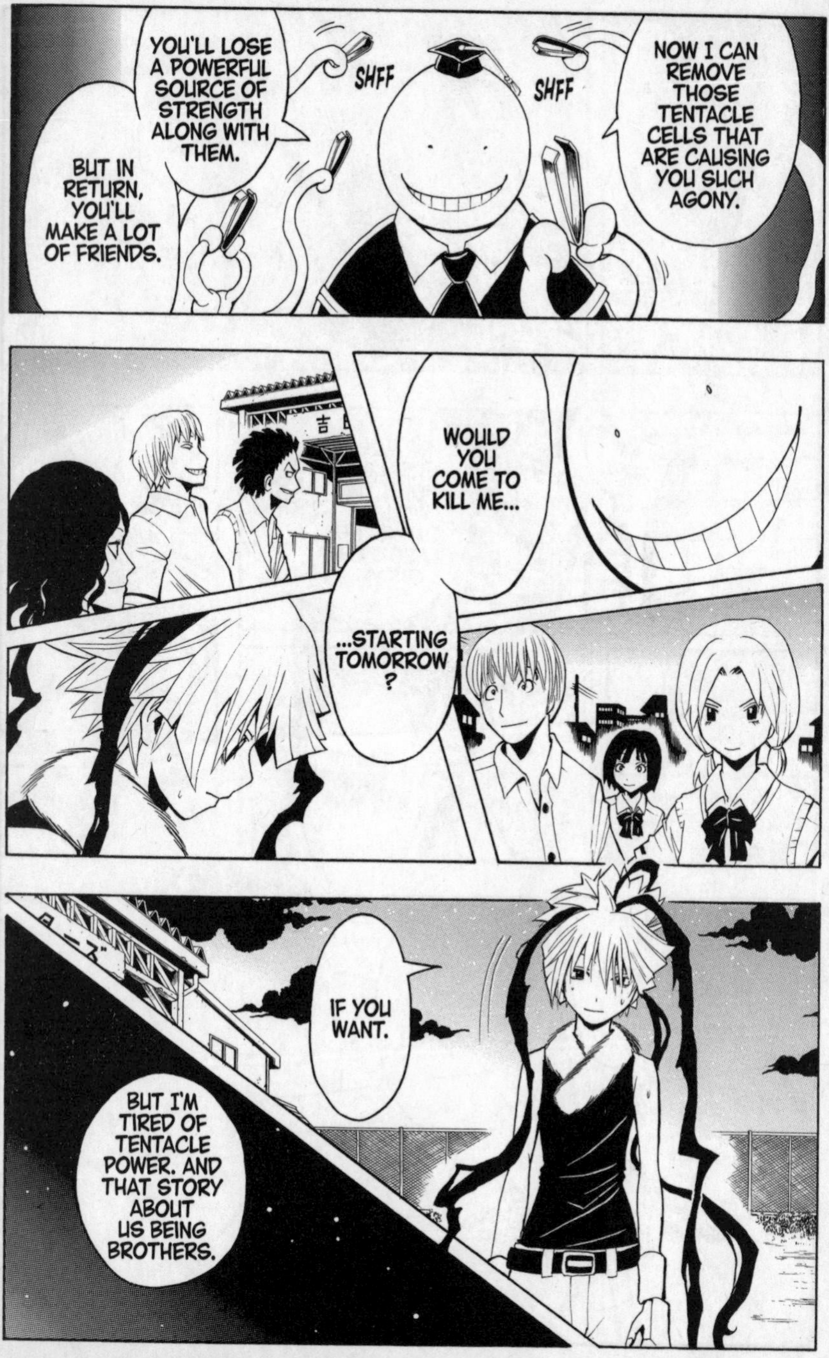
NOW I CAN REMOVE THOSE TENTACLE CELLS THAT ARE CAUSING YOU SUCH AGONY.
SHFF
SHFF
YOU'LL LOSE A POWERFUL SOURCE OF STRENGTH ALONG WITH THEM.
BUT IN RETURN, YOU'LL MAKE A LOT OF FRIENDS.
WOULD YOU COME TO KILL ME...
...STARTING TOMORROW?
IF YOU WANT.
BUT I'M TIRED OF TENTACLE POWER. AND THAT STORY ABOUT US BEING BROTHERS.

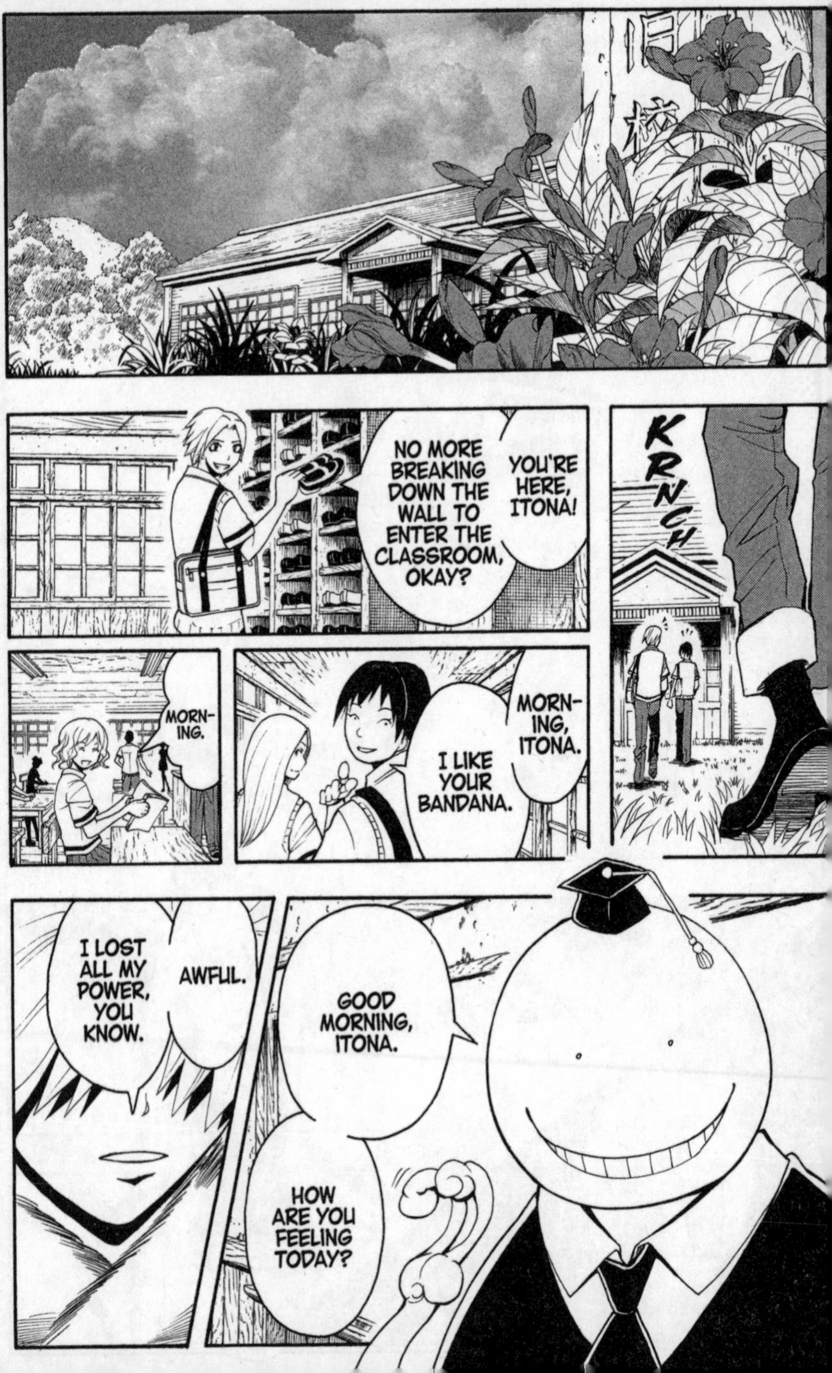
KRNCH
YOU'RE HERE, ITONA!
NO MORE BREAKING DOWN THE WALL TO ENTER THE CLASSROOM, OKAY?
MORNING, ITONA.
I LIKE YOUR BANDANA.
MORNING.
GOOD MORNING, ITONA.
HOW ARE YOU FEELING TODAY?
AWFUL.
I LOST ALL MY POWER, YOU KNOW.

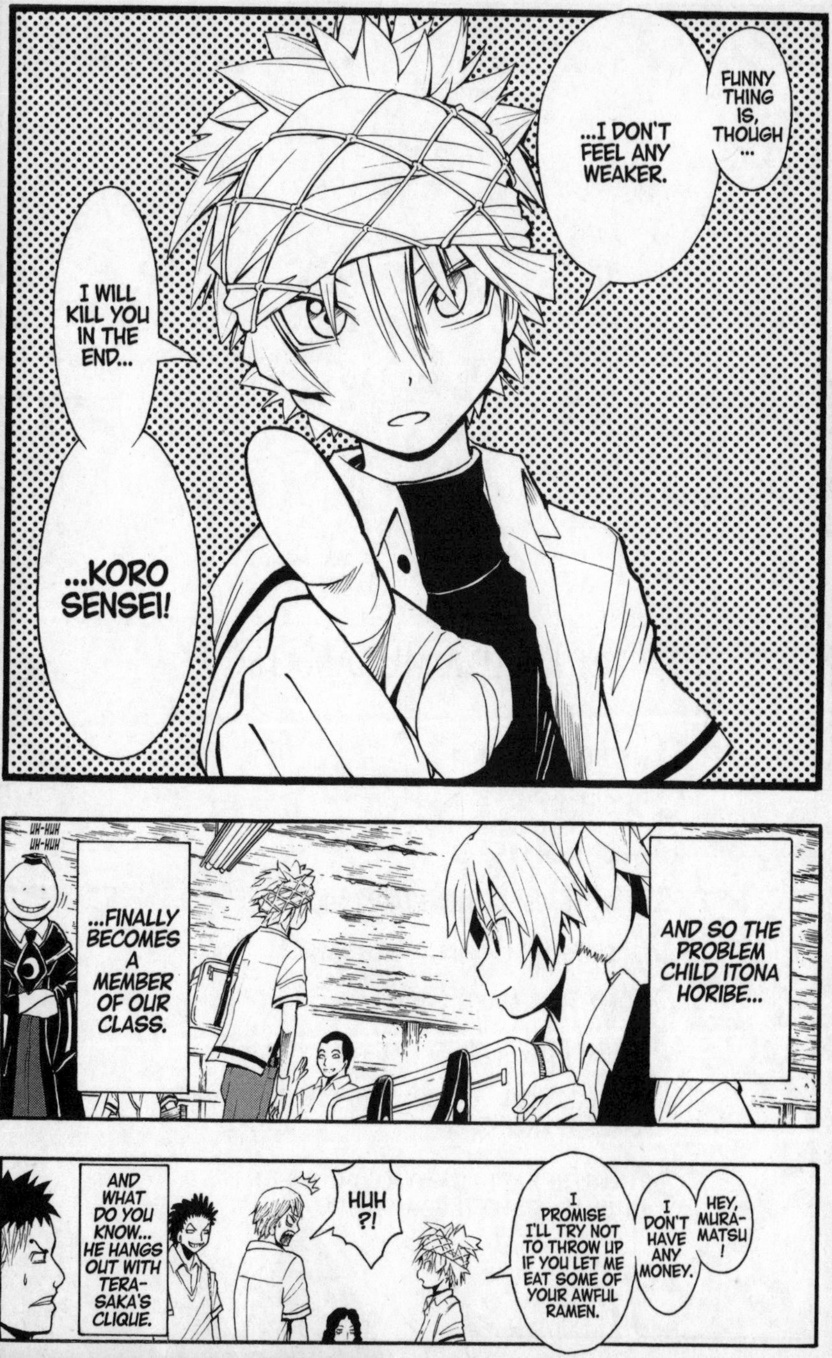
FUNNY THING IS, THOUGH...
...I DON'T FEEL ANY WEAKER.
I WILL KILL YOU IN THE END...
...KORO SENSEI!
AND SO THE PROBLEM CHILD ITONA HORIBE...
...FINALLY BECOMES A MEMBER OF OUR CLASS.
UH-HUH UH-HUH
HEY, MURA-MATSU!
I DON'T HAVE ANY MONEY.
I PROMISE I'LL TRY NOT TO THROW UP IF YOU LET ME EAT SOME OF YOUR AWFUL RAMEN.
HUH?!
AND WHAT DO YOU KNOW... HE HANGS OUT WITH TERA-SAKA'S CLIQUE.

E-24 TAKUYA MURAMATSU

- 🌑 BIRTHDAY: AUGUST 25

- 🌑 HEIGHT: 5' 9"

- 🌑 WEIGHT: 134 LBS.

- 🌑 FAVORITE SUBJECT: HOME ECONOMICS

- 🌑 LEAST FAVORITE SUBJECT: MATHEMATICS

- 🌑 HOBBY/SKILL: MANLY COOKING

- 🌑 FUTURE GOAL: BUSINESS MANAGEMENT MAJOR

- 🌑 ULTIMATE GOAL: TO BECOME THE CEO OF A GIGANTIC RAMEN FRANCHISE

- 🌑 THINGS HE HAS TO FIX TO ACCOMPLISH THAT: DITCH HIS STREET THUG AESTHETIC

Class 88 Time to Spin

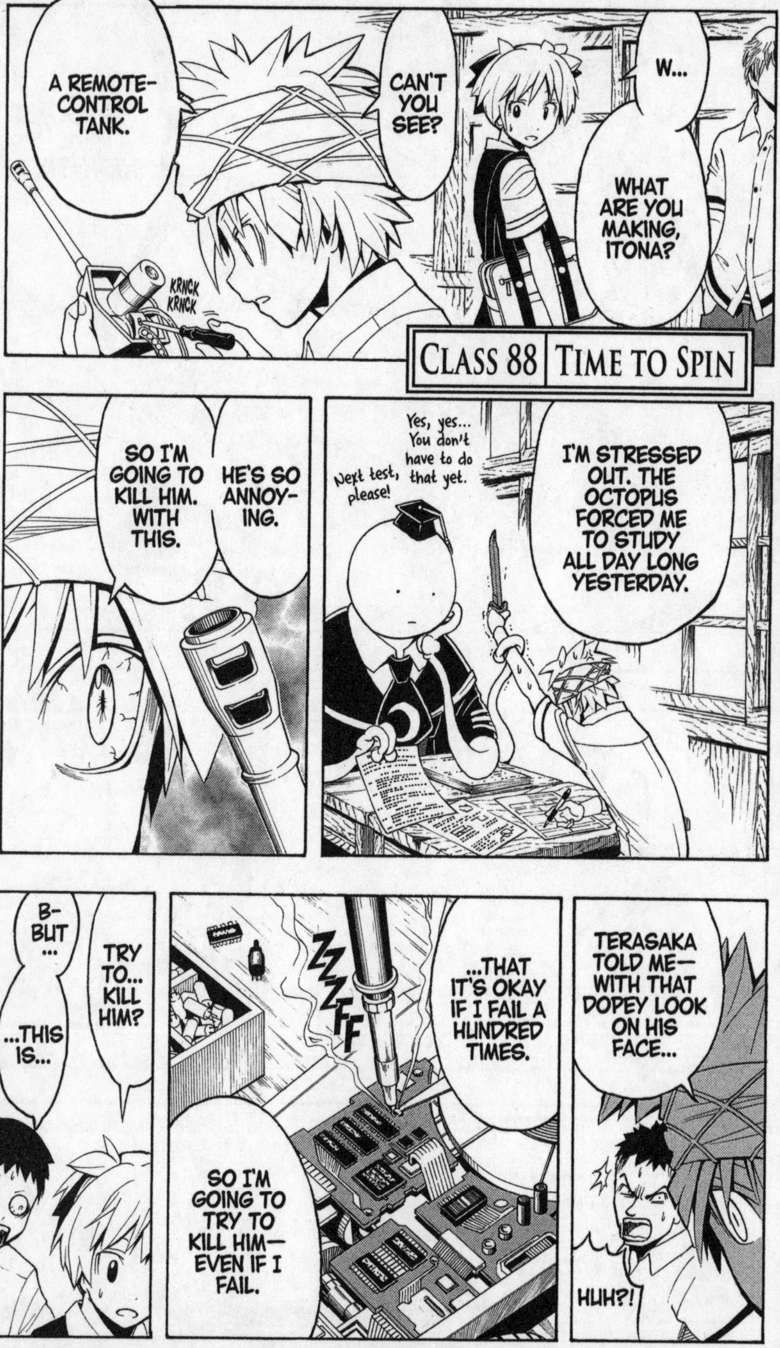
W...
WHAT ARE YOU MAKING, ITONA?
CAN'T YOU SEE?
A REMOTE-CONTROL TANK.
KRNCK KRNCK
I'M STRESSED OUT. THE OCTOPUS FORCED ME TO STUDY ALL DAY LONG YESTERDAY.
Yes, yes... You don't have to do that yet.
Next test, please!
HE'S SO ANNOY-ING.
SO I'M GOING TO KILL HIM. WITH THIS.
TERASAKA TOLD ME—WITH THAT DOPEY LOOK ON HIS FACE...
HUH?!
...THAT IT'S OKAY IF I FAIL A HUNDRED TIMES.
ZZZFF
SO I'M GOING TO TRY TO KILL HIM—EVEN IF I FAIL.
TRY TO... KILL HIM?
B-BUT...
...THIS IS...

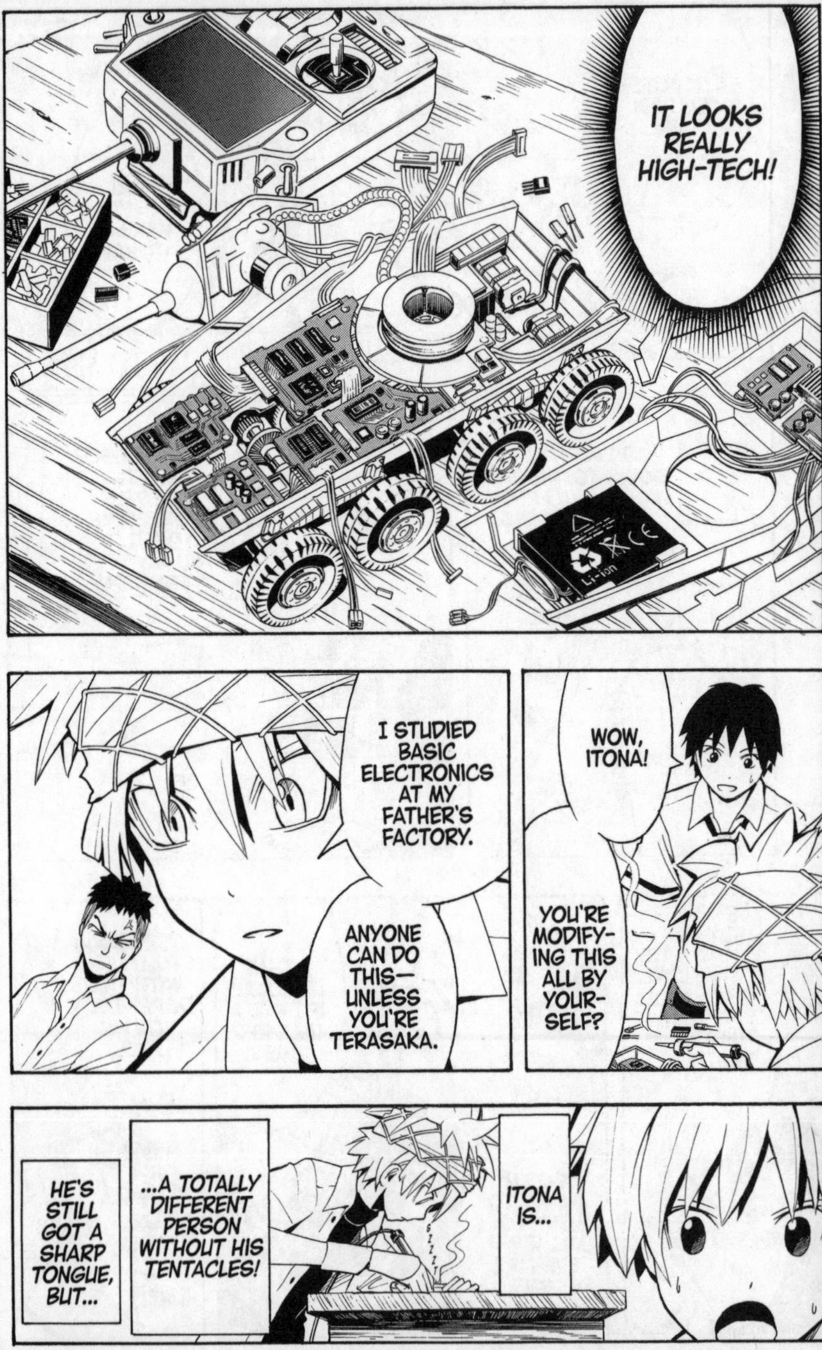
IT LOOKS REALLY HIGH-TECH!
Li-ion
WOW, ITONA!
YOU'RE MODIFYING THIS ALL BY YOURSELF?
I STUDIED BASIC ELECTRONICS AT MY FATHER'S FACTORY.
ANYONE CAN DO THIS—UNLESS YOU'RE TERASAKA.
ITONA IS...
...A TOTALLY DIFFERENT PERSON WITHOUT HIS TENTACLES!
HE'S STILL GOT A SHARP TONGUE, BUT...

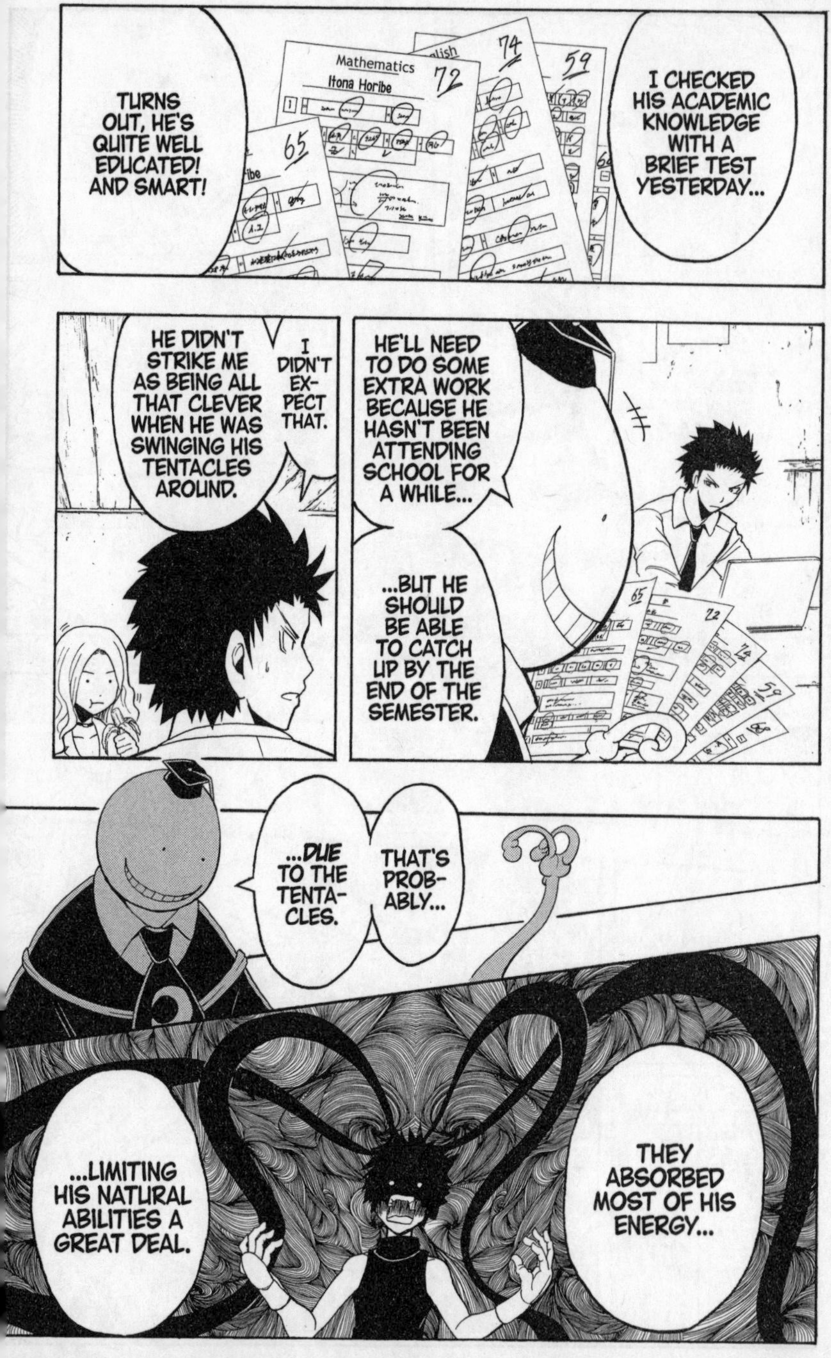
I CHECKED HIS ACADEMIC KNOWLEDGE WITH A BRIEF TEST YESTERDAY...
Mathematics
Itona Horibe
TURNS OUT, HE'S QUITE WELL EDUCATED! AND SMART!
HE'LL NEED TO DO SOME EXTRA WORK BECAUSE HE HASN'T BEEN ATTENDING SCHOOL FOR A WHILE...
...BUT HE SHOULD BE ABLE TO CATCH UP BY THE END OF THE SEMESTER.
I DIDN'T EX-PECT THAT.
HE DIDN'T STRIKE ME AS BEING ALL THAT CLEVER WHEN HE WAS SWINGING HIS TENTACLES AROUND.
THAT'S PROB-ABLY...
...DUE TO THE TENTA-CLES.
THEY ABSORBED MOST OF HIS ENERGY...
...LIMITING HIS NATURAL ABILITIES A GREAT DEAL.

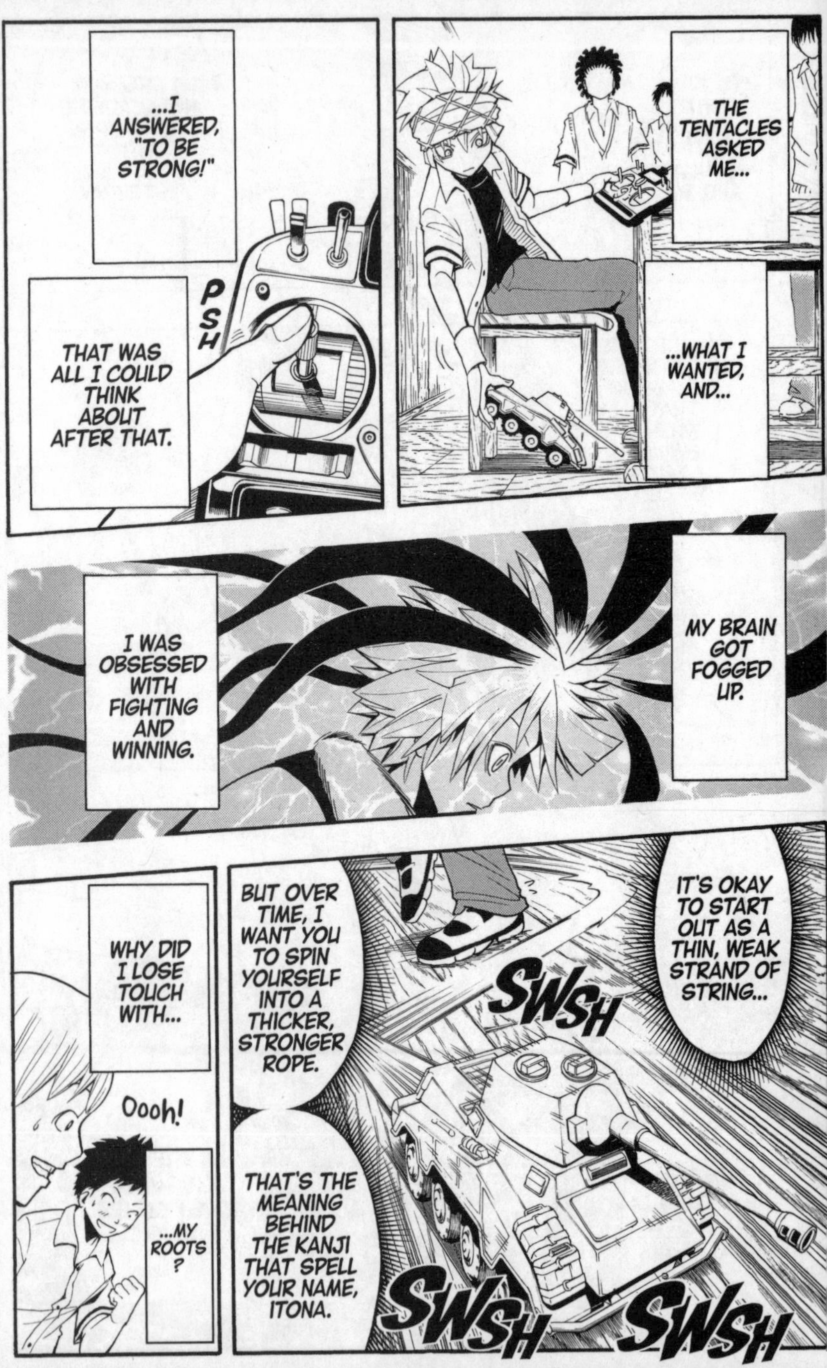
THE TENTACLES ASKED ME...
...WHAT I WANTED, AND...
...I ANSWERED, "TO BE STRONG!"
PSH
THAT WAS ALL I COULD THINK ABOUT AFTER THAT.
MY BRAIN GOT FOGGED UP.
I WAS OBSESSED WITH FIGHTING AND WINNING.
IT'S OKAY TO START OUT AS A THIN, WEAK STRAND OF STRING...
SWSH
BUT OVER TIME, I WANT YOU TO SPIN YOURSELF INTO A THICKER, STRONGER ROPE.
THAT'S THE MEANING BEHIND THE KANJI THAT SPELL YOUR NAME, ITONA.
SWSH
SWSH
WHY DID I LOSE TOUCH WITH...
Oooh!
...MY ROOTS?

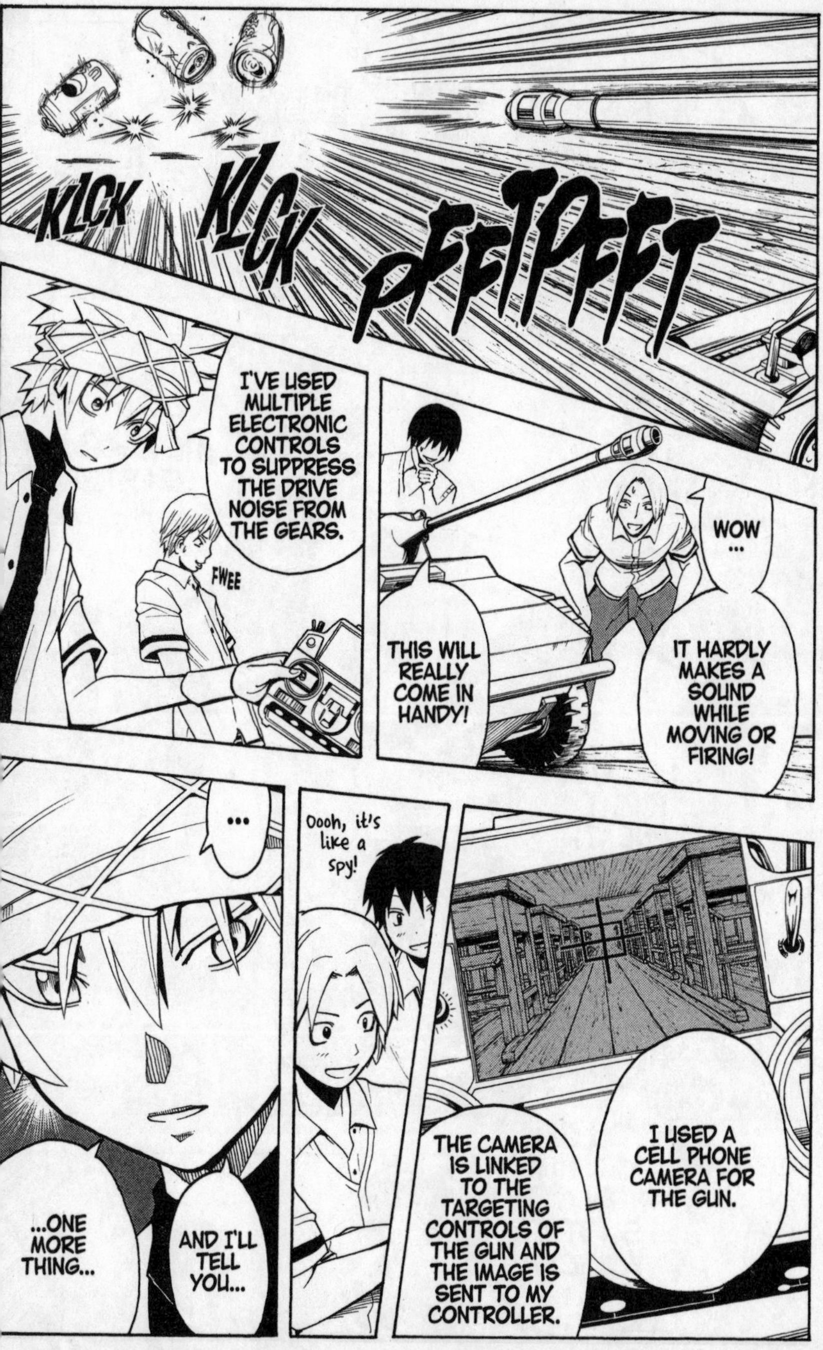
PFFTPFFT
KLCK
KLCK
WOW...
IT HARDLY MAKES A SOUND WHILE MOVING OR FIRING!
THIS WILL REALLY COME IN HANDY!
I'VE USED MULTIPLE ELECTRONIC CONTROLS TO SUPPRESS THE DRIVE NOISE FROM THE GEARS.
FWEE
I USED A CELL PHONE CAMERA FOR THE GUN.
THE CAMERA IS LINKED TO THE TARGETING CONTROLS OF THE GUN AND THE IMAGE IS SENT TO MY CONTROLLER.
Oooh, it's like a spy!
...
AND I'LL TELL YOU...
...ONE MORE THING...

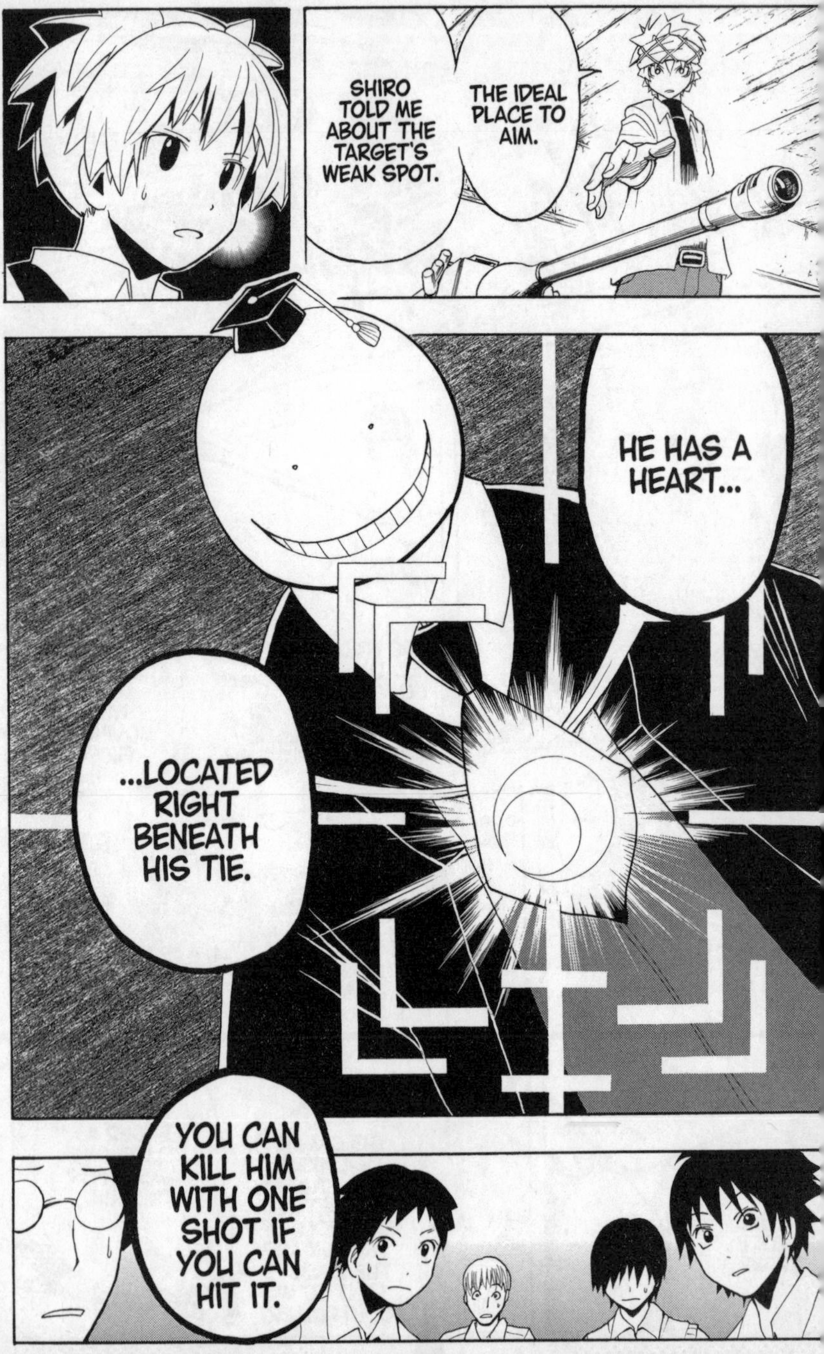
THE IDEAL PLACE TO AIM.
SHIRO TOLD ME ABOUT THE TARGET'S WEAK SPOT.
HE HAS A HEART...
...LOCATED RIGHT BENEATH HIS TIE.
YOU CAN KILL HIM WITH ONE SHOT IF YOU CAN HIT IT.

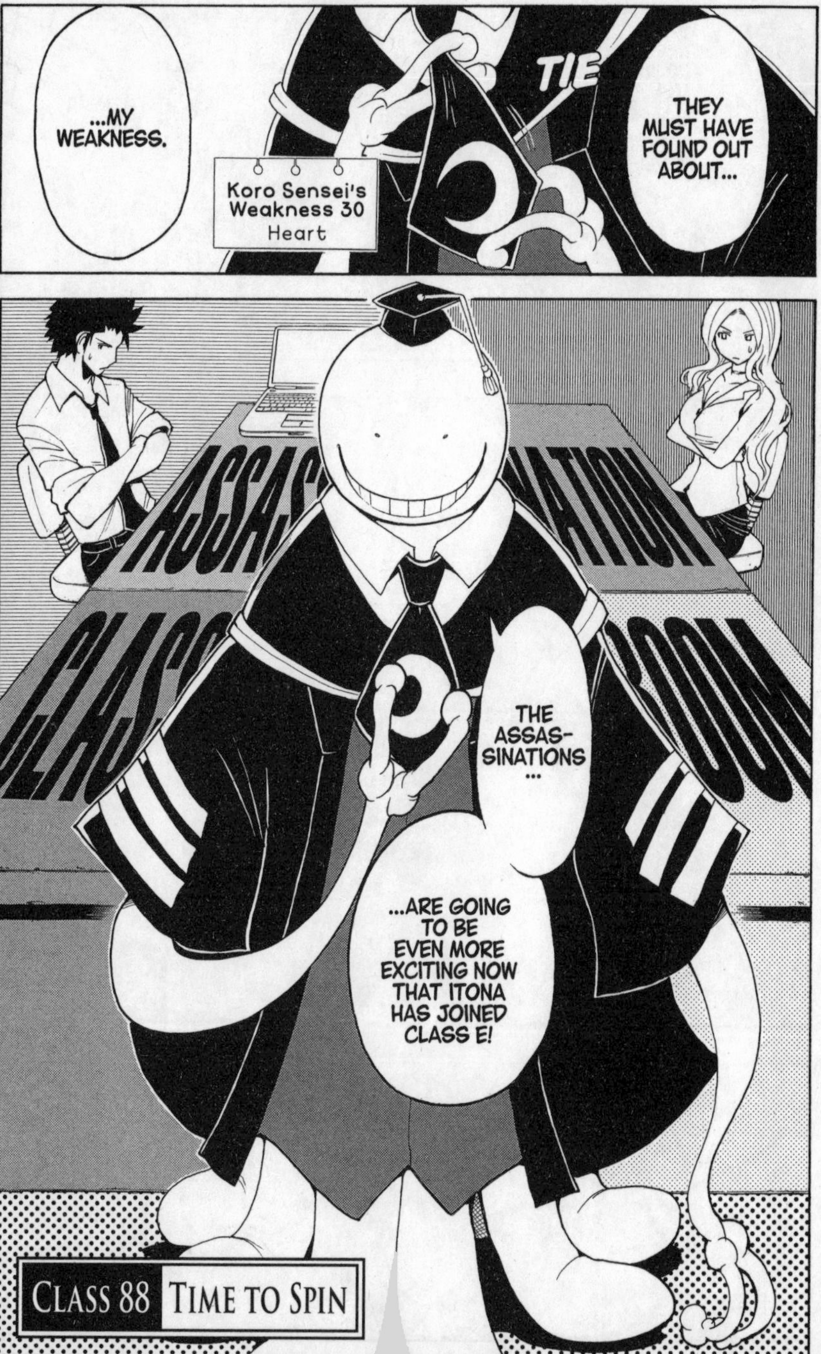
TIE
THEY MUST HAVE FOUND OUT ABOUT...
Koro Sensei's Weakness 30 Heart
...MY WEAKNESS.
THE ASSAS-SINATIONS ...
...ARE GOING TO BE EVEN MORE EXCITING NOW THAT ITONA HAS JOINED CLASS E!

CLASS 88 TIME TO SPIN

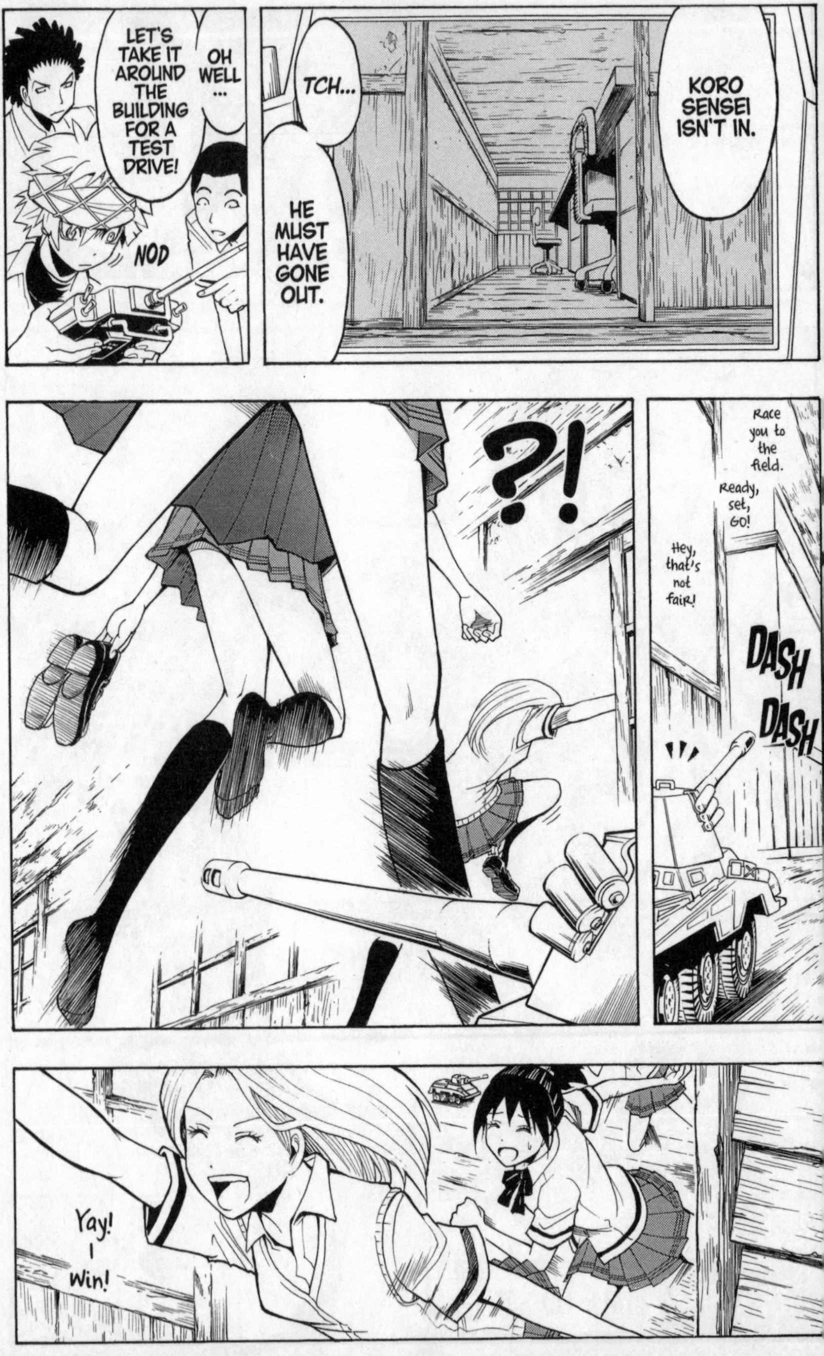
KORO SENSEI ISN'T IN.
TCH...
HE MUST HAVE GONE OUT.
OH WELL ...
LET'S TAKE IT AROUND THE BUILDING FOR A TEST DRIVE!
NOD
Race you to the field.
Ready, set, GO!
Hey, that's not fair!
DASH
DASH
?!
Yay! I win!

SH HH

ITS VIEW-FINDER RANGE IS TOO SMALL.

NO...

THE CAMERA COULDN'T CATCH UP WITH THEM.

DID YOU SEE IT?!

...USING A FISH-EYE LENS FOR THE CAMERA?

THEN HOW ABOUT...

HOW ABOUT ATTACHING A LARGER HIGH-PERFORM-ANCE CAMERA ON IT?

-Advisor-
Kotaro Takebayashi

Normally	
`1` `2` `3`	Only the front is visible

THAT WAY, YOU'LL BE ABLE TO GET A WIDE VIEW WITH A SMALL LENS.

YOU CAN CORRECT THE IMAGE DISTORTION WHEN IT GOES THROUGH THE CPU.

Fish-eye	
`1` `2` `3`	Wide view, but distorted image

...WHICH WOULD SLOW IT DOWN AND MAKE IT HARDER FOR ME TO FOLLOW THE TARGET.

THAT WOULD MAKE THE TANK HEAVIER...

Corrected Fish-eye	
`1` `2` `3` → `1 2 3`	Wide view with distortion corrected

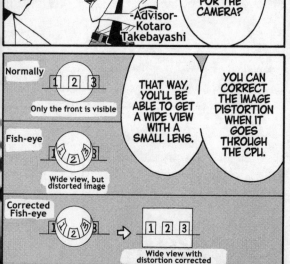

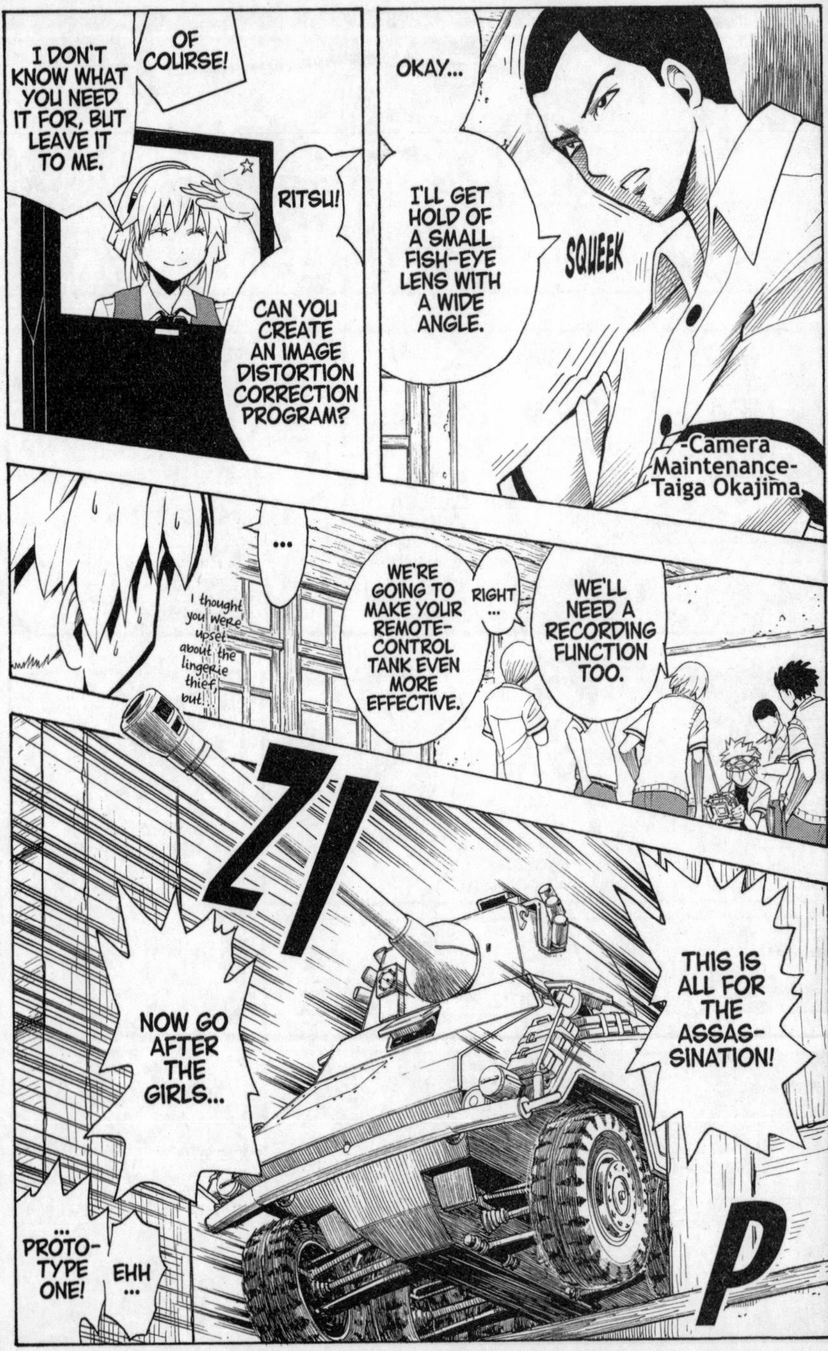
OKAY...
I'LL GET HOLD OF A SMALL FISH-EYE LENS WITH A WIDE ANGLE.
SQUEEK
-Camera Maintenance- Taiga Okajima
RITSU!
CAN YOU CREATE AN IMAGE DISTORTION CORRECTION PROGRAM?
OF COURSE!
I DON'T KNOW WHAT YOU NEED IT FOR, BUT LEAVE IT TO ME.
WE'LL NEED A RECORDING FUNCTION TOO.
RIGHT ...
WE'RE GOING TO MAKE YOUR REMOTE-CONTROL TANK EVEN MORE EFFECTIVE.
...
I thought you were upset about the lingerie thief, but...
P
THIS IS ALL FOR THE ASSAS-SINATION!
Z
NOW GO AFTER THE GIRLS...
EHH ...
... PROTO-TYPE ONE!

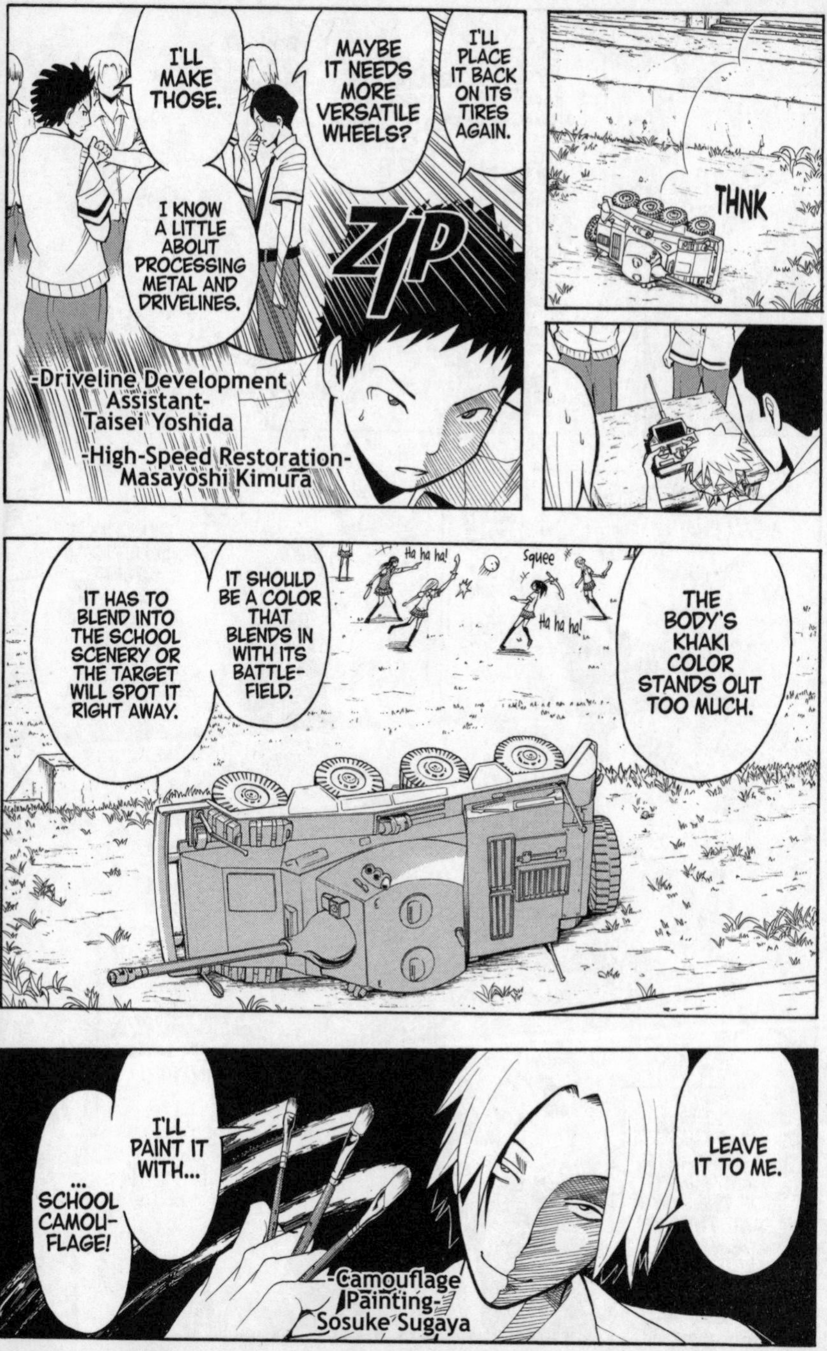
...
THNK
I'LL PLACE IT BACK ON ITS TIRES AGAIN.
MAYBE IT NEEDS MORE VERSATILE WHEELS?
ZIP
I'LL MAKE THOSE.
I KNOW A LITTLE ABOUT PROCESSING METAL AND DRIVELINES.
-Driveline Development Assistant- Taisei Yoshida
-High-Speed Restoration- Masayoshi Kimura
THE BODY'S KHAKI COLOR STANDS OUT TOO MUCH.
Squee
Ha ha ha!
Ha ha ha!
IT SHOULD BE A COLOR THAT BLENDS IN WITH ITS BATTLE-FIELD.
IT HAS TO BLEND INTO THE SCHOOL SCENERY OR THE TARGET WILL SPOT IT RIGHT AWAY.
LEAVE IT TO ME.
I'LL PAINT IT WITH...
... SCHOOL CAMOU-FLAGE!
-Camouflage Painting- Sosuke Sugaya

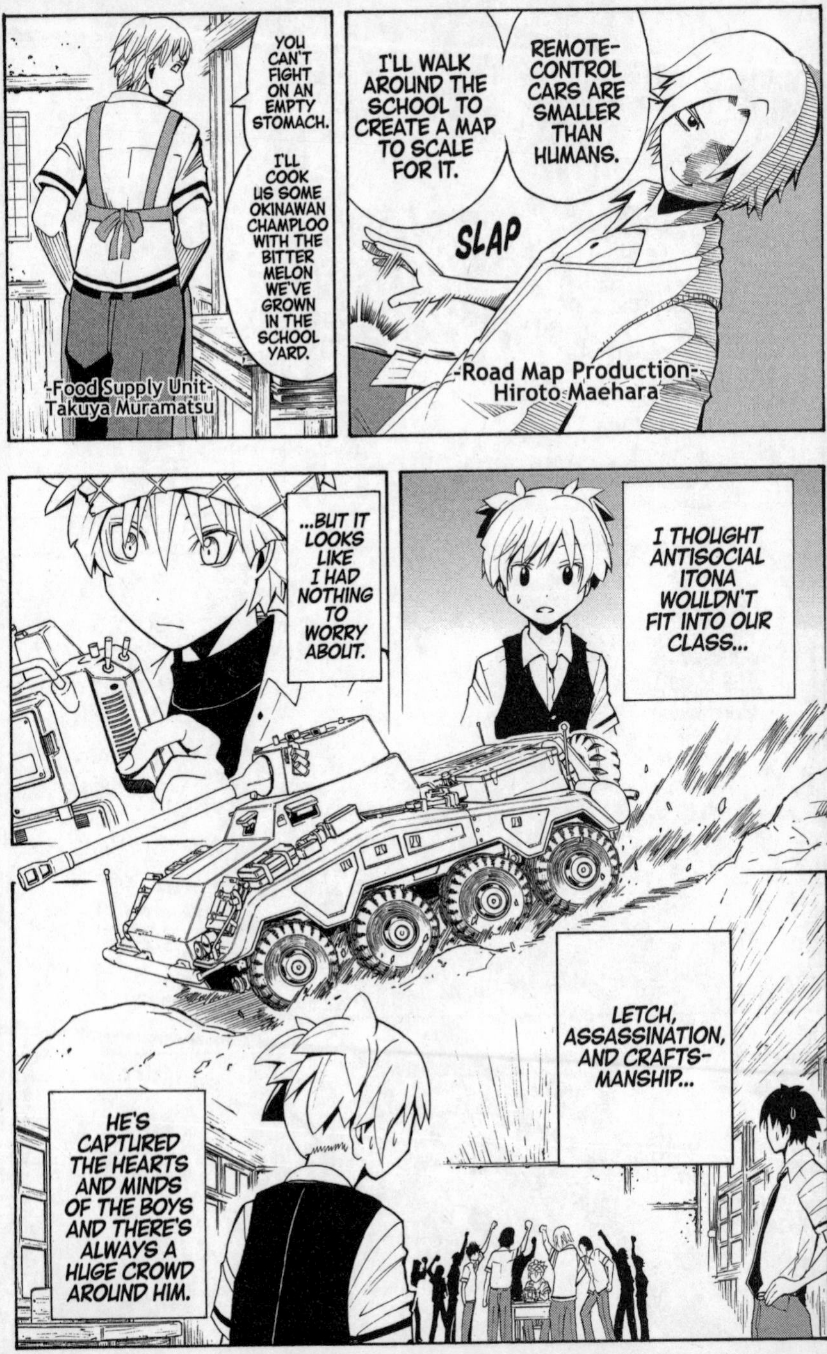
REMOTE-CONTROL CARS ARE SMALLER THAN HUMANS.
I'LL WALK AROUND THE SCHOOL TO CREATE A MAP TO SCALE FOR IT.
SLAP
-Road Map Production-
Hiroto Maehara
YOU CAN'T FIGHT ON AN EMPTY STOMACH.
I'LL COOK US SOME OKINAWAN CHAMPLOO WITH THE BITTER MELON WE'VE GROWN IN THE SCHOOL YARD.
-Food Supply Unit-
Takuya Muramatsu
I THOUGHT ANTISOCIAL ITONA WOULDN'T FIT INTO OUR CLASS...
...BUT IT LOOKS LIKE I HAD NOTHING TO WORRY ABOUT.
LETCH, ASSASSINATION, AND CRAFTSMANSHIP...
HE'S CAPTURED THE HEARTS AND MINDS OF THE BOYS AND THERE'S ALWAYS A HUGE CROWD AROUND HIM.

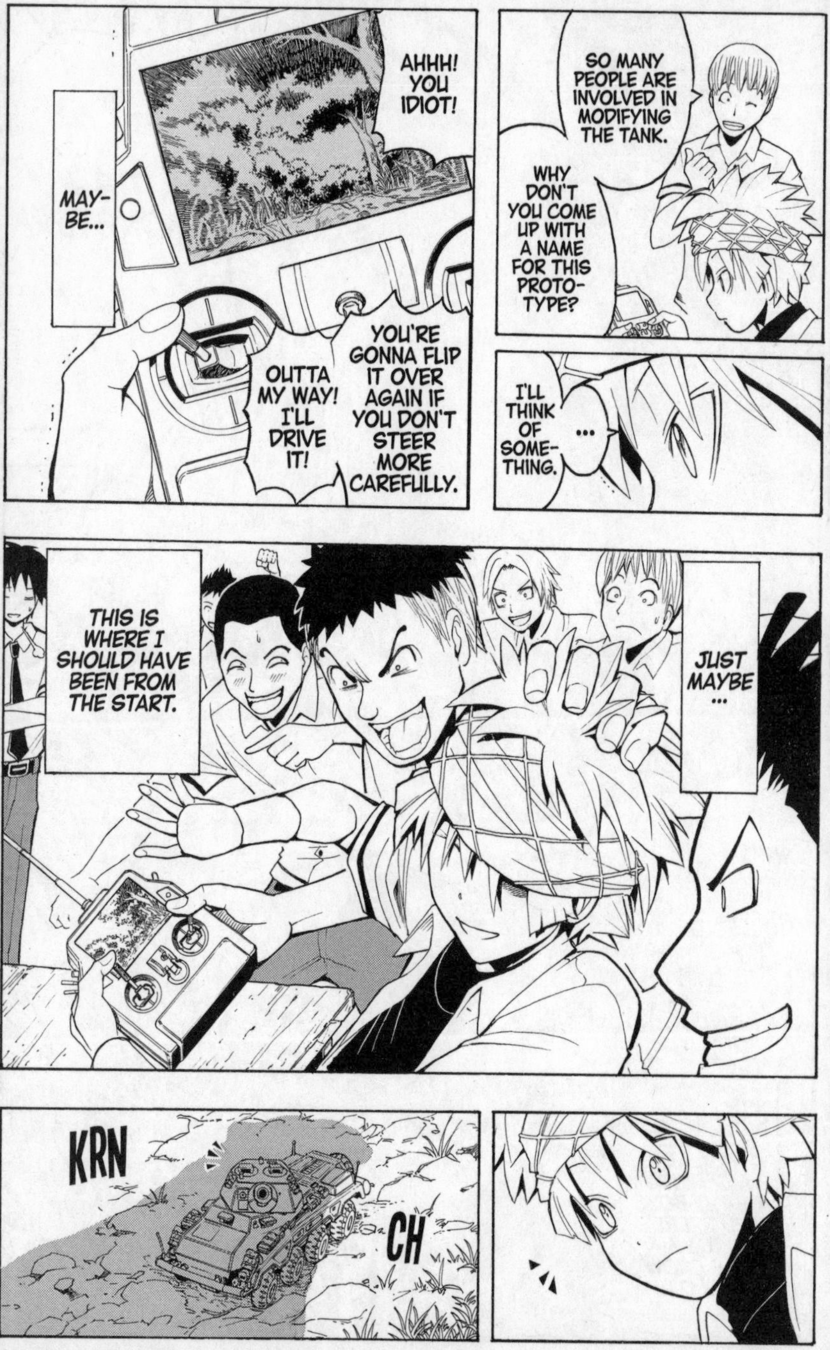
SO MANY PEOPLE ARE INVOLVED IN MODIFYING THE TANK.
WHY DON'T YOU COME UP WITH A NAME FOR THIS PROTO-TYPE?
...
I'LL THINK OF SOME-THING.
AHHH! YOU IDIOT!
YOU'RE GONNA FLIP IT OVER AGAIN IF YOU DON'T STEER MORE CAREFULLY.
OUTTA MY WAY! I'LL DRIVE IT!
MAY-BE...
JUST MAYBE ...
THIS IS WHERE I SHOULD HAVE BEEN FROM THE START.
KRN
CH

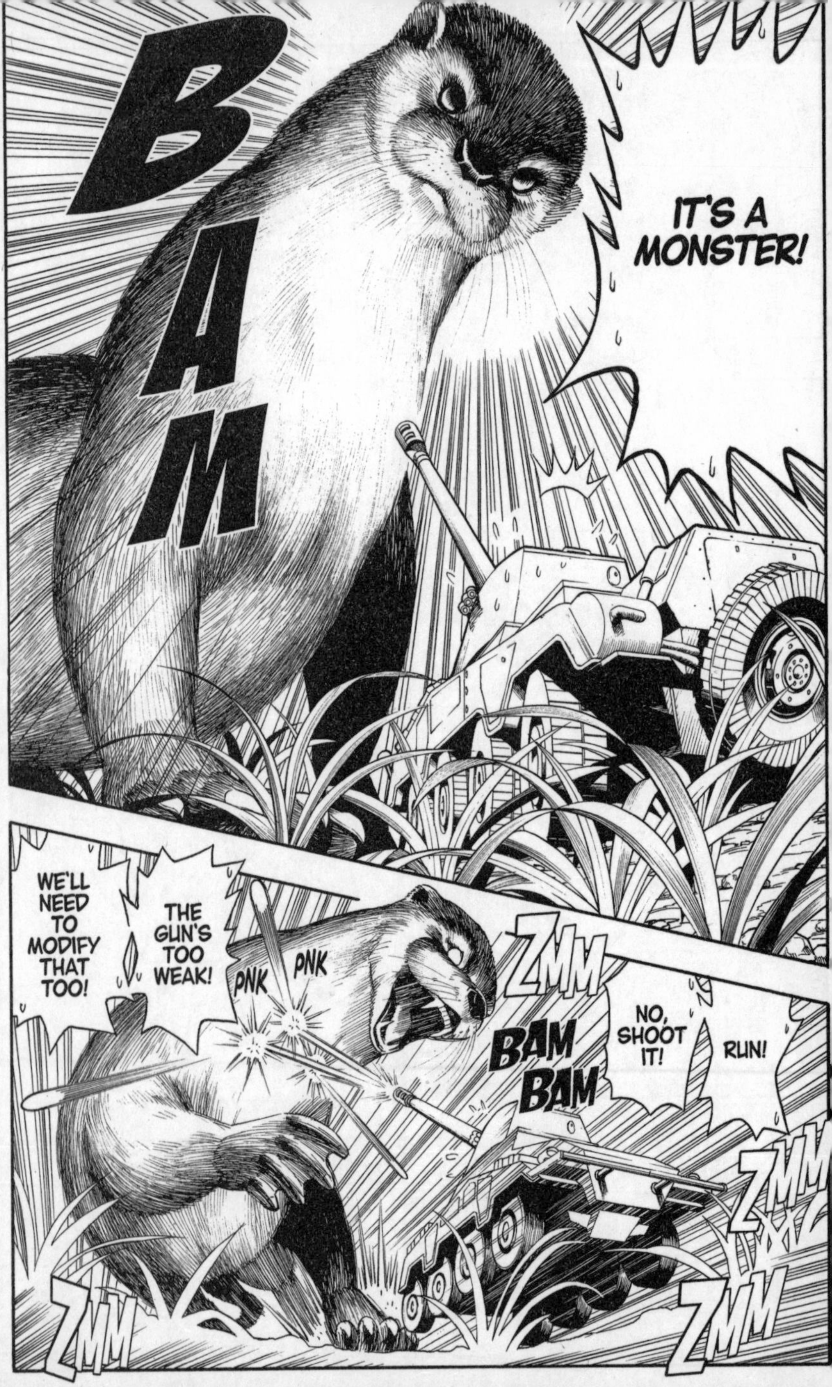
BAM
IT'S A MONSTER!
RUN!
NO, SHOOT IT!
ZMM
BAM BAM
PNK PNK
THE GUN'S TOO WEAK!
WE'LL NEED TO MODIFY THAT TOO!
ZMM
ZMM
ZMM

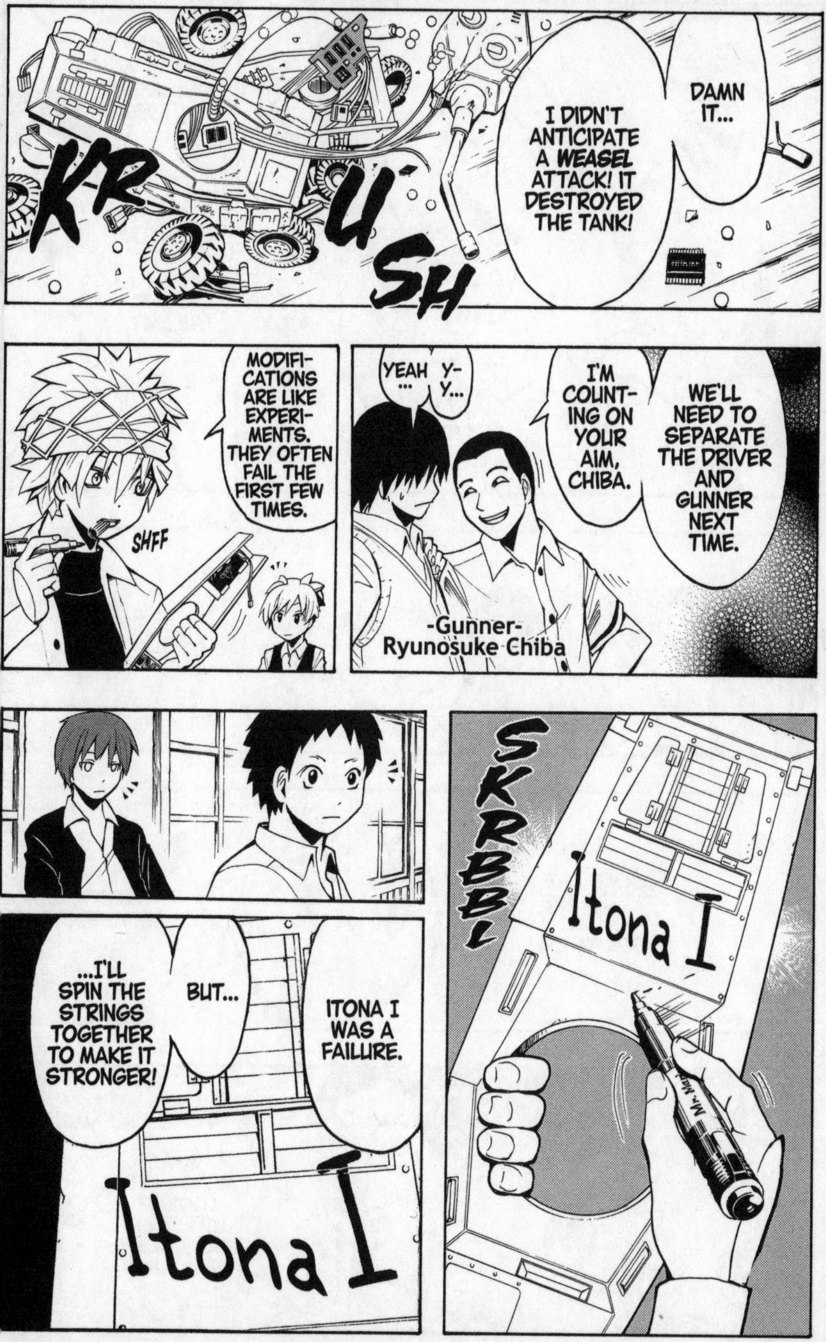
DAMN IT...
I DIDN'T ANTICIPATE A WEASEL ATTACK! IT DESTROYED THE TANK!
KRUSH
WE'LL NEED TO SEPARATE THE DRIVER AND GUNNER NEXT TIME.
I'M COUNTING ON YOUR AIM, CHIBA.
Y-Y...
YEAH...
-Gunner- Ryunosuke Chiba
MODIFICATIONS ARE LIKE EXPERIMENTS. THEY OFTEN FAIL THE FIRST FEW TIMES.
SHFF
SKRBBL
Itona I
ITONA I WAS A FAILURE.
BUT...
...I'LL SPIN THE STRINGS TOGETHER TO MAKE IT STRONGER!
Itona I

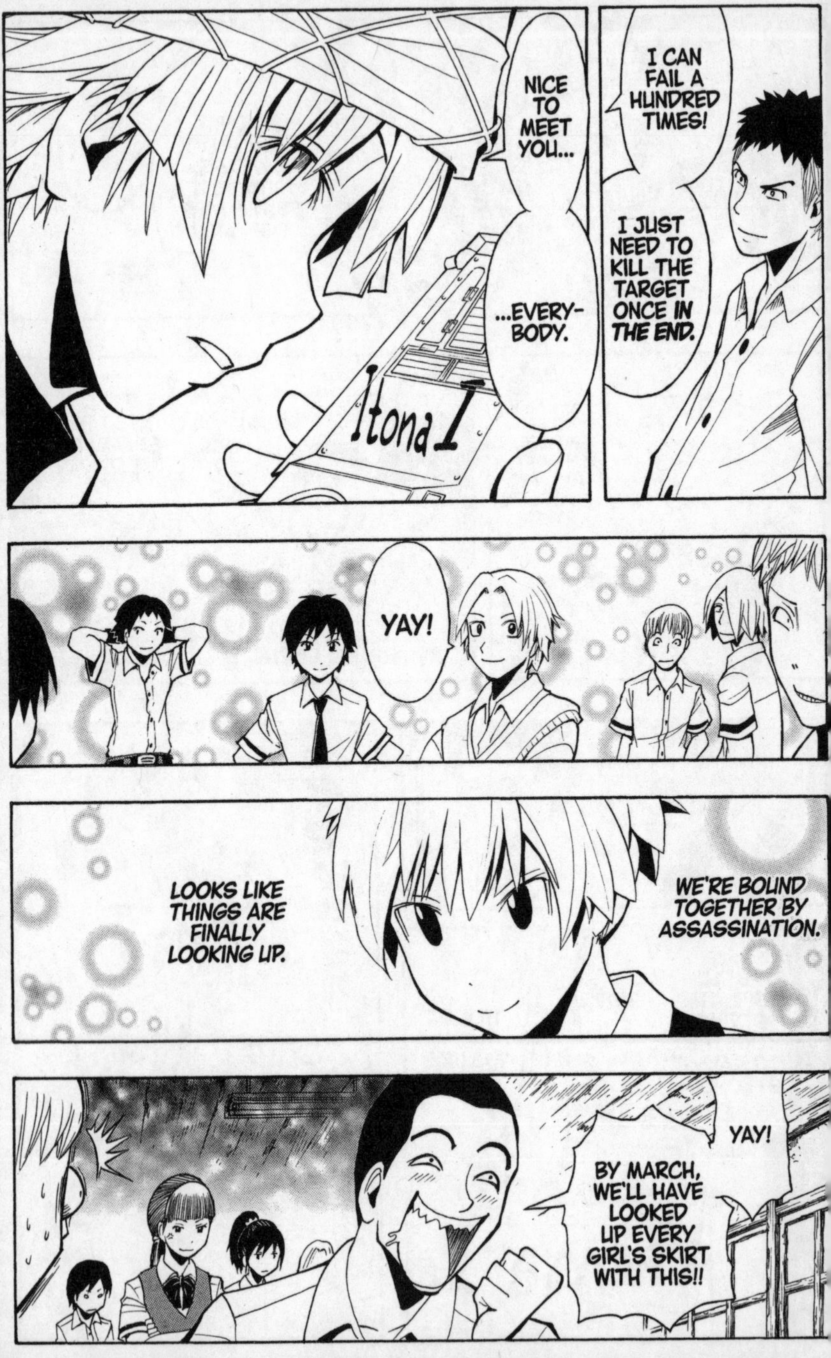
I CAN FAIL A HUNDRED TIMES!
I JUST NEED TO KILL THE TARGET ONCE IN THE END.
NICE TO MEET YOU...
...EVERYBODY.
Itona I
YAY!
WE'RE BOUND TOGETHER BY ASSASSINATION.
LOOKS LIKE THINGS ARE FINALLY LOOKING UP.
YAY!
BY MARCH, WE'LL HAVE LOOKED UP EVERY GIRL'S SKIRT WITH THIS!!

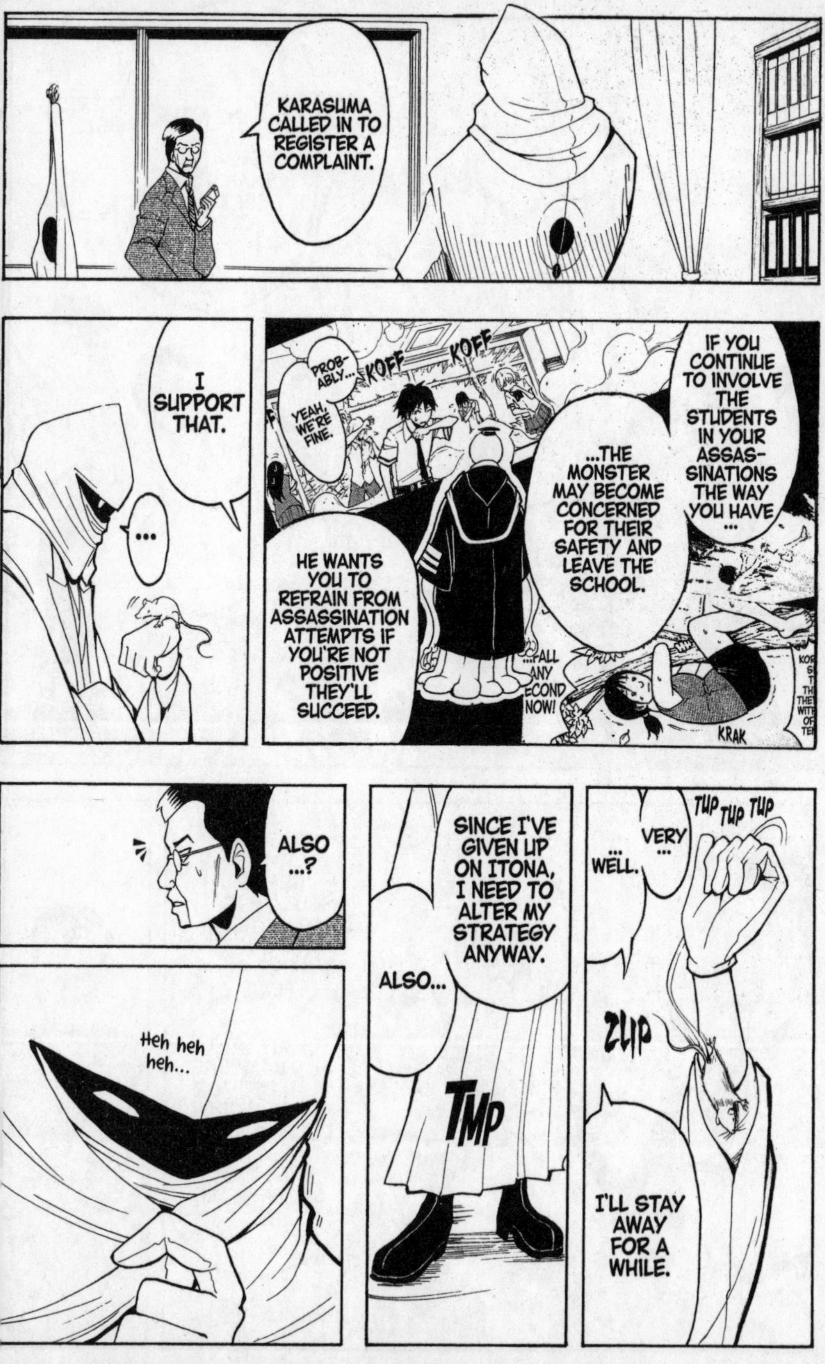
KARASUMA CALLED IN TO REGISTER A COMPLAINT.
IF YOU CONTINUE TO INVOLVE THE STUDENTS IN YOUR ASSAS-SINATIONS THE WAY YOU HAVE...
...THE MONSTER MAY BECOME CONCERNED FOR THEIR SAFETY AND LEAVE THE SCHOOL.
KOFF KOFF
PROB-ABLY...
YEAH, WE'RE FINE.
HE WANTS YOU TO REFRAIN FROM ASSASSINATION ATTEMPTS IF YOU'RE NOT POSITIVE THEY'LL SUCCEED.
KRAK
I SUPPORT THAT.
...
VERY... WELL.
TUP TUP TUP
ZLIP
I'LL STAY AWAY FOR A WHILE.
SINCE I'VE GIVEN UP ON ITONA, I NEED TO ALTER MY STRATEGY ANYWAY.
ALSO...
TMP
ALSO...?
Heh heh heh...

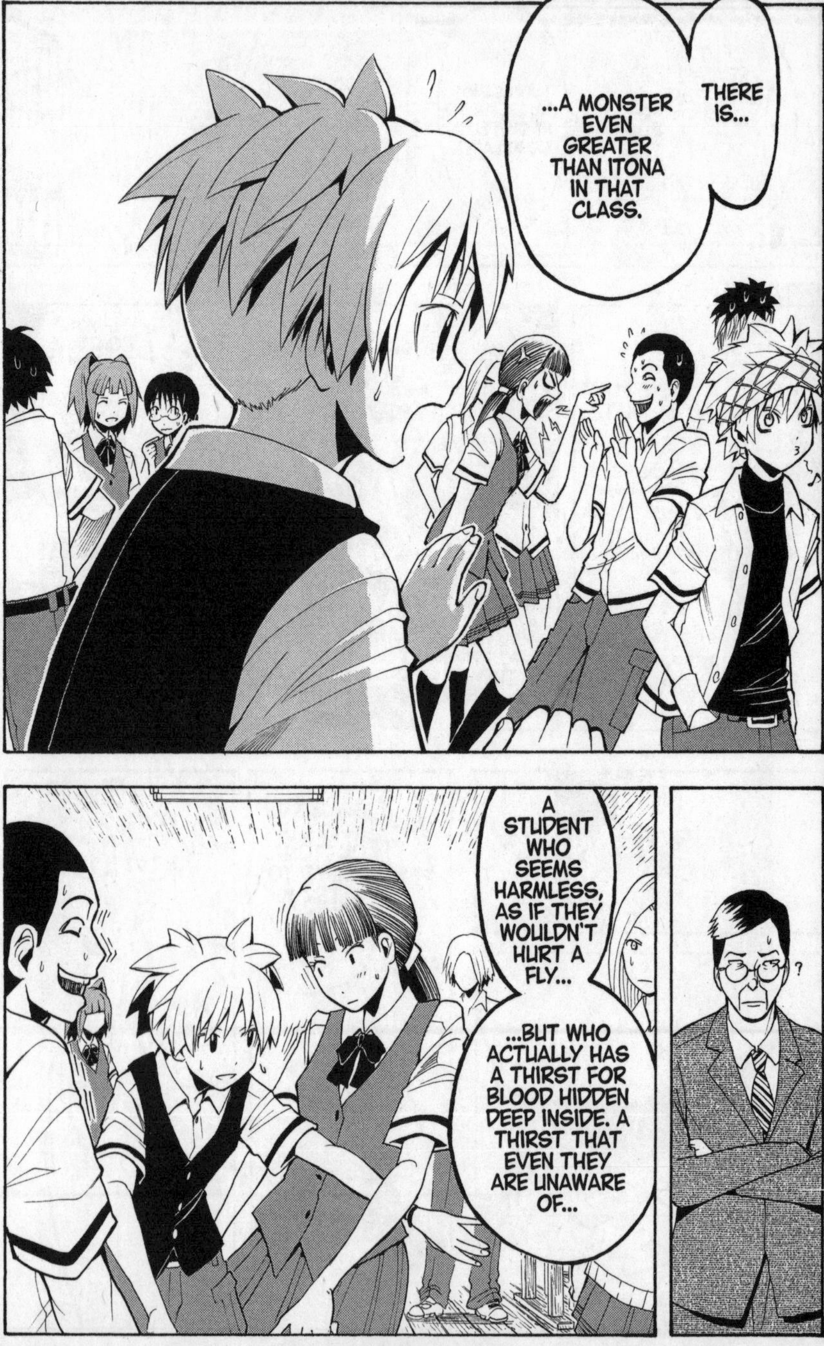
THERE IS...
...A MONSTER EVEN GREATER THAN ITONA IN THAT CLASS.
?
A STUDENT WHO SEEMS HARMLESS, AS IF THEY WOULDN'T HURT A FLY...
...BUT WHO ACTUALLY HAS A THIRST FOR BLOOD HIDDEN DEEP INSIDE. A THIRST THAT EVEN THEY ARE UNAWARE OF...

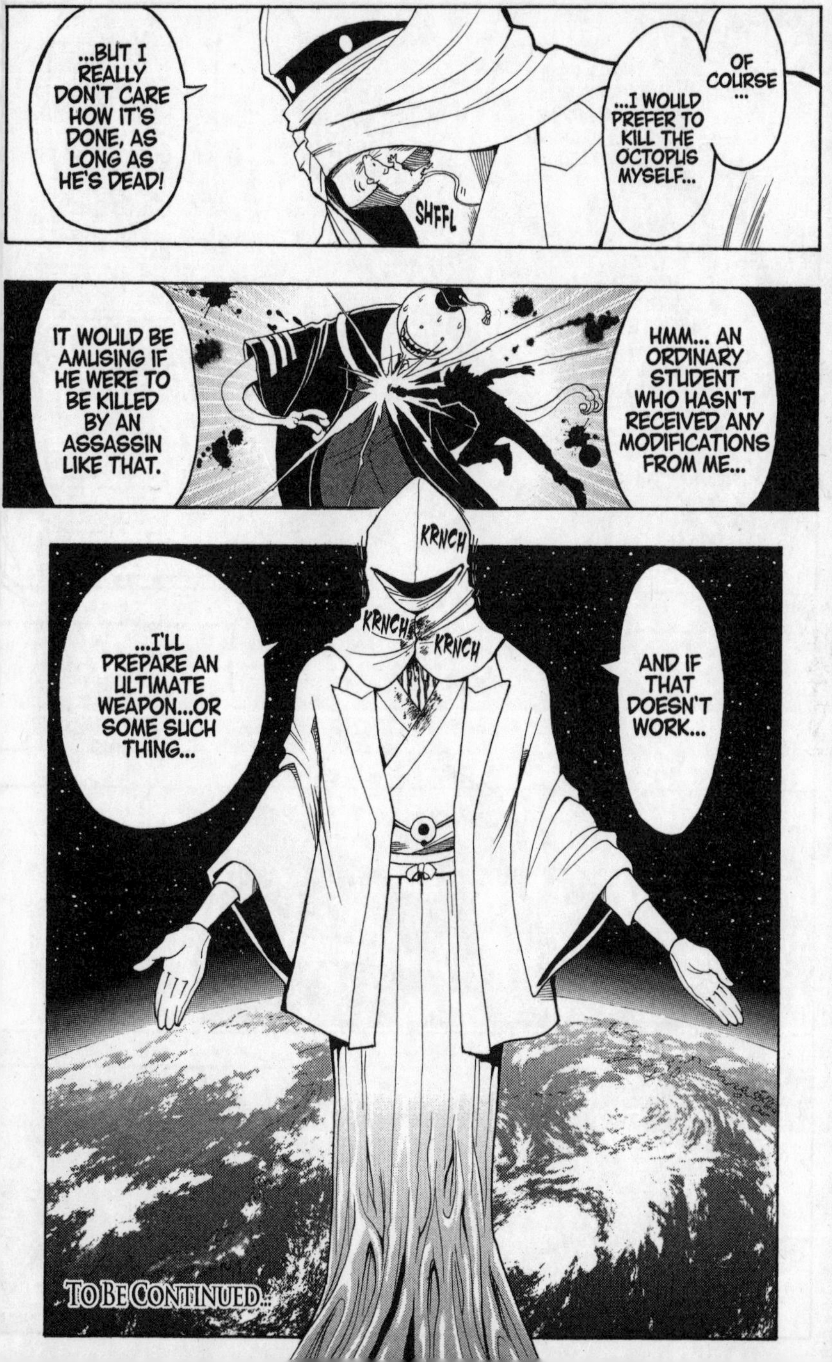
OF COURSE...
...I WOULD PREFER TO KILL THE OCTOPUS MYSELF...
SHFFL
...BUT I REALLY DON'T CARE HOW IT'S DONE, AS LONG AS HE'S DEAD!
HMM... AN ORDINARY STUDENT WHO HASN'T RECEIVED ANY MODIFICATIONS FROM ME...
IT WOULD BE AMUSING IF HE WERE TO BE KILLED BY AN ASSASSIN LIKE THAT.
KRNCH
KRNCH
KRNCH
AND IF THAT DOESN'T WORK...
...I'LL PREPARE AN ULTIMATE WEAPON...OR SOME SUCH THING...
TO BE CONTINUED...

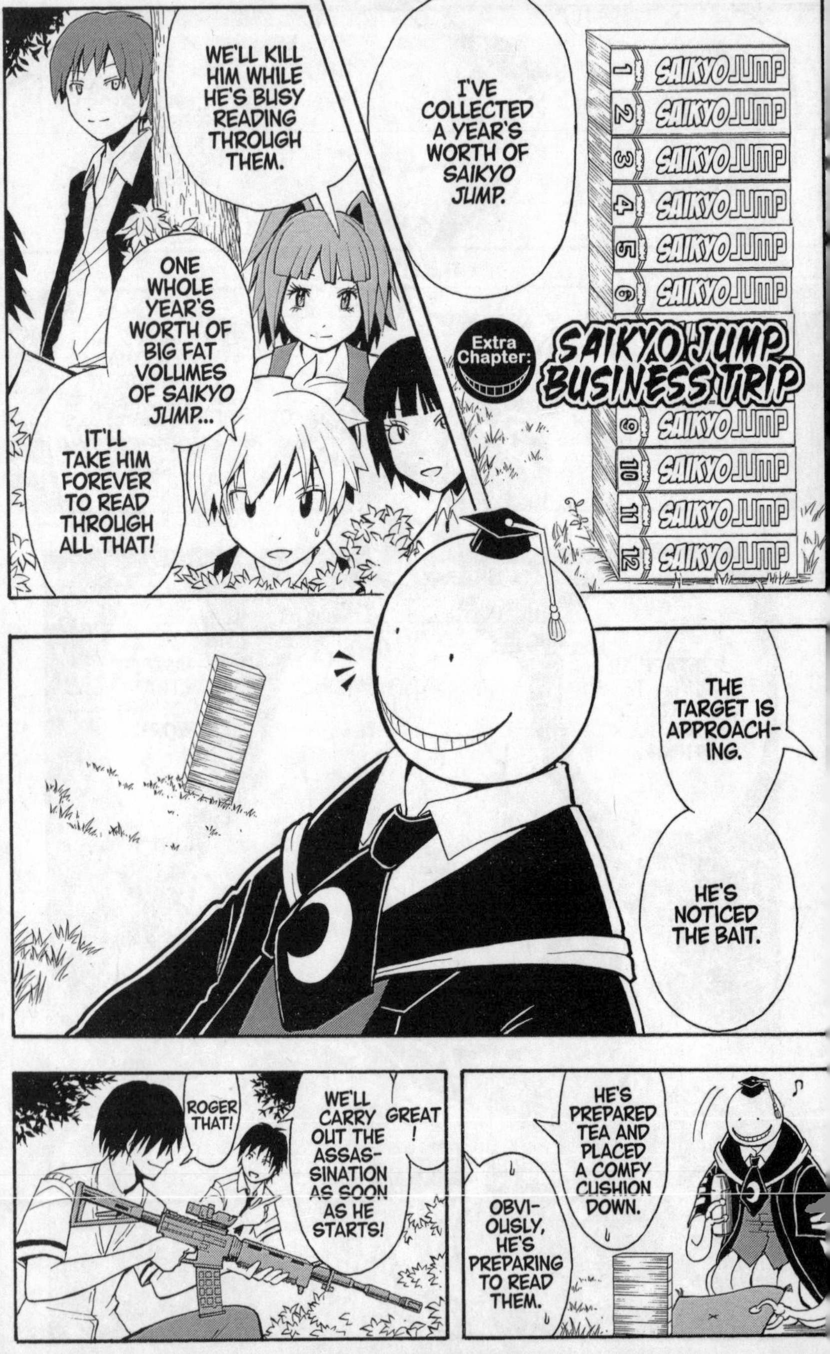
SAIKYO JUMP
Extra Chapter: SAIKYO JUMP BUSINESS TRIP
I'VE COLLECTED A YEAR'S WORTH OF SAIKYO JUMP.
WE'LL KILL HIM WHILE HE'S BUSY READING THROUGH THEM.
ONE WHOLE YEAR'S WORTH OF BIG FAT VOLUMES OF SAIKYO JUMP...
IT'LL TAKE HIM FOREVER TO READ THROUGH ALL THAT!
THE TARGET IS APPROACHING.
HE'S NOTICED THE BAIT.
HE'S PREPARED TEA AND PLACED A COMFY CUSHION DOWN.
OBVIOUSLY, HE'S PREPARING TO READ THEM.
GREAT!
WE'LL CARRY OUT THE ASSASSINATION AS SOON AS HE STARTS!
ROGER THAT!

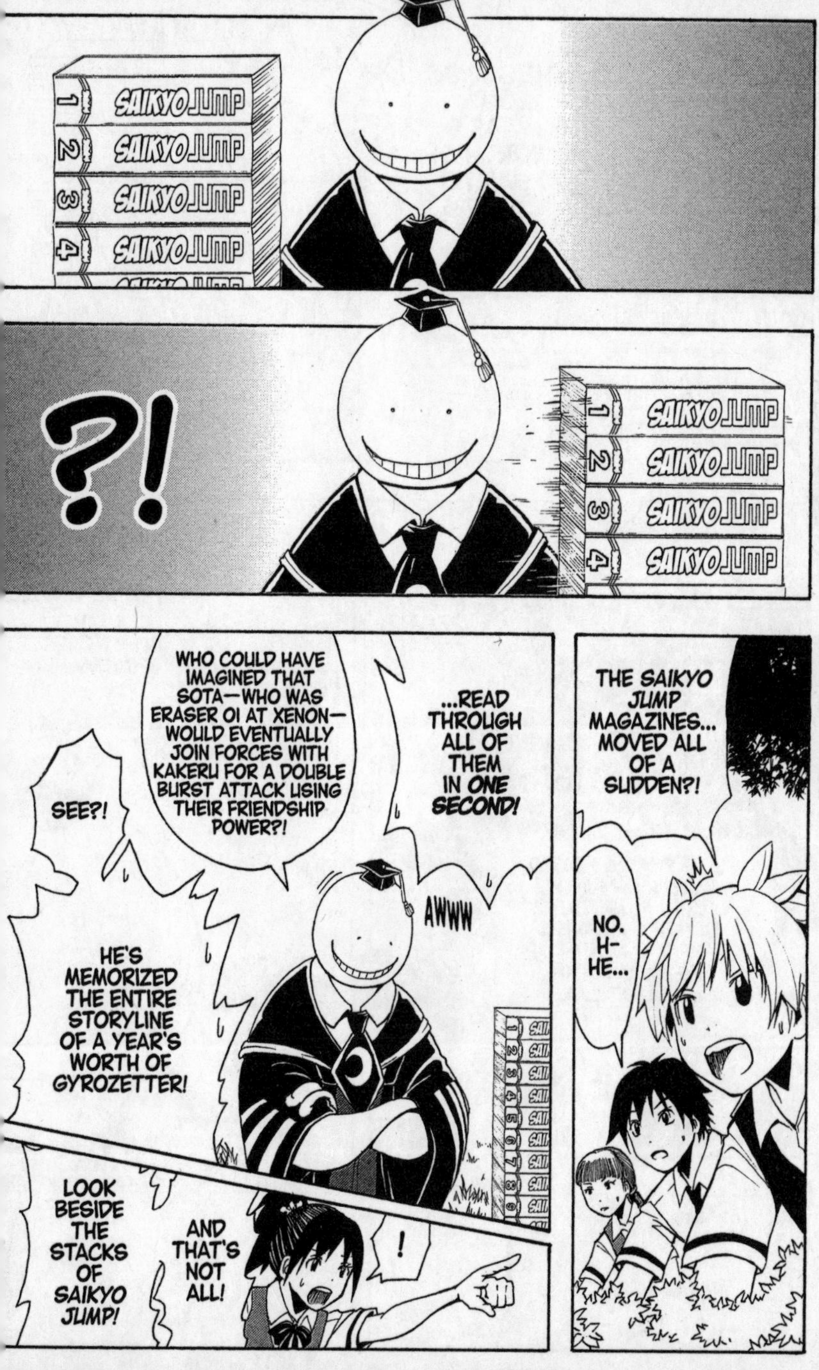
1 SAIKYO JUMP
2 SAIKYO JUMP
3 SAIKYO JUMP
4 SAIKYO JUMP
?!
1 SAIKYO JUMP
2 SAIKYO JUMP
3 SAIKYO JUMP
4 SAIKYO JUMP
THE SAIKYO JUMP MAGAZINES... MOVED ALL OF A SUDDEN?!
NO. H- HE...
...READ THROUGH ALL OF THEM IN ONE SECOND!
WHO COULD HAVE IMAGINED THAT SOTA—WHO WAS ERASER 01 AT XENON—WOULD EVENTUALLY JOIN FORCES WITH KAKERU FOR A DOUBLE BURST ATTACK USING THEIR FRIENDSHIP POWER?!
SEE?!
AWWW
HE'S MEMORIZED THE ENTIRE STORYLINE OF A YEAR'S WORTH OF GYROZETTER!
!
AND THAT'S NOT ALL!
LOOK BESIDE THE STACKS OF SAIKYO JUMP!

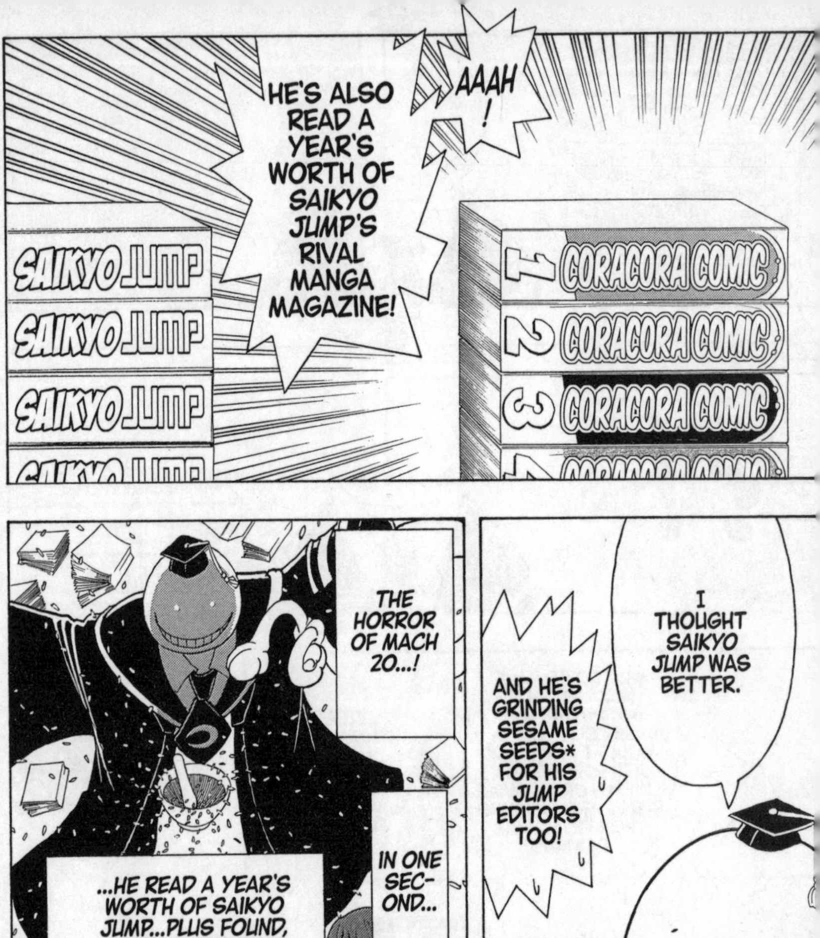
AAAH!
HE'S ALSO READ A YEAR'S WORTH OF SAIKYO JUMP'S RIVAL MANGA MAGAZINE!
1 CORACORA COMIC
2 CORACORA COMIC
3 CORACORA COMIC
SAIKYO JUMP
SAIKYO JUMP
SAIKYO JUMP
I THOUGHT SAIKYO JUMP WAS BETTER.
AND HE'S GRINDING SESAME SEEDS* FOR HIS JUMP EDITORS TOO!
GRNCH GRNCH
THE HORROR OF MACH 20...!
IN ONE SEC-OND...
...HE READ A YEAR'S WORTH OF SAIKYO JUMP...PLUS FOUND, BOUGHT, AND READ A YEAR'S WORTH OF ITS RIVAL MANGA MAGAZINE...AND KISSED UP!

*THE JAPANESE EXPRESSION "GRINDING SESAME SEEDS" = THE ENGLISH EXPRESSION "POLISHING APPLES" = KISSING UP TO SOMEO

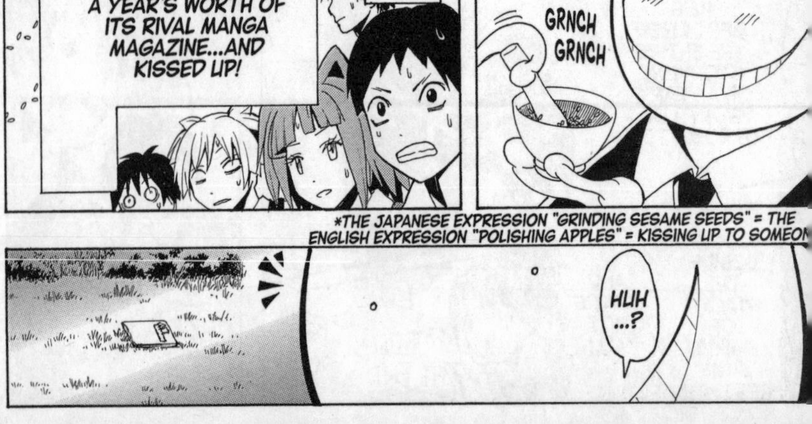
HUH ...?

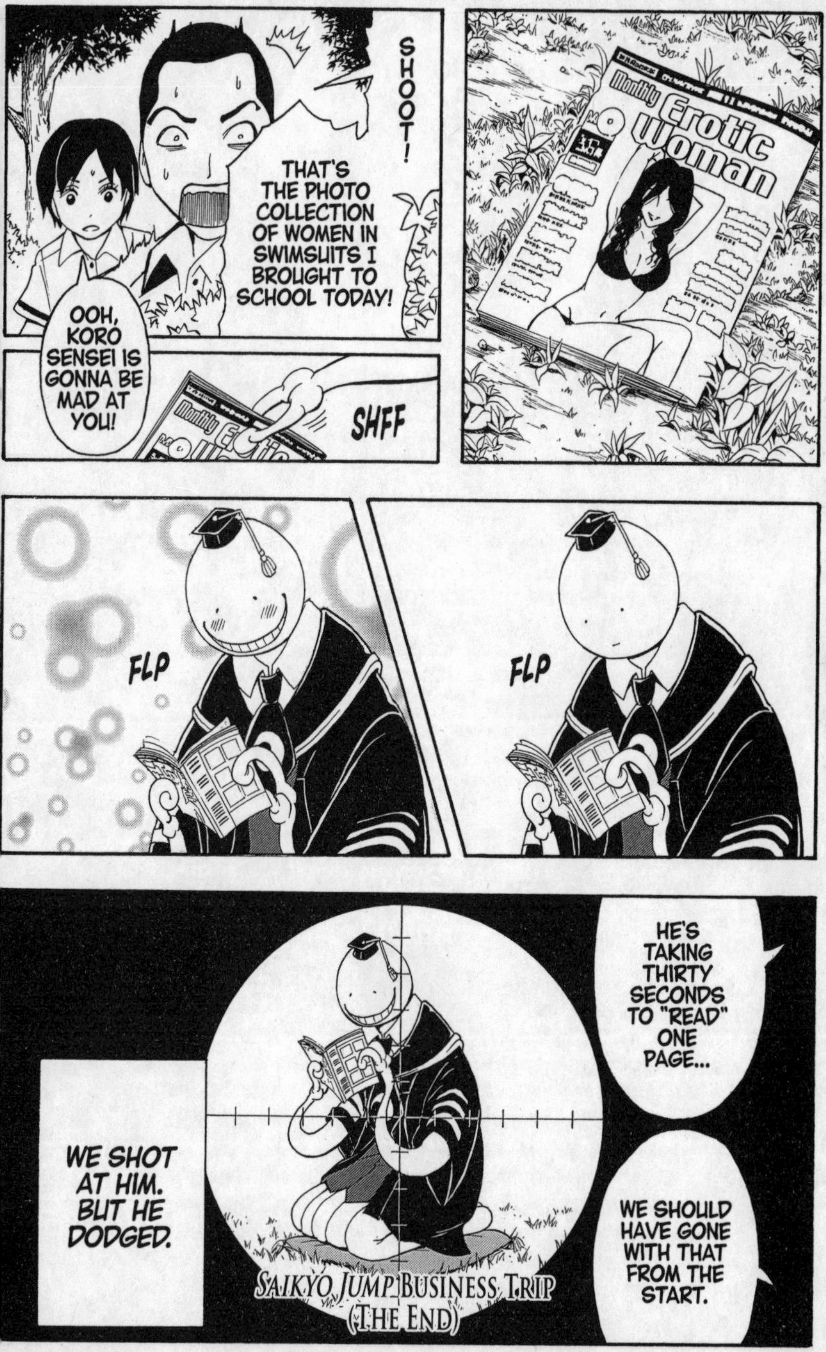
Monthly Erotic Woman
SHOOT!
THAT'S THE PHOTO COLLECTION OF WOMEN IN SWIMSUITS I BROUGHT TO SCHOOL TODAY!
OOH, KORO SENSEI IS GONNA BE MAD AT YOU!
SHFF
FLP
FLP
HE'S TAKING THIRTY SECONDS TO "READ" ONE PAGE...
WE SHOULD HAVE GONE WITH THAT FROM THE START.
SAIKYO JUMP BUSINESS TRIP
(THE END)
WE SHOT AT HIM. BUT HE DODGED.

A month after this graphic novel was published in Japan, *Assassination Classroom*'s special English vocabulary book *Koro Tan* ("Koro Vocab") was published as well.

Ever since the inception of this series, I wanted to publish a study guide. Since the series is about a teacher who helps you raise your academic grades, I wanted to create a fun yet serious study tool that could actually help students.

There are many words and phrases students need to learn for their Japanese high school entrance exams. This collection of all-new illustrations of Nagisa and Terasaka trying to plan their assassinations, combined with a variety of English sentences related to *Assassination Classroom*, is designed to help you have fun while you study English vocabulary.

I apologize for advertising this book here, but I sincerely want to use my skills as a manga artist to help people learn. If you're interested, please drop by the bookstore and check it out. I would be overjoyed if you found it helpful to you in your everyday studies!

—Yusei Matsui

Yusei Matsui was born on the last day of January in Saitama Prefecture, Japan. He has been drawing manga since elementary school. Some of his favorite manga series are *Bobobo-bo Bo-bobo*, *JoJo's Bizarre Adventure* and *Ultimate Muscle*. Matsui learned his trade working as an assistant to manga artist Yoshio Sawai, creator of *Bobobo-bo Bo-bobo*. In 2005, Matsui debuted his original manga *Neuro: Supernatural Detective* in *Weekly Shonen Jump*. In 2007, *Neuro* was adapted into an anime. In 2012, *Assassination Classroom* began serialization in *Weekly Shonen Jump*.

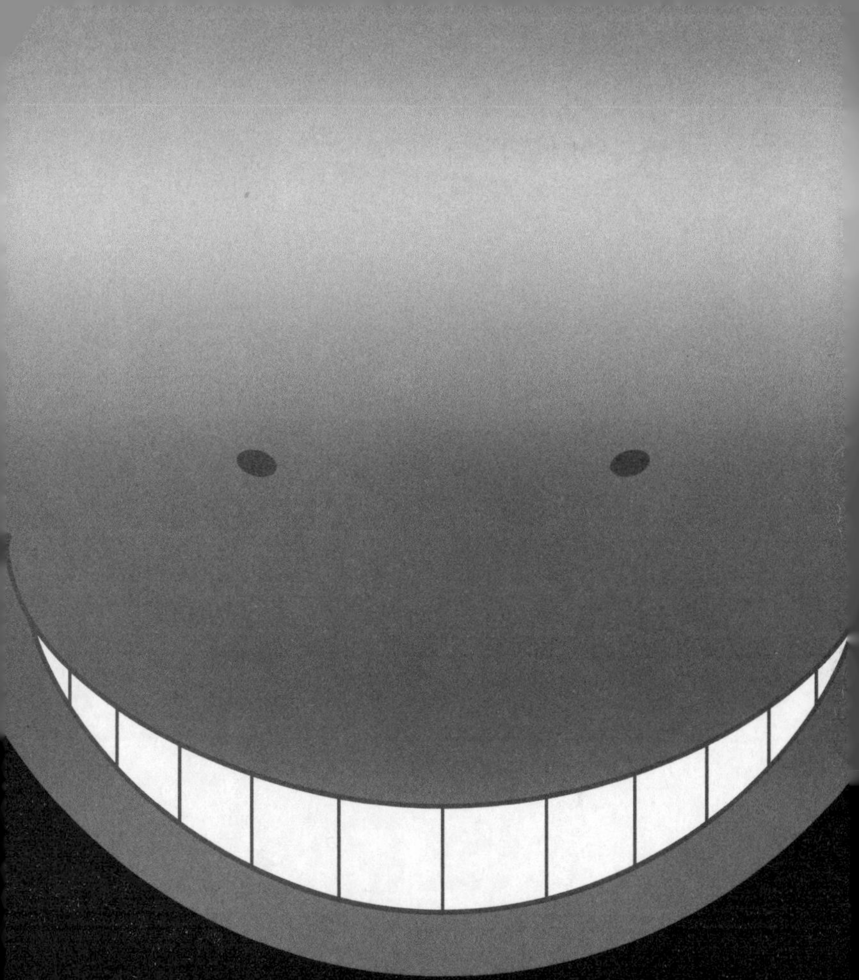

A Rainbow Face stands for everything! Happiness, anger, sorrow, pleasure, pain, good and evil, merits and demerits, past and present... A heartfelt thanks to all of you as the series reaches its 10th volume.

ASSASSINATION CLASSROOM

YUSEI MATSUI

⑩

TIME FOR ROBBERY

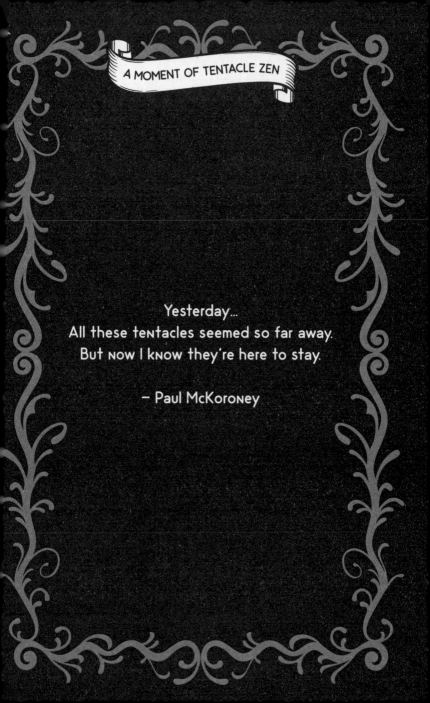

A MOMENT OF TENTACLE ZEN

Yesterday...
All these tentacles seemed so far away.
But now I know they're here to stay.

— Paul McKoroney

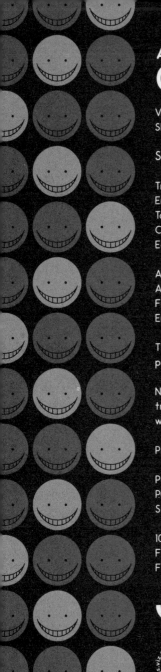

ASSASSINATION CLASSROOM

Volume 10
SHONEN JUMP Manga Edition

Story and Art by YUSEI MATSUI

Translation/Tetsuichiro Miyaki
English Adaptation/Bryant Turnage
Touch-up Art & Lettering/Stephen Dutro
Cover & Interior Design/Sam Elzway
Editor/Annette Roman

Printed in the U.S.A.

Published by VIZ Media, LLC
P.O. Box 77010
San Francisco, CA 94107

10 9 8 7 6 5
First printing, June 2016
Fifth printing, September 2020

VIZ MEDIA
viz.com

SHONEN JUMP
shonenjump.com

ratings.viz.com
RATED T+ OLDER TEEN

PARENTAL ADVISORY
ASSASSINATION CLASSROOM is rated T+ for Older Teen and is recommended for ages 16 and up. This volume contains realistic violence and suggestive situations.

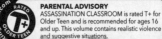

VICTORY!

3–E student Isogai breaks the school rules by working part-time to help support his family. When Gakushu and the rest of the Big Four students find out, they use his secret as leverage to force 3–E to participate in a bizarre sports-day competition. Soon it's time for the school's midterm competition as well, but when some 3–E students accidentally injure the elderly owner of a day care/after-school program, Koro Sensei forbids them from studying and orders them to replace the old codger until he recovers. Assassination is one thing, but *babysitting little kids*?! And then, our friends rescue a cat

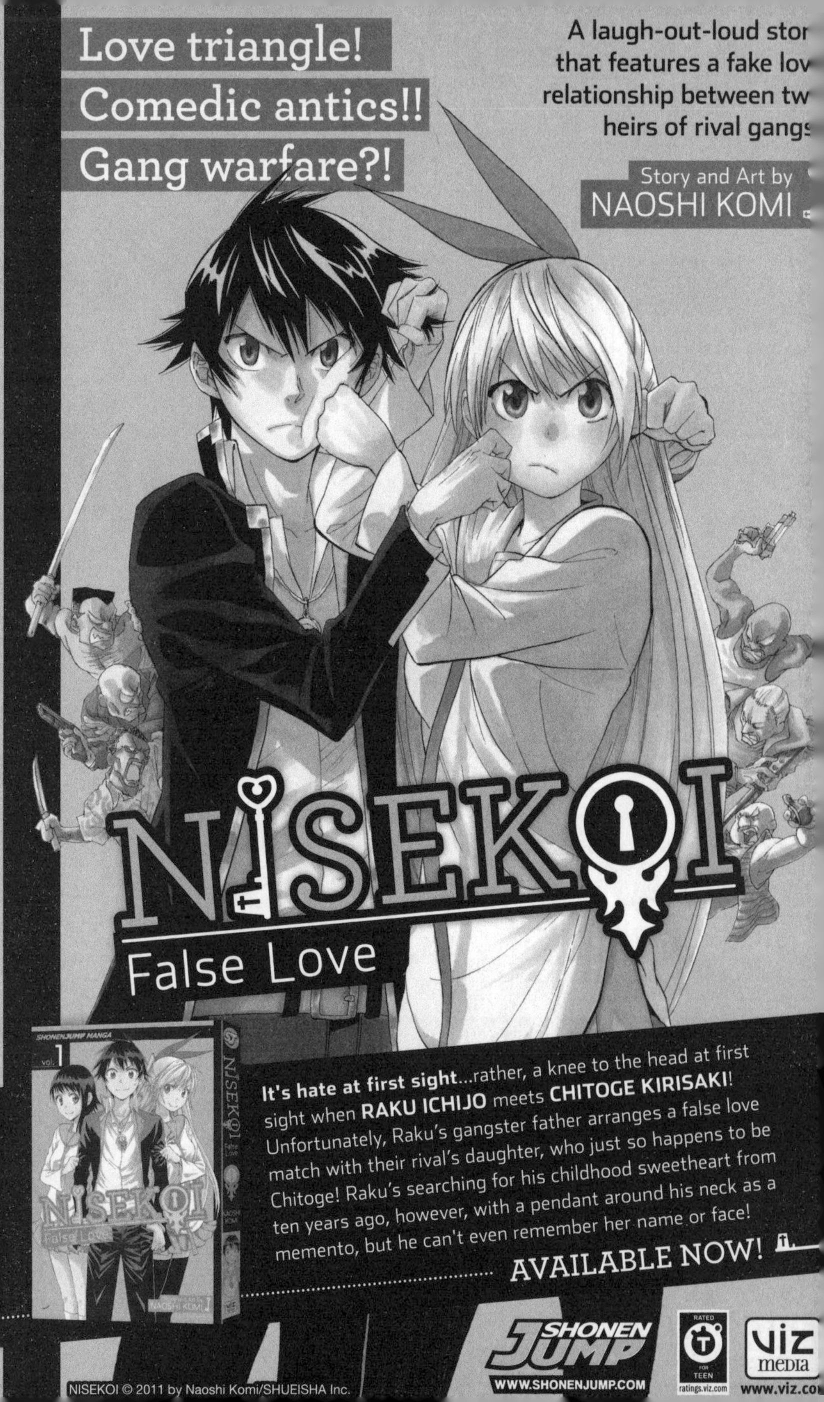

EYESHIELD 21

STORY BY RIICHIRO INAGAKI
ART BY YUSUKE MURATA

From the artist of *One-Punch Man!*

Wimpy Sena Kobayakawa has been running away from bullies all his life. But when the football gear comes on, things change—Sena's speed and uncanny ability to elude big bullies just might give him what it takes to become a great high school football hero! Catch all the bone-crushing action and slapstick comedy of Japan's hottest football manga!

You're Reading in the Wrong Direction!!

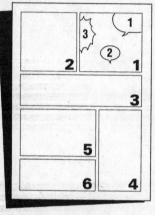

Whoops! Guess what? You're starting at the wrong end of the comic!

…It's true! In keeping with the original Japanese format, **Assassination Classroom** is meant to be read from right to left, starting in the upper-right corner.

Unlike English, which is read from left to right, Japanese is read from right to left, meaning that action, sound effects and word-balloon order are completely reversed… something which can make readers unfamiliar with Japanese feel pretty backwards themselves. For this reason, manga or Japanese comics published in the U.S. in English have sometimes been published "flopped"—that is, printed in exact reverse order, as though seen from the other side of a mirror.

By flopping pages, U.S. publishers can avoid confusing readers, but the compromise is not without its downside. For one thing, a character in a flopped manga series who once wore in the original Japanese version a T-shirt emblazoned with "M A Y" (as in "the merry month of") now wears one which reads "Y A M"! Additionally, many manga creators in Japan are themselves unhappy with the process, as some feel the mirror-imaging of their art skews their original intentions.

We are proud to bring you Yusei Matsui's **Assassination Classroom** in the original unflopped format.

For now, though, turn to the other side of the book and let the adventure begin…!

—Editor